肇庆学院学术著作出版资助金资助

罗尔德·达尔短篇故事品读及汉译探索
第 8 卷

An Interpretation of Short Stories by Roald Dahl and an Exploration of Their Chinese Translations
Volume 8

张跃伟　王永胜　著
ZHANG Yue-wei, WANG Yong-sheng

哈尔滨工业大学出版社

内容提要

本书系对英国作家罗尔德·达尔"非儿童类"(个别篇章具有"儿童类"文学特点,但由于是罗尔德·达尔早期作品,也被收录进来,作为研究的对象)短篇故事(小说)进行研究所著系列图书中的第8卷,也是最后一卷,包括七部短篇小说。这些小说长短不一、难易各异,按照不同的主题分成四章加以编排,分别为"非常之辈""事与愿违""生财之道"和"人生之路"。除第四章外,每章收录两篇作品,先做引导性的介绍,名为"原作导读",再给出小说的原文供读者阅读或作为翻译的参考,同时给出语言点及文化层面上的注释,以辅助理解,名为"原作释读",最后给出探索性的汉语译文,名为"翻译探索"。

本书适合英语专业大学本科生及研究生阅读、研究、翻译之用(不少小说也可供高中生阅读、学习),也适合广大的文学爱好者阅读,更适合从事英汉翻译或外国文学研究的学者、教师、学生等阅读、参考。

图书在版编目(CIP)数据

罗尔德·达尔短篇故事品读及汉译探索.第8卷/张跃伟,王永胜著.—哈尔滨:哈尔滨工业大学出版社,2016.12
　　ISBN 978-7-5603-6355-4

Ⅰ.①罗… Ⅱ.①张… ②王… Ⅲ.①短篇小说－小说研究－英国－现代 ②短篇小说－文学翻译－英国－现代 Ⅳ.①I561.074

中国版本图书馆CIP数据核字(2016)第295037号

策划编辑	田新华
责任编辑	陈　洁
封面设计	思　华　高永利
出版发行	哈尔滨工业大学出版社
社　　址	哈尔滨市南岗区复华四道街10号　邮编150006
传　　真	0451－86414749
网　　址	http://hitpress.hit.edu.cn
印　　刷	哈尔滨市工大节能印刷厂
开　　本	880mm×1230mm　1/32　印张11.375　字数407千字
版　　次	2016年12月第1版　2016年12月第1次印刷
书　　号	ISBN 978-7-5603-6355-4
定　　价	45.00元

(如因印装质量问题影响阅读,我社负责调换)

前　言

对于罗尔德·达尔（Roald Dahl，1916—1990），中国读者耳熟能详的恐怕是他的一些儿童文学作品，而且国内外对他称呼最多的莫过于"儿童文学作家"。他的儿童文学作品的确十分畅销，已被翻译成多国文字出版发行，知名度颇高。可以说，在儿童文学作家中，罗尔德·达尔是最为成功、最为知名的作家之一。达尔的儿童文学作品得到很多国家小朋友的喜爱，这样的作品包括《詹姆斯与大仙桃》（*James and the Giant Peach*）《查利与巧克力工厂》（*Charlie and the Chocolate Factory*）《魔法手指》（*The Magic Finger*）《查利与大玻璃升降机》（*Charlie and the Great Glass Elevator*）《了不起的狐狸爸爸》（*Fantastic Mr. Fox*）《特威特夫妇》（*The Twits*）《女巫》（*The Witches*）《好心眼儿的巨人》（*The BFG*，这部小说1983年获"惠特布雷德奖"，英文表述为"Whitbread Award"）《玛蒂尔达》（*Matilda*）等。

然而，作为英国儿童文学作家的罗尔德·达尔，还写过其他类型的文学作品，特别是那些"非儿童类"短篇小说（个别篇章具有"儿童类"文学特点，但由于是罗尔德·达尔早期作品，也被收录进来，作为研究的对象。也可以说"成人类"短篇小说，也就是说，为成年人写的文学作品。当然，这些作品中有些具有"成人"色彩——含有色情内容，但达尔"成人"作品中的"成人"内容大多是比较"隐晦"的。这样的"成人"作品，基本收录在他的《迷情乱性》[*Switch Bitch*]一书中）也同样精彩。称之为"非儿童类"，主要针对达尔"儿童类"作品耀眼的光环而言。其实，这些"非儿童类"短篇故事（小说）绝大多数是达尔转笔写儿童文学作品之前完成的。"儿童类"作品的耀眼光环或多或少掩盖了一些"非儿童类"作品的光芒，而在中国，这些"非儿童类"作品的"光芒"几乎没有散发出来,很少为中国广大读者所熟知。这些作品受到西方19世纪现实主义文学的影响,多数采用现实主义的创作手法。同时,达尔也从美国短篇小说家欧·亨利(O. Henry)那里汲取了一定的营养。就达尔作品本身对人物和景物的描写来看,可以说,他是"20世纪英国变形精神世界的一位工笔画家"[1]。同他的儿童文学作品一样,他早期的这些"非儿童类"作品同样具有结尾出奇、结局令人意想不到等特点,更进一步说,达尔的此类短篇小说这方面的特点尤为突出。这类作品充满奇思妙想,人物刻画细腻入微,其中不乏道貌岸然者、悲观主义者、心理变态者。此类作品也不乏荒谬、贪婪、邪恶、虚伪的成分,其中的人物大都在"机关用尽"之时,一不小心就"栽了跟头",或者在"聪明绝顶"之际,反而被自己的"聪明"所误。

罗尔德·达尔的父母是挪威人,但达尔本人1916年出生在英国格拉摩根郡的兰达夫(Llandaff, Glamorgan)[2],并在雷普顿公学(Repton School)接受教育。第二次世界大战爆发,他应征入伍,加入英国皇家空军,驻扎在内罗毕。后来,他加入了驻利比亚的一个战斗机中队,受了重伤。之后,又作为一名战斗机飞行员到希腊和叙利亚参加战斗。1942年,达尔作为英国大使馆的空军助理专员去了华盛顿。华盛顿成为他人生的转折点,因为在那里他开始了自己的创作生涯。随后,他被调到情报部。战争结束的时候,他成为英国皇家空军中校。他的第一批短篇小说共有12篇,都是根据自己在战争期间的经历所写。这12篇作品首先发表在美国的一些主流杂志上,后来编撰成书出版,书名为《向你飞跃》(*Over to You*)。

罗尔德·达尔所有受到高度赞誉的作品都被译成多种文字,成为全世界的畅销书。安格利亚电视台(Anglia Television)将他的一些短篇小说改编成电视系列剧,冠以标题《出乎意料的故事集》(*Tales*

---

[1] 参见"陈钰,1985(4):66",这里只不过将其中的"二十世纪",规范性修改成"20世纪"。

[2] 格拉摩根原来是英国南威尔士的一个郡。

of the Unexpected)。他的作品还包括两本自传——《男孩时代》(*Boy*)和《独闯天下》(*Going Solo*),还有赢得很多赞誉的小说《我的叔叔奥斯瓦尔德》(*My Uncle Oswald*)以及《罗尔德·达尔倾心的鬼怪故事集》(*Roald Dahl's Book of Ghost Stories*)。最后一本是他自己编辑出版的。在生命的最后一年,他收集了一些奇闻轶事,并跟妻子弗利西蒂(*Felicity*)一起,整理了一些烹饪食谱,汇编成一本书。这本书1996年由企鹅出版集团出版,书名为《罗尔德·达尔的烹饪书》(*Roald Dahl's Cookbook*)①。

罗尔德·达尔于1990年11月23日去世。英国《泰晤士报》(*The Times*)称其为"我们这一代人中最有影响力的作家之一,也是拥有极其广泛读者群的作家之一"(One of the most widely read and influential writers of our generation),并在写给他的讣告中写道:"孩子喜欢他写的故事,把他当成自己心目中最喜爱的人……他的作品将成为未来的经典之作"(Children loved his stories and made him their favourite... They will be classics of the future)。据报道,在2000年英国的"世界图书日"(World Book Day)投票中,罗尔德·达尔当选为"读者最喜爱的作家"(Favourite Author)②。

对于20世纪的英国作家罗尔德·达尔及其作品,《爱尔兰时报》(*Irish Times*)的一篇评论,可谓一语中的:"Roald Dahl is one of the few writers I know whose work can accurately be described as addictive. Through his tales runs a vein of macabre malevolence, the more effective because it springs from the slightest, almost inconsequential everyday things. The result is a black humour of the most sophisticated kind."(罗尔德·达尔是我所认识的为数不多的作家之一,可以准确无误地说,其作品令人沉醉、上瘾。他的作品始终贯穿着一条主线,这条主线充

---

① 参见"Roald Dahl. *The Best of Roald Dahl* [M]. London: Penguin Books Ltd., 2006"。

② 参见"Roald Dahl. *The Collected Short Stories of Roald Dahl* [M]. London: Penguin Books Ltd., 1992"。

满恶意和凶险,令人毛骨悚然,但却更加行之有效,因为其来源是一些不起眼的、几乎微不足道的日常事物。结果,最为错综复杂的黑色幽默便应运而生了)①。

抛开后来"儿童类"作品的耀眼光环不说,罗尔德·达尔在上一世纪中叶之所以蜚声世界,就是因为他所创作的这些"非儿童类"的短篇小说(当然,个别篇章具有"儿童类"文学特点,预示性地展露出达尔后来作为儿童文学作家的一丝"光芒")。但是,当时中国翻译出版业不是很发达,对他的作品的译介也不是很多。就算是有所译介,也处于零星的"散兵作战"状态,不成体系。在全球化浪潮滚滚而来的今天,研究罗尔德·达尔的这部分作品,并系统地进行翻译研究,如同打开尘封已久的大门,门内的景色依然会令当代中国读者惊喜不已。对于广大的英语学习者和文学爱好者来说,阅读达尔的这部分作品将会带来迥然不同的人生体验。

其实,罗尔德·达尔这部分短篇小说的实质和绝妙,可以从英美主流媒体的评价窥见一斑:

"Roald Dahl is the prince of storytellers."—*Daily Mail*
"罗尔德·达尔是位讲故事的王子。"——(英国)《每日邮报》

"The absolute master of the twist-in-the-tale"—*The Observer*
"绝对的大师,其故事的结局出人意料。"——(英国)《观察家报》

"These stories pack their punch."—*The Observer*
"这些故事蓄满了惊人之力。"——(英国)《观察家报》

---

① 著者译自 Roald Dahl (1916—1990) 的 "*The Best of Roald Dahl*"(《罗尔德·达尔小说精品集》)一书的封底(back cover)。此书由英国"Penguin Books Ltd."出版公司于2006年出版发行。

"An unforgettable read, don't miss it."—*Sunday Times*
"一次难忘的阅读体验,不可错过。"

——(英国)《星期日泰晤士报》

"Dahl is too good a storyteller to become predictable, so you never know whether the tyrant or the tyrannized will win in the end."

—*Daily Telegraph*

"达尔的故事讲得太精彩了,结局简直令人无法预测。因此,你永远都无法得知,最后的赢家是残暴的人,还是受到残暴对待的人。"

——(英国)《每日电讯报》

"Dahl has the mastery of plot and characters possessed by great writers of the past, along with a wildness and wryness of his own. One of his trademarks is writing beautifully about the ugly, even the horrible."

—*The Los Angeles Times*

"达尔拥有以往伟大作家的资质——善于营造情节、精于刻画人物,但达尔也拥有自己荒诞不经的一面,以及自己的一套挖苦讥讽的手段。其中的一个标志就是他对丑陋之人的精妙刻画,更有甚者是对恐怖之人的精妙刻画。" ——(美国)《洛杉矶时报》

"An ingenious imagination, a fascination with odd and ordinary detail, and a lust for its thorough exploitation are the… strengths of Dahl's storytelling." —*The New York Times Book Review*

"达尔写作的影响力在于其独特的想象力,在于其对稀奇古怪和平淡无奇的细节的着迷程度,在于其对细节完完全全加以利用的欲望。" ——(美国)《纽约时报·书评》

"The mind of Roald Dahl is quintessentially nasty and wicked."

—*The Washington Post*

"罗尔德·达尔的思维具有典型的特点,那就是肮脏和邪恶。"
——(美国)《华盛顿邮报》

在此前提下,研究并翻译罗尔德·达尔的"非儿童类"短篇小说,将具有一定的学术价值和社会价值,会为中国文学的百花园增添一个品种,会为文学爱好者和翻译者提供一个可供参考的文本。

在历时三年多对罗尔德·达尔"非儿童类"短篇小说进行研究和翻译的过程中,共收集到长短不一的此类作品60篇,并站在一定的角度,根据著者个人的理解,细加编排,精心安排,详加注释,最终通过翻译,引介给中国读者。

本书在对罗尔德·达尔短篇小说的翻译探索中,采取了严谨的翻译态度,形成了以下基本的翻译思路:

(1)人名、地名按照一定的标准进行"异化"式处理(极个别人名作了"归化"式处理),主要依据《世界人名翻译大辞典》(新华社译名室编,中国对外翻译出版公司1993年第一版或2007年第二版)以及《世界地名翻译大辞典》(周定国主编,中国出版集团、中国对外翻译出版公司2008年第一版)等,个别的人名、地名的翻译兼顾了流行的译法。

(2)绝大多数非国际化的度量衡单位,特别是英制的度量衡单位,采用"同化"或"归化"的处理方法,以便汉语思维者能形象化地加以理解。

(3)每一篇的题目都采用汉语四字格来处理,以求汉语的工整,发挥汉语四字格表达的优势,但同时最大限度地兼顾原文题目的字面含义。

(4)就汉语译文整体而言,尽量杜绝"翻译腔",以保持汉语语言的纯洁性和规范性,但前提是确保对达尔小说原文的"忠实"。

(5)尽量完美地再现原文的风格,虽然做到这一点并不是轻而易举的事情。原文有些风格,在翻译中只能退其次而求之——基本上采用"归化"处理手法,照顾了汉语的通畅性。比如,原文中很多非标准的英语表达,汉译时就没有在"风格"上充分加以体现,这也是以后有待继续探索的一个翻译问题。

当然,"金无足赤,人无完人",匆忙且蹒跚的步履必将会迈出"不和谐"的步伐。在对罗尔德·达尔的"非儿童类"短篇小说进行研究、翻译并成书的过程中,不当甚至错误之处在所难免,还望读者不吝赐教,多多批评,特别是多做文学翻译方面的批评。

需要特别声明的是,本系列书中所引用的罗尔德·达尔原著内容以及所做的翻译探索,旨在学术研究,不做商业用途。涉及相关版权的地方,已经做了引用和标注。

张跃伟　王永胜
2016 年 9 月 16 日

目 录

第一章 非常之辈 ········· 1

第一节 《搭车怪客》*The Hitch-hiker* ········· 2
一、原作导读 ········· 2
二、原作释读 ········· 4
三、翻译探索 ········· 25

第二节 《捕鼠者说》*The Ratcatcher* ········· 39
一、原作导读 ········· 39
二、原作释读 ········· 41
三、翻译探索 ········· 63

第二章 事与愿违 ········· 78

第一节 《大兵"救美"》*Madame Rosette* ········· 79
一、原作导读 ········· 79
二、原作释读 ········· 82
三、翻译探索 ········· 128

第二节 《小菜一碟》*A Piece of Cake* ········· 159
一、原作导读 ········· 160
二、原作释读 ········· 163
三、翻译探索 ········· 183

第三章 生财之道 ········· 197

第一节 《管家之谋》*The Butler* ········· 198
一、原作导读 ········· 198

二、原作释读 ………………………………… 200
　　三、翻译探索 ………………………………… 207
  第二节　《卖伞男子》*The Umbrella Man* ………… 211
　　一、原作导读 ………………………………… 212
　　二、原作释读 ………………………………… 214
　　三、翻译探索 ………………………………… 226
第四章　人生之路 …………………………………… 234
  第一节　《幸运开局》(上部) *Lucky Break（Part A）* … 235
　　一、原作导读 ………………………………… 236
　　二、原作释读 ………………………………… 237
　　三、翻译探索 ………………………………… 265
  第二节　《幸运开局》(下部) *Lucky Break（Part B）* … 281
　　一、原作导读 ………………………………… 281
　　二、原作释读 ………………………………… 283
　　三、翻译探索 ………………………………… 310

参考文献 ……………………………………………… 325
附录 …………………………………………………… 327
  附录1　生平时间轴 …………………………… 327
  附录2　罗尔德·达尔去世后作品出版时间轴 …… 333
  附录3　《罗尔德·达尔短篇故事品读及汉译探索》全系列
　　　　目录总览 ………………………………… 335
后记 …………………………………………………… 347

第一章 非常之辈

非常之辈,乃异乎寻常、非寻常之人,非常人也。非常之辈,非泛泛之辈、无名之辈,而是具有特殊才干的人。

非常之辈,也许是胸怀大志、不鸣则已,一鸣惊人的人,在机遇没有到来的时候忙忙碌碌,却似乎碌碌无为,但机遇一来便豪气冲天,顿时展露出鸿鹄之志。正如孟浩然在《送陈七赴西军》中所言:

吾观非常者,碌碌在目前。
君负鸿鹄志,蹉跎书剑年。
一闻边烽动,万里忽争先。
余亦赴京国,何当献凯还。①

当然,在一定的语境下,非常之辈也许就是身怀"绝技"的无名鼠辈。他们的技能非同小可,甚至匪夷所思。在英国作家罗尔德·达尔的笔下,可以寻到这样非常之辈的踪影。一个鼠模鼠样的"搭车怪客",自诩为专业"手指匠",非比常人,可谓"非常之辈";在《捕鼠者说》中,另一个鼠模鼠样的"非常之辈"自诩为"啮齿类动物消灭技

---

① 转引自《全唐诗》第159卷第019首。

工",他的技能更是令吾等平常之人瞠目结舌。

走近罗尔德·达尔笔下的"非常之辈",去观看"搭车怪客"的精彩杂耍,去倾听令人咂舌的"捕鼠者说"吧。

第一节 《搭车怪客》The Hitch-hiker

罗尔德·达尔的《搭车怪客》(The Hitch-hiker)被收录在《〈非凡亨利〉及另外六篇故事集》(The Wonderful Story of Henry Sugar and Six More)《罗尔德·达尔短篇故事集锦》(The Collected Short Stories of Roald Dahl)《完全出人意料故事集》(Completely Unexpected Tales)以及《后续出人意料故事集》(Further Tales of the Unexpected)等书中。此外,这部小说也被改编成电视系列剧——1980年3月22日播映的《出乎意料的故事集》(Tales of the Unexpected)第二部中的第4集(Episode 2.4),可见其影响力之大。

一、原作导读

这篇小说是以第一人称"我"(姓名未知)的视角展开的,但叙述者"我"是"隐身"的——地位无足轻重,起到了"纽带"或者"桥梁"的作用,可以看成作家罗尔德·达尔本人的化身。

"我"买了辆豪华的新车。六月里的一天,"我"驱车驶向伦敦,途中遇到一位搭车的,动了恻隐之心,让他上了车。搭车的是一名男子,模样酷似一只老鼠。他说要去伦敦的赛马场,但不是去看赛马,不是去赌马,也不是去调试那些赌马售票机。于是,"我"的兴趣被激发起来了,主动告诉对方说,"我"是一名作家。"我"跟他谈起了"我"新买的车,并就车速打了个赌,结果因为超速把警察招来了,一番盘问之后,开具票据罚了款。警察走后,"我"因为罚款的事闷闷不乐,但那个搭车的却劝我说,不要为这事儿担心。

继续上路之后,"我"跟对方的话题又回到了各自的职业上面。

第一章 非常之辈 第一节 《搭车怪客》The Hitch-hiker

打过一些哑谜之后,搭车的最终说,他是一名"手指匠"——神不知鬼不觉地将"我"的裤袋、鞋带、车内的钟表等东西"变"走。

"那么,你怎么称呼你自己呢?"

"我?我是一名手指匠,而且是专业的。"说这话的时候,他显得很庄严、很自豪,那架势好像是对我说,他是皇家外科学院的院长,或者是坎特伯雷大主教。

"What do you call yourself, then?"

"Me? I'm a fingersmith. I'm a professional fingersmith." He spoke the words solemnly and proudly, as though he were telling me he was the President of the Royal College of Surgeons or the Archbishop of Canterbury.

刚才开罚单的时候,那名警察把"我"和搭车人的细节都记录到本子上去了,对此我忧心忡忡,但是搭车人却还是说不用担心之类的话语,并说警察的记忆力没有那么好。

"记忆力与记录本有什么关系?"我问。"细节都记录到他的本子上了,难道不是吗?"

"是的,老板,是在本子上。但麻烦的是,他把本子弄丢了,两个本子都弄丢了,一个记着我的名字,还有一个记着你的名字。"

这名男子右手纤细、修长的手指得意洋洋地举起从警察衣兜里掏出的那两个本子。"我干过的最为轻松的活儿,"他自豪地宣布。

"What's memory got to do with it?" I asked. "It's written down in his book, isn't it?"

"Yes, guv'nor, it is. But the trouble is, 'ee's lost the book. 'Ee's lost both books, the one with my name in it *and* the one with yours."

In the long delicate fingers of his right hand, the man was holding up in triumph the two books he had taken from the policeman's pockets.

"Easiest job I ever done," he announced proudly.

二、原作释读

这篇小说阅读难度不是很大，主要是要理解好人物对话中的一些非标准的表达，以及这些表达所反映出的人物的性格特点。

The Hitch-hiker[①]

I had a new car. It was an exciting toy, a big B. M. W.[②] 3. 3 Li, which means 3. 3 litre, long wheelbase[③], fuel injection[④]. It had a top speed of 129 m. p. h. and terrific acceleration. The body was pale blue. The seats inside were darker blue and they were made of leather, genuine soft leather of the finest quality. The windows were electrically operated and so was the sunroof. The radio aerial popped up when I switched on the radio, and disappeared when I switched it off. The powerful engine

---

[①] 本部小说原文出自"DAHL, R. *The Wonderful Story of Henry Sugar and Six More* [M]. London: Penguin Books Ltd., 2002"。

hitch-hiker or hitchhiker: *Noun* a person who travels by getting free rides from passing vehicles 搭便车的旅行者

[②] B. M. W. or BMW: *Abbreviation* Bavarian Motor Works（德国）宝马汽车公司

[③] wheelbase: *Noun* the distance between the front and rear axles of a vehicle （汽车的）轴距

[④] fuel injection: *Noun* [mass noun] the direct introduction of fuel under pressure into the combustion units of an internal-combustion engine 燃油喷射；喷油

growled① and grunted② impatiently at slow speeds, but at sixty miles an hour the growling stopped and the motor began to purr③ with pleasure.

  I was driving up to London by myself. It was a lovely June day. They were haymaking in the fields and there were buttercups④ along both sides of the road. I was whispering along at seventy miles an hour, leaning back comfortably in my seat, with no more than a couple of fingers resting lightly on the wheel to keep her steady. Ahead of me I saw a man thumbing a lift. I touched the footbrake and brought the car to a stop beside him. I always stopped for hitch-hikers. I knew just how it used to feel to be standing on the side of a country road watching the cars go by. I hated the drivers for pretending they didn't see me, especially the ones in big cars with three empty seats. The large expensive cars seldom stopped. It was always the smaller ones that offered you a lift, or the old rusty ones, or the ones that were already crammed full of children and the driver would say, "I think we can squeeze in one more."

  The hitch-hiker poked his head through the open window and said,

---

  ① growl：*Verb*（of a thing）make a low or harsh rumbling sound, typically one that is felt to be threatening（事物）发轰隆声（e.g. Thunder growls without warning from a summer sky. 夏日的天空中突然雷声隆隆。）

  ② grunt：*Verb*［no obj.］（of an animal, especially a pig）make a low, short guttural sound（动物，尤指猪）发出呼噜声

  ③ purr：*Verb*［no obj., with adverbial of direction］（of a vehicle or engine）move smoothly while making such a sound（车辆或发动机）咕隆咕隆地平稳转动（e.g. A sleek blue BMW purred past him. 一辆豪华蓝色宝马牌汽车咕隆咕隆从他身旁驶过。）

  ④ buttercup：*Noun* a herbaceous plant with bright yellow cup-shaped flowers, which is common in grassland and as a garden weed. All kinds are poisonous and generally avoided by livestock 毛茛；金凤花（e.g. The fields were golden with buttercups. 田里是一片金黄色的金凤花。）

"Going to London, guv'nor?"

"Yes," I said, "Jump in."

He got in and I drove on.

He was a small ratty-faced man with grey teeth. His eyes were dark and quick and clever, like a rat's eyes, and his ears were slightly pointed at the top. He had a cloth cap on his head and he was wearing a greyish-coloured jacket with enormous pockets. The grey jacket, together with the quick eyes and the pointed ears, made him look more than anything like some sort of a huge human rat.

"What part of London are you headed for?" I asked him.

"I'm goin'① right through London and out the other side," he said. "I'm goin' to Epsom②, for the races. It's Derby③ Day today."

"So it is," I said. "I wish I were going with you. I love betting on horses."

"I never bet on horses," he said. "I don't even watch 'em run. That's a stupid silly business."

"Then why do you go?" I asked.

He didn't seem to like that question. His little ratty face went absolutely blank and he sat there staring straight ahead at the road, saying nothing.

---

① goin' = going

② Epsom: *Noun* a town in Surrey, SE England; pop. 68,500 (1981). The annual Derby and Oaks horse races are held at its racecourse on Epsom Downs. 埃普瑟姆(英国东南部萨里郡的一个城镇,1981年人口68,500,一年一度的德比马赛和欧可斯马赛在埃普索姆唐斯赛马场举行。)

③ Derby: *Noun* an annual flat horse race for three-year-olds, founded in 1780 by the 12th Earl of Derby. The race is run on Epsom Downs in England in late May or early June. 德比马赛(一年一度的三岁马平地速跑比赛,于1780年由德比伯爵第十二世发起,每年5月底或6月初在英格兰埃普索姆唐斯举行。)

第一章 非常之辈 第一节 《搭车怪客》The Hitch-hiker

"I expect you help to work the betting machines or something like that," I said.

"That's even sillier," he answered. "There's no fun working them lousy① machines and selling tickets to mugs②. Any fool could do that."

There was a long silence. I decided not to question him any more. I remembered how irritated I used to get in my hitch-hiking days when drivers kept asking *me* questions. Where are you going? Why are you going there? What's your job? Are you married? Do you have a girl-friend? What's her name? How old are you? And so on and so forth. I used to hate it.

"I'm sorry," I said. "It's none of my business what you do. The trouble is, I'm a writer, and most writers are terrible nosey parkers③."

"You write books?" he asked.

"Yes."

"Writin'④ books is okay," he said. "It's what I call a skilled trade. I'm in a skilled trade too. The folks I despise⑤ is them that spend all their lives doin'⑥ crummy⑦ old routine jobs with no skill in em' at all. You see what I mean?"

---

① lousy: *Adjective* used to express anger, contempt, or annoyance(用以表达愤怒、轻蔑或不快)讨厌的;卑鄙的;该死的

② mug: *Noun* (Brit. informal) a stupid or gullible person(英国英语非正式用法)笨蛋;易受骗的人

③ nosey parker or nosy-parker: a person who is nosy 爱管闲事的人

④ writin' = writing

⑤ despise: *Verb* [with obj.] feel contempt or a deep repugnance for 鄙视;厌恶(e. g. He despised himself for being selfish. 他厌恶自己的自私。)

⑥ doin' = doing

⑦ crummy or crumby: *Adjective* dirty, unpleasant, or of poor quality 肮脏的;令人不快的;质量低劣的

"Yes."

"The secret of life," he said, "is to become very very good at somethin'① that's very very 'ard② to do."

"Like you," I said.

"Exactly. You and me both."

"What makes you think that *I'm* any good at my job?" I asked. "There's an awful lot of bad writers around."

"You wouldn't be drivin'③ about in a car like this if you weren't no good at it," he answered. "It must've cost a tidy④ packet⑤, this little job."

"It wasn't cheap."

"What can she do flat out⑥?" he asked.

"One hundred and twenty-nine miles an hour," I told him.

"I'll bet she won't do it."

"I'll bet she will."

"All car makers is liars," he said. "You can buy any car you like and it'll never do what the makers say it will in the ads."

---

① somethin' = something

② 'ard = hard

③ drivin' = driving

④ tidy: *Adjective* [attrib.] (informal) (of an amount, especially of money) considerable(非正式用法)(数量)相当大的;(尤指钱)相当多的(e.g. The book will bring in a tidy sum. 这本书将带来一笔可观的收入。)

⑤ packet: *Noun* (informal, chiefly Brit.) a large sum of money(主要为英国英语的非正式表达)一笔巨款;大笔款项(e.g. That car cost me a packet. 那辆小汽车花了我一大笔钱。)

⑥ flat out: as fast or as hard as possible 尽可能快;尽最大努力;竭尽全力 (e.g. The whole team is working flat out to satisfy demand. 整个团队正竭尽全力来满足需求。)

"This one will."

"Open 'er① up then and prove it," he said. "Go on, guv'nor, open 'er right up and let's see what she'll do."

There is a roundabout② at Chalfont St Peter and immediately beyond it there's a long straight section of dual carriageway. We came out of the roundabout on to the carriageway and I pressed my foot down on the accelerator. The big car leaped forward as though she'd been stung. In ten seconds or so, we were doing ninety.

"Lovely!" he cried. "Beautiful! Keep goin'!"

I had the accelerator jammed right down against the floor and I held it there.

"One hundred!" he shouted... "A hundred and five!... A hundred and ten!... A hundred and fifteen! Go on! Don't slack off!"

I was in the outside lane and we flashed past several cars as though they were standing still—a green Mini③, a big cream-coloured Citroën④, a white Land-Rover⑤, a huge truck with a container on the back, an orange-coloured Volkswagen⑥ Minibus...

"A hundred and twenty!" my passenger shouted, jumping up and down. "Go on! Go on! Get 'er up to one-two-nine!"

At that moment, I heard the scream of a police siren.

---

① 'er = her

② roundabout: *Noun* (Brit.) a road junction at which traffic moves in one direction round a central island to reach one of the roads converging on it(英国用法) 环行交叉;环行交通枢纽

③ Mini:一个汽车的品牌,一般译作"米妮"。

④ Citroën or Citroen:一个著名汽车的品牌,通常译作"雪铁龙"。

⑤ Land-Rover:一个著名汽车的品牌,通常译作"路虎"。

⑥ Volkswagen:一个著名汽车的品牌,通常译作"大众"。

It was so loud it seemed to be right inside the car, and then a policeman on a motor-cycle loomed up alongside us on the inside lane and went past us and raised a hand for us to stop.

"Oh, my sainted aunt!① " I said. "That's torn it!②"

The policeman must have been doing about a hundred and thirty when he passed us, and he took plenty of time slowing down. Finally, he pulled into the side of the road and I pulled in behind him. "I didn't know police motor-cycles could go as fast as that," I said rather lamely③.

"That one can," my passenger said. "It's the same make as yours. It's a B. M. W. R90S. Fastest bike on the road. That's what they're usin'④ nowadays."

The policeman got off his motor-cycle and leaned the machine sideways on to its prop stand. Then he took off his gloves and placed them carefully on the seat. He was in no hurry now. He had us where he wanted us and he knew it.

"This is real trouble," I said. "I don't like it one bit."

"Don't talk to 'im⑤ any more than is necessary, you understand,"

---

① my sainted aunt!: (informal, chiefly Brit.) an exclamation expressing surprise or disbelief(主要为英国英语非正式用法)哎呀！天呐！(表示惊讶或不相信)

② That's torn it: (Brit. informal) used to express dismay when something unfortunate has happened to disrupt someone's plans(英国英语非正式用法)这下完蛋了；那就糟了

③ lame: Adjective (of an explanation or excuse) unconvincingly feeble(理由)站不住脚的；无说服力的

④ usin' = using

⑤ 'im = him

my companion said. "Just sit tight and keep mum①."

Like an executioner② approaching his victim, the policeman came strolling slowly towards us. He was a big meaty③ man with a belly, and his blue breeches④ were skintight⑤ around his enormous thighs. His goggles were pulled up on the helmet, showing a smouldering red face with wide cheeks.

We sat there like guilty schoolboys, waiting for him to arrive.

"Watch out for this man," my passenger whispered. "'Ee⑥ looks mean as the devil."

The policeman came round to my open window and placed one meaty hand on the sill. "What's the hurry?" he said.

"No hurry, officer," I answered.

"Perhaps there's a woman in the back having a baby and you're rushing her to hospital? Is that it?"

"No, officer."

"Or perhaps your house is on fire and you're dashing home to rescue the family from upstairs?" His voice was dangerously soft and mocking.

"My house isn't on fire, officer."

---

① keep mum: (informal) remain silent, especially so as not to reveal a secret(非正式)(尤指为保密)保持沉默;守口如瓶(e.g. He was keeping mum about a possible move to West Ham. 他对可能搬到西哈姆一事不发一言。)

② executioner: Noun an official who carries out a sentence of death on a legally condemned person 行刑人

③ meaty: Adjective fleshy; brawny 肥硕的;粗壮的(e.g. the tall, meaty young man 高大、强壮的年轻人)

④ breeches: Plural Noun short trousers fastened just below the knee, now chiefly worn for riding or as part of ceremonial dress 及膝短裤;马裤

⑤ skintight: Adjective (of a garment) very close-fitting(衣服)非常紧身的

⑥ 'Ee = He

"In that case," he said, "you've got yourself into a nasty mess, haven't you? Do you know what the speed limit is in this country?"

"Seventy," I said.

"And do you mind telling me exactly what speed you were doing just now?"

I shrugged and didn't say anything.

When he spoke next, he raised his voice so loud that I jumped. "*One hundred and twenty miles per hour*!" he barked. "That's *fifty* miles an hour over the limit!"

He turned his head and spat out a big gob① of spit. It landed on the wing② of my car and started sliding down over my beautiful blue paint. Then he turned back again and stared hard at my passenger. "And who are you?" he asked sharply.

"He's a hitch-hiker," I said. "I'm giving him a lift."

"I didn't ask you," he said. "I asked him."

"'Ave③ I done somethin' wrong?" my passenger asked. His voice was as soft and oily as haircream.

"That's more than likely," the policeman answered. "Anyway, you're a witness. I'll deal with you in a minute. Driving-licence," he snapped, holding out his hand.

I gave him my driving-licence.

---

① gob: *Noun* (Brit.) a lump or clot of a slimy or viscous substance(英国用法)(黏性或黏稠物质的)一块;一团

② wing: *Noun* (Brit.) a raised part of the body of a car or other vehicle above the wheel(英国用法)(汽车等的)挡泥板;翼子板

③ 'Ave = Have

第一章 非常之辈　第一节 《搭车怪客》*The Hitch-hiker*

He unbuttoned the left-hand breast-pocket of his tunic① and brought out the dreaded books of tickets. Carefully, he copied the name and address from my licence. Then he gave it back to me. He strolled round to the front of the car and read the number from the number-plate and wrote that down as well. He filled in the date, the time and the details of my offence. Then he tore out the top copy of the ticket. But before handing it to me, he checked that all the information had come through clearly on his own carbon copy②. Finally, he replaced the book in his tunic pocket and fastened the button.

"Now you," he said to my passenger, and he walked around to the other side of the car. From the other breast-pocket he produced a small black notebook. "Name?" he snapped.

"Michael Fish," my passenger said.

"Address?"

"Fourteen, Windsor Lane, Luton③."

"Show me something to prove this is your real name and address." the policeman said.

My passenger fished in his pockets and came out with a driving-licence of his own. The policeman checked the name and address and handed it back to him. "What's your job?" he asked sharply.

---

① tunic: *Noun* a close-fitting short coat as part of a uniform, especially a police or military uniform(尤指警察、军人的)紧身短上衣

② carbon copy: a copy of written or typed material made with carbon paper 复写本;副本

③ Luton: *Noun* an industrial town to the north-west of London, a unitary council formerly in Bedfordshire; pop. 167,300 (1991) 卢顿(伦敦西北一工业城镇,原为贝德福德郡内的一个单一制地方议会;1991年人口167,300。)

"I'm an 'od① carrier②."

"A what?"

"An 'od carrier."

"Spell it."

"H – O – D C – A – ..."

"That'll do. And what's a hod carrier, may I ask?"

"An 'od carrier, officer, is a person 'oo③ carries the cement up the ladder to the bricklayer④. And the 'od is what 'ee carries it in. It's got a long 'andle⑤ and on the top you've got two bits of wood set at an angle..."

"All right, all right. Who's your employer?"

"Don't 'ave one. I'm unemployed."

The policeman wrote all this down in the black notebook. Then he returned the book to its pocket and did up the button. "When I get back to the station I'm going to do a little checking up on you," he said to my passenger.

"Me? What've I done wrong?" the rat-faced man asked.

"I don't like your face, that's all," the policeman said. "And we just might have a picture of it somewhere in our files." He strolled round the car and returned to my window.

---

① 'od = hod：*Noun* a builder's V-shaped open trough on a pole, used for carrying bricks and other building materials（搬运砖块和其他建筑材料的 V 型）砖斗；灰砂斗；灰浆桶

② hod carrier or hodman：(Building) a labourer who carries the materials in a hod for a plasterer, bricklayer, etc.（建筑）灰泥砖瓦搬运工；小工；苦工

③ 'oo = who

④ bricklayer：*Noun* a person whose job is to build walls, houses, and other structures with bricks 泥瓦匠；砌砖工人

⑤ 'andle = handle

"I suppose you know you're in serious trouble," he said to me.

"Yes, officer."

"You won't be driving this fancy car of yours again for a very long time, not after *we've* finished with you. You won't be driving *any* car again come to that① for several years. And a good thing, too. I hope they lock you up for a spell into the bargain②."

"You mean prison?" I asked, alarmed.

"Absolutely," he said, smacking his lips. "In the clink③. Behind the bars. Along with all the other criminals who break the law. *And* a hefty④ fine into the bargain. Nobody will be more pleased about that than me. I'll see you in court, both of you. You'll be getting a summons to appear."

He turned away and walked over to his motor-cycle.

He flipped the prop stand back into position with his foot and swung his leg over the saddle. Then he kicked the starter and roared off up the road out of sight.

"Phew⑤!" I gasped. "That's done it."

---

① come to that (or if it comes to that): (informal) in fact (said to introduce an additional point)（非正式用法）事实上；其实（用于引出另一点）(e. g. There isn't a clock on the mantelpiece—come to that, there isn't a mantelpiece! 壁炉架上并没有钟——事实上，也根本没有壁炉架。)

② into the bargain: in addition to what has been already mentioned or was expected 另外还；而且还(e. g. I am now tired and extremely hungry—with a headache into the bargain. 我现在又累又饿，而且还头疼。)

③ clink: *Noun* [in sing.] (informal) prison(非正式用法)监狱

④ hefty: *Adjective* (of a number or amount) impressively large(数目或数量)相当大的

⑤ phew: *Exclamation* (informal) expressing a strong reaction of relief(非正式用法)咳；唷；哦(表示松一口气)(e. g. Phew, what a year! 唷，又打发了一年！)

"We was caught," my passenger said. "We was caught good and proper."

"I was caught, you mean."

"That's right," he said. "What you goin' to do now, guv'nor?"

"I'm going straight up to London to talk to my solicitor," I said. I started the car and drove on.

"You mustn't believe what 'ee said to you about goin' to prison," my passenger said. "They don't put nobody in the clink just for speedin'①."

"Are you sure of that?" I asked.

"I'm positive," he answered. "They can take your licence away and they can give you a whoppin'② big fine, but that'll be the end of it."

I felt tremendously relieved.

"By the way," I said, "why did you lie to him?"

"Who, me?" he said. "What makes you think I lied?"

"You told him you were an unemployed hod carrier. But you told *me* you were in a highly-skilled trade."

"So I am," he said. "But it don't pay to tell everythin'③ to a copper."

"So what *do* you do?" I asked him.

"Ah," he said slyly. "That'd be tellin'④, wouldn't it?"

---

① speedin' = speeding

② whoppin' = whopping: Adjective (informal) very large(非正式用法)巨大的;庞大的

③ everythin' = everything

④ tellin' = telling

That would be telling: (informal) used to convey that one is not prepared to divulge secret or confidential information(非正式用法)不走漏风声;不泄密

"Is it something you're ashamed of?"

"Ashamed?" he cried. "Me, ashamed of my job? I'm about as proud of it as anybody could be in the entire world!"

"Then why won't you tell me?"

"You writers really is nosey parkers, aren't you?" he said. "And you ain't① goin' to be 'appy②, I don't think, until you've found out exactly what the answer is?"

"I don't really care one way or the other," I told him, lying.

He gave me a crafty little ratty look out of the sides of his eyes. "I think you do care," he said. "I can see it in your face that you think I'm in some kind of a very peculiar trade and you're just achin'③ to know what it is."

I didn't like the way he read my thoughts. I kept quiet and stared at the road ahead.

"You'd be right, too," he went on. "I *am* in a very peculiar trade. I'm in the queerest peculiar trade of 'em all."

I waited for him to go on.

"That's why I'as to be extra careful 'oo I'm talkin'④ to, you see. 'Ow⑤ am I to know, for instance, you're not another copper in plain clothes?"

"Do I look like a copper?"

"No," he said. "You don't. And you ain't. Any fool could tell

---

① ain't = aren't

② 'appy = happy

③ achin' = aching

ache: *Verb* feel an intense desire for 渴望(e. g. She ached for his touch. 她渴望他的抚摸。)

④ talkin' = talking

⑤ 'Ow = How

that."

He took from his pocket a tin of tobacco and a packet of cigarette papers and started to roll a cigarette. I was watching him out of the corner of one eye, and the speed with which he performed this rather difficult operation was incredible. The cigarette was rolled and ready in about five seconds. He ran his tongue along the edge of the paper, stuck it down and popped the cigarette between his lips. Then, as if from nowhere, a lighter appeared in his hand. The lighter flamed. The cigarette was lit. The lighter disappeared. It was altogether a remarkable performance.

"I've never seen anyone roll a cigarette as fast as that," I said.

"Ah," he said, taking a deep suck of smoke. "So you noticed."

"Of course I noticed. It was quite fantastic."

He sat back and smiled. It pleased him very much that I had noticed how quickly he could roll a cigarette. "You want to know what makes me able to do it?" he asked.

"Go on then."

"It's because I've got fantastic fingers. These fingers of mine," he said, holding up both hands high in front of him, "are quicker and cleverer than the fingers of the best piano player in the world!"

"Are you a piano player?"

"Don't be daft," he said. "Do I look like a piano player?"

I glanced at his fingers. They were so beautifully shaped, so slim and long and elegant, they didn't seem to belong to the rest of him at all. They looked more like the fingers of a brain surgeon or a watchmaker.

"My job," he went on, "is a hundred times more difficult than playin'① the piano. Any twerp② can learn to do that. There's titchy③ little kids learnin'④ to play the piano in almost any 'ouse⑤ you go into these days. That's right, ain't it?"

"More or less," I said.

"Of course it's right. But there's not one person in ten million can learn to do what I do. Not one in ten million! 'Ow about that?"

"Amazing," I said.

"You're darn right it's amazin'⑥," he said.

"I think I know what you do." I said. "You do conjuring⑦ tricks. You're a conjurer."

"Me?" he snorted⑧. "A conjurer? Can you picture me goin' round crummy⑨ kids' parties makin'⑩ rabbits come out of top 'ats⑪?"

———

① playin' = playing

② twerp or twirp: *Noun* (informal) a silly or annoying person(非正式用法)笨蛋;讨厌的家伙

③ titchy: *Adjective* (Brit. informal) very small(英国英语非正式用法)极小的

④ learnin' = learning

⑤ 'ouse = house

⑥ amazin' = amazing

⑦ conjuring: *Noun* [mass noun] [often as modifier] the performance of tricks which are seemingly magical, typically involving sleight of hand 变戏法;魔术表演

⑧ snort: *Verb* [no obj.] make a sudden sound through one's nose, especially to express indignation or derision (尤指因气愤、蔑视而)哼鼻子(e.g. "How perfectly ridiculous!" he snorted. 简直是无稽之谈!"他嗤之以鼻。)

⑨ crummy or crumby: *Adjective* dirty, unpleasant, or of poor quality 肮脏的;令人不快的;质量低劣的

⑩ makin' = making

⑪ 'ats = hats

"Then you're a card player. You get people into card games and deal yourself marvellous hands."

"Me! A rotten card-sharper!" he cried. "That's a miserable racket if ever there was one."

"All right. I give up."

I was taking the car along slowly now, at no more than forty miles an hour, to make quite sure I wasn't stopped again. We had come on to the main London-Oxford road and were running down the hill towards Denham.

Suddenly, my passenger was holding up a black leather belt in his hand. "Ever seen this before?" he asked. The belt had a brass buckle of unusual design.

"Hey!" I said. "That's mine, isn't it? It is mine! Where did you get it?"

He grinned and waved the belt gently from side to side. "Where d'you think I got it?" he said. "Off the top of your trousers, of course."

I reached down and felt for my belt. It was gone.

"You mean you took it off me while we've been driving along?" I asked, flabbergasted.

He nodded, watching me all the time with those little black ratty eyes.

"That's impossible," I said. "You'd have to undo the buckle and slide the whole thing out through the loops all the way round. I'd have seen you doing it. And even if I hadn't seen you, I'd have felt it."

"Ah, but you didn't, did you?" he said, triumphant. He dropped the belt on his lap, and now all at once there was a brown shoelace dangling from his fingers. "And what about this, then?" he exclaimed, waving the shoelace.

"What about it?" I said.

"Anyone round 'ere① missin'② a shoelace?" he asked, grinning.

I glanced down at my shoes. The lace of one of them was missing. "Good grief!" I said. "How did you do that? I never saw you bending down." "You never saw nothin'③," he said proudly. "You never even saw me move an inch. And you know why?"

"Yes," I said. "Because you've got fantastic fingers."

"Exactly right!" he cried. "You catch on pretty quick, don't you?" He sat back and sucked away at his homemade cigarette, blowing the smoke out in a thin stream against the windshield. He knew he had impressed me greatly with those two tricks, and this made him very happy. "I don't want to be late," he said. "What time is it?"

"There's a clock in front of you," I told him.

"I don't trust car clocks," he said. "What does your watch say?"

I hitched up my sleeve to look at the watch on my wrist. It wasn't there. I looked at the man. He looked back at me, grinning.

"You've taken that, too," I said.

He held out his hand and there was my watch lying in his palm. "Nice bit of stuff, this," he said. "Superior quality. Eighteen-carat gold. Easy to flog④, too. It's never any trouble gettin'⑤ rid of quality goods."

---

① 'ere = here

② missin' = missing

③ nothin' = nothing

④ flog: *Verb* (Brit. informal) sell or offer for sale(英国英语非正式用法)卖;出售(e. g. He made a fortune flogging beads to hippies. 他靠卖珠子给嬉皮士们发了财。)

⑤ gettin' = getting

"I'd like it back, if you don't mind," I said rather huffily①.

He placed the watch carefully on the leather tray in front of him. "I wouldn't nick② anything from you, guv'nor," he said. "You're my pal. You're giving me a lift."

"I'm glad to hear it." I said.

"All I'm doin' is answerin'③ your questions," he went on. "You asked me what I did for a livin'④ and I'm showin'⑤ you."

"What else have you got of mine?"

He smiled again, and now he started to take from the pocket of his jacket one thing after another that belonged to me—my driving-licence, a key-ring with four keys on it, some pound notes, a few coins, a letter from my publishers, my diary, a stubby⑥ old pencil, a cigarette-lighter, and last of all, a beautiful old sapphire⑦ ring with pearls around it belonging to my wife. I was taking the ring up to the jeweller in London because one of the pearls was missing.

"Now *there's* another lovely piece of goods," he said, turning the ring over in his fingers. "That's eighteenth century, if I'm not mistaken, from the reign of King George the Third."

---

① huffy：*Adjective* annoyed or irritated and quick to take offence at petty things 易动怒的；易生气的

② nick：*Verb*（Brit. informal）steal(英国英语非正式用法)偷(e. g. He'd had his car nicked by joyriders. 他的车被兜风族偷走了。)

③ answerin' = answering

④ livin' = living

⑤ showin' = showing

⑥ stubby：*Adjective* short and thick 又短又粗的(e. g. Blufton pointed with a stubby finger. 布拉夫顿用又短又粗的手指头指点着。)

⑦ sapphire：*Noun* a transparent precious stone, typically blue, which is a variety of corundum (aluminium oxide) 蓝宝石

"You're right," I said, impressed. "You're absolutely right."

He put the ring on the leather tray with the other items.

"So you're a pickpocket," I said.

"I don't like that word," he answered. "It's a coarse and vulgar word. Pickpockets is coarse and vulgar people who only do easy little amateur jobs. They lift money from blind old ladies."

"What do you call yourself, then?"

"Me? I'm a fingersmith. I'm a professional fingersmith." He spoke the words solemnly and proudly, as though he were telling me he was the President of the Royal College of Surgeons or the Archbishop of Canterbury.

"I've never heard that word before," I said. "Did you invent it?"

"Of course I didn't invent it," he replied. "It's the name given to them who's risen to the very top of the profession. You've 'eard[①] of a goldsmith and a silversmith, for instance. They're experts with gold and silver. I'm an expert with my fingers, so I'm a fingersmith."

"It must be an interesting job."

"It's a marvellous job," he answered. "It's lovely."

"And that's why you go to the races?"

"Race meetings is easy meat[②]," he said. "You just stand around after the race, watchin'[③] for the lucky ones to queue up and draw their money. And when you see someone collectin'[④] a big bundle of notes, you

---

① 'eard = heard

② easy meat: (informal) a person or animal that is easily overcome or outwitted (非正式用法) 容易对付的人（或动物）

③ watchin' = watching

④ collectin' = collecting

simply follows after 'im and 'elps① yourself. But don't get me wrong, guv'nor. I never takes nothin' from a loser. Nor from poor people neither. I only go after them as can afford it, the winners and the rich."

"That's very thoughtful of you," I said. "How often do you get caught?"

"Caught?" he cried, disgusted. "*Me* get caught! It's only pickpockets get caught. Fingersmiths never. Listen, I could take the false teeth out of your mouth if I wanted to and you wouldn't even catch me!"

"I don't have false teeth," I said.

"I know you don't," he answered. "Otherwise I'd 'ave 'ad 'em out long ago!"

I believed him. Those long slim fingers of his seemed able to do anything.

We drove on for a while without talking.

"That policeman's going to check up on you pretty thoroughly," I said. "Doesn't that worry you a bit?"

"Nobody's checkin'② up on me," he said.

"Of course they are. He's got your name and address written down most carefully in his black book."

The man gave me another of his sly, ratty little smiles. "Ah," he said. "So 'ee 'as. But I'll bet 'ee ain't got it all written down in 'is③ memory as well. I've never known a copper yet with a decent memory. Some of 'em can't even remember their own names."

"What's memory got to do with it?" I asked. "It's written down in his book, isn't it?"

---

① 'elps = helps
② checkin' = checking
③ 'is = his

"Yes, guv'nor, it is. But the trouble is, 'ee's① lost the book. 'Ee's lost both books, the one with my name in it *and* the one with yours."

In the long delicate fingers of his right hand, the man was holding up in triumph the two books he had taken from the policeman's pockets. "Easiest job I ever done," he announced proudly.

I nearly swerved the car into a milk-truck, I was so excited.

"That copper's got nothin' on either of us now," he said.

"You're a genius!" I cried.

"'Ee's got no names, no addresses, no car number, no nothin'," he said.

"You're brilliant!"

"I think you'd better pull in off this main road as soon as possible," he said. "Then we'd better build a little bonfire and burn these books."

"You're a fantastic fellow," I exclaimed.

"Thank you, guv'nor," he said. "It's always nice to be appreciated."

三、翻译探索

本篇小说的翻译中,那位搭车怪客的语言风格的传达是个可以探索的翻译问题。在这方面,下面的译文只是做了常规性的处理,未能做到风格上的"对等"传达,有待进一步探索。

搭车怪客

我买了辆新车,也就是一个令人兴奋不已的大玩具——宝马3.3Li,数字和字母指的是排量,为"3.3升"。这是一辆燃油喷射式的长轴距大个头车,最高时速为206公里,而且加速奇快。车身颜色为淡蓝色,内部座椅颜色为深蓝色,座椅是皮制的,而且是质量上乘

---

① 'ee's = he has

的真皮做的。车窗以及天窗都是电动的。一开收音机,收音天线就弹出来;一关收音机,天线就收回去。低速行驶时,强大的引擎会发出"轰隆隆""呼噜噜"的、好似不耐烦的声响,但是,速度达到每小时96公里时,轰隆声就骤然停止,马达就开始平稳地发出"呼噜、呼噜"欢快的声响。

六月里风和日丽的一天,我自己开着车,驶向伦敦。人们在田野里晾晒干草,路的两旁开满了金凤花。车轻轻松松地行驶着,车速每小时112公里,我则舒舒服服倚靠在驾驶座位上,只有两三根手指轻轻地放在方向盘上,控制着爱车平稳前进。我看到车前方有一名男子竖起大拇指要搭车,我踩下脚刹车,把车停在他身旁。看见搭车的,我总是会停下,因为我知道以前我搭车时的滋味:站在乡村的路边,看着一辆辆车驶过。我憎恨那些对搭车的我故意视而不见的司机,特别是那些开着大车的司机,他们的车上还有三个空座呢。大个头的、价格昂贵的车很少停下让人搭车,停下与人方便的总是那些小个头的车,或者是老得生了锈的车,或者是那些挤满了孩子的车。尽管车里挤满了孩子,司机还会说:"我想,我们这里还能挤进一位。"

搭车的男子将脑袋伸进开着的车窗,问道:"老板,是去伦敦吗?"

"是的,"我说,"上来吧。"

他上来后,我继续开车。

他个子矮矮,牙齿灰灰,面如鼠脸,目如鼠眼——颜色很黑、转动飞快、聪明伶俐,两只尖耳朵微微向上竖起。他头戴一顶布帽子,穿着一件浅灰色的夹克衫,上面缝了几个大大的口袋。灰色的夹克衫、快速转动的眼睛、竖起的尖耳朵,这些令他看起来简直就像一只人形鼠。

"你要去伦敦的什么地方?"我问他。

"我要穿过伦敦,去另一头,"他回答。"我要去的是埃普瑟姆镇。今天是德比赛马日。"

"是的,没错,"我说。"真希望我能跟你一起去,我酷爱赌马。"

"我从来不赌马,"他说,"我甚至也不看马赛,赛马这个行当无

第一章 非常之辈 第一节 《搭车怪客》The Hitch-hiker

聊得很,蠢到了家。"

"那么,你为什么还要去?"我问。

他似乎不太喜欢这个问题。他那张小鼠脸毫无表情,坐在那儿直勾勾盯着前方的路,什么都没有说。

"我估计,你是去帮助弄赌马机器,或者干点类似的活吧,"我说。

"那更是蠢到了家,"他回答,"摆弄那些讨厌的机器,卖票给那些讨厌的家伙,一点意思都没有,那是傻子都能干的活。"

一段长时间的沉默过后,我决定不再问这问那了。我记得,在我搭车的日子里,司机问我这个、问我那个时,我是多么不快和气恼!你去哪儿?为什么去那儿?你是干什么的?你结婚了吗?有女朋友了吗?女朋友叫什么名字?你多大了?问题一箩筐,我一度憎恨这一点。

"我很抱歉。"我说。"你做什么,不关我的事。可问题是,我是一个作家,多数作家都是喜欢打探、爱管闲事的。"

"你写书吗?"他问。

"是的。"

"写书不错啊,"他说。"那是高技能的行当,我从事的也是高技能的行当。我鄙视的是那些一生时间都做些低劣的、老掉牙的、一成不变的工作的人,那些工作根本没有什么技能而言。你明白我的意思吗?"

"是的。"

"生活的秘密,"他说,"就在于要变得很擅长、很擅长去做某个很难、很难做到的事情。"

"就像你那样,"我说。

"正是。就像我和你这样。"

"是什么让你认为,我擅长我的工作呢?"我问,"周围徒有其表的作家有的是啊。"

"要是你不擅长的话,你就不会坐在这样的一辆车里到处走了,"他回答,"就你的小差事所赚的钱而言,这车一定是价格不菲。"

"这车不便宜。"

"开足马力跑,它能有多快?"他问。

"每小时206公里,"我对他说。

"我敢打赌,它跑不了那么快。"

"我敢打赌,能跑那么快。"

"所有的汽车制造商都在说谎,"他说,"随你去买哪一辆车,它将永远也达不到制造商在广告中所说的速度。"

"但这辆车能。"

"跑起来,证明一下,"他说,"来呀,老板,立刻跑起来,让我们看看它能跑多少。"

在查尔芬特圣彼得处有一个环状交叉路,这条路一过,就是一段长长的双向直行路。我们驶过交叉路,开上了直行路,于是,我就踩下了油门。这辆大车猛地向前一跃,就好像被什么东西蜇了一下似的。约摸十秒钟的工夫,我们速度就达到了每小时144公里。

"不错!"他喊道。"漂亮!继续啊!"

我将油门踩到了底儿,并保持住。

"160!"他喊道……"168!……176!184!继续啊!不要松懈!"

我是在外车道行驶,车窗外有好几辆车一闪而过:有一辆绿色的米妮牌车,有一辆大个头淡黄色的雪铁龙,有一辆白色的路虎,有一辆后面拖着货柜的大卡车,还有一辆橘黄色的大众牌面包车……

"192!"我的这位乘客上下跳跃,大叫起来,"继续!继续啊!跑到206啊!"

就在那一刻,我听到警笛的尖叫声,声音很响,就好像从车内响起一般。紧接着,在内侧的车道上,隐隐约约地出现了一名骑着摩托车的警察,逐渐跟我们并驾齐驱,随后超过我们,并举起一只手示意我们停车。

"哎呀,我的天哪!"我喊道。"这下可玩完啦!"

警车超过我们的时候,速度一定有208了,以至于用了很长时间才减慢下来。最后,警察将车靠路边停下,我随即停到他的后面。

"我真不知道警察的摩托车能跑得如此快,"我说,感觉底气有些不足。

"那辆可以的,"搭车的人说道,"那车跟你的是一个牌子的,但型号是'宝马R90S',是公路上最快的摩托车,警察现在都骑这种车。"

警察下了摩托车,放下车支脚,将车原地斜放好。然后,他摘下手套,细心地放到车座上。现在,他用不着着急了,他知道他已经如愿控制住我们。

"这下可真的麻烦了,"我说,"我一点都不喜欢这样。"

"不要跟他多说什么无关紧要的话,你明白的,"我的同伴告诫道,"只管坐正,守口如瓶。"

警察慢悠悠地向我们这边溜达,就像一个执行死刑的人走向死刑犯似的。这位警察块头很大、脑满肠肥、大腹便便,那条蓝色的马裤在大腿部位绷得紧紧的,他把护目镜拉了上去,搭到了头盔上,露出一副闷得发红的面孔,脸颊宽宽的。

我俩像愧疚的学生一样坐在那儿,等着他的到来。

"留意一下这个伙计,"搭车的人小声说,"他看起来如同凶神恶煞一般。"

这名警察走到我那扇开着的车窗跟前,将一只肉乎乎的手放到车窗横梁上。"有什么事如此着忙?"他问。

"没有着忙啊,警官,"我回答。

"或许,车后面坐着一位妇女,要生孩子了,你急着要将她送往医院?是这样的吗?"

"不是的,警官。"

"或者是你家房子着火了,你急着往回飞奔,要救二楼的家人?"他的语调和缓,却暗藏危险,充满嘲弄之意。

"我家房子没有着火,警官。"

"那样的话,"他说,"你麻烦就大啦,难道不是吗?你知道这个郡的限速是多少吗?"

"112,"我回答。

"你介意告诉我一下,你刚才开多少吗?"

我耸了耸肩,什么也没有说。

他再一次说话的时候,嗓门提高了,把我吓了一跳。"每小时192公里啊!"他大声吼叫。"每小时超过限速80公里啊!"

他转过头,张嘴一吐,一大团痰就吐到了我的车的侧翼,然后开始沿着漂亮的蓝色油漆表面向下滑落。他又转过身,使劲盯着搭车的乘客。"那么,你又是谁?"他尖锐地问道。

"他就是一个搭车的,"我说,"是我让他搭车的。"

"我没有问你,"他说,"我问的是他。"

"我做错什么事儿了吗?"我的乘客问。他的声音和缓,但却像发乳一样油滑。

"极其有可能,"警察回答。"不管怎么说,你是证人,稍后我再问你。驾照,"他伸出一只手,厉声说道。

我将驾照递给他。

他将警服左边胸袋上的纽扣解开,从中取出可怕的罚单簿,然后,仔细地从驾照上抄写姓名和地址,然后就将驾照还给了我。他溜达到车的前部,看了看车牌上的号码,然后写了下来,填写好日期和时间,以及我违规的细节,就随手撕下最上面那一页。但是,在递给我之前,他检查了一下复写页,以确保所写的内容都清晰可辨。最后,他将罚单簿放回警服衣兜里,扣上了纽扣。

"听着,你,"他绕到车的另一侧,对我的乘客说。随后,从另一只胸袋里掏出一个小小的黑色笔记本,"你的名字?"他厉声问道。

"迈克尔·菲什,"我的乘客回答。

"地址?"

"卢顿镇温莎街十四号。"

"给我看点能证明你身份的东西,"警察说。

我的这位乘客摸了一个衣兜又一个衣兜,拿出了他自己的驾照。

警察核实完,递还给他。"你是做什么工作的?"他尖声问道。

"我是一个搬运小工。"

"什么小工?"

"搬运小工。"

"怎么写?"

"提手旁的'搬',走之旁的……"

"会写了。我可以问问,搬运小工是干什么的吗?"

"警官,搬运小工就是一个将混凝土沿着梯子搬运给大泥瓦匠的人。搬运用的是灰浆桶,它有一根长柄,桶的顶部有两片木头,呈一定的角度……"

"好啦,好啦。你的老板是谁?"

"没有老板,我失业了。"

警察将所有这一切都写到那个黑色的笔记本里,然后将其放回衣兜,扣上了纽扣。

"回到警局,我要把你说的稍微核实一下,"他对我的这位乘客说。

"核实我? 我做错了什么?"鼠脸男子问。

"我不喜欢你那张脸,仅此而已,"警察说,"我们档案的某个地方,或许有这样一张脸的图片。"他又溜达着回到了我这一侧。

"我想,你知道你麻烦可不小啊,"他对我说道。

"是的,警官。"

"会有很长一段时间,不允许你开你的这辆名贵车了,你这次违规我们一处理完,你就开不了了。事实上,会有好几年的时间,你什么车也别想开了。这也是一件好事儿,而且我希望,他们会将你关上一阵子。"

"你意思是在监狱里?"我有些惶恐地问道。

"绝对没错,"他咂巴着嘴唇说道。"蹲在大牢里,关进大狱中,跟其他触犯法律的罪犯一同关进去,而且还要交纳一笔巨额罚款。为这事儿,没有谁比我更开心的啦。我要把你送上法庭,你们两个。

你们会被传唤出庭的。"

他转身向摩托车走去。他用脚一踢,收回了支架,随即腿一挥,跨上了鞍座,脚一蹬启动器,驾着摩托车呼啸而去,消失不见了。

"喔唷!"我喘着粗气说,"完蛋了。"

"我俩被逮了,"搭车人说。"我俩被逮个正着,跑不掉。"

"你意思是说,我被逮住了。"

"没错,"他说。"老板,现在你打算怎么办?"

"我要径直开到伦敦,跟我的律师谈谈,"说完,我发动汽车,开走了。

"你莫信他说的蹲监狱之类的话,"我的这位乘客说道,"单单因为超速,他们是不会把谁送进大牢的。"

"你肯定吗?"我问。

"我肯定,"他回答。"他们会没收你的驾照,罚你一大笔钱,也就是这个样子。"

我感到大大地松了口气。

"随便问一句,"我说,"你为什么跟他撒谎?"

"谁撒谎?我吗?"他反问。"你凭什么认为我撒谎了?"

"你对他说,你是一个失业的搬运小工,但是,你对我说,你是从事高技能行当的。"

"我是的,没错,"他说。"但是,跟警察全盘托出,划不来的。"

"那么,你做的到底是什么?"我问他。

"哦,"他不好意思说道,"我不想到处宣扬,不可以吗?"

"说出来,会令你感到羞耻吗?"

"羞耻?"他大叫道。"我?对我的工作感到羞耻?我对我工作的自豪感,不亚于这个世界上任何一个人!"

"那么,为什么不肯告诉我?"

"你们这些当作家的,真的是喜欢打探、爱管闲事,不是吗?"他说。"我想,你得到了准确的答案,你就不会那么开心了,对吗?"

"不管怎样,我真的不在意,"我言不由衷地说。

他用鼠目的余光看了我一下,露出狡诈的神情。"我想,你肯定会在意的,"他说,"从你的脸上我看得出,你认为我所从事的是某种很奇特的行当,而且你渴望知道那到底是什么行当。"

我不喜欢他用这种方式揣摩我的心思,于是我就盯着前方的路,一言不发。

"你想得也对,"他继续说。"我从事的的确是很奇特的行当。我所从事的是全世界所有行当中最为奇特的行当。"

我等着他继续往下说。

"说什么话,我要看对象是谁,那也就是我格外谨小慎微的原因所在,你明白的。比方说,我怎么会知道你不是警察,一个穿便衣的警察呢?"

"我看起来像警察吗?"

"不像,"他说,"你不像。你也不是警察,傻子都能看出来你不是。"

他从衣兜里掏出一个装了烟草的锡罐,还有一叠卷烟纸,开始卷起烟来。我从一只眼角处看着他,发现他卷烟的速度快得令人称奇,大约五秒钟的时间他就把烟卷好了。他用舌头在卷烟纸的边缘一舔,将烟纸封好,往嘴里"啪"的一扔,两只嘴唇就将烟叼住了。接下来,也不知道他从什么地方一下子取来一个打火机,握在手中。随即打着了火机,点燃了香烟,但火机却不见了。这完完全全是一场令人拍手叫绝的表演。

"我可从来没有看到谁卷烟的速度会有那么快,"我说。

"哦,"他深深吸了口香烟说道,"这么说,你注意到了。"

"我当然注意到了,相当了不起啊。"

他微笑着在座位上向后一靠。我注意到他卷烟速度之快,令他很开心,"你想知道,我为什么能够卷得这么快吗?"他问。

"继续说。"

"那是因为我有了不起的手指。我手上的这些手指,"他将双手在面前高高举起说道,"比世界上最优秀的钢琴弹奏家的手指都快速和灵巧!"

"你是弹钢琴的吗?"

"不要犯傻,"他说,"我看起来像是弹钢琴的吗?"

我向他的手指瞥了一眼,发现那些手指确实漂亮、苗条、修长、雅致,似乎跟他身体的其余部位特别不相配,看起来更像是脑外科医生或者钟表匠的手指。

"我工作的难度,"他继续说,"是弹钢琴难度的一百倍,任何一个傻蛋都能学会弹钢琴。现如今,只要你走进几乎任何一家的家门,都会发现里面有非常小的小孩子在学弹钢琴。事实如此,对吧?"

"八九不离十吧,"我说。

"当然如此,但是,一千万个人当中,没有一个能学会做我的工作。一千万人当中,不会有一个人啊!怎么样呢?"

"令人称奇,"我说。

"令人称奇,你完全说对了,"他说。

"我想,我知道你是做什么的啦,"我说,"你是变戏法的,你是魔术家。"

"我?"他嗤之以鼻。"魔术家?我到处逛游,在那些聚会上,到处都是孩子,脏兮兮的,从帽子顶部变出兔子来,你能想象得出吗?"

"那么,你就是纸牌高手。你让人们参与牌类游戏,你发一手漂亮的牌。"

"我是这样的人啊!耍纸牌,搞欺诈,令人厌烦!"他大叫,"我要是这样一个人的话,那也是一个悲惨的诈骗犯。"

"好吧,我不猜啦。"

现在,我开车的速度很慢,时速也就是64公里,我可不想再次被拦。我们驶上了伦敦至牛津的主路,正行驶在通往德纳姆的下坡路上。

突然之间,我的这位乘客手里举起了一条黑色的皮带。"以前见过这个没?"他问。那条皮带的带扣是黄铜质的,设计独特。

"嘿!"我说,"那是我的,对吗?是我的皮带啊!你从哪儿弄到手的?"

他露齿一笑,将皮带从一边挥舞到另一边。"你认为我会从哪儿搞到手?"他问,"当然是从你裤子上。"

我伸手摸裤带,但裤带不见了。

"你的意思是说,我们行驶过程中,你从我身上抽掉了裤带?"我问,感觉有点大惊失色。

他点了点头,始终用他那双小小的、黑色的老鼠眼睛看着我。

"这怎么可能啊,"我说。"你必须得将扣带解开,将整条裤带沿着裤带环抽出来。你要是这样做,我会看见的。即使我没看见,也能感觉到。"

"噢,可是你没有,对吧?"他说,一副旗开得胜的样子。他将皮带放到膝盖上,突然之间一根棕色鞋带从他的手指上垂了下来。"那么,这个呢?"他挥舞着鞋带,大声问道。

"这个怎么了?"我说。

"这儿有谁丢鞋带没?"他露出牙齿,微笑着问。

我低头瞅了眼自己的鞋,发现其中一只的鞋带不见了。"哎呀呀!"我说,"你是怎么做到的? 我可从没看到你弯腰啊。"

"你什么都没有看到,"他无比自豪地说,"你从来都没有看到我移动一丁点儿。你知道为什么吗?"

"是的,"我说。"因为你有了不起的手指。"

"千真万确!"他大声说,"你感悟很快,难道不是吗?"他向后坐去,吸了口自制的香烟,将烟雾从口中喷出,一缕细细的烟雾喷向车窗玻璃。他清楚,他露的这两手令我印象深刻,这令他十分开心。"我不想去晚了,"他说,"现在几点了?"

"你前面有一个时钟,"我对他说。

"我不信任车内的钟表,"他说,"你的手表是几点了?"

我急忙抖开衣袖,要看看手腕上的表,但表不见了。我看了他一眼,他看了看我,露出牙齿笑了起来。

"你把表也拿走了啊,"我说。

他伸出手,我的手表就躺在他的手掌上。"很不错的东西,这块表,"他说,"质量上乘,镶嵌十八克拉黄金,也很容易贩卖出手。高质量的货物从来都不费劲儿就能出手。"

"要是你不介意的话,我想把表拿回来,"我说,一副被惹恼的样子。

他将表小心地放到前面的皮制托盘上。"老板,我不会从你那儿偷拿任何东西,"他说,"你是我的同伴,你让我搭车。"

"听到这话,我很高兴,"我说。

"我刚才所做的一切,都是为了回答你的问题,"他继续说,"你当时问,我做什么工作谋生,我给你形象地展示出来了。"

"你还拿了我什么东西?"

他又微笑起来,随后开始从他的夹克衫兜子里一样一样地拿出属于我的东西:驾照、挂有四把钥匙的钥匙环、几张一英镑钞票、几枚硬币、一封出版商写给我的信、我的日记、一支又短又粗的旧铅笔、一个点香烟的打火机,最后拿出的是一枚漂亮的、年代久远的蓝宝石戒指,上面镶了一圈珍珠,那是我妻子的戒指。我这次将其带到身上,是想送到伦敦的珠宝商那儿修理一下,因为上面的一颗珍珠丢掉了。

"现在,这儿又有一个可爱的物件了,"他将这枚戒指用手指翻了过来,说道。"如果我没看错的话,它是十八世纪的,是国王乔治三世时期的东西。"

"没错,"我有些佩服地说道。"你说的绝对没错。"

他将戒指跟皮制托盘上的其他东西放到了一起。

"这么说来,你是扒手了,"我说。

"我不喜欢那个词,"他回应,"那是一个很粗俗、很丑陋的词。扒手都很粗俗、很丑陋,他们只是小打小闹,做一些轻松的、业余性的工作,只会从眼睛看不见的、年迈的女性身上弄钱。"

"那么,你怎么称呼你自己呢?"

"我?我是一名手指匠,而且是专业的。"说这话的时候,他显得很庄严、很自豪,那架势好像是对我说,他是皇家外科学院的院长,或者是坎特伯雷大主教。

"这个词儿我从来没听说过,是你自己发明创造的吗?"

"当然不是我的发明创造,"他回答,"这个名字是用来称呼那些在这一专业领域上升到顶尖层次的人。举例来说,你早已听说过金器匠和银器匠,他们都是金器、银器方面的行家里手。我则是将我的手指运用自如的专家,所以嘛,我就是一名手指匠。"

"这个工作一定很有意思。"

"这个工作美妙之至,"他回答,"很惹人喜爱。"

"那也就是你去赛马场的原因吗?"

"赛马时,这份工作易如反掌,"他说,"比赛过后,你只需在周围站立,观察一下有没有幸运的家伙前来排队领取赌金。一旦看到有谁领取一大笔钞票,你就跟随他,从那家伙身上愿意取多少你就取多少。但是,老板,你不要曲解我的意思,我从来不取输家身上的钱,也不取穷人身上的钱,我只跟随那些能付得起钱的人,也就是那些赢家和富有的人。"

"你真的很善解人意,"我说,"多长时间,你会被逮着一次呢?"

"逮着?"他很反感地大声问,"我,被逮着?被逮着的,只有扒手,而手指匠却从来都不会的。听着,如果我愿意,可以从你的嘴里将你的假牙取出来,也不会被逮着的!"

"我没有假牙,"我说。

"我知道你没有,"他回答,"否则的话,我早就会把假牙取出来啦!"

我信他的话。他那些修长的、苗条的手指似乎无所不能。

我们向前行驶了一会,彼此没有说话。

"那个警察对你检查的是相当彻底,"我说,"那是,你是否有点担心呢?"

"没有谁会对我彻底检查的,"他说。

"他们当然是彻底检查了。那个警察把你的名字和住址都仔仔细细地写到他的黑色笔记本上了。"

这名男子小小的鼠目看着我,又冲我奸诈地微笑起来。"哦,"他说,"他是记下了,但是,我敢打赌,他不会记住他所有写下的东西。记忆力还算不错的警察,我从来没有遇到过,有些警察甚至连自己的名字都记不住。"

"记忆力与记录本有什么关系?"我问。"细节都记录到他的本子上了,难道不是吗?"

"是的,老板,是在本子上。但麻烦的是,他把本子弄丢了,两个本子都弄丢了,一个记着我的名字,还有一个记着你的名字。"

这名男子右手纤细、修长的手指得意洋洋地举起从警察衣兜里掏出的那两个本子。"我干过的最为轻松的活儿,"他自豪地宣布。

我简直是太兴奋了,车几乎偏离方向,差点撞到一辆运送牛奶的卡车上。

"现在,那个警察手里既没有你的把柄,也没有我的把柄了,"他说。

"你真是天才啊!"我叫道。

"他手里没有名字,没有住址,没有车牌号码,什么都没有了,"他说。

"你真棒啊!"

"我想呢,你最好靠边行驶,尽快开离主路,"他说。"然后,我们最好点起一小堆篝火,将本子烧掉。"

"你真是一个了不起的伙计,"我叹道。

"谢谢夸奖,老板,"他说。"有人感激、夸奖,感觉总是不错的。"

第二节 《捕鼠者说》The Ratcatcher

罗尔德·达尔的《捕鼠者说》(The Ratcatcher)被收录在《罗尔德·达尔短篇故事集锦》(The Collected Short Stories of Roald Dahl)《如你之人》(Someone Like You)《罗尔德·达尔小说精品集》(The Best of Roald Dahl)《五部畅销书集》(5 Bestsellers)《罗尔德·达尔选集》(The Roald Dahl Omnibus)以及《罗尔德·达尔二十九篇成人故事集》(Twenty Nine Kisses from Roald Dahl)等书中,可见其影响力之大。

这篇是罗尔德·达尔乡村故事"克劳德的狗"(Claud's Dog)系列中的一篇。另外,这篇小说中的克劳德等人物,在达尔这一系列的其他作品以及这个系列之外的作品如《奥妙生活》(Ah Sweet Mystery of Life)中也出现过。这说明作家罗尔德·达尔对"素材"善于加以充分利用,也可以说,达尔很"贪材"——充分甚至反复利用已有的素材。在《捕鼠者说》中,捕鼠者声称的关于大工厂和巧克力商用老鼠血来制作诱人美味的说法,在其后来的自传作品《男孩时代》(Boy)中也有所提及。所以说,对于自己的"好点子",达尔做到了"物尽其用",直至"榨干"其"骨髓"。

一、原作导读

这篇小说是以第一人称"我"(名叫"戈登")的视角展开的,但叙述者"我"是"隐身"的——地位无足轻重,是"看热闹"或"围观"的,起到了"纽带"或者"桥梁"的作用,可以看成作家达尔本人的化身。

一天,戈登和克劳德待在加油站的时候,捕鼠者来了,说是卫生局官员派他来处理鼠患问题。本身就像一只大老鼠的这个捕鼠的家伙开始大谈特谈各种捕鼠的方法,还说聪明过人的老鼠是多么多么难以捕捉。克劳德对他说,他要捕捉的老鼠生活在马路对过的草垛里。于是，他又讲出各种捕捉草垛里老鼠的方法，然后跟戈登和克劳德一起到现场实际操作起来。

　　三天后，捕鼠者前来准备为自己毒死的老鼠收尸，却发现对自己撒下的有毒燕麦，老鼠连碰都没有碰一下。于是，他念念有词地说，这些老鼠肯定有其他的食物来源①，要不然，这些老鼠不会不吃自己撒下的那些难以抗拒的诱饵。

　　为了挽回一些面子，捕鼠者接下来展示了一些自己捕鼠的"绝活"。由于是专业的捕鼠者，四处游走为人捕鼠，他的衣兜里总是会揣上几只活蹦乱跳的老鼠或白鼬之类的小动物。他从一个衣兜里掏出一只老鼠，从另一个衣兜里掏出一只白鼬，把这两只小动物塞进自己衬衫，任其在自己的衬衫里追逐、打斗……

　　现在，他一只手伸进衬衫拉出白鼬，另一只手则把死老鼠拽了出来。白鼬的鼻口部位沾染了斑斑血迹。
　　Now he reached one hand down into his shirt and pulled out the ferret; with the other he took out the dead rat. There were traces of blood around the white muzzle of the ferret.

　　这个"绝活"表演完毕，捕鼠者觉得还不过瘾，还要展示一下另一个"绝活"，要跟戈登和克劳德赌一把：不用手、胳膊、腿和脚也能杀死一只老鼠，以充分挽回自己一只老鼠也没有捕捉到的败局。他又掏出一只年迈的老鼠，将它用细绳拴到一辆汽车风挡的雨刷上，让它无处可逃，然后一点点向它靠拢，跟它对视起来……

　　接着，他冷不防发起了进攻。

---

　　① 捕鼠者的这个说法为乡村故事"克劳德的狗"（Claud's Dog）系列中的第二篇《草垛之灾》（Rummins）埋下了伏笔，感兴趣的读者可以参阅《罗尔德·达尔短篇故事品读及汉译探索（第2卷）》第二章第二节。

他像蛇一样发起了攻击,下半身肌肉积聚的力量瞬间爆发,将头向前猛地一冲,如刀一般快速划过。就在这一瞬间,我瞥眼看过去,看到他那张嘴张得宽宽的,露出那两颗黄黄的门牙,整个脸部由于张嘴时过于用力而扭曲变形。

Then suddenly he struck.

He struck as a snake strikes, darting his head forward with one swift knifelike stroke that originated in the muscles of the lower body, and I had a momentary glimpse of his mouth opening very wide and two yellow teeth and the whole face contorted by the effort of mouth-opening.

二、原作释读

在类似这样的小说中,作家罗尔德·达尔大量使用了一些非标准的词汇和具有英国英语特点的表达,这给阅读和理解造成了一定的困难。阅读中,读者还需体会好这样的词汇和表达对于人物性格刻画所起的作用。

The Ratcatcher[①]

In the afternoon the ratcatcher came to the filling station. He came

---

① 本部小说原文出自"DAHL, R. *The Best of Roald Dahl* [M]. London: Penguin Books Ltd., 2006"。

ratcatcher: *Noun* one who catches rats; particularly one who does so professionally 捕鼠者;(专业)灭鼠者

sidling up the driveway① with a stealthy②, soft-treading gait③, making no noise at all with his feet on the gravel. He had an army knapsack④ slung over one shoulder and he was wearing an old-fashioned black jacket with large pockets. His brown corduroy⑤ trousers were tied around the knees with pieces of white string.

"Yes?" Claud asked, knowing very well who he was.

"Rodent⑥ operative⑦." His small dark eyes moved swiftly over the premises.

"The ratcatcher?"

"That's me."

The man was lean and brown with a sharp face and two long sul-

---

① driveway or drive: *Noun* a short road leading from a public road to a house（由住宅通向公路的）私人车道

② stealthy: *Adjective* behaving, done, or made in a cautious and surreptitious manner, so as not to be seen or heard 暗中进行的；隐秘的；偷偷摸摸的(e.g. stealthy footsteps 悄悄的脚步声)

③ gait: *Noun* a person's manner of walking 步态(e.g. the easy gait of an athlete 运动员般轻松的步态)

④ knapsack: *Noun* a soldier's or hiker's bag with shoulder straps, carried on the back, and typically made of canvas or other weatherproof material（士兵或徒步旅行者用的帆布等防水材料做的）背包

⑤ corduroy: *Noun*（corduroys）trousers made of corduroy 灯芯绒裤

⑥ rodent: *Noun* a gnawing mammal of an order that includes rats, mice, squirrels, hamsters, porcupines, and their relatives, distinguished by strong constantly growing incisors and no canine teeth. They constitute the largest order of mammals 啮齿目动物

⑦ operative: *Noun* a worker, especially a skilled one in a manufacturing industry（尤指制造业中的）技术工

phur①-coloured teeth that protruded from the upper jaw, overlapping the lower lip, pressing it inward. The ears were thin and pointed and set far back on the head, near the nape② of the neck. The eyes were almost black, but when they looked at you there was a flash of yellow somewhere inside them.

"You've come very quick."

"Special orders from the Health Officer."

"And now you're going to catch all the rats?"

"Yep③."

The kind of dark furtive④ eyes he had were those of an animal that lives its life peering out cautiously and forever from a hole in the ground.

"How are you going to catch 'em?"

"Ah-h-h," the ratman said darkly. "That's all accordin'⑤ to where they is."

"Trap 'em, I suppose."

"Trap 'em!" he cried, disgusted. "You won't catch many rats that way! Rats isn't rabbits, you know."

---

① sulphur or sulfur: *Noun* a pale greenish-yellow colour 硫磺色;淡黄绿色 (e.g. the bird's sulphur-yellow throat. 鸟儿淡黄绿色的颈前部)

② nape: *Noun* (also called "nape of the/one's neck") the back of a person's neck 项背;后颈

③ yep or yup: *Exclamation & Noun* non-standard spelling of yes, representing informal pronunciation(非规范及非正式用法)同"yes"

④ furtive: *Adjective* attempting to avoid notice or attention, typically because of guilt or a belief that discovery would lead to trouble; secretive 偷偷摸摸的;鬼鬼祟祟的;秘密的;遮遮掩掩的

⑤ accordin' = according

He held his face up high, sniffing the air with a nose that twitched① perceptibly② from side to side.

"No," he said, scornfully. "Trappin's③ no way to catch a rat. Rats is clever, let me tell you that. If you want to catch 'em, you got to know 'em. You got to know rats on this job."

I could see Claud staring at him with a certain fascination.

"They're more clever'n④ dogs, rats is."

"Get away."

"You know what they do? They watch you! All the time you're goin' round preparin'⑤ to catch 'em, they're sittin'⑥ quietly in dark places, watchin' you." The man crouched, stretching his stringy neck far forward.

"So what do you do?" Claud asked, fascinated.

"Ah! That's it, you see. That's where you got to know rats."

"How d'you catch 'em?"

"There's ways," the ratman said, leering. "There's various ways."

---

① twitch: *Verb* give or cause to give a short, sudden jerking or convulsive movement 抽动；使抽动 (e. g. He saw her lips twitch and her eyelids flutter. 他看见她嘴唇抽搐，眼皮颤动。)

② perceptible: *Adjective* (especially of a slight movement or change of state) able to be seen or noticed (尤指轻微的活动或状态变化) 可感觉的；可感知的；可辨的；看得出的 (e. g. a perceptible decline in public confidence 公众信心的明显下降)

③ Trappin's = Trapping's = Trapping is

④ clever'n = clever than

⑤ preparin' = preparing

⑥ sittin' = sitting

· 44 ·

He paused, nodding his repulsive head sagely① up and down. "It's all dependin'②," he said, "on where they is. This ain't a sewer job, is it?"

"No, it's not a sewer job."

"Tricky things, sewer jobs. Yes," he said, delicately sniffing the air to the left of him with his mobile nose-end, "sewer jobs is very tricky things."

"Not especially, I shouldn't think."

"Oh-ho. You shouldn't, shouldn't you! Well, I'd like to see *you* do a sewer job! Just exactly how would *you* set about it, I'd like to know?"

"Nothing to it. I'd just poison 'em, that's all."

"And where exactly would you put the poison, might I ask?"

"Down the sewer. Where the hell you think I put it!"

"There!" the ratman cried, triumphant. "I knew it! Down the sewer! And you know what'd happen then? Get washed away, that's all. Sewer's like a river, y'know③."

"That's what *you* say," Claud answered. "That's only what *you* say."

"It's facts."

"All right, then, all right. So what would *you* do, Mr. Know-all?"

"That's exactly where you got to know rats, on a sewer job."

"Come on then, let's have it."

"Now listen. I'll tell you." The ratman advanced a step closer, his

---

① sage: *Adjective* having, showing, or indicating profound wisdom 贤明的; 睿智的(e. g. They nodded in agreement with these sage remarks. 他们点头同意那些明智的话语。)

② dependin' = depending

③ y'know = you know

voice became secretive and confidential, the voice of a man divulging① fabulous professional secrets. "You works on the understandin'② that a rat is a gnawin'③ animal, see. Rats *gnaws*. Anythin'④ you give 'em, don't matter what it is, anythin' new they never seen before, and what do they do? They *gnaws* it. So now! There you are! You get a sewer job on your hands. And what d'you do?"

His voice had the soft throaty⑤ sound of a croaking⑥ frog and he seemed to speak all his words with an immense wet-lipped relish⑦, as though they tasted good on the tongue. The accent was similar to Claud's, the broad soft accent of the Buckinghamshire countryside, but his voice was more throaty, the words more fruity⑧ in his mouth.

"All you do is you go down the sewer and you take along some ordinary paper bags, just ordinary brown paper bags, and these bags is filled

---

① divulge：*Verb* [with obj.] make known (private or sensitive information) 泄漏(秘密或敏感信息)(e.g. I am too much of a gentleman to divulge her age. 以我的绅士身份我做不出泄漏她年龄的事。)

② understandin' = understanding

③ gnawin' = gnawing

  gnaw：*Verb* [no obj.] bite at or nibble something persistently 咬；啃；啮

④ anythin' = anything

⑤ throaty：*Adjective* (of a sound such as a person's voice or the noise of an engine) deep and rasping(嗓音，引擎声)低沉洪亮的

⑥ croak：*Verb* (of a frog or crow) make a characteristic deep hoarse sound (蛙或鸦)呱呱叫

⑦ relish：*Noun* [mass noun] great enjoyment 享受；乐趣(e.g. She swigged a mouthful of wine with relish. 她津津有味地喝了一大口酒。)

⑧ fruity：*Adjective* (of a voice or sound) mellow, deep, and rich(嗓音或声音)圆润的(e.g. Jeffery had a wonderfully fruity voice. 杰弗里的嗓音非常圆润。)

第一章 非常之辈 第二节 《捕鼠者说》The Ratcatcher

with plaster① of Paris powder. Nothin'② else. Then you suspend the bags from the roof of the sewer so they hang down not quite touchin'③ the water. See? Not quite touchin', and just high enough so a rat can reach 'em."

Claud was listening, rapt.

"There you are, y'see④. Old rat comes swimmin'⑤ along the sewer and sees the bag. He stops. He takes a sniff at it and it don't smell so bad anyway. So what's he do then?"

"He *gnaws* it," Claud cried, delighted.

"There! That's it! That's exactly it! He starts *gnawin'* away at the bag and the bag breaks and the old rat gets a mouthful of powder for his pains."

"Well?"

"That does him."

"What? Kills him?"

"Yep. Kills him stony!"

"Plaster of Paris ain't poisonous, you know."

"Ah! There you are! That's exactly where you're wrong, see. This powder swells. When you wet it, it swells. Gets into the rat's tubes⑥ and

---

① plaster: *Noun* [mass noun] the powder from which such a substance is made 石膏粉

② nothin' = nothing

③ touchin' = touching

④ y'see = you see

⑤ swimmin' = swimming

⑥ tube: *Noun* [usu. with adj. or noun modifier] (Anatomy, Zoology & Botany) a hollow cylindrical organ or structure in an animal body or in a plant (e.g. a Eustachian tube, a sieve tube) (解剖学、动物学以及植物学)管状器官;管(如咽鼓管、筛管)

swells right up and kills him quicker'n① anythin' in the world."

"That's where you got to know rats."

The ratman's face glowed with a stealthy pride, and he rubbed his stringy fingers together, holding the hands up close to the face. Claud watched him, fascinated.

"Now—where's them rats?" The word "rats" came out of his mouth soft and throaty, with a rich fruity relish as though he were gargling② with melted butter. "Let's take a look at them *rraats*."

"Over there in the hayrick across the road."

"Not in the house?" he asked, obviously disappointed.

"No. Only around the hayrick. Nowhere else."

"I'll wager③ they're in the house too. Like as not gettin' in all your food in the night and spreadin'④ disease and sickness. You got any disease here?" he asked, looking first at me, then at Claud.

"Everyone fine here."

"Quite sure?"

"Oh yes."

"You never know, you see. You could be sickenin'⑤ for it weeks and weeks and not feel it. Then all of a sudden—bang! —and it's got you. That's why Dr Arbuthnot's so particular. That's why he sent me out so quick, see. To stop the spreadin' of disease."

---

① quicker'n = quicker than

② gargle: *Verb* [no obj.] wash one's mouth and throat with a liquid kept in motion by breathing through it 漱口;漱喉 (e. g. He had gargled with alcohol for toothache. 因为牙痛他用酒漱了漱口。)

③ wager: *Noun & Verb* more formal term for bet "bet" 较正式的形式

④ spreadin' = spreading

⑤ sickenin' = sickening

第一章 非常之辈 第二节 《捕鼠者说》The Ratcatcher

He had now taken upon himself the mantle of the Health Officer. A most important rat he was now, deeply disappointed that we were not suffering from bubonic plague①.

"I feel fine," Claud said, nervously.

The ratman searched his face again, but said nothing.

"And how are you goin' to catch 'em in the hayrick?"

The ratman grinned, a crafty② toothy grin. He reached down into his knapsack and withdrew a large tin which he held up level with his face. He peered around one side of it at Claud.

"Poison!" he whispered. But he pronounced it *pye-zn*, making it into a soft, dark, dangerous word. "Deadly *pye-zn*, that's what this is!" He was weighing the tin up and down in his hands as he spoke. "Enough here to kill a million men!"

"Terrifying," Claud said.

"Exactly it! They'd put you inside③ for six months if they caught you with even a spoonful of this," he said, wetting his lips with his tongue. He had a habit of craning his head forward on his neck as he spoke.

"Want to see?" he asked, taking a penny from his pocket, prising open the lid. "There now! There it is!" He spoke fondly, almost lovingly of the stuff, and he held it forward for Claud to look.

"Corn? Or barley is it?"

---

① bubonic plague: the commonest form of plague in humans, characterized by fever, delirium, and the formation of buboes 腹股沟淋巴结鼠疫;淋巴腺鼠疫

② crafty: *Adjective* clever at achieving one's aims by indirect or deceitful methods 狡诈的;诡计多端的(e.g. A crafty crook faked an injury to escape from prison. 狡猾的骗子假装受伤逃出了监狱。)

③ inside: *Preposition & Adverb* (informal) in prison(非正式用法)在狱中 (e.g. He was sentenced to three years inside. 他被判三年监禁。)

"It's oats①. Soaked in deadly *pye-zn*. You take just one of them grains in your mouth and you'd be a gonner② in five minutes."

"Honest?"

"Yep. Never out of me sight, this tin."

He caressed it with his hands and gave it a little shake so that the oat grains rustled softly inside.

"But not today. Your rats don't get this today. They wouldn't have it anyway. That they wouldn't. There's where you got to know rats. Rats is suspicious. Terrible suspicious, rats is. So today they gets some nice clean tasty oats as'll do 'em no harm in the world. Fatten 'em, that's all it'll do. And tomorrow they gets the same again. And it'll taste so good there'll be all the rats in the districk③ comin'④ along after a couple of days."

"Rather clever."

"You got to be clever on this job. You got to be cleverer'n⑤ a rat and that's sayin'⑥ something."

"You've almost got to be a rat yourself," I said. It slipped out in error, before I had time to stop myself, and I couldn't really help it because I was looking at the man at the time. But the effect upon him was surprising.

---

① oat: *Noun* an Old World cereal which is cultivated chiefly in cool climates and is widely used for animal feed(作为饲料的)燕麦

② 此处的"gonner"疑为"goner"之误,可能由于捕鼠者说话不标准所致。
goner: *Noun* (informal) a person or thing that is doomed or cannot be saved(非正式用法)完蛋的人(或物);不可救药的人(或物)

③ 这里的"districk"应是"district"的非标准发音的拼写形式。

④ comin' = coming

⑤ cleverer'n = cleverer than

⑥ sayin' = saying

"There!" he cried. "Now you got it! Now you really said something! A good ratter's got to be more like a rat than anythin' else in the world! Cleverer even than a rat, and that's not an easy thing to be, let me tell you!"

"Quite sure it's not."

"All right, then let's go. I haven't got all day, you know. There's Lady Leonora Benson asking for me urgent up there at the Manor."

"She got rats, too?"

"Everybody's got rats," the ratman said, and he ambled off down the driveway, across the road to the hayrick and we watched him go. The way he walked was so like a rat it made you wonder—that slow, almost delicate ambling walk with a lot of give① at the knees and no sound at all from the footsteps on the gravel. He hopped nimbly over the gate into the field, then walked quickly round the hayrick scattering handfuls of oats on to the ground.

The next day he returned and repeated the procedure.

The day after that he came again and this time he put down the poisoned oats. But he didn't scatter these; he placed them carefully in little piles at each corner of the rick.

"You got a dog?" he asked when he came back across the road on the third day after putting down the poison.

"Yes."

"Now if you want to see your dog die an 'orrible② twistin'③ death, all you got to do is let him in that gate some time."

---

① give: *Noun* [mass noun] capacity to bend or alter in shape under pressure; elasticity(在压力下)弯曲或变形的能力;弹性

② 'orrible = horrible

③ twistin' = twisting

"We'll take care," Claud told him. "Don't you worry about that."

The next day he returned once more, this time to collect the dead.

"You got an old sack?" he asked. "Most likely we goin' to need a sack to put 'em in."

He was puffed① up and important now, the black eyes gleaming with pride. He was about to display the sensational② results of his catch to the audience.

Claud fetched a sack and the three of us walked across the road, the ratman leading. Claud and I leaned over the gate, watching. The ratman prowled around the hayrick, bending over to inspect his little piles of poison.

"Somethin' wrong here," he muttered. His voice was soft and angry.

He ambled over to another pile and got down on his knees to examine it closely.

"Somethin' bloody wrong here."

"What's the matter?"

He didn't answer, but it was clear that the rats hadn't touched his bait.

"These are very clever rats here," I said.

"Exactly what I told him, Gordon. These aren't just no ordinary kind of rats you're dealing with here."

---

① puff: *Verb* [with obj.] (usu. as "be puffed up") (figurative) cause to become conceited(比喻用法)使傲慢; 使自负(e. g. He was never puffed up about his writing. 他从不吹嘘自己的写作。)

② sensational: *Adjective* (of an event, a person, or a piece of information) causing great public interest and excitement(事件、人或消息)轰动性的(e. g. a sensational murder trial 一次轰动性的谋杀审判)

The ratman walked over to the gate. He was very annoyed and showed it on his face and around the nose and by the way the two yellow teeth were pressing down into the skin of his lower lip. "Don't give me that crap①," he said, looking at me. "There's nothing wrong with these rats except somebody's feedin'② 'em. They got somethin' juicy to eat somewhere and plenty of it. There's no rats in the world'll turn down oats unless their bellies is full to burstin'③."

"They're clever," Claud said.

The man turned away, disgusted. He knelt down again and began to scoop up the poisoned oats with a small shovel, tipping them carefully back into the tin. When he had done, all three of us walked back across the road.

The ratman stood near the petrol-pumps, a rather sorry, humble ratman now whose face was beginning to take on a brooding④ aspect⑤. He had withdrawn into himself and was brooding in silence over his failure, the eyes veiled and wicked, the little tongue darting out to one side of the two yellow teeth, keeping the lips moist. It appeared to be essential that the lips should be kept moist. He looked up at me, a quick surrepti-

---

① crap: *Noun* [mass noun] nonsense; rubbish 废话;垃圾
② feedin' = feeding
③ burstin' = bursting
④ brooding: *Adjective* showing deep unhappiness of thought 忧思的;哀思的(e.g. He stared with brooding eyes. 他用一双沉思的眼睛盯着看。)
⑤ aspect: *Noun* [in sing., with modifier] a particular appearance or quality 外表;特性

tious① glance, then over at Claud. His nose-end twitched, sniffing the air. He raised himself up and down a few times on his toes, swaying gently, and in a voice soft and secretive, he said: "Want to see somethin'?" He was obviously trying to retrieve his reputation.

"What?"

"Want to see somethin' amazin'②?" As he said this he put his right hand into the deep poacher's pocket of his jacket and brought out a large live rat clasped tight between his fingers.

"Good God!"

"Ah! That's it, y'see!" He was crouching slightly now and craning his neck forward and leering③ at us and holding this enormous brown rat in his hands, one finger and thumb making a tight circle around the creature's neck, clamping its head rigid so it couldn't turn and bite.

"D'you usually carry rats around in your pockets?"

"Always got a rat or two about me somewhere." With that he put his free hand into the other pocket and produced a small white ferret④.

"Ferret," he said, holding it up by the neck.

The ferret seemed to know him and stayed still in his grasp.

---

① surreptitious: *Adjective* kept secret, especially because it would not be approved of 私下的;偷偷摸摸的(尤指因为不会被批准)(e.g. Low wages were supplemented by surreptitious payments from tradesmen. 商人私下付的报酬补充了低工资。)

② amazin' = amazing

③ leer: *Verb* [no obj.] look or gaze in an unpleasant, malign, or lascivious way 斜睨;讨厌(或恶意、挑逗)地看(e.g. Bystanders were leering at the nude painting. 旁观者斜眼看着裸体画。)

④ ferret: *Noun* a domesticated polecat used chiefly for catching rabbits. It is typically albino in coloration, but sometimes brown 白鼬;雪貂

"There's nothin'll① kill a rat quicker'n a ferret. And there's nothin' a rat's more frightened of either."

He brought his hands close together in front of him so that the ferret's nose was within six inches of the rat's face. The pink beady eyes of the ferret stared at the rat. The rat struggled, trying to edge away from the killer.

"Now," he said. "Watch!"

His khaki shirt was open at the neck and he lifted the rat and slipped it down inside his shirt, next to his skin. As soon as his hand was free, he unbuttoned his jacket at the front so that the audience could see the bulge the body of the rat made under his shirt. His belt prevented it from going down lower than his waist.

Then he slipped the ferret in after the rat.

Immediately there was a great commotion inside the shirt. It appeared that the rat was running around the man's body, being chased by the ferret. Six or seven times they went around, the small bulge chasing the larger one, gaining on it slightly each circuit and drawing closer and closer until at last the two bulges seemed to come together and there was a scuffle② and a series of shrill shrieks.

Throughout this performance the ratman had stood absolutely still with legs apart, arms hanging loosely, the dark eyes resting on Claud's face. Now he reached one hand down into his shirt and pulled out the ferret; with the other he took out the dead rat. There were traces of blood

---

① nothin'll = nothing'll = nothing will

② scuffle: Noun a short, confused fight or struggle at close quarters 厮打；扭打(e.g. There were minor scuffles with police. 有过同警方的小冲突。)

around the white muzzle① of the ferret.

"Not sure I liked that very much."

"You never seen anythin' like it before, I'll bet you that."

"Can't really say I have."

"Like as not② you'll get yourself a nasty little nip in the guts one of these days," Claud told him. But he was clearly impressed, and the ratman was becoming cocky③ again.

"Want to see somethin' far more *amazin* 'n④ that?" he asked. "You want to see somethin' you'd never even *believe* unless you seen it with your own eyes?"

"Well?"

We were standing in the driveway out in front of the pumps and it was one of those pleasant warm November mornings. Two cars pulled in for petrol, one right after the other, and Claud went over and gave them what they wanted.

"You want to see?" the ratman asked.

I glanced at Claud, slightly apprehensive. "Yes," Claud said. "Come on then, let's see."

The ratman slipped the dead rat back into one pocket, the ferret into the other. Then he reached down into his knapsack and produced—If you please—a second live rat.

---

① muzzle: *Noun* the projecting part of the face, including the nose and mouth, of an animal such as a dog or horse（四足动物,如犬、马等的)鼻口部;吻

② (as) like as not: probably 很可能 (e.g. She would be in bed by now, like as not. 她现在很可能在床上了。)

③ cocky: *Adjective* conceited or arrogant, especially in a bold or cheeky way 自以为是的;傲慢自负的(尤指以无礼、无耻的方式表现出来)

④ 'n = than

"Good Christ!" Claud said.

"Always got one or two rats about me somewhere," the man announced calmly. "You got to know rats on this job, and if you want to know 'em you got to have 'em round you. This is a sewer rat, this is. An old sewer rat, clever as buggery①. See him watchin' me all the time, wonderin'② what I'm goin' to do? See him?"

"Very unpleasant."

"What are you going to do?" I asked. I had a feeling I was going to like this one even less than the last.

"Fetch me a piece of string."

Claud fetched him a piece of string.

With his left hand, the man looped the string around one of the rat's hind legs. The rat struggled, trying to turn its head to see what was going on, but he held it tight around the neck with finger and thumb.

"Now!" he said, looking about him. "You got a table inside?"

"We don't want the rat inside the house," I said.

"Well—I need a table. Or somethin' flat like a table."

"What about the bonnet③ of that car?" Claud said.

We walked over to the car and the man put the old sewer rat on the bonnet. He attached the string to the windshield wiper so that the rat was

---

① buggery: *Noun* (Brit. vulgar slang) used in various expressions as an intensifier(英国英语中的粗俗俚语)在各种表述中起加强语气作用(e.g. Drive like buggery if you know what's good for you. 你要是知道什么对你有好处，就开他妈的车吧。)

② wonderin' = wondering

③ bonnet: *Noun* (Brit.) a metal part covering the engine of a motor vehicle (英国用法)(汽车)引擎罩

now tethered[①].

At first it crouched, unmoving and suspicious, a big-bodied grey rat with bright black eyes and a scaly tail that lay in a long curl upon the car's bonnet. It was looking away from the ratman, but watching him sideways to see what he was going to do. The man stepped back a few paces and immediately the rat relaxed. It sat up on its haunches[②] and began to lick the grey fur on its chest. Then it scratched its muzzle with both front paws. It seemed quite unconcerned about the three men standing near by.

"Now—how about a little bet?" the ratman asked.

"We don't bet," I said.

"Just for fun. It's more fun if you bet."

"What d'you want to bet on?"

"I'll bet you I can kill that rat without usin'[③] my hands. I'll put my hands in my pockets and not use 'em."

"You'll kick it with your feet," Claud said.

It was apparent that the ratman was out to earn some money. I looked at the rat that was going to be killed and began to feel slightly sick, not so much because it was going to be killed but because it was going to be killed in a special way, with a considerable degree of relish.

"No," the ratman said. "No feet."

"Nor arms?" Claud asked.

---

① tether: *Verb* [with obj.] tie (an animal) with a rope or chain so as to restrict its movement(用绳、链)拴(动物)(e.g. The horse had been tethered to a post. 马被拴在一根柱子上。)

② sit on one's haunches: squat with the haunches resting on the backs of the heels 蹲坐

③ usin' = using

"Nor arms. Nor legs, nor hands neither."

"You'll sit on it."

"No. No squashin'①."

"Let's see you do it."

"You bet me first. Bet me a quid."

"Don't be so bloody daft②," Claud said. "Why should we give you a quid③?"

"What'll you bet?"

"Nothin'."

"All right. Then it's no go."

He made as if to untie the string from the windshield wiper.

"I'll bet you a shilling," Claud told him. The sick gastric④ sensation in my stomach was increasing, but there was an awful magnetism⑤ about this business and I found myself quite unable to walk away or even move.

"You too?"

"No," I said.

"What's the matter with you?" the ratman asked.

"I just don't want to bet you, that's all."

---

① squashin' = squashing: *Verb* [with obj.] crush or squeeze (something) with force so that it becomes flat, soft, or out of shape 把……压扁(或压烂、压变形)

② daft: *Adjective* (informal, chiefly Brit.) silly; foolish(主要为英国英语的非正式用法)傻的;愚蠢的

③ quid: *Noun* (Brit. informal) one pound sterling(英国英语非正式用法)一英镑

④ gastric: *Adjective* of the stomach 胃(部)的

⑤ magnetism: *Noun* (figurative) the ability to attract and charm people(比喻用法)吸引力;魅力

"So you want me to do this for a lousy shillin'①?"

"I don't want you to do it."

"Where's the money?" he said to Claud.

Claud put a shilling piece on the bonnet, near the radiator. The ratman produced two sixpences and laid them beside Claud's money. As he stretched out his hand to do this, the rat cringed②, drawing its head back and flattening itself against the bonnet.

"Bet's on," the ratman said.

Claud and I stepped back a few paces. The ratman stepped forward. He put his hands in his pockets and inclined his body from the waist so that his face was on a level with the rat, about three feet away.

His eyes caught the eyes of the rat and held them. The rat was crouching, very tense, sensing extreme danger, but not yet frightened. The way it crouched, it seemed to me it was preparing to spring forward at the man's face; but there must have been some power in the ratman's eyes that prevented it from doing this, and subdued③ it, and then gradually frightened it so that it began to back away, dragging its body backwards with slow crouching steps until the string tautened④ on its hind leg. It tried to struggle back further against the string, jerking its leg to free it. The man leaned forward towards the rat, following it with his face,

---

① shillin' = shilling

② cringe: *Verb* [no obj.] bend one's head and body in fear or apprehension or in a servile or obsequious manner（因害怕、恐惧或担心）蜷缩；卑躬屈膝；阿谀奉承（e.g. He cringed away from the blow. 他害怕挨打而缩成一团。）

③ subdue: *Verb* [with obj.] overcome, quieten, or bring under control（a feeling or person）克制；抑制；控制（e.g. She managed to subdue an instinct to applaud. 她终于克制住鼓掌的冲动。）

④ tauten: *Verb* to make or become taut or tense（使某物）变紧；拉紧；绷紧；紧张（e.g. The skin of her cheeks tautened. 她紧绷着脸。）

watching it all the time with his eyes, and suddenly the rat panicked and leaped sideways in the air. The string pulled it up with a jerk that must almost have dislocated its leg.

It crouched again, in the middle of the bonnet, as far away as the string would allow, and it was properly frightened now, whiskers quivering, the long grey body tense with fear.

At this point, the ratman again began to move his face closer. Very slowly he did it, so slowly there wasn't really any movement to be seen at all except that the face just happened to be a fraction closer each time you looked. He never took his eyes from the rat. The tension was considerable and I wanted suddenly to cry out and tell him to stop. I wanted him to stop because it was making me feel sick inside, but I couldn't bring myself to say the word. Something extremely unpleasant was about to happen I was sure of that. Something sinister and cruel and ratlike, and perhaps it really would make me sick. But I had to see it now.

The ratman's face was about eighteen inches from the rat. Twelve inches. Then ten, or perhaps it was eight, and then there was not more than the length of a man's hand separating their faces. The rat was pressing its body flat against the car bonnet, tense and terrified. The ratman was also tense, but with a dangerous active tensity① that was like a tight-wound spring. The shadow of a smile flickered around the skin of his mouth.

Then suddenly he struck.

He struck as a snake strikes, darting his head forward with one swift knifelike stroke that originated in the muscles of the lower body, and I had a momentary glimpse of his mouth opening very wide and two yellow

---

① tensity: *Noun* the state of being tense; tenseness 张力; 紧张(度)

teeth and the whole face contorted① by the effort of mouth-opening.

More than that I did not care to see. I closed my eyes, and when I opened them again the rat was dead and the ratman was slipping the money into his pocket and spitting to clear his mouth.

"That's what they makes lickerish out of," he said. "Rat's blood is what the big factories and the chocolate-people use to make lickerish."

Again the relish, the wet-lipped, lip-smacking relish as he spoke the words, the throaty richness of his voice and the thick syrupy② way he pronounced the word *lickerish*.

"No," he said, "there's nothin' wrong with a drop of rat's blood."

"Don't talk so absolutely disgusting," Claud told him.

"Ah! But that's it, you see. You eaten it many a time. Penny sticks and lickerish bootlaces is all made from rat's blood."

"We don't want to hear about it, thank you."

"Boiled up, it is, in great cauldrons③, bubblin'④ and steamin'⑤ and men stirrin'⑥ it with long poles. That's one of the big secrets of the chocolate-makin' factories, and no one knows about it—no one except the ratters supplyin'⑦ the stuff."

Suddenly he noticed that his audience was no longer with him, that our faces were hostile and sick-looking and crimson with anger and dis-

---

① contort：*Verb* twist or bend out of its normal shape(使)歪曲；(使)扭曲

② syrupy or sirupy：*Adjective* having the consistency or sweetness of syrup 糖浆般的(e.g. syrupy puddings 像糖浆般甜的布丁)

③ cauldron or caldron：*Noun* a large metal pot with a lid and handle, used for cooking over an open fire(放在火堆上用来煮食物的有盖和带柄的)大锅

④ bubblin' = bubbling

⑤ steamin' = steaming

⑥ stirrin' = stirring

⑦ supplyin' = supplying

· 62 ·

gust. He stopped abruptly, and without another word he turned and sloped off① down the driveway out on to the road, moving with the slow, that almost delicate ambling walk that was like a rat prowling, making no noise with his footsteps even on the gravel of the driveway.

三、翻译探索

本篇小说的翻译中,值得探索的部分就是对于一些风格的再现,如对于体现出捕鼠者性格特点的口语表达的翻译,很不容易把握——处理不好,往往会弄巧成拙。这种在翻译中风格的再现,有待进一步探索。

捕鼠者说

下午的时候,捕鼠者来到了加油站。他当时好像是沿着车道滑行而上,脚底如同踩上棉花一般悄无声息,踏着砾石路走起路来一点声响也没有。他的一只肩上搭着一只军用背包,上身穿着一件过了时的黑色夹克,夹克上面缝了几个大大的兜子,下身穿一条棕色的灯芯绒裤子。在膝盖部位,裤子跟腿用一根根白绳绑到了一起。

"你谁啊?"克劳德明知故问,其实他心里十分清楚来者为何人。

"啮齿类动物消灭技工。"他那双黑色的小眼睛快速转动起来,察看四周的场所。

"捕鼠的?"

"正是我。"

捕鼠之人精瘦,皮肤呈棕色,脸尖尖的;上颚的两颗硫磺色的门牙凸了出来,贴到下唇,把下唇向嘴内挤去;他的两只耳朵很薄、很

---

① slope off: (informal) leave unobtrusively, typically in order to evade work or duty (非正式)悄悄溜走(尤指逃避工作或值班) (e.g. The men sloped off looking ashamed of themselves. 那些人悄悄溜走了,满脸羞愧的样子。)

尖,使劲地向脑袋后部生长,快长到后脖颈那儿了;两只眼睛接近黑色,但看人的时候,眼里的某个地方会闪现出一点儿黄颜色来。

"你来得够快的。"

"管卫生的下了特别命令。"

"所有的老鼠都能逮住吗?"

"是耶。"

他那双黑黑的、鬼鬼祟祟的眼睛类似于某种动物的眼睛,这种动物一生之中,一直穴居地下,小心谨慎地向洞穴外窥探。

"怎么捕呢?"

"哦——咳——咳,"捕鼠者神秘兮兮地说道,说话不是很标准。"那全看它们所处的位置。"

"设陷阱,我猜。"

"设陷阱!"他有些反感地叫道,"那样做,逮不了多少的!你知道,老鼠可不是什么野兔。"

他将脸高高仰起,用鼻子嗅着空气,鼻子抽动着,嗅嗅这边,嗅嗅那边,边嗅边感觉着。

"不是那样,"他说,露出了蔑视的神情,"捕老鼠,陷阱可使不得,老鼠很聪明。我跟你说说啊,要想逮住它们,你要了解它们。干这一行的,要了解老鼠才行。"

我看得出,克劳德盯着捕鼠者看,有点被吸引住了。

"它们可比狗聪明多了,我是指老鼠。"

"没有的事。"

"你知道它们干什么吗? 它们观察你! 你在周围转悠要捕捉它们的时候,它们一直静静地蹲在暗处,观察着你。"捕鼠者蹲伏下来,将伸展性很强的脖子远远地向前拉伸着。

"所以嘛,你做什么?"克劳德问,已经入了迷。

"噢! 你明白,就是这样。那就是你要了解老鼠的原因所在。"

"到底怎么逮呢?"

"自然有方法的,"捕鼠者斜视一眼说道,"方法多种多样。"

他暂停下来,自作聪明地上下点着头,那样子令人反胃。"那完全要看,"他说,"它们所处的位置。这可不是在下水道里干活,对吗?"

"不,不是在下水道里干活。"

"下水道里的活,需要细心和技巧。是的,没错。"说完,用他那转动灵活的鼻尖嗅着身体左侧的空气。"需要细心和技巧来做下水道里的活。"

"我想,这活不是特别需要细心和技巧。"

"噢——嚄,你不应该那样想,不应该的想法啊!好吧,我倒想看看你怎么做下水道里的活!我想一五一十地知道,你如何着手干这个活呢?"

"这有什么呀。直接把它们毒死,就这样。"

"那么,我可否问问,毒药到底投放在什么位置呢?"

"顺着下水道放进去。你以为我会把毒药放到哪儿啊!"

"瞧瞧!"捕鼠者喊道,一副得意洋洋的样子,"我就知道你会这样说!顺着下水道放进去呀!那样的话,你知道会发生什么吗?会被冲跑的,就这样。你知道,下水道就像一条河。"

"那是你的说法,"克劳德回答,"那仅仅是你的说法。"

"事实如此。"

"好吧,那么,好吧。万事通先生,你会怎么做呢?"

"在干下水道活这方面,你要了解老鼠,那就是原因所在。"

"那么,赶快,我们开始吧。"

"现在,听着啊,我告诉你。"捕鼠者向前跨出一步,靠近一些。他说起话来有些遮遮掩掩,一副高度保密的样子,好像是在吐露重大而非凡的行业机密。"做这项工作,你要明确的前提是,老鼠是啃咬型动物。要知道,它又啃又咬。只要你给它们东西吃,不管是什么样的东西,也不管是不是它们以前从来没有见过的新东西,它们会做什么呢?它们一味地啃咬。所以嘛,现在,你就瞧好吧!你手头就有了份下水道的活要干,那么,你要做什么呢?"

他的声音轻柔而低沉,如同一只青蛙在呱呱地叫着。他说起话来嘴唇湿漉漉的,就好像那些话语滋味美妙,沾沾自喜之情溢于言表。他的口音轻柔、宽厚,类似克劳德的口音,属于白金汉郡乡下人的口音。但是,他的嗓音更加低沉,嘴里说出的话更加圆润。

"所有你需要做的,就是顺着下水道下去,随身携带一些普普通通的纸袋,就是一些普普通通的棕色纸袋,里面装满巴黎香氛型石膏粉,其他的什么都不用装。然后,你就从下水道的顶部把这些袋子吊起来,要让袋子往下垂,但不要碰到水面,明白吗?不要碰到水面,但离水面的高度要刚好合适,老鼠可以够到袋子。"

克劳德听着,神情变得痴迷起来。

"你明白了吧,就是这个样子。一只年长的公老鼠沿着下水道游过来,看见袋子,停下来,鼻子吸口气嗅一嗅,嗅来嗅去,感觉味道还不赖。所以嘛,它接下来会做什么呢?"

"它会啃咬袋子,"克劳德大声说道,一副兴高采烈的样子。

"正是!说的没错!正如你所言呀!他开始啃咬起袋子来,袋子破裂,老家伙辛苦的努力换来一嘴的粉末。"

"然后呢?"

"就这样玩完了。"

"什么?置它于死地了吗?"

"是耶,杀它个没商量!"

"要知道啊,巴黎香氛型石膏粉是无毒的。"

"噢啊!你算是说到位啦!知道吗,那正是你搞错的地方。这种粉末会膨胀,一遇湿就膨胀。一进入老鼠的管状器官,就立刻膨胀,杀死他的速度比世界上任何东西都要快。"

"不会吧!"

"你要了解老鼠,这就是原因所在。"

捕鼠者的脸上暗自闪现出一丝自豪之情。他把双手举起靠近脸部,细长的手指相互摩擦起来。克劳德看着他,为之着迷。

"现在,哪儿有老鼠呢?"从他的嘴里说出这句话的时候,"老鼠"

这两个字咬得既轻柔又低沉,嗓音圆润,显得沾沾自喜,就好像含着融化的黄油漱口似的。"我们看一眼这些老——鼠吧。"

"就在那边,就在马路对面的干草垛里面。"

"房子里没有吗?"他问,明显带有一些失望的神情。

"没有。就在干草垛周边,别处没有。"

"我敢打赌,房子里也有。比如说,夜晚钻没钻进你们的食物,传播疾病,致人生病。这儿,你们谁也没得什么疾病吗?"他先看了看我,接着,看了看克劳德,问道。

"这儿,大家都很好。"

"十分肯定吗?"

"哦,是的。"

"你知道的,你永远无法察觉得病与否。你可能得了病,一周又一周过去,但你却察觉不到。然后,犹如晴天霹雳——'砰'的一声巨响——你就没得跑。阿巴斯诺特医生对这事要求得特别严格,派我火速赶来,原因就在于此,明白吧,来制止疾病的传播。"

现在,他主动承担起卫生人员的职责来了。眼下,他仿佛是一只大个头老鼠,得知我们大家都没有得上淋巴腺鼠疫,感到失望之极。

"我感觉还好,"克劳德有点神情紧张地说道。

这位捕鼠者又打量一下他的脸,但什么也没说。

"既然老鼠在干草垛里,那你怎么去捕捉呢?"

捕鼠者张嘴一笑,这一笑露出了很多牙齿,一副诡计多端的样子。他把手伸进背包,取出一只大大的锡罐,举到跟脸部齐平的位置上。然后,从罐子的一侧,瞥了克劳德一眼。

"毒药!"他小声说,但是,这个词他发得很轻微、很神秘,听起来成了一个危险的字眼"夺腰"。"致命的'夺腰',就是它啦!"他一边说,一边在手里上下掂量着罐子。"里面的药量足以毒死一百万个人!"

"真可怕,"克劳德说。

"说得一点不差!这东西即便是你用上一勺的量,被他们逮住,也得把你监禁个半年的时间,"他边说,边用舌头将嘴唇舔湿。他有一个习惯,就是说话时,将头向前拉伸。

"想看一看吗?"他问。随后,从衣兜里掏出一便士硬币,撬开盖子。"现在看看,就是它啦!"他满怀深情地说,对这东西表露出一副近于无比喜爱的样子,还把罐子向前一举,让克劳德看个清楚。

"玉米?或者是大麦?"

"是燕麦,在致命的'夺腰'里浸泡过。只要把其中的一粒放进你嘴里,不出五分钟,你就一命呜呼啦!"

"果真如此?"

"是耶。这只锡罐,我是从不敢离身的。"

他双手轻轻地爱抚着罐子,然后轻轻地晃动一下,罐里的燕麦粒就轻轻地发出"沙沙"的声音。

"但是,不是今天用。今天,不给你们的老鼠吃这个。无论如何,它们是不肯吃的,就是不肯吃。你们要了解老鼠,这就是原因所在。老鼠生性多疑,忒生性多疑,这就是老鼠。所以嘛,今天给它们一些干净的好燕麦,很好吃的燕麦,对他们毫无伤害,将它们催肥,这样就可以啦。明天,还是一样的做法。这样,它们吃到了好处,两三天过后,整个这一地区的老鼠都会接踵而至。"

"不一般的聪明。"

"你干这一行,也会聪明起来。你要变得比老鼠更聪明,那就能说明问题啦。"

"你本人几乎就是一只老鼠了,"我说。话音一落,我就知道自己说走了嘴,但要收回去已经来不及。当时我正看着这位捕鼠者,看着看着,话就情不自禁溜出了口,但是,我的失言对他产生的效果,却出乎我的意料。

"对啦!"他大叫道,"现在,你总算弄明白啦!你的的确确说到点子上啦!优秀的捕鼠者要比这个世界上的任何东西,更要像一只老鼠!聪明度要超过老鼠,这可不容易做到,我就给你说道说道吧。"

"十分肯定,老鼠赶不上你聪明。"

第一章　非常之辈　第二节　《捕鼠者说》The Ratcatcher

"那么,好吧,跟我去吧。你知道,我一整天没有捕鼠了。庄园那边有一位莱奥诺拉·本森太太正急着要我过去呢。"

"她那儿也有老鼠?"

"谁那儿都有老鼠的,"捕鼠者说,然后悠闲地沿着车道走开,穿过马路,走到干草垛那儿,而我们则一直看着他走过去。他走路的姿态太像老鼠了,令你禁不住浮想联翩:步态缓慢而敏捷,近乎于悠闲的漫步,膝盖部位弹性很大,脚踏在砾石路面上,一点声音也没有。他利索敏捷地跳过篱笆门进入田野,然后快速绕着干草垛走了一圈,同时随手一把一把地将燕麦洒向地面。

第二天,他又过来了,把同样的过程如法炮制一番。

第三天,他也过来了,但这次,他洒的是毒药浸泡过的燕麦,并不是像前两次那样随意抛洒,而是在干草垛的每一个角上仔仔细细地放上一小滩儿。

"你有狗吗?"第三天下完毒药,穿过马路,走过来后,他问道。

"有。"

"现在起,要是你想看到你的狗扭曲身体、倒地而死的惨状,你可以找个时间,只需把狗通过那扇篱笆门放进去,就可以啦。"

"我们会当心的,"克劳德对他说,"你大可不必担心。"

接下来一天,他又来了。这次,他是来收拾死老鼠的。

"你有旧麻袋吗?"他问。"极有可能的是,我们需要一条麻袋装尸体。"

现在,他开始趾高气扬,让人感到显赫尊贵起来,一双黑黑的眼睛闪耀着自豪的光芒。他就要向在场的观众展示他的精湛技艺所带来的轰动效应了。

克劳德取来一条麻袋,接着我们三个人穿过马路,捕鼠者走在前头。我和克劳德没有进去,倚身篱笆门上方,看着捕鼠者。只见他小心翼翼地绕着干草垛,边走边弯腰察看他留下的那一小滩一小滩的毒药。

"这儿有什么不对劲儿的地方,"他嘟囔着说道,说话的声音既轻柔又气愤。

他悠闲地走到另一摊毒药那儿,跪下来仔细检查起来。

"这儿有什么要命的不对劲儿的地方啦。"

"怎么啦?"

他没有回答,但明显老鼠并没有碰他设下的诱饵。

"这儿的这些老鼠都很聪明,"我说。

"戈登,那正是我跟他说过的。这儿你处理的这些,可不是普普通通的鼠辈。"

捕鼠者朝篱笆门走过来。他很是恼怒,恼怒之情写到了脸上,以及鼻子的周围。还有,他那两颗黄色的门牙把下嘴唇的皮肤使劲向里挤压,也表明他很恼怒。"不要说废话、扯淡了,"他看着我说道。"这些老鼠肯定没有什么不对劲儿的地方,除非有人喂东西给它们吃。它们从某个地方吃到了某种多汁的美味,而且还吃了不少。这个世界上的老鼠没有一个会将燕麦拒之门外,除非它们的肚子塞得满满的,快要爆炸。"

"它们聪明得很,"克劳德说。

这话令捕鼠者反感,于是他转身,又一次跪下来,开始用一把小铲子把毒药浸泡过的燕麦粒一铲铲地铲起,仔仔细细地装回锡罐。装完后,我们三个人又穿过马路走了回去。

捕鼠者站在靠近加油泵的位置上,看起来相当愧疚,抬不起头,脸上阴森森的,开始沉思起来。他独自一人待在那儿,一声不吱,思考着自己失手的原因所在。只见他眼露凶光,眼神朦胧,小小的舌头伸出来,伸到那两颗黄色的门牙的一边,不断舔着双唇来保湿。看起来,双唇保湿是至关重要的。他快速看了我一眼,也可以说,偷偷摸摸瞥了一眼,然后又看了看克劳德。他抽动鼻子尖,嗅着空气,还有好几次踮起脚尖,把身体抬高又放下,同时身体还轻轻地摆动。接着,他轻柔地,又颇为神秘兮兮地说:"想看点东西吗?"很明显,他想尽力挽回声誉。

"看什么?"

"想看点大开眼界的吗?"他一边说,一边将右手伸进夹克上一个深长的兜子里,掏出一只大个头的、活蹦乱跳的老鼠,他把老鼠紧紧夹在手指之间。

"老天啊!"

"噢哈!就是它啦,你们开眼吧!"现在,他稍微蹲伏一下身体,脖子向前伸展,斜视着我们。他两手握着这只棕色的大老鼠,其中一根手指和大母指组成一个圆环,紧紧地套住了这家伙的脖子。这样的话,它的头部就被紧紧地夹住,无法转动,也无法啃咬什么。

"你四处转悠,兜子里通常会揣些老鼠吗?"

"我身体什么地方总会放上一两只老鼠的。"

说这番话的时候,他腾出一只手,伸进另一个衣兜,拿出一只小白鼬。

"白鼬,"他握紧它的脖子说道。

那只白鼬似乎认识他,任由他紧紧握着,一动不动。

"杀死老鼠速度最快的莫过于白鼬啦,也没有什么比白鼬更令老鼠恐惧不已的啦。"

他把两只手靠拢,举到眼前。这时,白鼬的鼻子离老鼠的面部只有十五厘米的距离,白鼬的那双粉红色的小圆眼睛盯着这只老鼠。老鼠挣扎着,想尽力摆脱这位杀手。

"现在,"他说。"看着啊!"

他那件黄色卡其布衬衫领口处没有系扣。只见他举起老鼠从领口那儿将其紧贴着皮肤滑了进去。这只手一腾出来,就把夹克前面的扣子解开,好让现场的观众看到衬衫里那只老鼠身体鼓包、凸起的样子。有裤带挡着,老鼠是不会滑到腰部以下的。

紧接着,他把那只白鼬也滑了进去。

转瞬之间,衬衫内部骚动一片。看来,老鼠一直绕着捕鼠者的上身跑,那是白鼬追击的结果。小鼓包紧紧追赶大一点的鼓包,跑了约有六七圈,每跑完一圈,间距就稍微拉近一点,而且,越拉越近、越拉越近。最后,两个鼓包似乎融到一起,一通撕扯、扭打,发出阵阵刺耳的尖叫声。

整个表演过程中,捕鼠者双腿叉开静静站立,纹丝不动,两只胳膊松垮地悬垂着,而双眼却落在克劳德的脸上。现在,他一只手伸进衬衫拉出白鼬,另一只手则把死老鼠拽了出来。白鼬的鼻口部位沾染了斑斑血迹。

"不敢说,我很喜欢这一幕。"

"我敢打赌,此类场景你从来都没有看到过。"

"的确不敢说我见到过。"

"很有可能的是,说不定哪一天,你的肠子会被狠狠咬一下,"克劳德告诫他说。但是,很显然,他大饱了眼福,捕鼠者也再度高傲自大起来。

"想看看比这个更令你大开眼界的吗?"他问,"有些东西,若不是你亲眼所见的话,你甚至永远都无法相信,想看吗?"

"是吗?"

我们当时站在车道上,就站在加油泵的前面。正值十一月,但那天上午却是一个好天气,暖洋洋的,很令人愉快。有两辆车前后停靠在那儿等待加油。于是,克劳德走过去,给它们加了油。

"你们想看看吗?"捕鼠者问道。

我看了克劳德一眼,稍微感觉有点恐惧不安。"看,"克劳德回应,"那就快点让我们看看吧。"

捕鼠者将死老鼠滑回一只兜子,再将白鼬滑入另一只兜子。然后,他把手伸进背包,掏出另一只活蹦乱跳的老鼠——竟然还有一只。

"老天爷啊!"克劳德说。

"我身体什么地方总会放上一两只老鼠的,"捕鼠者从容不迫地宣布道。"干这一行,你要了解老鼠,要把它们带在左右。这是一只下水道公老鼠,真的。虽说上了年纪,但姜还是老的辣,这家伙真他妈的聪明。他一直盯着我,心里纳闷我要干什么,看到了吗?看到没有?"

"令人感到很不舒服。"

"你要做什么?"我问,我有一种预感,感觉不会太喜欢这次表演。

"给我取一根细绳来。"

克劳德应声取来一根细绳。

捕鼠者用左手将细绳套到老鼠的一条后腿上,老鼠挣扎着,想尽力扭头看看后面发生了什么情况,但是,他却用手指和拇指紧紧夹住了老鼠的脖子。

"瞧吧!"他说完,向四周看看,"屋内有桌子吗?"

"我们不想让老鼠进屋,"我说。

"噢——我需要一张桌子,或者某个像桌子一样扁平的东西也可以。"

"那辆车的引擎罩可以吗?"克劳德问。

我们走到那辆车跟前,捕鼠者将上了年纪的下水道老鼠放到引擎罩上面,把细绳栓到风挡的雨刷上,现在老鼠就跑不了了。

刚开始的时候,这只老鼠蹲伏在那儿,一动不动,但疑虑重重。这是一只大块头的灰色老鼠,黑黑的眼睛很是明亮,长长的尾巴干燥而粗糙,打了一个卷儿翘在引擎罩的上方。老鼠没有正面观瞧捕鼠者,但却用眼睛的余光观察着,看看他要做些什么。他向后跨出了几步远,老鼠就立刻放松许多。于是,老鼠就蹲坐起来,开始舔胸部灰色的软毛。接着,用两只前爪挠鼻口部位,而对附近站着的三名男子似乎并不在意。

"现在嘛——小赌一把怎么样呢?"捕鼠者提议。

"我们不赌博的,"我说。

"只是玩玩而已嘛。要是赌一赌,会有更多乐趣的。"

"你想赌什么?"

"我要赌的是,一只手都不用,我也能杀死那只老鼠。我把两只手插进衣兜,不用。"

"你会用双脚将它踢死,"克劳德说。

显而易见,捕鼠者存心想赢点钱了。看着那只要命丧黄泉的老鼠,我开始轻微感到有点不适,这倒不是因为老鼠要丢掉性命,而是因为老鼠要以一种特殊的方式丧命,有人却因此而自享其乐,沾沾自喜。

"不会,"捕鼠者说,"不会用脚。"

"也不用胳膊吗?"克劳德问。

"不用。也不用腿,更不用手,都不用。"

"你会坐到它上面。"

"不坐。不坐也不压。"

"那你开始吧,我们瞧瞧。"

"先下注啊。跟我赌一英镑吧。"

"真是蠢得要命啊你,"克劳德说,"凭什么我们要给你一英镑呢?"

"那你拿什么赌?"

"什么都不拿。"

"好吧。那么,这可就没有什么可玩的啦。"

看他那架势,好像要把细绳从风挡雨刷上解下来。

"我拿一先令跟你赌,"克劳德对他说。此时,我胃部那种不适感开始翻腾起来,但是,这个赌局却有着一股极大的磁性引力吸引着我,令我无法拔腿走开,甚至无法挪动脚步。

"你也一样吗?"

"不,"我回答。

"你怎么回事呢?"捕鼠者问。

"我只是不想跟你赌,仅此而已。"

"最终,为了区区一先令,你想让我杀死一只老鼠吗?"

"我可不想让你这么做。"

"钱在哪儿呢?"他问克劳德。

克劳德将一先令硬币放到引擎罩上,放在靠近散热器的位置上。随后,捕鼠者拿出两枚六便士硬币,放到克劳德钱的旁边。他伸手放硬币的时候,这只老鼠蜷缩一下,收缩脑袋,放平了身体,紧紧贴到引

第一章 非常之辈 第二节 《捕鼠者说》The Ratcatcher

擎罩上。

"开赌,"捕鼠者说。

我和克劳德向后退出几步远,捕鼠者则向前跨步。只见他双手插入衣兜,腰部以上的身体倾斜着,这样,他的脸就跟老鼠齐平,与老鼠相距大约九十厘米。

他与老鼠四目相对,紧盯不放。老鼠蹲伏在那儿,绷紧神经,觉察到有极端的危险存在,但还没有惊恐万分。老鼠蹲伏的样子在我看来,它正准备向前跳跃,跃到捕鼠者的脸上,但是,他的眼中一定露出某种力量,阻止它这样做,迫使它屈从,令它逐渐恐惧不安起来。结果是,它开始后退了:蹲伏着身体,向后慢慢迈动脚步退去。随着它的后退,一条后腿上系的那根细绳就被拉紧了。于是,它进一步后退,挣扎着猛拉后腿,意欲挣脱细绳。捕鼠者向前倾斜身体靠近老鼠,脸紧紧跟随着它移动,眼睛始终盯着它。突然之间,老鼠一下子惊慌失措起来,向一侧的空中跳去,但是,细绳猛地将它拉住,这一拉十有八九会将它的腿关节拉脱白。

它又蹲伏下来,就爬在引擎罩的中间,细绳已经拉到了最大的限度。现在,老鼠可算是惊恐万状了,胡须颤动,由于恐惧害怕,它那长长的灰色身体也绷得紧紧的。

此时此刻,捕鼠者又开始把脸靠近了一些,靠近的速度很是缓慢,慢到你根本觉察不到他的脸是在移动,但是,你每次看过去,就会发现,他的脸刚好靠近了一点点。他的眼睛从来就没有离开过它,气氛紧张得让人承受不了,弄得我突然间想大叫一声,喊"停"。我之所以想让他停下,是因为我体内的不适感翻腾得让我受不了,但是,我还是下不了决心对他喊出这个字。令人不快的极端的事情即将发生,这一点我有把握。某种险恶的、残忍的、只有老鼠才能做得出的事情即将发生,这件事情或许会真的令我感觉不适而呕吐,可现在我必须忍耐,继续看下去。

捕鼠者的脸离老鼠约四十五厘米……三十厘米……二十五厘米……二十厘米。很快,他跟老鼠的间距不足一只手的长度了。这只老鼠放平身体,紧紧贴在车的引擎罩上,绷紧神经,恐惧异常。捕鼠者也绷紧了神经,但是,他绷紧的强度却充满威胁并且活力十足,就像一根发条,弦上得紧紧的。他嘴周边的皮肤上残留着一丝若隐若现的微笑。

接着,他冷不防发起了进攻。

他像蛇一样发起了攻击,下半身肌肉积聚的力量瞬间爆发,将头向前猛地一冲,如刀一般快速划过。就在这一瞬间,我瞥眼看过去,看到他那张嘴张得宽宽的,露出那两颗黄黄的门牙,整个脸部由于张嘴时过于用力而扭曲变形。

除了这一幕,其他的我不愿意再看下去。于是,我闭上双眼。再次睁开时,我看到老鼠已经死了,捕鼠者将钱滑入衣兜,吐了几口,算是将嘴清理干净。

"他们就是用那东西做诱人美味的,"他说。"老鼠血,就是大工厂和巧克力商用来制作诱人美味的东西。"

他又得意洋洋起来。他说那话的时候,得意洋洋地咂巴着嘴唇,弄得双唇湿乎乎的。说"诱人美味"这个词的时候,嗓音听起来过于低沉,感觉是在吃黏稠的糖浆。

"不,"他说,"老鼠的一滴血,没有什么不对劲儿的地方。"

"不要把话说得让人感到如此恶心和反胃,"克劳德对他说。

"噢!可是你知道,事情就是这样子。这种东西你吃过无数次了。一便士的细棒糖和香甜诱人的靴带巧克力都是用老鼠血做成的。"

"谢谢你,但是我们不想听这个。"

"注入大大的锅中,将其煮开,鼓起阵阵泡泡,冒出腾腾热气,还有一些人用长长的杆子搅拌着。这可是巧克力制造工厂里天大的秘密,神不知鬼不觉的秘密,除了提供这种东西的捕鼠者,没有人知道的。"

突然,他注意到,现场的观众不再拥护他了。我们面露敌意,厌恶透顶。由于气愤和反感,我们的脸都涨红了。于是,他戛然而止,一个字也没有多说就转过身,沿着车道,夹着尾巴,灰溜溜向马路走去。他走起路来,步伐缓慢,几乎是在悠闲而敏捷地散步,就像是一只老鼠在小心翼翼地游走。他走起路来,即便是踏在砾石路上,一点声响也没有发出来。

第二章 事与愿违

　　事情的发展没有按照预定的方向进行,或者按照预定的方向进行,却突然发生了没有预料的转变,这都是所谓的"事与愿违"。"竹林七贤"之一,三国(魏)嵇康在其四言诗《幽愤》中这样写道:"嗷嗷鸣雁,奋翼北游。顺时而动,得意忘忧。嗟我愤叹,曾莫能俦。事与愿违,遘兹淹留。"几个英国皇家空军的飞行员大兵萌生了"救美"的念头,但是,"救美"于"水火"的使命尚未完成之际,却发生了"抱得美人归"的出人意料的结局。这就是英国作家罗尔德·达尔笔下颇具讽刺意义的《大兵"救美"》里的精彩情节。

　　事情的发展与愿望相反,这也是所谓的"事与愿违",这种"事与愿违"的结果也许就"适得其反"。老资格飞行员再三叮嘱即将升空执行战斗任务的英国皇家空军年轻飞行员:要谨慎行事。但年轻的飞行员却不以为意,认为执行这样的任务简直就是"小菜一碟"——易如反掌。可是,结果呢? 恰恰相反。这名年轻的飞行员遇到了大麻烦,飞机被击中,飞行员受伤严重,失去了知觉。这就是罗尔德·达尔笔下颇具意识流色彩的《小菜一碟》里的"事与愿违"的故事。

　　走进罗尔德·达尔的世界,去体会《大兵"救美"》中事与愿违的突然转变,去品尝《小菜一碟》中事与愿违的沉重代价。

第一节 《大兵"救美"》Madame Rosette

罗尔德·达尔的《大兵"救美"》(Madame Rosette)首次发表在全球知名杂志《时尚芭莎》(Harper's Bazaar)1945年8月号上。后来,这篇小说被收录到《向你飞跃》(Over to You)《罗尔德·达尔短篇故事集锦》(The Collected Short Stories of Roald Dahl)《罗尔德·达尔小说精品集》(The Best of Roald Dahl)以及《五部畅销书集》(5 Bestsellers)等书中。

一、原作导读

虽说本篇小说是有关达尔"飞行"方面的故事,讲的是皇家空军三个飞行员在短暂休假期间发生的事情,但多少涉及一些所谓"成人"方面的内容,如与罗塞特夫人开的那家名声不大好的妓院有关的内容。因此,不建议儿童在没有指导的情况下阅读,年轻读者也应谨慎阅读。

斯塔非和斯塔格是英国皇家空军某个飞行中队的飞行员,在他们执行飞行任务的间隙,有幸得到批准,短暂休假一次。于是,他俩就到了开罗,一起住进一家宾馆,先洗洗澡,放松一下身心。然后,出去逛街。斯塔非买了一副太阳镜,迷上卖给他太阳镜的那个埃及女孩,要约她出来。于是,他向斯塔格求助,问斯塔格如何才能将那个女孩子约出来。

斯塔格说,他听说有一个女人神通广大,人称"罗塞特夫人"。要想跟城里的哪个女子幽会,只要找她,她都能设法安排成功。斯塔非给罗塞特夫人打了个电话,谈好了价钱,跟斯塔格回到宾馆等待回信。但是,没过多久,斯塔非改变了主意,反悔了。于是,他说服了斯塔格,求斯塔格给罗塞特夫人回电话,取消了跟那个埃及女孩幽会的要求。

斯塔格跟斯塔非闲来无事,就去酒吧喝酒。在一个酒吧,他俩结识了皇家空军第三十三飞行中队的飞行员威廉。他们三个人结伴而行,要喝遍开罗所有酒吧。酒吧打烊之际,他们三个喝得也差不多了,虽然喝了很多,但都没有喝成酩酊大醉的状态。返回的路上,他们想到了一个疯狂的计划:从罗塞特夫人那儿救走所有的"美女"。

他们设法打了一辆埃及当地的出租马车,赶到罗塞特夫人开的那家妓院,将罗塞特夫人锁到办公室,救走了妓院里所有十四名"美女"。

三个大兵护送十四名"美女"走到埃及一家咖啡馆前面的时候,斯塔格发话了:

"年轻的女士,"他一边说,一边微笑着,"对军方而言,总会有一些拘泥于形式的东西,这是不可避免的。对此,我十分抱歉。但是,骑士风范也是有的。而且,你们必须了解的是,皇家空军具有很伟大的骑士风范。因此,现在你们要是进去,跟我们喝一杯啤酒的话,我们将不胜荣幸。这就是军人的骑士风范。"他向前跨出一步,打开咖啡馆的门说道:"看在上帝的份上,我们喝一杯吧。谁想喝一杯呢?"

"Mesd'moiselles," he said, and his voice was smiling. "With the military there always has to be formality. It is something unavoidable. It is something that I regret exceedingly. But there can be chivalry also. And you must know that with the RAF there is great chivalry. So now it will be a pleasure if you will all come in here and take with us a glass of beer. It is the chivalry of the military." He stepped forward, opened the door of the café and said, "Oh for God's sake, let's have a drink. Who wants a drink?"

众"美女"迷惑不解,你看看我,我看看你,但是很快,她们就心领神会了。

第二章 事与愿违 第一节 《大兵"救美"》Madame Rosette

女孩们突然间明白了一切,她们明白整个事件的来龙去脉了。这都是在一瞬间弄明白的。突然明白之后,她们吃惊不已。她们考虑了片刻,彼此看了看,又看了看斯塔格,又转身看了看斯塔非和威廉。看着后两位时,她们看到他俩的眼神,听到他俩发出的笑声。顿时,女孩们开始大笑起来,威廉和斯塔非也开始大笑起来,大家一起涌进咖啡馆。

Suddenly the girls saw it all. They saw the whole thing as it was, all of them at once. It took them by surprise. For a second they considered. Then they looked at one another, then they looked at the Stag, then they looked around at Stuffy and at William, and when they looked at those two they caught their eyes, and the laughter that was in them. All at once the girls began to laugh and William laughed and Stuffy laughed and they moved forward and poured into the café.

三个皇家空军飞行员掏腰包请"美女"们喝啤酒。她们乐开了怀,有说有笑喝着啤酒。期间,斯塔格拿出纸笔,要求"美女"写下姓名和电话号码,说是要带回去给中队里的其他人。最后,斯塔格一敲桌子,说道:

"年轻的女士们,"他说,"护送你们回家,我们将不胜荣幸。我送五个。"他都已经计算好了。"斯塔非送五个,娃娃脸威廉送四个。我们打三辆出租马车。你们五个坐我打的马车,到家一个,下一个。"

"Mesd'moiselles," he said. "It will be a pleasure for us to escort you home. I will take five of you,"—he had worked it all out—"Stuffy will take five, and Jamface will take four. We will take three gharries and I will take five of you in mine and I will drop you home one at a time.

他怕斯塔非不明白,就冲他说道:

"斯塔非,这样安排可以吗?你送五个。谁最后下,你说了算。"

"Stuffy, is that all right? You take five. It's up to you whom you drop off last."

二、原作释读

这部作品中,达尔为突出人物的性格特点,在对话中使用了一些不规范的表达,特别是主人公跟埃及人的对话中的不规范表达,要注意理解和把握。另外,还要在阅读中理解好主人公前后态度的转变,体会好作家达尔对一些场景的细腻描写。

Madame Rosette[①]

"Oh Jesus, this is wonderful," said the Stag.

He was lying back in the bath with a Scotch[②] and soda in one hand and a cigarette in the other. The water was right up to the brim and he was keeping it warm by turning the tap with his toes.

He raised his head and took a little sip of his whisky, then he lay back and closed his eyes.

"For God's sake, get out," said a voice from the next room. "Come on, Stag, you've had over an hour." Stuffy was sitting on the edge of the bed with no clothes on, drinking slowly and waiting his turn.

The Stag said, "All right. I'm letting the water out now," and he

---

① 本部小说原文出自"DAHL, R. *The Best of Roald Dahl* [M]. England: Penguin Books Ltd., 2006"。

② scotch(usu. as "Scotch"): *Noun* short for Scotch whisky "苏格兰威士忌"的简称

第二章 事与愿违 第一节 《大兵"救美"》Madame Rosette

stretched out a leg and flipped① up the plug with his toes.

Stuffy stood up and wandered into the bathroom holding his drink in his hand. The Stag lay in the bath for a few moments more, then, balancing his glass carefully on the soap rack, he stood up and reached for a towel. His body was short and square, with strong thick legs and exaggerated calf muscles. He had coarse curly ginger hair and a thin, rather pointed face covered with freckles. There was a layer of pale ginger hair on his chest.

"Jesus," he said, looking down into the bathtub, "I've brought half the desert with me."

Stuffy said, "Wash it out and let me get in. I haven't had a bath for five months."

This was back in the early days when we were fighting the Italians in Libya. One flew very hard in those days because there were not many pilots. They certainly could not send any out from England because there they were fighting the Battle of Britain②. So one remained for long periods out in the desert, living the strange unnatural life of the desert, living in the same dirty little tent, washing and shaving every day in a mug full of one's own spat-out tooth water, all the time picking flies out of one's tea and out of one's food, having sandstorms which were as much in the tents as outside them so that placid men became bloody-minded and

---

① flip: *Verb* turn over or cause to turn over with a sudden sharp movement 翻转;使翻转

② Battle of Britain: *Noun* the prolonged bombardment of British cities by the German Luftwaffe during World War II and the aerial combat that accompanied it(第二次世界大战期间的)不列颠之战

· 83 ·

lost their tempers with their friends and with themselves; having dysentery① and gippy tummy② and mastoid③ and desert sores④, having some bombs from the Italian S. 79s⑤, having no water and no women, having no flowers growing out of the ground; having very little except sand sand sand. One flew old Gloster Gladiators against the Italian C. R. 42s, and when one was not flying, it was difficult to know what to do.

　　Occasionally one would catch scorpions, put them in empty petrol cans and match them against each other in fierce mortal combat. Always there would be a champion scorpion in the squadron⑥, a sort of Joe Louis⑦ who was invincible⑧ and won all his fights. He would have a name; he would become famous and his training diet would be a great secret known only to the owner. Training diet was considered very important

---

　　① dysentery：*Noun* an infection of the intestines marked by severe diarrhea 痢疾

　　② gippy tummy：*Noun* [in sing.] (Brit. informal) diarrhea affecting visitors to hot countries(英国英语非正式用法)(热带国家游客所患的)热带腹泻

　　③ mastoid：*Noun* process of the temporal bone behind the ear at the base of the skull；(informal) mastoiditis 乳般突起；(非正式用法)乳突炎

　　④ desert sore：*Noun* (Med.) An infective sore mostly on the hands and feet, often contracted in walking on the veldt and apparently due to a specific microorganism(医学)沙漠疮

　　⑤ 本段中提到的"S. 79""Gloster Gladiator""C. R. 42"都是二战时期一些战斗机的型号。

　　⑥ squadron：*Noun* an operational unit in an air force consisting of two or more flights of aircraft and the personnel required to fly them(空军)中队

　　⑦ Joe Louis：*Noun* United States prizefighter who was world heavyweight champion for 12 years (1914—1981) 乔·路易斯(美国职业拳击手,连续12年保持世界重量级拳王的称号)

　　⑧ invincible：*Adjective* too powerful to be defeated or overcome 不可战胜的；不能征服的；不能克服的(e.g. an invincible warrior 不可战胜的勇士)

第二章 事与愿违 第一节 《大兵"救美"》Madame Rosette

with scorpions. Some were trained on corned beef, some on a thing called Machonachies, which is an unpleasant canned meat stew, some on live beetles and there were others who were persuaded to take a little beer just before the fight, on the premise that it made the scorpion happy and gave him confidence. These last ones always lost. But there were great battles and great champions, and in the afternoons when the flying was over, one could often see a group of pilots and airmen standing around in a circle on the sand, bending over with their hands on their knees, watching the fight, exhorting① the scorpions and shouting at them as people shout at boxers or wrestlers in a ring. Then there would be a victory, and the man who owned the winner would become excited. He would dance around in the sand yelling, waving his arms in the air and extolling in a loud voice the virtues of the victorious animal. The greatest scorpion of all was owned by a sergeant called Wishful who fed him only on marmalade②. The animal had an unmentionable name, but he won forty-two consecutive fights and then died quietly in training just when Wishful was considering the problem of retiring him to stud③.

So you can see that because there were no great pleasures while living in the desert, the small pleasures became great pleasures and the pleasures of children became the pleasures of grown men. That was true

---

① exhort: Verb [with obj. and infinitive] strongly encourage or urge (someone) to do something 敦促;激励;勉励;规劝(e. g. The media have been exhorting people to turn out for the demonstration. 媒体激励人们走上街头进行示威。)

② marmalade: Noun [mass noun] a preserve made from citrus fruit, especially bitter oranges, prepared like jam (用柑橘类水果制成的)橘皮酱

③ stud (Also as "stud horse"): Noun a stallion 种马(这里用作动词,带点玩笑之意,意思是想要那只蝎子做"种公畜"。)

for everyone; for the pilots, the fitters①, the riggers②, the corporals③ who cooked the food, and the men who kept the stores. It was true for the Stag and for Stuffy, so true that when the two of them wangled④ a forty eight hour pass and a lift by air into Cairo⑤, and when they got to the hotel, they were feeling about having a bath rather as you would feel on the first night of your honeymoon.

The Stag had dried himself and was lying on the bed with a towel round his waist, with his hands up behind his head, and Stuffy was in the bath, lying with his head against the back of the bath, groaning and sighing with ecstasy.

The Stag said, "Stuffy."

"Yes."

"What are we going to do now?"

"Women," said Stuffy. "We must find some women to take out to supper."

① fitter: Noun a person who puts together or installs machinery, engine parts, or other equipment 装配工;钳工(e.g. a qualified gas fitter 一位合格的煤气装配工)

② rigger: Noun a person who rigs or attends to the rigging of a sailing ship, aircraft, or parachute(帆船)索具操纵工;(飞机或降落伞)装配工

③ corporal: Noun a rank of non-commissioned officer in the army, above lance corporal or private first class and below sergeant 下士

④ wangle: Verb [with obj.] obtain (something that is desired) by persuading others to comply or by manipulating events 设法获得;骗取(想要之物)(e.g. I wangled an invitation to her flat. 我设法使她邀请我去她的公寓。)

⑤ Cairo: Noun the capital of Egypt, a port on the Nile near the head of its delta; pop. 13,300,000 (est. 1991). Arabic name Al Qahira 开罗(埃及首都,尼罗河三角洲入口附近港口,1991 年估计人口 13,300,000,阿拉伯语名"Al Qahira"。)

第二章 事与愿违 第一节 《大兵"救美"》*Madame Rosette*

The Stag said, "Later. That can wait till later." It was early afternoon.

"I don't think it can wait," said Stuffy.

"Yes," said the Stag, "it can wait."

The Stag was very old and wise; he never rushed any fences. He was twenty-seven, much older than anyone else in the squadron, including the C. O.①, and his judgement was much respected by the others.

"Let's do a little shopping first," he said.

"Then what?" said the voice from the bathroom.

"Then we can consider the other situation."

There was a pause.

"Stag?"

"Yes."

"Do you know any women here?"

"I used to. I used to know a Turkish② girl with very white skin called Wenka, and a Yugoslav③ girl who was six inches taller than I, called Kiki, and another who I think was Syrian. I can't remember her name."

"Ring them up," said Stuffy.

"I've done it. I did it while you were getting the whisky. They've all gone. It isn't any good."

"It's never any good," Stuffy said.

The Stag said, "We'll go shopping first. There is plenty of time."

---

① C. O. = Commanding Officer 指挥官

② Turkish: *Adjective* of or relating to Turkey or to the Turks or their language 土耳其(人)的;土耳其式的;土耳其语的

③ Yugoslav: *Adjective* of or relating to Yugoslavia, its former constituent republics, or its people 南斯拉夫的;南斯拉夫人的

In an hour Stuffy got out of the bath. They both dressed themselves in clean khaki① shorts and shirts and wandered downstairs, through the lobby of the hotel and out into the bright hot street. The Stag put on his sunglasses.

Stuffy said, "I know. I want a pair of sunglasses."

"All right. We'll go and buy some."

They stopped a gharry②, got in and told the driver to go to Cicurel. Stuffy bought his sunglasses and the Stag bought some poker dice, then they wandered out again on to the hot crowded street.

"Did you see that girl?" said Stuffy.

"The one that sold us the sunglasses?"

"Yes. That dark one."

"Probably Turkish," said Stag.

Stuffy said, "I don't care what she was. She was terrific. Didn't you think she was terrific?"

They were walking along the Sharia Kasr-el-Nil with their hands in their pockets, and Stuffy was wearing the sunglasses which he had just bought. It was a hot dusty afternoon, and the sidewalk was crowded with Egyptians and Arabs and small boys with bare feet. The flies followed the small boys and buzzed around their eyes, trying to get at the inflamma-

---

① khaki: *Noun* a sturdy twilled cloth of a yellowish brown color used especially for military uniforms 黄卡其布

② gharry: *Noun* (in the Indian subcontinent) a horse-drawn carriage available for hire(印度次大陆)出租马车

tion① which was in them, which was there because their mothers had done something terrible to those eyes when the boys were young, so that they would not be eligible for military conscription when they grew older. The small boys pattered along beside the Stag and Stuffy shouting, "Baksheesh②, baksheesh," in shrill insistent voices, and the flies followed the small boys. There was the smell of Cairo, which is not like the smell of any other city. It comes not from any one thing or from any one place; it comes from everything everywhere; from the gutters and the sidewalks, from the houses and the shops and the things in the shops and the food cooking in the shops, from the horses and the dung③ of the horses in the streets and from the drains; it comes from the people and the way the sun bears down upon the people and the way the sun bears down upon the gutters and the drains and the horses and the food and the refuse in the streets. It is a rare, pungent④ smell, like something which is sweet and rotting and hot and salty and bitter all at the same time, and it is never absent, even in the cool of the early morning.

The two pilots walked along slowly among the crowd.

"Didn't you think she was terrific?" said Stuffy. He wanted to know what the Stag thought.

---

① inflammation: *Noun* [mass noun] a localized physical condition in which part of the body becomes reddened, swollen, hot, and often painful, especially as a reaction to injury or infection 发炎；炎（症）(e. g. chronic inflammation of the nasal cavities 慢性鼻腔炎)

② baksheesh: *Noun* a relatively small amount of money given for services rendered (as by a waiter)（中东地区）小费；赏钱

③ dung: *Noun* [mass noun] the excrement of animals; manure（动物的）粪；粪肥

④ pungent: *Adjective* having a sharply strong taste or smell 有刺激性气味（或味道）的；辣的(e. g. the pungent smell of frying onions 炸洋葱的辣味)

"She was all right."

"Certainly she was all right. You know what, Stag?"

"What?"

"I would like to take that girl out tonight."

They crossed over a street and walked on a little farther.

The Stag said, "Well, why don't you? Why don't you ring up Rosette?"

"Who in the hell's Rosette?"

"Madame Rosette," said the Stag. "She is a great woman."

They were passing a place called Tim's Bar. It was run by an Englishman called Tim Gilfillan who had been a quartermaster① sergeant in the last war and who had somehow managed to get left behind in Cairo when the army went home.

"Tim's," said the Stag. "Let's go in."

There was no one inside except for Tim, who was arranging his bottles on shelves behind the bar.

"Well, well, well," he said, turning around, "Where you boys been all this time?"

"Hello, Tim."

He did not remember them, but he knew by their looks that they were in from the desert.

"How's my old friend Graziani?" he said, leaning his elbows on the counter.

"He's bloody close," said the Stag. "He's outside Mersah."

"What you flying now?"

---

① quartermaster: *Noun* a regimental officer, usually commissioned from the ranks, responsible for administering barracks, laying out the camp, and looking after supplies 军需官

"Gladiators."

"Hell, they had those here eight years ago."

"Same ones still here," said the Stag. "They're clapped out." They got their whisky and carried the glasses over to a table in the corner.

Stuffy said, "Who's this Rosette?"

The Stag took a long drink and put down the glass.

"She's a great woman," he said.

"Who is she?"

"She's a filthy old Syrian Jewess①."

"All right," said Stuffy, "all right, but what about her."

"Well," said Stag, "I'll tell you. Madame Rosette runs the biggest brothel② in the world. It is said that she can get you any girl that you want in the whole of Cairo."

"Bullshit."

"No, it's true. You just ring her up and tell her where you saw the woman, where she was working, what shop and at which counter, together with an accurate description, and she will do the rest."

"Don't be such a bloody fool," said Stuffy.

"It's true. It's absolutely true. Thirty-three squadron told me about her."

"They were pulling your leg."

"All right. You go and look her up in the phone book."

"She wouldn't be in the phone book under that name."

"I'm telling you she is," said Stag. "Go and look her up under Ro-

---

① Jewess: *Noun* (often offensive) a Jewish woman or girl(常带冒犯之意)犹太女人

② brothel: *Noun* a house where men visit prostitutes 妓院

sette. You'll see I'm right."

Stuffy did not believe him, but he went over to Tim and asked him for a telephone directory and brought it back to the table. He opened it and turned the pages until he came to R-o-s. He ran his finger down the column. Roseppi... Rosery... Rosette. There it was, Rosette, Madame and the address and number, clearly printed in the book. The Stag was watching him.

"Got it?" he said.

"Yes, here it is. Madame Rosette."

"Well, why don't you go and ring her up?"

"What shall I say?"

The Stag looked down into his glass and poked the ice with his finger.

"Tell her you are a Colonel①," he said. "Colonel Higgins; she mistrusts pilot officers. And tell her that you have seen a beautiful dark girl selling sunglasses at Cicurel's and that you would like, as you put it, to take her out to dinner."

"There isn't a telephone here."

"Oh yes there is. There's one over there."

Stuffy looked around and saw the telephone on the wall at the end of the bar.

"I haven't got a piastre② piece."

"Well, I have," said Stag. He fished in his pocket and put a pias-

---

① colonel: *Noun* a rank of officer in the army and in the US air force, above a lieutenant colonel and below a brigadier or brigadier general（陆军和美国空军中的）上校（这里指的应该是陆军上校）

② piaster: *Noun* The piastre was the currency of Egypt until 1834 皮亚斯特（埃及的货币单位）

tre on the table.

"Tim will hear everything I say."

"What the hell does that matter? He probably rings her up himself. You're windy①," he added.

"You're a shit," said Stuffy.

Stuffy was just a child. He was nineteen; seven whole years younger than the Stag. He was fairly tall and he was thin, with a lot of black hair and a handsome wide-mouthed face which was coffee brown from the sun of the desert. He was unquestionably the finest pilot in the squadron, and already in these early days, his score was fourteen Italians confirmed destroyed. On the ground he moved slowly and lazily like a tired person and he thought slowly and lazily like a sleepy child, but when he was up in the air his mind was quick and his movements were quick, so quick that they were like reflex actions. It seemed, when he was on the ground, almost as though he was resting, as though he was dozing a little in order to make sure that when he got into the cockpit② he would wake up fresh and quick, ready for that two hours of high concentration. But Stuffy was away from the aerodrome③ now and he had something on his mind which had waked him up almost like flying. It might not last, but for the moment anyway, he was concentrating.

He looked again in the book for the number, got up and walked slowly over to the telephone. He put in the piastre, dialled the number

---

① windy: *Adjective* (Brit. informal) (of a person) nervous or anxious about something(英国英语非正式)(人)紧张的;忧虑的

② cockpit: *Noun* a compartment for the pilot, and sometimes also the crew, in an aircraft or spacecraft(飞机或航天器的)飞行员座舱(或机组人员座舱)

③ aerodrome: *Noun* (Brit.) a small airport or airfield(英国)小型飞机(降落)场

and heard it ringing the other end. The Stag was sitting at the table looking at him and Tim was still behind the bar arranging his bottles. Tim was only about five yards away and he was obviously going to listen to everything that was said. Stuffy felt rather foolish. He leaned against the bar and waited, hoping that no one would answer.

Then click, the receiver was lifted at the other end and he heard a woman's voice saying, "Allo①."

He said, "Hello, is Madame Rosette there?" He was watching Tim. Tim went on arranging his bottles, pretending to take no notice, but Stuffy knew that he was listening.

"This ees② Madame Rosette. Oo③ ees it?" Her voice was petulant④ and gritty⑤. She sounded as if she did not want to be bothered with anyone just then.

Stuffy tried to sound casual. "This is Colonel Higgins."

"Colonel oo?"

"Colonel Higgins." He spelled it.

"Yes, Colonel. What do you want?" She sounded impatient. Obviously this was a woman who stood no nonsense. He still tried to sound casual.

"Well, Madame Rosette, I was wondering if you would help me over a little matter."

Stuffy was watching Tim. He was listening all right. You can always

---

① 这里的"allo"是"hallo"非标准发音的拼写形式。
② 这里的"ees"是"is"非标准发音的拼写形式。
③ 这里的"oo"是"who"非标准发音的拼写形式。
④ petulant: Adjective (of a person or their manner) childishly sulky or bad-tempered(人或其举止)任性的;脾气坏的
⑤ gritty: Adjective containing or covered with grit 含砂的;布满沙砾的

第二章 事与愿违 第一节 《大兵"救美"》*Madame Rosette*

tell if someone is listening when he is pretending not to. He is careful not to make any noise about what he is doing and he pretends that he is concentrating very hard upon his job. Tim was like that now, moving the bottles quickly from one shelf to another, watching the bottles, making no noise, never looking around into the room. Over in the far corner the Stag was leaning forward with his elbows on the table, smoking a cigarette. He was watching Stuffy, enjoying the whole business and knowing that Stuffy was embarrassed because of Tim. Stuffy had to go on.

"I was wondering if you could help me," he said. "I was in Cicurel's today buying a pair of sunglasses and I saw a girl there whom I would very much like to take out to dinner."

"What's 'er① name?" The hard, rasping voice was more business-like than ever.

"I don't know," he said, sheepishly.

"What's she look like?"

"Well, she's got dark hair, and tall and, well, she's very beautiful."

"What sort of dress was she wearing?"

"Er, let me see. I think it was a kind of white dress with red flowers printed all over it." Then, as a brilliant afterthought, he added, "She had a red belt." He remembered that she had been wearing a shiny red belt.

There was a pause. Stuffy watched Tim who wasn't making any noise with the bottles; he was picking them up carefully and putting them down carefully.

Then the loud gritty voice again, "It may cost you a lot."

"That's all right." Suddenly he didn't like the conversation any

---

① 这里的"'er"是"her"非标准发音的拼写形式。

more. He wanted to finish it and get away.

"Might cost you six pounds, might cost you eight or ten. I don't know till I've seen her. That all right?"

"Yes yes, that's all right."

"Where you living, Colonel?"

"Metropolitan Hotel," he said without thinking.

"All right, I give you a ring later." And she put down the receiver, bang.

Stuffy hung up, went slowly back to the table and sat down.

"Well," said Stag, "that was all right, wasn't it?"

"Yes, I suppose so."

"What did she say?"

"She said that she would call me back at the hotel."

"You mean she'll call Colonel Higgins at the hotel."

Stuffy said, "Oh Christ."

Stag said, "It's all right. We'll tell the desk that the Colonel is in our room and to put his calls through to us. What else did she say?"

"She said it may cost me a lot, six or ten pounds."

"Rosette will take ninety per cent of it," said Stag. "She's a filthy old Syrian Jewess."

"How will she work it?" Stuffy said.

He was really a gentle person and now he was feeling worried about having started something which might become complicated.

"Well," said Stag, "she'll dispatch one of her pimps[①] to locate the girl and find out who she is. If she's already on the books, then it's easy.

---

① pimp: *Noun* a man who controls prostitutes and arranges clients for them, taking a percentage of their earnings in return 男皮条客

If she isn't, the pimp will proposition① her there and then over the counter at Cicurel's. If the girl tells him to go to hell, he'll up the price, and if she still tells him to go to hell, he'll up the price still more, and in the end she'll be tempted by the cash and probably agree. Then Rosette quotes you a price three times as high and takes the balance herself. You have to pay her, not the girl. Of course, after that the girl goes on Rosette's books, and once she's in her clutches② she's finished. Next time Rosette will dictate the price and the girl will not be in a position to argue."

"Why?"

"Because if she refuses, Rosette will say, 'All right, my girl, I shall see that your employers, that's Cicurel's, are told about what you did last time, how you've been working for me and using their shop as a market place. Then they'll fire you.' That's what Rosette will say, and the wretched girl will be frightened and do what she's told."

Stuffy said, "Sounds like a nice person."

"Who?"

"Madame Rosette."

"Charming," said Stag. "She's a charming person."

It was hot. Stuffy wiped his face with his handkerchief

---

① proposition：*Verb* [with obj.] (informal) make a suggestion of sexual intercourse to (someone with whom one is not sexually involved), especially in an unsubtle or offensive way(非正式)(尤指以猥亵无礼的方式)提出性要求；求欢 (e.g. She had been propositioned at the party by a subeditor with bad breath. 晚会上一个口臭的小编辑向她提出非分的要求。)

② clutch：*Noun* (someone's clutches) a person's power or control, especially when perceived as cruel or inescapable(尤指某人残酷或无法逃脱的)掌握；控制；魔爪；毒手(e.g. He had narrowly escaped the clutches of the Nazis. 他侥幸逃脱了纳粹的魔爪。)

"More whisky," said Stag. "Hi, Tim, two more of those."

Tim brought the glasses over and put them on the table without saying anything. He picked up the empty glasses and went away at once. To Stuffy it seemed as though he was different from what he had been when they first came in. He wasn't cheery any more, he was quiet and offhand. There wasn't any more "Hi, you fellows, where you been all this time" about him now, and when he got back behind the counter he turned his back and went on arranging the bottles.

The Stag said, "How much money you got?"

"Nine pounds, I think."

"May not be enough. You gave her a free hand, you know. You ought to have set a limit. She'll sting you now."

"I know," Stuffy said.

They went on drinking for a little while without talking. Then Stag said, "What you worrying about, Stuffy?"

"Nothing," he answered. "Nothing at all. Let's go back to the hotel. She may ring up."

They paid for their drinks and said good-bye to Tim, who nodded but didn't say anything. They went back to the Metropolitan and as they went past the desk, the Stag said to the clerk, "If a call comes in for Colonel Higgins, put it through to our room. He'll be there." The Egyptian said, "Yes, sir," and made a note of it.

In the bedroom, the Stag lay down on his bed and lit a cigarette. "And what am I going to do tonight?" he said.

Stuffy had been quiet all the way back to the hotel. He hadn't said a word. Now he sat down on the edge of the other bed with his hands still in his pockets and said, "Look, Stag, I'm not very keen on this Rosette deal any more. It may cost too much. Can't we put it off?"

The Stag sat up. "Hell no," he said. "You're committed. You

can't fool about with Rosette like that. She's probably working on it at this moment. You can't back out now."

"I may not be able to afford it," Stuffy said.

"Well, wait and see."

Stuffy got up, went over to the parachute bag and took out the bottle of whisky. He poured out two, filled the glasses with water from the tap in the bathroom, came back and gave one to the Stag.

"Stag," he said. "Ring up Rosette and tell her that Colonel Higgins has had to leave town urgently, to rejoin his regiment in the desert. Ring her up and tell her that. Say the Colonel asked you to deliver the message because he didn't have time."

"Ring her up yourself"

"She'd recognize my voice. Come on, Stag, you ring her."

"No," he said, "I won't."

"Listen," said Stuffy suddenly. It was the child Stuffy speaking. "I don't want to go out with that woman and I don't want to have any dealings with Madame Rosette tonight. We can think of something else."

The Stag looked up quickly. Then he said, "All right. I'll ring her."

He reached for the phone book, looked up her number and spoke it into the telephone. Stuffy heard him get her on the line and he heard him giving her the message from the Colonel. There was a pause, then the Stag said, "I'm sorry Madame Rosette, but it's nothing to do with me. I'm merely delivering a message." Another pause; then the Stag said the same thing over again and that went on for quite a long time, until he must have got tired of it, because in the end he put down the receiver and lay back on his bed. He was roaring with laughter.

"The lousy old bitch," he said, and he laughed some more.

Stuffy said, "Was she angry?"

"Angry," said Stag. "Was she angry? You should have heard her. Wanted to know the Colonel's regiment① and God knows what else and said he'd have to pay. She said you boys think you can fool around with me but you can't."

"Hooray②," said Stuffy. "The filthy old Jewess."

"Now what are we going to do?" said the Stag. "It's six o'clock already."

"Let's go out and do a little drinking in some of those Gyppi places."

"Fine. We'll do a Gyppi pub crawl③."

They had one more drink, then they went out. They went to a place called the Excelsior, then they went to a place called the Sphinx, then to a small place called by an Egyptian name, and by ten o'clock they were sitting happily in a place which hadn't got a name at all, drinking beer and watching a kind of stage show. At the Sphinx they had picked up a pilot from Thirty-three squadron, who said that his name was William. He was about the same age as Stuffy, but his face was younger, for he had not been flying so long. It was especially around his mouth that he was younger. He had a round schoolboy face and a small turned-up nose and his skin was brown from the desert.

---

① regiment: *Noun* a permanent unit of an army typically commanded by a lieutenant colonel and divided into several companies, squadrons, or batteries and often into two battalions(军队)团

② hooray: *Exclamation* another word for hurrah 同"hurrah"

hurrah: *Exclamation* used to express joy or approval 好哇;好;万岁(用于表示喜悦、赞扬)(e.g. Hurrah! She's here at last! 好呀! 她终于来了!)

③ pub crawl: *Noun* a tour of bars or public houses (usually taking one drink at each stop) 逛遍酒店喝酒

第二章 事与愿违 第一节 《大兵"救美"》Madame Rosette

The three of them sat happily in the place without a name drinking beer, because beer was the only thing that they served there. It was a long wooden room with an unpolished wooden sawdust① floor and wooden tables and chairs. At the far end there was a raised wooden stage where there was a show going on. The room was full of Egyptians, sitting drinking black coffee with the red tarbooshes② on their heads.

There were two fat girls on the stage dressed in shiny silver pants and silver brassieres③. One was waggling④ her bottom in time to the music. The other was waggling her bosom in time to the music. The bosom waggler was most skilful. She could waggle one bosom without waggling the other and sometimes she would waggle her bottom as well. The Egyptians were spellbound⑤ and kept giving her a big hand. The more they clapped the more she waggled and the more she waggled the faster the music played, and the faster the music played, the faster she waggled, faster and faster and faster, never losing the tempo, never losing the

---

① sawdust: *Noun* [mass noun] powdery particles of wood produced by sawing 锯末；木屑

② tarboosh: *Noun* a man's cap similar to a fez, typically of red felt with a tassel at the top 塔布什帽

③ brassiere: *Noun* an undergarment worn by women to support their breasts 奶罩

④ waggle: *Noun* causing to move repeatedly from side to side 来回摇摆

⑤ spellbound: *Adjective* bound by or as if by a spell; enchanted, entranced, or fascinated 入迷的；出神的 (e.g. The children were spellbound by the circus performance. 孩子们被马戏表演迷住了。)

fixed brassy① smile that was upon her face, and the Egyptians clapped more and more and louder and louder as the speed increased. Everyone was very happy.

When it was over William said, "Why do they always have those dreary fat women? Why don't they have beautiful women?"

The Stag said, "The Gyppies like them fat. They like them like that."

"Impossible," said Stuffy.

"It's true," Stag said. "It's an old business. It comes from the days where there used to be lots of famines here, and all the poor people were thin and all the rich people and the aristocracy were well fed and fat. If you got someone fat you couldn't go wrong; she was bound to be high-class."

"Bullshit," said Stuffy.

William said, "Well, we'll soon find out. I'm going to ask those Gyppies." He jerked his thumb towards two middle-aged Egyptians who were sitting at the next table, only about four feet away.

"No," said Stag. "No, William. We don't want them over here."

"Yes," said Stuffy.

"Yes," said William. "We've got to find out why the Gyppies like fat women."

He was not drunk. None of them was drunk, but they were happy with a fair amount of beer and whisky, and William was the happiest. His brown schoolboy face was radiant with happiness, his turned-up nose

---

① brassy: *Adjective* resembling brass in color; bright or harsh yellow 黄铜色的(e. g. She was an iodine-dark Indian woman with brassy peroxided hair and a dead-tired disposition. 她是一个紫棠面皮、黄铜色漂发、总是一副倦怠模样的印第安女人。)

seemed to have turned up a little more, and he was probably relaxing for the first time in many weeks. He got up, took three paces over to the table of the Egyptians and stood in front of them, smiling.

"Gentlemen," he said, "my friends and I would be honoured if you would join us at our table."

The Egyptians had dark greasy skins and podgy① faces. They were wearing the red hats and one of them had a gold tooth. At first, when William addressed them, they looked a little alarmed. Then they caught on, looked at each other, grinned and nodded.

"Pleess②," said one.

"Pleess," said the other, and they got up, shook hands with William and followed him over to where the Stag and Stuffy were sitting.

William said, "Meet my friends. This is the Stag. This is Stuffy. I am William."

The Stag and Stuffy stood up, they all shook hands, the Egyptians said "Pleess" once more and then everyone sat down.

The Stag knew that their religion forbade them to drink. "Have a coffee," he said.

The one with the gold tooth grinned broadly, raised his palms upward and hunched his shoulders a little. "For me," he said, "I am accustomed. But for my frient③," and he spread out his hands towards the other, "for my frient—I cannot speak."

---

① podgy: *Adjective* (Brit. informal)(of a person or part of their body) rather fat; chubby(英国英语非正式用法)(人或人体部位)很胖的;胖乎乎的(e.g. He put a podgy arm round Alan's shoulders. 他把一只胖乎乎的手臂搭在了艾伦的肩上。)

② 这里的"pleess"是"please"非标准发音的拼写形式。

③ 这里的"frient"是"friend"非标准发音的拼写形式。

The Stag looked at the friend. "Coffee?" he asked.

"Pleess," he answered. "I am accustomed."

"Good," said Stag. "Two coffees."

He called a waiter. "Two coffees," he said. "And, wait a minute. Stuffy, William, more beer?"

"For me," Stuffy said, "I am accustomed. But for my friend," and he turned towards William, "for my friend—I cannot speak."

William said, "Please. I am accustomed." None of them smiled.

The Stag said, "Good. Waiter, two coffees and three beers." The waiter fetched the order and the Stag paid. The Stag lifted his glass towards the Egyptians and said, "Bung ho①."

"Bung ho," said Stuffy.

"Bung ho," said William.

The Egyptians seemed to understand and they lifted their coffee cups. "Pleess," said the one. "Thank you," said the other. They drank.

The Stag put down his glass and said, "It is an honour to be in your country."

"You like?"

"Yes," said the Stag. "Very fine."

The music had started again and the two fat women in silver tights

---

① bung ho or bung-ho: "Bung-ho" was old British slang for "until we meet again, au revoir"(英国古老的土语)再见(从上下文来看,这里的意思似乎为"幸会"更为恰当)

were doing an encore. The encore was a knockout①. It was surely the most remarkable exhibition of muscle control that has ever been witnessed; for although the bottom-waggler was still just waggling her bottom, the bosom-waggler was standing like an oak tree in the centre of the stage with her arms above her head. Her left bosom she was rotating in a clockwise direction and her right bosom in an anticlockwise direction. At the same time she was waggling her bottom and it was all in time to the music. Gradually the music increased its speed, and as it got faster, the rotating and the waggling got faster and some of the Egyptians were so spellbound by the contra-rotating bosoms of the woman that they were unconsciously following the movements of the bosoms with their hands, holding their hands up in front of them and describing circles in the air. Everyone stamped their feet and screamed with delight and the two women on the stage continued to smile their fixed brassy smiles.

Then it was over. The applause gradually died down.

"Remarkable," said the Stag.

"You like?"

"Please, it was remarkable."

"Those girls," said the one with the gold tooth, "very special."

William couldn't wait any longer. He leaned across the table and said, "Might I ask you a question?"

"Pleess," said Golden Tooth. "Pleess."

"Well," said William, "How do you like your women? Like this—slim?" and he demonstrated with his hands. "Or like this—fat?"

---

① knockout: *Noun* [in sing](informal) an extremely attractive or impressive person or thing(非正式)异常动人的人(或物);给人留下深刻印象的人(或物)(e.g. He must have been a knockout when he was young. 他年轻的时候一定非常引人注目。)

The gold tooth shone brightly behind a big grin. "For me, I like this, fat," and a pair of podgy hands drew a big circle in the air.

"And your friend?" said William.

"For my frient," he answered, "I cannot speak."

"Pleess," said the friend. "Like this." He grinned and drew a fat girl in the air with his hands.

Stuffy said, "Why do you like them fat?"

Golden Tooth thought for a moment, then he said, "You like them slim, eh?"

"Please," said Stuffy. "I like them slim."

"Why you like them slim? You tell me."

Stuffy rubbed the back of his neck with the palm of his hand. "William," he said, "why do we like them slim?"

"For me," said William, "I am accustomed."

"So am I," Stuffy said. "But why?"

William considered. "I don't know," he said. "I don't know why we like them slim."

"Ha," said Golden Tooth, "You don't know." He leaned over the table towards William and said triumphantly, "And me, I do not know either."

But that wasn't good enough for William. "The Stag," he said, "says that all rich people in Egypt used to be fat and all poor people were thin."

"No," said Golden Tooth, "No no no. Look those girls up there. Very fat; very poor. Look queen of Egypt, Queen Farida. Very thin; very rich. Quite wrong."

"Yes, but what about years ago?" said William.

"What is this, years ago?"

William said, "Oh all right. Let's leave it."

· 106 ·

第二章 事与愿违 第一节 《大兵"救美"》Madame Rosette

The Egyptians drank their coffee and made noises like the last bit of water running out of the bathtub. When they had finished, they got up to go.

"Going?" said the Stag.

"Pleess," said Golden Tooth.

William said, "Thank you." Stuffy said, "Pleess." The other Egyptian said, "Pleess" and the Stag said, "Thank you." They all shook hands and the Egyptians departed.

"Ropey[①] types," said William.

"Very," said Stuffy. "Very ropey types."

The three of them sat on drinking happily until midnight, when the waiter came up and told them that the place was closing and that there were no more drinks. They were still not really drunk because they had been taking it slowly, but they were feeling healthy.

"He says we've got to go."

"All right. Where shall we go? Where shall we go, Stag?"

"I don't know. Where do you want to go?"

"Let's go to another place like this," said William. "This is a fine place."

There was a pause. Stuffy was stroking the back of his neck with his hand. "Stag," he said slowly, "I know where I want to go. I want to go to Madame Rosette's and I want to rescue all the girls there."

"Who's Madame Rosette?" William said.

"She's a great woman," said the Stag.

"She's a filthy old Syrian Jewess," said Stuffy.

"She's a lousy old bitch," said the Stag.

---

① ropey or ropy: *Adjective* slang for suspicious or of poor quality 怀疑的;质量差的

"All right," said William. "Let's go. But who is she?"

They told him who she was. They told him about their telephone calls and about Colonel Higgins, and William said, "Come on, let's go. Let's go and rescue all the girls."

They got up and left. When they went outside, they remembered that they were in a rather remote part of the town.

"We'll have to walk a bit," said Stag. "No gharries here."

It was a dark starry night with no moon. The street was narrow and blacked-out. It smelled strongly with the smell of Cairo. It was quiet as they walked along, and now and again they passed a man or sometimes two men standing back in the shadow of a house, leaning against the wall of the house, smoking.

"I say," said William, "ropey, what?"

"Very," said Stuffy. "Very bad types."

They walked on, the three of them walking abreast; square short ginger-haired Stag, tall dark Stuffy, and tall young William who went bareheaded because he had lost his cap. They headed roughly towards the centre of the town where they knew that they would find a gharry to take them on to Rosette.

Stuffy said, "Oh, won't the girls be pleased when we rescue them?"

"Jesus," said the Stag, "it ought to be a party."

"Does she actually keep them locked up?" William said.

"Well, no," said Stag. "Not exactly. But if we rescue them now, they won't have to work any more tonight anyway. You see, the girls she has at her place are nothing but ordinary shop girls who still work during the day in the shops. They have all of them made some mistake or other which Rosette either engineered or found out about, and now she has put

第二章 事与愿违 第一节 《大兵"救美"》Madame Rosette

the screws on them①; she makes them come along in the evening. But they hate her and they do not depend on her for a living. They would kick her in the teeth if they got the chance."

Stuffy said, "We'll give them the chance."

They crossed over a street. William said, "How many girls will there be there, Stag?"

"I don't know. I suppose there might be thirty."

"Good God," said William. "This will be a party. Does she really treat them very badly?"

The Stag said, "Thirty-three squadron told me that she pays them nothing, about twenty akkers a night. She charges the customers a hundred or two hundred akkers② each. Every girl earns for Rosette between five hundred and a thousand akkers every night."

"Good God," said William. "A thousand piastres a night and thirty girls. She must be a millionaire."

"She is. Someone calculated that not even counting her outside business, she makes the equivalent of about fifteen hundred pounds a week. That's, let me see, that's between five and six thousand pounds a month. Sixty thousand pounds a year."

Stuffy came out of his dream. "Jesus," he said, "Jesus Christ. The filthy old Syrian Jewess."

"The lousy old bitch," said William.

They were coming into a more civilized section of the town, but still there were no gharries.

---

① put the screws on: (informal) exert strong psychological pressure on (someone) so as to intimidate them into doing something (非正式用法) 给(某人)施加心理压力;强迫(某人)。

② 这里的"akker"是埃及使用过的货币单位的英式拼法。

The Stag said, "Did you hear about Mary's House?"

"What's Mary's House?" said William.

"It's a place in Alexandria①. Mary is the Rosette of Alex."

"Lousy old bitch," said William.

"No," Stag said. "They say she's a good woman. But anyway, Mary's House was hit by a bomb last week. The navy was in port at the time and the place was full of sailors, nautic② types."

"Killed?"

"Lots of them killed. And d'you know what happened? They posted them as killed in action."

"The Admiral③ is a gentleman," said Stuffy.

"Magnificent," said William.

Then they saw a gharry and hailed it.

Stuffy said, "We don't know the address."

"He'll know it," said Stag. "Madame Rosette," he said to the driver.

The driver grinned and nodded. Then William said, "I'm going to drive. Give me the reins, driver, and sit up here beside me and tell me where to go."

The driver protested vigorously, but when William gave him ten piastres, he gave him the reins. William sat high up on the driver's seat

---

① Alexandria: *Noun* the chief port of Egypt; pop. 3,170,000 (est. 1990). Alexandria was a major centre of Hellenistic culture 亚历山大(埃及主要港口,1990年估计人口 3,170,000,曾是希腊文化的重要中心。)

② nautical: *Adjective* of or concerning sailors or navigation; maritime 航海的;海员的;船舶的;海上的;海事的

③ admiral: *Noun* the supreme commander of a fleet; ranks above a vice admiral and below a fleet admiral 海军将领;舰队司令

第二章 事与愿违 第一节 《大兵"救美"》 *Madame Rosette*

with the driver beside him. The Stag and Stuffy got in the back of the carriage.

"Take off," said Stuffy. William took off. The horses began to gallop①.

"No good," shrieked the driver. "No good. Stop."

"Which way Rosette?" shouted William.

"Stop," shrieked the driver.

William was happy. "Rosette," he shouted. "Which way?"

The driver made a decision. He decided that the only way to stop this madman was to get him to his destination. "This way," he shrieked. "Left." William pulled hard on the left rein and the horses swerved around the corner. The gharry took it on one wheel.

"Too much bank②," shouted Stuffy from the back seat.

"Which way now?" shouted William.

"Left," shrieked the driver. They took the next street to the left, then they took one to the right, two more to the left, then one to the right again and suddenly the driver yelled, "Here pleess, here Rosette. Stop."

William pulled hard on the reins and gradually the horses raised their heads with the pulling and slowed down to a trot.

"Where?" said William.

"Here," said the driver. "Pleess." He pointed to a house twenty yards ahead. William brought the horses to a stop right in front of it.

"Nice work, William," said Stuffy.

---

① gallop: *Verb* (of a horse) go at the pace of a gallop(马)飞跑;疾驰

② bank: *Noun* a transverse slope given to a road, railway, or sports track to enable vehicles or runners to maintain speed round a curve(公路、铁路或跑道的横向、用以帮助车辆或运动员在弯道处保持速度的)斜坡

"Jesus," said the Stag. "That was quick."

"Marvellous," said William. "Wasn't it?" He was very happy.

The driver was sweating through his shirt and he was too frightened to be angry.

William said, "How much?"

"Pleess, twenty piastres."

William gave him forty and said, "Thank you very much. Fine horses." The little man took the money, jumped up on to the gharry, and drove off. He was in a hurry to get away.

They were in another of those narrow, dark streets, but the houses, what they could see of them, looked huge and prosperous. The one which the driver had said was Rosette's was wide and thick and three storeys high, built of grey concrete, and it had a large thick front door which stood wide open. As they went in, the Stag said, "Now leave this to me. I've got a plan."

Inside there was a cold grey dusty stone hall, lit by a bare electric light bulb in the ceiling, and there was a man standing in the hall. He was a mountain of a man, a huge Egyptian with a flat face and two cauliflower[①] ears[②]. In his wrestling days he had probably been billed as Abdul the Killer or The Poisonous Pasha, but now he wore a dirty white cotton suit.

The Stag said, "Good evening. Is Madame Rosette here?"

Abdul looked hard at the three pilots, hesitated, then said, "Mad-

---

① cauliflower: Noun a plant having a large edible head of crowded white flower buds 花椰菜；菜花

② cauliflower ear: Noun a person's ear that has become thickened or deformed as a result of repeated blows, typically in boxing or rugby（尤指在拳击或橄榄球赛中因多次受击而肿胀或变形的）开花耳朵

第二章 事与愿违 第一节 《大兵"救美"》Madame Rosette

ame Rosette top floor."

"Thank you," said Stag. "Thank you very much." Stuffy noticed that the Stag was being polite. There was always trouble for somebody when he was like that. Back in the squadron, when he was leading a flight, when they sighted the enemy and when there was going to be a battle, the Stag never gave an order without saying "Please" and he never received a message without saying "Thank you." He was saying "Thank you" now to Abdul.

They went up the bare stone steps which had iron railings. They went past the first landing and the second landing, and the place was as bare as a cave. At the top of the third flight of steps, there was no landing; it was walled off①, and the stairs ran up to a door. The Stag pressed the bell. They waited a while, then a little panel② in the door slid back and a pair of small black eyes peeked through. A woman's voice said, "What you boys want?" Both the Stag and Stuffy recognized the voice from the telephone. The Stag said, "We would like to see Madame Rosette." He pronounced the Madame in the French way because he was being polite.

"You officers? Only officers here," said the voice. She had a voice like a broken board.

"Yes," said Stag. "We are officers."

"You don't look like officers. What kind of officers?"

---

① wall something off: to build a wall around a place 用墙把……隔开(e.g. This room is walled off from the rest of the house. 这个房间和屋里的其他房间隔了开来。)

② panel: *Noun* a thin, typically rectangular piece of wood or glass forming or set into the surface of a door, wall, or ceiling 镶板;嵌板;玻璃片

"R. A. F.①"

There was a pause. The Stag knew that she was considering. She had probably had trouble with pilots before, and he hoped only that she would not see William and the light that was dancing in his eyes; for William was still feeling the way he had felt when he drove the gharry. Suddenly the panel closed and the door opened.

"All right, come in," she said. She was too greedy, this woman, even to pick her customers carefully.

They went in and there she was. Short, fat, greasy, with wisps of untidy black hair straggling② over her forehead; a large, mud-coloured face, a large wide nose and a small fish mouth, with just the trace of a black moustache above the mouth. She had on a loose black satin③ dress.

"Come into the office, boys," she said, and started to waddle④ down the passage to the left. It was a long wide passage, about fifty yards long and four or five yards wide. It ran through the middle of the house, parallel with the street, and as you came in from the stairs, you had to turn left along it. All the way down there were doors, about eight or ten

---

① R. A. F. or RAF: *Abbreviation* Royal Air Force 英国皇家空军

② straggle: *Verb* grow, spread, or be laid out in an irregular, untidy way 蔓生；四散；散落(e.g. Her hair was straggling over her eyes. 她的头发凌乱地搭盖在双眼上。)

③ satin: *Noun* [mass noun] a smooth, glossy fabric, usually of silk, produced by a weave in which the threads of the warp are caught and looped by the weft only at certain intervals(通常由丝织成的)缎子

[as modifier] a blue satin dress 一件蓝缎子连衣裙

④ waddle: *Verb* [no obj., with adverbial of direction] walk with short steps and a clumsy swaying motion 蹒跚而行；摇摇摆摆地行走(e.g. Three geese waddled across the road. 三只鹅摇摇摆摆地穿过公路。)

第二章 事与愿违 第一节 《大兵"救美"》Madame Rosette

of them on each side. If you turned right as you came in from the stairs, you ran into the end of the passage, but there was one door there too, and as the three of them walked in, they heard a babble① of female voices from behind that door. The Stag noted that it was the girls' dressing-room.

"This way, boys," said Rosette. She turned left and slopped down the passage, away from the door with the voices. The three followed her, Stag first, then Stuffy, then William, down the passage which had a red carpet on the floor and huge pink lampshades② hanging from the ceiling. They got about halfway down the passage when there was a yell from the dressing-room behind them. Rosette stopped and looked around.

"You go on, boys," she said, "into the office, last door on the left. I won't be a minute." She turned and went back towards the dressing-room door. They didn't go on. They stood and watched her, and just as she got to the door, it opened and a girl rushed out. From where they stood, they could see that her fair hair was all over her face and that she had on an untidy-looking green evening dress. She saw Rosette in front of her and she stopped. They heard Rosette say something, something angry and quick spoken, and they heard the girl shout something back at her. They saw Rosette raise her right arm and they saw her hit the girl smack③ on the side of the face with the palm of her hand. They saw her draw back her hand and hit her again in the same place. She hit her hard.

---

① babble: *Noun* [in sing.] the sound of a person or a group of people babbling 嘈杂的谈话声;七嘴八舌(e.g. a babble of protest 七嘴八舌的抗议)

② lampshade: *Noun* a protective ornamental shade used to screen a light bulb from direct view 灯罩

③ smack: *Adverb* in a sudden and violent way 猛然地(e.g. I ran smack into the back of a parked truck. 我猛地撞到了一辆停靠的卡车的车尾。)

The girl put her hands up to her face and began to cry. Rosette opened the door of the dressing-room and pushed her back inside.

"Jesus," said the Stag. "She's tough." William said, "So am I." Stuffy didn't say anything.

Rosette came back to them and said, "Come along, boys. Just a bit of trouble, that's all." She led them to the end of the passage and in through the last door on the left. This was the office. It was a medium-sized room with two red plush sofas, two or three red plush armchairs and a thick red carpet on the floor. In one corner was a small desk, and Rosette sat herself behind it, facing the room.

"Sit down, boys," she said.

The Stag took an armchair, Stuffy and William sat on a sofa.

"Well," she said, and her voice became sharp and urgent. "Let's do business."

The Stag leaned forward in his chair. His short ginger hair looked somehow wrong against the bright red plush. "Madame Rosette," he said, "it is a great pleasure to meet you. We have heard so much about you." Stuffy looked at the Stag. He was being polite again. Rosette looked at him too, and her little black eyes were suspicious. "Believe me," the Stag went on, "we've really been looking forward to this for quite a time now."

His voice was so pleasant and he was so polite that Rosette took it.

"That's nice of you boys," she said. "You'll always have a good time here. I see to that. Now—business."

William couldn't wait any longer. He said slowly. "The Stag says that you're a great woman."

"Thanks, boys."

Stuffy said, "The Stag says that you're a filthy old Syrian Jewess."

William said quickly, "The Stag says that you're a lousy old bitch."

第二章 事与愿违 第一节 《大兵"救美"》Madame Rosette

"And I know what I'm talking about," said the Stag.

Rosette jumped to her feet. "What's this?" she shrieked, and her face was no longer the colour of mud; it was the colour of red clay. The men did not move. They did not smile or laugh; they sat quite still, leaning forward a little in their seats, watching her.

Rosette had had trouble before, plenty of it, and she knew how to deal with it. But this was different. They didn't seem drunk, it wasn't about money and it wasn't about one of her girls. It was about herself and she didn't like it.

"Get out," she yelled. "Get out unless you want trouble." But they did not move.

For a moment she paused, then she stepped quickly from behind her desk and made for the door. But the Stag was there first and when she went for him, Stuffy and William each caught one of her arms from behind.

"We'll lock her in," said the Stag. "Let's get out."

Then she really started yelling and the words which she used cannot be written down on paper, for they were terrible words. They poured out of her small fish mouth in one long unbroken high-pitched stream, and little bits of spit and saliva[①] came out with them. Stuffy and William pulled her back by the arms towards one of the big chairs and she fought and yelled like a large fat pig being dragged to the slaughter. They got her in front of the chair and gave her a quick push so that she fell backwards into it. Stuffy nipped across to her desk, bent down quickly and jerked the telephone cord from its connection. The Stag had the door

---

① saliva: *Noun* a clear liquid secreted into the mouth by the salivary glands and mucous glands of the mouth; moistens the mouth and starts the digestion of starches 唾液；口水

open and all three of them were out of the room before Rosette had time to get up. The Stag had taken the key from the inside of the door, and now he locked it. The three of them stood outside in the passage.

"Jesus," said the Stag. "What a woman!"

"Mad as hell," William said. "Listen to her."

They stood outside in the passage and they listened. They heard her yelling, then she began banging on the door, but she went on yelling and her voice was not the voice of a woman, it was the voice of an enraged but articulate① bull.

The Stag said, "Now quick. The girls. Follow me. And from now on you've got to act serious. You've got to act serious as hell."

He ran down the passage towards the dressing room, followed by Stuffy and William. Outside the door he stopped, the other two stopped and they could still hear Rosette yelling from her office. The Stag said, "Now don't say anything. Just act serious as hell," and he opened the door and went in.

There were about a dozen girls in the room. They all looked up. They stopped talking and looked up at the Stag, who was standing in the doorway. The Stag clicked his heels and said, "This is the Military Police. *Les Gendarmes Milltaires*②." He said it in a stern voice and with a straight face and he was standing there in the doorway at attention with his cap on his head. Stuffy and William stood behind him.

"This is the Military Police," he said again, and he produced his i-

---

① articulate: *Adjective* (of a person or their words) having or showing the ability to speak fluently and coherently(人或其言语)流利连贯的(e. g. She was not very articulate. 她说话不怎么流利连贯。)

② Les Gendarmes Milltaires：法语,相当于前一句"This is the Military Police"的意思。

dentification card and held it up between two fingers.

The girls didn't move or say anything. They stayed still in the middle of what they were doing and they were like a tableau① because they stayed so still. One had been pulling on a stocking and she stayed like that, sitting on a chair with her leg out straight and the stocking up to her knee with her hands on the stocking. One had been doing her hair in front of a mirror and when she looked round she kept her hands up to her hair. One was standing up and had been applying lipstick and she raised her eyes to the Stag but still held the lipstick to her mouth. Several were just sitting around on plain wooden chairs, doing nothing, and they raised their heads and turned them to the door, but they went on sitting. Most of them were in some sort of shiny evening dress, one or two were half-clothed, but most of them were in shiny green or shiny blue or shiny red or shiny gold, and when they turned to look at the Stag, they were so still that they were like a tableau.

The Stag paused. Then he said, "I am to state on behalf of the authorities that they are sorry to disturb you. My apologies, mesd'moiselles②. But it is necessary that you come with us for purposes of registration, et cetera. Afterwards you will be allowed to go. It is a mere formality. But now you must come, please. I have conversed with Madame."

The Stag stopped speaking, but still the girls did not move.

"Please," said the Stag, "get your coats. We are the military." He

---

① tableau：Noun a group of models or motionless figures representing a scene from a story or from history; a tableau vivant(由一群模特儿或静止不动的人扮演的故事或历史中的)画面；场景；活人造型

② mesd'moiselles：法语,意思为"my young ladies"(年轻的女士们)

stepped aside and held open the door. Suddenly the tableau dissolved①, the girls got up, puzzled and murmuring, and two or three of them moved towards the door. The others followed. The ones that were half-clothed quickly slipped into dresses, patted their hair with their hands and came too. None of them had coats.

"Count them," said the Stag to Stuffy as they filed out of the door. Stuffy counted them aloud and there were fourteen.

"Fourteen, sir," said Stuffy, who was trying to talk like a sergeant-major②.

The Stag said, "Correct," and he turned to the girls who were crowded in the passage. "Now, mesd'moiselles, I have the list of your names from Madame, so please do not try to run away. And do not worry. This is merely a formality of the military."

William was out in the passage opening the door which led to the stairs, and he went out first. The girls followed and the Stag and Stuffy brought up the rear. The girls were quiet and puzzled and worried and a little frightened and they didn't talk, none of them talked except for a tall one with black hair who said, "Mon Dieu,③ a formality of the military. Mon Dieu, mon Dieu, what next." But that was all and they went on down. In the hall they met the Egyptian who had a flat face and two cau-

---

① dissolve: Verb [no obj.] (of a solid) become incorporated into a liquid so as to form a solution(固体)溶解(e.g. Glucose dissolves easily in water. 葡萄糖在水中易溶解。)

② sergeant-major or sergeant major: Noun a warrant officer in the British army whose job is to assist the adjutant of a regiment or battalion (regimental sergeant major) or a subunit commander (company sergeant major, battery sergeant major, etc.)(英军)军士长

③ Mon Dieu: 法语,意思为"My God"(我的天啊;上帝)

liflower ears. For a moment it looked as though there would be trouble. But the Stag waved his identification card in his face and said, "The Military Police," and the man was so surprised that he did nothing and let them pass.

And so they came out into the street and the Stag said, "It is necessary to walk a little way, but only a very little way," and they turned right and walked along the sidewalk with the Stag leading, Stuffy at the rear and William walking out on the road guarding the flank①. There was some moon now. One could see quite well and William tried to keep in step with Stag and Stuffy tried to keep in step with William, and they swung their arms and held their heads up high and looked very military, and the whole thing was a sight to behold. Fourteen girls in shiny evening dresses, fourteen girls in the moonlight in shiny green, shiny blue, shiny red, shiny black and shiny gold, marching along the street with the Stag in front, William alongside and Stuffy at the rear. It was a sight to behold.

The girls had started chattering. The Stag could hear them, although he didn't look around. He marched on at the head of the column and when they came to the crossroads he turned right. The others followed and they had walked fifty yards down the block when they came to an Egyptian café. The Stag saw it and he saw the lights burning behind the blackout② curtains. He turned around and shouted "Halt!" The girls stopped, but they went on chattering and anyone could see that there was

---

① flank: *Noun* the right or left side of a body of people such as an army, a naval force, or a soccer team(陆军、海军或足球队的)侧翼;翼侧(e.g. the left flank of the Russian Third Army 俄罗斯第三军的左翼)

② blackout: *Noun* the extinguishing or concealment of all visible lights, usu. as a precaution against air raids 不透光窗罩(窗帘)

mutiny① in the ranks. You can't make fourteen girls in high heels and shiny evening dresses march all over town with you at night, not for long anyway, not for long, even if it is a formality of the military. The Stag knew it and now he was speaking.

"Mesd'moiselles," he said, "listen to me." But there was mutiny in the ranks and they went on talking and the tall one with dark hair was saying, "Mon Dieu, what is this? "What in hell's name sort of a thing is this, oh mon Dieu?"

"Quiet," said the Stag. "Quiet!" and the second time he shouted it as a command. The talking stopped.

"Mesd'moiselles," he said, and now he became polite. He talked to them in his best way and when the Stag was polite there wasn't anyone who didn't take it. It was an extraordinary thing because he could make a kind of smile with his voice without smiling with his lips. His voice smiled while his face remained serious. It was a most forcible② thing because it gave people the impression that he was being serious about being nice.

"Mesd'moiselles," he said, and his voice was smiling. "With the military there always has to be formality. It is something unavoidable. It is something that I regret exceedingly. But there can be chivalry③ also. And you must know that with the RAF there is great chivalry. So now it

---

① mutiny: *Noun* open rebellion against constituted authority（especially by seamen or soldiers against their officers）(尤指士兵或船员的)哗变；暴动

② forcible: *Adjective* vigorous and strong; forceful 强有力的；有说服力的（e.g. They could only be deterred by forcible appeals. 只有强力呼吁才能阻止他们。）

③ chivalry: *Noun* [mass noun] the medieval knightly system with its religious, moral, and social code(中世纪)骑士制度(包括其宗教、道德和社交规范)

第二章 事与愿违 第一节 《大兵"救美"》*Madame Rosette*

will be a pleasure if you will all come in here and take with us a glass of beer. It is the chivalry of the military." He stepped forward, opened the door of the café and said, "Oh for God's sake, let's have a drink. Who wants a drink?"

Suddenly the girls saw it all. They saw the whole thing as it was, all of them at once. It took them by surprise. For a second they considered. Then they looked at one another, then they looked at the Stag, then they looked around at Stuffy and at William, and when they looked at those two they caught their eyes, and the laughter that was in them. All at once the girls began to laugh and William laughed and Stuffy laughed and they moved forward and poured into the café.

The tall one with dark hair took the Stag by the arm and said, "Mon Dieu, Military Police, mon Dieu, oh mon Dieu," and she threw her head back and laughed and the Stag laughed with her. William said, "It is the chivalry of the military," and they moved into the café.

The place was rather like the one that they had been in before, wooden and sawdusty, and there were a few coffee-drinking Egyptians sitting around with the red tarbooshes on their heads. William and Stuffy pushed three round tables together and fetched chairs. The girls sat down. The Egyptians at the other tables put down their coffee cups, turned around in their chairs and gaped①. They gaped like so many fat muddy fish, and some of them shifted their chairs round facing the party so that they could get a better view and they went on gaping.

A waiter came up and the Stag said, "Seventeen beers. Bring us seventeen beers." The waiter said "Pleess" and went away.

---

① gape: *Verb* [no obj.] stare with one's mouth open wide, typically in amazement or wonder 目瞪口呆地凝视(e.g. They gaped at her as if she was an alien. 他们目瞪口呆地看着她,好像她是个外星人。)

As they sat waiting for the drinks the girls looked at the three pilots and the pilots looked at the girls. William said, "It is the chivalry of the military," and the tall dark girl said, "Mon Dieu, you are crazy people, oh mon Dieu."

The waiter brought the beer. William raised his glass and said, "To the chivalry of the military." The dark girl said, "Oh mon Dieu." Stuffy didn't say anything. He was busy looking around at the girls, sizing them up①, trying to decide now which one he liked best so that he could go to work at once. The Stag was smiling and the girls were sitting there in their shiny evening dresses, shiny red, shiny gold, shiny blue, shiny green, shiny black and shiny silver, and once again it was almost a tableau, certainly it was a picture, and the girls were sitting there sipping their beer, seeming quite happy, not seeming suspicious any more because to them the whole thing now appeared exactly as it was and they understood.

"Jesus," said the Stag. He put down his glass and looked around him. "Oh Jesus, there's enough here for the whole squadron. How I wish the whole squadron was here!" He took another drink, stopped in the middle of it and put down his glass quickly. "I know what," he said. "Waiter, oh waiter."

"Pleess."

"Get me a big piece of paper and a pencil."

"Pleess." The waiter went away and came back with a sheet of paper. He took a pencil from behind his ear and handed it to the Stag. The Stag banged the table for silence.

---

① size up: *Phrasal Verb* to look at critically or searchingly, or in minute detail; to make an estimate, opinion, or judgment of 估量;估计;迅速对……做出判断(评价)

第二章 事与愿违 第一节 《大兵"救美"》*Madame Rosette*

"Mesd'moiselles," he said, "for the last time there is a formality. It is the last of all the formalities."

"Of the military," said William.

"Oh mon Dieu," said the dark girl.

"It is nothing," the Stag said. "You are required to write your name and your telephone number on this piece of paper. It is for my friends in the squadron. It is so that they can be as happy as I am now, but without the same trouble beforehand." The Stag's voice was smiling again. One could see that the girls liked his voice. "You would be very kind if you would do that," he went on, "for they too would like to meet you. It would be a pleasure."

"Wonderful," said William.

"Crazy," said the dark girl, but she wrote her name and number on the paper and passed it on. The Stag ordered another round of beer. The girls certainly looked funny sitting there in their dresses, but they were writing their names down on the paper. They looked happy and William particularly looked happy, but Stuffy looked serious because the problem of choosing was a weighty one and it was heavy on his mind. They were good-looking girls, young and good-looking, all different, completely different from each other because they were Greek and Syrian and French and Italian and light Egyptian and Yugoslav and many other things, but they were good-looking, all of them were good-looking and handsome.

The piece of paper had come back to the Stag now and they had all written on it; fourteen strangely written names and fourteen telephone numbers. The Stag looked at it slowly. "This will go on the squadron notice-board," he said, "and I will be regarded as a great benefactor[①]."

---

① benefactor: *Noun* a person who gives money or other help to a person or cause 施惠者;捐助人;施主;恩人

William said, "It should go to headquarters. It should be mimeographed① and circulated to all squadrons. It would be good for morale②."

"Oh mon Dieu," said the dark girl. "You are crazy."

Slowly Stuffy got to his feet, picked up his chair, carried it round to the other side of the table and pushed it between two of the girls. All he said was "Excuse me. Do you mind if I sit here?" At last he had made up his mind, and now he turned towards the one on his right and quietly went to work. She was very pretty; very dark and very pretty and she had plenty of shape. Stuffy began to talk to her, completely oblivious③ to the rest of the company, turning towards her and leaning his head on his hand. Watching him, it was not so difficult to understand why he was the greatest pilot in the squadron. He was a young concentrator, this Stuffy; an intense athletic concentrator who moved towards what he wanted in a dead straight line. He took hold of winding roads and carefully he made them straight, then he moved over them with great speed and nothing stopped him. He was like that, and now he was talking to the pretty girl but no one could hear what he was saying.

Meanwhile the Stag was thinking. He was thinking about the next move, and when everyone was getting towards the end of their third beer,

---

① mimeograph: *Verb* print copies from (a prepared stencil) using a mimeograph 用誊写版印刷机印刷；油印

② morale: *Noun* [mass noun] the confidence, enthusiasm, and discipline of a person or group at a particular time 士气；精神面貌(e.g. Their morale was high. 他们士气高昂。)

③ oblivious: *Adjective* not aware of or not concerned about what is happening around one 不注意的；未察觉到的；不知不觉的；不关心的(e.g. She became absorbed, oblivious to the passage of time. 她变得全神贯注起来，没有注意到时间在消逝。)

he banged the table again for silence.

"Mesd'moiselles," he said. "It will be a pleasure for us to escort you home. I will take five of you,"—he had worked it all out—"Stuffy will take five, and Jamface will take four. We will take three gharries and I will take five of you in mine and I will drop you home one at a time."

William said, "It is the chivalry of the military."

"Stuffy," said the Stag. "Stuffy, is that all right? You take five. It's up to you whom you drop off last."

Stuffy looked around. "Yes," he said. "Oh yes. That suits me."

"William, you take four. Drop them home one by one; you understand."

"Perfectly," said William. "Oh perfectly."

They all got up and moved towards the door. The tall one with dark hair took the Stag's arm and said, "You take me?"

"Yes," he answered. "I take you."

"You drop me off last?"

"Yes. I drop you off last."

"Oh mon Dieu," she said. "That will be fine."

Outside they got three gharries and they split up into parties. Stuffy was moving quickly. He got his girls into the carriage quickly, climbed in after them and the Stag saw the gharry drive off down the street. Then he saw William's gharry move off, but it seemed to start away with a sudden jerk, with the horses breaking into a gallop at once. The Stag looked again and he saw William perched[①] high up on the driver's seat with the

---

① perch: Verb (of a person) sit somewhere, especially on something high or narrow(尤指人在高处或很窄的地方)稍坐;暂歇(e.g. Eve perched on the side of the armchair. 伊夫坐在扶手椅的边上。)

reins in his hands.

The Stag said, "Let's go," and his five girls got into their gharry. It was a squash①, but everyone got in. The Stag sat back in his seat and then he felt an arm pushing up and under and linking with his. It was the tall one with dark hair. He turned and looked at her.

"Hello," he said. "Hello, you."

"Ah," she whispered. "You are such goddam crazy people." And the Stag felt a warmness inside him and he began to hum a little tune as the gharry rattled② on through the dark streets.

三、翻译探索

这部小说的翻译中,对于一些形象化的场景,要力求做到真实再现。一些对话中的非标准的表达,处理起来并非易事。对于埃及的一些小地名,也要认真对待,一一查实,实在落实不了的,就只能创造性地翻译。对于人物对话风格的再现,实属难事,有待广大译者做进一步的翻译探索。

大兵"救美"

"噢,天啊!这简直是太享受了,"斯塔格说道。

此时,斯塔格仰躺在浴缸里,一手拿着一杯兑了苏打水的苏格兰威士忌,一手夹着一支香烟。水正好漫到浴缸边缘。他用脚趾扳水

---

① squash: Noun [in sing.] a state of being squeezed or forced into a small or restricted space 硬挤;硬塞(e.g. It was a bit of a squash but he didn't seem to mind. 有点挤,但他似乎并不介意。)

② rattle: Verb [with adverbial of direction] (of a vehicle or its driver or passengers) move or travel somewhere while making such sounds(车辆、司机或乘客)咔嚓、咔嚓行进(e.g. Trains rattled past at frequent intervals. 火车每过一会儿就咔嚓、咔嚓飞驰而过。)

第二章 事与愿违 第一节 《大兵"救美"》Madame Rosette

龙头放水,不让温度降下来。

他抬头喝了一小口威士忌,就又仰回去,闭上了眼睛。

"看在上帝的份上,别洗了,"隔壁房间有人说道,"得啦,斯塔格。你已经泡一个多小时了。"说话的人是斯塔非,正赤身坐在床边,一边慢慢喝着,一边等着。

这位斯塔格回应说:"好吧,这就把水放掉。"说完,伸出一条腿,用脚趾"嗲"地拔起塞子。

斯塔非应声而起,手里握着刚才喝的威士忌,溜溜达达走进浴室。可是,斯塔格在浴缸里多躺了几分钟才小心地把酒杯放到肥皂架上,生怕掉下去。然后,站起身来,够了条毛巾。斯塔格个头矮小,人却敦实,双腿粗壮,小腿肌肉块非常显眼。他长着一头粗糙的姜黄色卷发,一张尖尖的瘦脸布满了雀斑,胸部长了一层姜黄色的毛,只是色调淡了点。

"天啊,"斯塔格边喊边看浴缸,"我身上洗掉了半个沙漠啊!"

斯塔非说:"赶紧冲干净,我好进去。五个月没洗澡了。"

这话还得从头说起。那时候一开始的几天里,我方在利比亚跟意大利军队作战。那些日子里,执行飞行任务是很艰难的,因为没有那么多飞行员。当然,英格兰本土也派不出飞行员,他们都投入到"不列颠之战"中去了。所以在这里,只能长时间待在沙漠里,过着令人难以理解的、不近人情的沙漠生活。总是住在那顶小小的、脏脏的帐篷里;每天用自己吐出来的那缸刷牙水来洗脸、刮胡子;总能从茶、饭里挑出苍蝇来;帐篷外的沙尘暴多大,帐篷里就多大。结果呢,心平气和的也变得残忍无比,动不动就跟朋友甚至自己发脾气,或者患上痢疾、热带腹泻、乳般突起以及沙漠疮等病症。更有甚者,意大利式(简称"意式"——译者注)"S. 79"型飞机还来狂轰滥炸;没有水,没有女人;地上长不出鲜花;除了沙子,还是沙子,别的几乎什么都没有,只有沙子。飞行员开的是古旧的"格洛斯特格斗士"型战机来对付意式"C.R. 42"型战机。更何况,不飞的时候,想要找出点什么能做的事儿,简直比登天还难啊。

有的时候,就逮几只蝎子,放到空油罐儿里,让它们对阵,激烈地打斗,最后弄个你死我活的。一群蝎子中总有一个会所向披靡、场场必胜,最后夺得冠军,成为乔·路易斯一般的重量级拳王。这样的话,这位蝎子冠军就得起个名字,那名气就大啦。主人就为其配备训练餐,至于究竟吃什么,那可是大秘密,只有主人知道的。训练餐对蝎子是十分重要的。训练时,给有些蝎子喂细碎的牛肉;有些喂一种叫作"莫乔瑙基"的东西——味道不太好的罐装炖肉;有些喂点甲壳虫;有些在打斗前设法给蝎子灌点啤酒,其根据是:啤酒会让蝎子开心,增添信心。可后几种东西喂出来的蝎子总会输掉比赛,但终归会有精彩的打斗场面,总会有伟大的冠军。下午飞行结束的时候,经常会看到三五成群的飞行员和机组成员在沙子里围城一圈,弯下腰,手扶膝盖站立,一边观看渐渐耗尽体力的蝎子打斗,一边大喊大叫,那架势,简直就像是对着赛台上的拳击手或摔跤手大喊大叫。打斗总会有胜出,每每此时,蝎子的主人就兴奋不已,在沙子里一边转圈舞蹈,一边挥动手臂喊叫,大声称赞其冠军宝贝这也好、那也好的。其中一只最了不起的蝎子的主人是一个叫威如意的中士,他只喂蝎子果酱吃。他的爱蝎有个名字,但那名字有点说不出口。尽管如此,小家伙连续赢了四十二场比赛,却在随后的训练中悄无声息地死去了,而当时威如意正考虑让它退役,做配种之用呢。

这下明白了吧:在沙漠里生活没有什么大的乐趣。所以,在那里,小乐趣成了大乐趣,小孩的乐趣成了大人的乐趣了。沙漠里,大家都是这样过的,而不管什么身份不身份的:什么飞行员、装配员、机身装配工、做饭的下士还是店铺的卖货兵,都是一样的。斯塔格和斯塔非也不例外。他俩甚至连哄带骗弄到一张四十八小时休假的通行证,搭乘便机飞到了开罗。一住进宾馆,就想痛快地洗个澡,那想法非常的强烈,就像新婚夫妇企盼着蜜月的第一个夜晚。

这位斯塔格擦干身子,腰间围上一条毛巾,躺到床上,双手捂着头。斯塔非就进了浴室洗开了。他头枕着浴缸的后背,嘴里哼哼着,开心陶醉地舒了口气。

第二章　事与愿违　第一节　《大兵"救美"》Madame Rosette

斯塔格叫了声:"斯塔非。"

"啊。"

"现在去干点什么呢?"

"找女人呗,"斯塔非应道,"找几个女人出去吃晚饭,必须的。"

斯塔格说:"不着急,一会儿再说。"这个时候,下午还没过去多少呢。

"我想啊,我是等不了啦,"斯塔非说。

"不,"斯塔格说,"可以等等的。"

斯塔格老兄老练而睿智,从不鲁莽行事。他才二十七岁,但在整个飞行中队里,比任何人都老,包括那位指挥官。况且,他的判断力可是颇受尊重的。

"咱俩先买点东西吧,"他说。

浴室里传来一句,"然后呢?"

"然后,再考虑做其他事情。"

沉默了一会。

"斯塔格,在听吗?"

"说吧。"

"你认识这地方的女人吗?"

"以前认识几个。记得有一个土耳其女孩儿,名叫温卡,皮肤很白;还有一个南斯拉夫女孩,叫基基,比我高十五厘米还多呢;还有另一个女孩我认识,是叙利亚的,名字记不得啦。"

"给他们打电话啊,"斯塔非要求。

"打过了。你买威士忌的时候,我打的。她们都不在啊。白打了。"

"哎,总是白打,"斯塔非回应道。

斯塔格说,"咱俩先买东西吧。时间有的是。"

一小时后,斯塔非从浴缸里出来。他俩各自穿好黄色的卡其布短裤和衬衫,往楼下溜达,穿过宾馆前厅,走上阳光明媚的大街。天很热,斯塔格戴上太阳镜。

斯塔非说,"我知道买什么了,一副太阳镜。"
"好吧。我们去买吧。"

他们拦了一辆出租马车,上了车,告诉赶车的去西屈雷尔。在那里,斯塔非买了太阳镜,斯塔格买了些扑克骰子。然后,两人又溜达到大街上,热烘烘的,很是拥挤。

"看到那女孩儿了吗?"斯塔非问。

"卖给我们太阳镜的那个?"

"对啊,就是黑头发的那个。"

"可能是土耳其人吧,"斯塔格说。

斯塔非说:"我才不管是哪里人呢。女孩很棒,你说呢?"

他们手插衣兜,沿着沙里亚·卡瑞尼尔大街走着。斯塔非戴上了刚买的太阳镜。时值午后,很热,尘土飞扬的。人行道上挤满了埃及人、阿拉伯人,还有光着脚走路的小男孩。苍蝇跟着那些小男孩舞来舞去,在他们眼前嗡嗡地晃悠,趁机叮一口他们眼里发炎的地方。之所以发炎,是小男孩很小的时候,母亲对其眼睛下毒手的原因。因为发了炎,长大应征当兵就不合格了。这帮小男孩"噼里啪啦"地跟在斯塔格和斯塔非后面,叫嚷着:"赏钱,赏钱。"语调刺耳,声声逼人。苍蝇对孩子们也穷追不舍。到处充斥着开罗的味道,这味道与其他任何城市的味道都不一样。任何东西、任何地方都能散发出这种味道;无论看到什么、走到哪里,都能闻到这样的味道。这味道无所不在:排水沟里、人行道上、住房里、商店里,还有商店卖的东西上、饭馆里烹饪的食物上、马匹身上、大街上的马粪里还有下水道里。人身上散发出这味道,甚至太阳晒到人身上也散发出这味道;太阳晒到排水沟、下水道、马身体、食物以及大街上的垃圾,也散发出这味道。这种味道稀有罕见,却酸辣刺鼻,就像某种甜甜的、热热的、咸咸的、苦苦的东西行将腐烂之际,一起扑鼻而来的味道。这种味道总是不期而至,哪怕是在一大早很清爽的时候。

这两个飞行员在人群中慢悠悠地走着。

"你不认为她很棒吗?"斯塔非问道。他想知道斯塔格老兄的看法。

"还算可以吧。"

"当然是可以的啦。斯塔格,你知道那什么吗?"

"什么呢?"

"今晚我要把那女孩约出来。"

他们横穿过大街,又走了一段。

斯塔格说:"好吧。何不这样呢?何不给罗塞特夫人打个电话?"

"罗塞特?何许人也?"

"是罗塞特夫人,"斯塔格补充道,"这个女人能耐大着呢。"

说这话时,他们正经过一个地方,名叫"蒂姆酒吧"。酒吧是一个叫蒂姆·吉尔菲兰的英国人开的。上一场战争中,这个人曾经是一个中士,掌管军需品,但部队回国时这个人不知怎么搞的,最终留在了开罗。

"你看,蒂姆酒吧,"斯塔格说,"我们进去瞧瞧。"

酒吧里除了蒂姆,别无他人。蒂姆在吧台后面,正往架子上放酒。

"哇,哇,哇,"蒂姆一边喊,一边转过身来,"这段时间,你们两小子都跑到哪里去了?"

"嗨,蒂姆,你好!"

蒂姆不认识他俩,但从外表来看,他知道他俩是从沙漠里出来的。

"我的老朋友格拉齐亚尼怎么样了?"他问道。两个胳膊肘支到吧台上,看着他俩。

"他离这儿近得很,"斯塔格回答,"他还没进默萨呢。"

"你们现在开什么飞机?"

"格斗士型战机。"

"真见鬼,他们八十年前就开这种飞机了。"

"还是那机型,"斯塔格说,"老掉牙了。"

他俩要了威士忌,拿着杯子坐到一个角落的桌子前。

斯塔非问:"罗塞特是谁呢?"

斯塔格喝了一大口,放下杯子,说道:

"这个女人可了不得。"

"她是什么样的人?"

"她是一个乌七八黑的老妓女。"

"打住,"斯塔非说,"就算是吧。那又怎么啦?"

"怎么说呢,"斯塔格回应道,"这样对你说吧。罗塞特夫人经营着世界上最大的一家妓院。据说,整个开罗你要什么样的女孩,她就能为你找来什么样的女孩。"

"胡扯。"

"不是胡扯,真的。你只需打电话告诉她:你在哪里看到一个女的,她在什么地方干活,哪个商店的什么柜台。而且,只要描述准确无误,那么其余的事儿就交给她好了。"

"别那么傻儿巴叽了,"斯塔非说。

"真的,绝对真实可靠。三十三中队的人跟我讲过她的事了。"

"他们拿你开涮呢。"

"别说了。你去拿电话簿查查她的号码。"

"她才不会用那个名字登记的。"

"我跟你说,她会登记的,"斯塔格说,"去查啊,在'罗塞特'下面找找。找到了,你就知道我说的没错。"

斯塔非虽是不信,却也走到蒂姆那儿,要了电话册,带回到酒桌这边来。他打开册子,"哗啦啦"翻了起来,翻到了"罗塞"所在的页码,急切地移动手指往下查找:罗塞皮……罗塞瑞……罗塞特。哇,真有啊。写的是"罗塞特夫人",还有地址和号码,都清晰地印在册子上。斯塔格盯着他看。

"找到了?"斯塔格问。

"是的。你看,'罗塞特夫人'。"

"那么,怎么不去给她打电话?"

"打电话说什么呢?"

第二章 事与愿违 第一节 《大兵"救美"》Madame Rosette

斯塔格低头看了看酒杯,用手指拨弄了一下冰块。

"跟她说,你是个陆军上校,"他指点道,"对,就说你是希金斯上校。她不信任当官的飞行员。跟她说,你看上了一个漂亮的、黑头发的女孩,那女孩在西屈雷尔的商店卖太阳镜。就像刚才你说的,跟她说,你想约那女孩出去吃晚饭。"

"这连电话都没有啊。"

"啊!不是吧。那边就有一部电话啊。"

斯塔非朝周围看了一眼,看到酒吧尽头的墙上挂了一部话机。

"可我身上没有埃及皮亚斯特硬币啊。"

"噢,我有啊,"斯塔格说。他在兜里摸了摸,捻出一枚硬币放到桌子上。

"跟她一说话,蒂姆不就听到了呀。"

"那有什么屁关系呢?蒂姆或许自己也给她打过电话呢。你话怎么这么多啊。"斯塔格补充道。

"你才放屁呢。"斯塔非说。

斯塔非还只是个孩子,才十九岁,整整比斯塔格小六岁。但他个子相当高,人很瘦,黑发居多;嘴很大,长了一张英俊的脸,但被沙漠的阳光晒成了咖啡棕色。毫无疑问,他是中队里最帅气的飞行员了。况且,在最初那些天里,他成绩喜人,击毁了十四架意式战机,并得到了证实。在地面,他行动缓慢,慢得像一个筋疲力尽的人;他思维缓慢,慢得像一个昏昏欲睡的孩童。但是,一旦升空,他就思维敏捷、动作飞快了,快得如同自动反射一般。在地面,他似乎在静心休养,好像是在稍微打打盹,为的是一旦钻进座舱就立马醒来,时刻精神抖擞地准备做两个小时的高强度飞行。然而,此时的斯塔非尽管不在机场,脑子里却有某种想法像飞行一样让他立马醒来。这种想法虽然一闪而过,但当时却是全神贯注地想过的。

他又看了眼册子里的号码,站起身来,慢慢地走向话机,塞入硬币,拨了号码,听到另一端铃声响起。斯塔格坐在酒桌旁,盯着他,而蒂姆还在吧台后边摆放酒瓶。蒂姆离话机才四米半,很显然是想一字不漏地听听斯塔非在电话里说什么。斯塔非更是不知所措,他倚靠着吧台,等待着,希望另一头无人接听。

紧接着,"咔嗒"一声,另一端有人拿起了电话听筒。他听到一个女人的声音:"喂,哈喽。"发音不是很标准。

他一边回应:"你好!是罗塞特夫人吗?"一边看着蒂姆,而蒂姆自顾继续摆放酒瓶,假装没有听,但斯塔非知道他在听。

"俺是罗塞特夫人。你谁啊,找俺?"听起来声音有些沙哑,显得有点急躁的样子。听那意思,此时此刻她好像不想让任何人打扰。

斯塔非尽量说得很随意:"我是希金斯上校。"

"啥上校?"

"希金斯上校。"他把名字拼了一下。

"知道了,上校。有什么事吗?"听起来,她有些不耐烦。很显然,这个女人不能忍受有人无理取闹的,但他还是尽量说得很随意。

"这样的,罗塞特夫人。有一件小事,我想知道你是否能帮我一下。"

斯塔非看着蒂姆,他确确实实在听。要是一个人假装没有听,而实际在听,总是能看出来的。其表现就是,做事轻手轻脚,不弄出任何响动,并假装集中精力努力做手头的事情。看看蒂姆吧,正是如此:快速地把瓶子从一个架子上挪到另一架子上,死盯着瓶子,不弄出任何声响,且始终不去环视酒吧。酒吧更远的角落里,斯塔格抽着烟,两个胳膊肘挂在酒桌上,两眼看着斯塔非,心里暗自发笑,因为他知道斯塔非会因为蒂姆的存在而进退维谷,但又不得不硬着头皮继续把电话打下去。

"我想知道,你能否帮帮我,"他继续说,"我今天去了趟西屈雷尔,在那儿买了副太阳镜,看到了一个女孩,很想约她出来吃晚饭。"

"那妞儿的名字呢?"跟起先比较起来,那强硬、嘶哑的声音更具有要做生意的意思了。

"我不知道啊。"他有点怯生生地说。

"她长什么样呢?"

第二章 事与愿违 第一节 《大兵"救美"》Madame Rosette

"她呀,一头黑发,个子高挑。她么,人很漂亮的。"

"她穿什么样的衣服呢?"

"这个呀,容我想想。我想,她穿的是一种白色的衣服,上面印满了红色的花。"接着,他又想起了什么,事后诸葛般补充说,"她系了一条红带子。"他记得,她一直系着一条闪闪发亮的红带子。

通话暂停了一下。这时,斯塔非看着蒂姆,只见他搬弄酒瓶一点声响也不弄出来,轻轻地拿起来,又轻轻地放下。

紧接着,嘶哑的声音又大声传了过来,"你得花一大笔钱的。"

"可以的。"突然之间,他不想继续说下去了。他想结束通话,然后脱身一走了之。

"你得付六英镑,或许八英镑,或许十英镑。数目不好确定。得看到她本人,才能定下来。可不可以呢?"

"行啊,行啊,可以的。"

"上校,你住哪儿?"

"大都市宾馆,"他不假思索地答道。

"就这样吧。我稍后打给你。"她随后挂断了电话,发出"嘭"的一声。

斯塔非挂上电话,慢慢走到酒桌旁,坐了下来。

"妥了,"斯塔格说,"就这样办妥了,是吧?"

"是啊,我想是成了。"

"她怎么说?"

"她说,她会把电话打到宾馆找我。"

"你意思是说,她会打到宾馆,找希金斯上校?"

斯塔非说:"啊,老天啊!"

斯塔格说:"没关系的。我们对前台说,上校在我们房间,打给他的电话转给我们就行了。她还说什么了?"

"她还说,我得破费了,要掏六到十英镑的。"

"罗塞特会从中抽取百分之九十的,"斯塔格说,"这个老妓女,乌七八黑的。"

"她会如何去运作呢?"斯塔非问。

斯塔非真是一个谨慎之人,现在他开始担心:事情才刚刚开始,局面会变得无法收拾。

"是这样的,"斯塔格说,"她会派她的一个拉皮条的出去,探出女孩的住处,查查女孩是何许人也。要是女孩已经登记在册,就好办了。要是没有记录,他就当场向她提要求,然后一路跟到她工作的西屈雷尔商店的柜台那儿向她提要求。如果女孩对他说'滚蛋吧',他就提高价格;如果女孩还对他说'滚蛋吧',他就再把价格提高一些。最终,她会禁不住钞票的诱惑,或许会同意。然后,罗塞特会向你报出比原价多出三倍的价格,她自己则赚得中间的差价。你必须把钱付给她,而不是那女孩。当然,自那之后,那女孩就登记到罗塞特的册子里了。一旦罗塞特把她抓到手里,她便不由自主了。下次揽到活,罗塞特告诉她多少钱就是多少钱,她将无力还价了。"

"为什么啊?"

"因为要是她拒绝的话,罗塞特就会说,'那行吧,我的乖乖。我告诉你西屈雷尔商店的老板一声,告诉老板你上次的所作所为,说你一直用老板的店铺作为交易的场所,为我工作。下一步,老板就该炒你鱿鱼了。'罗塞特就会像这样说,可怜兮兮的女孩就会害怕起来,对她言听计从了。"

斯塔非说:"听起来人还不错。"

"谁不错?"

"罗塞特夫人啊。"

"有魅力的,"斯塔格说,"她可是魅力四射啊。"

天很热,斯塔非用手绢擦了一把脸。

"再来点儿威士忌,"斯塔格喊道。"嗨,蒂姆,再来两杯威士忌。"

蒂姆一言不发,拿过来两杯酒,放到桌上,拾起空杯子,转身走开。在斯塔非看来,蒂姆看起来似乎与他们刚进来时判若两人:不再那么兴高采烈,而是默不作声,对人不搭不理的;不再逢人就喊"嗨,

第二章　事与愿违　第一节　《大兵"救美"》Madame Rosette

老兄,这段时间跑哪里去了?"回到吧台后面,就背过身去,继续摆弄那些酒瓶子。

斯塔格问:"你身上带多少钱?"

"有九英镑吧,我想。"

"或许不够啊。知道吗?你让她漫天要价了。你真应该设定一个限额。现在啊,她敲定你这根竹杠了。"

"我知道,"斯塔非说。

他们谁也没有再说什么,继续喝了一会。接着,斯塔格吱声了,"斯塔非,你有什么可担心的吗?"

"没什么,"他回答,"啥也不担心。回宾馆吧,她可能要打电话了。"

他们付了酒钱,跟蒂姆道别。蒂姆只是点头,一句话也没说。回到大都市宾馆经过前台时,斯塔格对埃及接待员说,"要是有电话找希金斯上校,麻烦接到我们房间,上校在我们那儿。"这位接待员回答,"遵命,先生。"然后,顺手记到便签上。

回到卧室,斯塔格躺在床上,点了支烟,说道,"今晚我干点什么呢?"

斯塔非在回宾馆的路上一直沉闷不语,一声不吭。回来后,双手也没有从兜里掏出来,一屁股坐到另一张床边,说道,"瞧瞧,斯塔格。跟罗塞特这笔交易我不再那么感兴趣,太贵了。我们能不能推推?"

斯塔格一下子坐起来:"真见鬼,不会吧,"他说,"你做出承诺了,可不能这样耍罗塞特。此刻,她也许正在运作呢。你现在可不能打退堂鼓。"

"或许,我拿不出那么多钱,"斯塔非说。

"那样的话,就等等看吧。"

斯塔非站起来,取来降落伞包,掏出一瓶威士忌,往两个杯子里倒了点,然后走到浴室,拧开水龙头,再把杯子灌满水,又回到卧室,把其中一杯递给斯塔格。

"斯塔格,"他说,"给罗塞特打电话,告诉她希金斯上校有急事要离开这座城镇,到沙漠里与军团会合。打给她,就这样说。告诉她说,上校要你传口信,是因为他走得急。"

"还是你自己打吧。"

"她会听出我的声音。拜托,斯塔格,你打吧。"

"不行啊,"他说,"我不能打的。"

"听好了,"斯塔非冷不防说道,流露出斯塔非孩子一面的口气。"今晚我不想约那个女孩出去,也不想跟罗塞特夫人做什么交易。我们想出点别的什么事来做。"

斯塔格立即站起来,说道:"行吧,我给她打。"

他拿起电话簿,查到她的号码,对着话机向接线员念了出来。斯塔非听到她接了电话,听到他传达了上校的口信。稍微停顿之后,斯塔格对着话机又说道,"很抱歉,罗塞特夫人,但这事与我无关。我只是一个传口信的。"又停顿了一会之后,斯塔格重复了一遍抱歉的话,并且抱歉了很长时间。最后,他一定累坏了,因为一放下话机,他就倒在床上,放声大笑起来。

"这个差劲的臭婊子,"他骂道,又大笑几声。

斯塔非问:"她发火了吗?"

"还发火呢,"斯塔格回答,"能不发火吗?你没有听到,她想知道上校军团的名称吗?天呐,我哪里知道。还说,他必须付钱。她说'你们这帮家伙把我耍来耍去,休想'。"

"好家伙,"斯塔非叫道,"这个乌七八黑的老妓女。"

"现在我们做什么?"斯塔格问,"已经六点了。"

"我们出去,到埃及佬开的那些酒吧喝一点。"

"好的。我们要把埃及佬的酒吧喝个遍。"

他们又喝了些威士忌,然后出去了。他们先去了一家叫"埃克塞尔西奥"的地方,紧接着去了一个叫"斯芬克斯"的地方,随后又到了一家写着埃及语店名的地方。到十点的时候,他俩坐在一个根本没有名字的地方,一边喝着啤酒,一边观看某种舞台表演,很是开心。在斯芬克斯酒吧,他俩带上了三十三中队的一个飞行员。这个人说他名叫威廉,跟斯塔非年纪相仿,但是看他那张脸可年轻多了,因为他飞行时间不长。特别是能从他的嘴周围区域,看出他年轻一些的。他长了一张圆圆的学生脸;鼻子很小,向上翘起;由于身处沙漠,皮肤晒得黝黑。

他们仨儿坐在那个没有名字的酒吧喝着啤酒,十分开心,因为那里只卖啤酒。这个酒吧其实就是一间长长的木屋,里面摆放的是木头桌椅,木头地板没有抛光,上面还有碎锯末。屋子的另一端有一个高于地板的木制舞台,正在进行一场表演。一屋子坐满了头戴红色无边圆塔帽的埃及人,他们喝的是黑咖啡。舞台上表演的是两个胖女孩,都穿着闪闪发光的银白色短裤,戴着银白色的奶罩。一个随着音乐节奏来回摇摆屁股,另一个随着音乐节奏来回摇摆奶子。摇摆奶子的女孩技巧最娴熟:她可以摇摆一个奶子,而另一个不动;有时候,也摇摆屁股。台下的埃及人如同着了魔,一个劲地用力拍手。他们越拍,她就越摇,音乐演奏得就越快;音乐演奏得越快,她摇得就越快,而且不断地加快、加快、加快,一个节拍也不会落下,铜黄色的脸上总带着一成不变的微笑。随着她摇得越来越快,台下埃及人拍得也越来越快、越来越响。人人都开心得不得了。

表演结束时,威廉说:"怎么总用那些胖女人表演?多乏味啊。怎么不用苗条漂亮的呢?"

斯塔格说:"埃及佬喜欢胖女人。女人像那样胖,他们喜欢。"

"不可能啊,"斯塔非说。

"千真万确,"斯塔格说,"这是一个古老的行当啦。追根溯源,这里以前有些日子里,人们经常挨饿。所有的穷人都骨瘦如柴,所有的富人和贵族都吃得好,长得胖。要是你得到一个胖女孩,你就万无一失了,她注定高人一等的。"

"扯淡,"斯塔非说。

威廉说:"光说没用,一会儿我们就会搞清楚的。我过去问问那些埃及佬。"他猛地朝两个中年埃及人晃了晃大拇指。那两个人坐在邻桌,跟他相距不过一米二。

"别啊,"斯塔格说。"别,威廉。别让他们过来。"

"无妨,"斯塔非说。

"无妨的,"威廉应道,"我们倒要看看埃及佬为什么喜欢胖女人。"

威廉没喝醉,谁都没有喝醉。但是,喝下了一定量的啤酒和威士忌,他们很开心,而威廉是最开心的。他那张晒得黝黑的学生脸洋溢着开心的表情,上翘的鼻子似乎又翘起了一点。好几个星期以来,或许这是他第一次这么放松。他站起来,三步迈到两个埃及人面前,朝他俩微笑着。

"尊贵的先生,"他说,"要是你们到我们座位上共饮的话,我和我的朋友将不胜荣幸。"

这两个人皮肤黑黑,泛着油光;脸很短、很胖。他们戴着红帽子,其中一个镶了一颗金牙。威廉一开始称呼时,他俩看起来有点惊恐不安。紧接着,他俩弄明白了,彼此相视,露齿一笑,就点头同意了。

"勤,"一个说道,发音不很标准,把"请"发成了"勤"。

"勤",另一个回应道,发音一样的不标准。两人随即站起,同威廉握手,跟着他走到斯塔格和斯塔非坐的位置。

威廉介绍道:"认识一下我的朋友。这位叫斯塔格,这位叫斯塔非。我叫威廉。"

斯塔格和斯塔非站起来,相互握手。两个埃及人又说了句"勤",然后大家都坐了下来。

斯塔格知道,埃及的宗教信仰不允许喝酒,就说:"来杯咖啡吧。"

镶金牙的略微张大一点嘴巴笑了笑,抬起双手,手掌朝上,双肩稍微隆起,回答:"我嘛,可以来一杯,我已经习惯了。但,我的朋友嘛,"他向同伴摊开双手,继续说:"我的朋友嘛,我没法说。"

斯塔格看了看他的朋友,问道:"来杯咖啡吗?"

"勤,"他回答,"我已经习惯了。"

"妥了,"斯塔格说,"两杯咖啡。"

他喊来服务生,吩咐道:"来两杯咖啡。嗯,等等。斯塔非,威廉,

第二章　事与愿违　第一节　《大兵"救美"》Madame Rosette

你俩还要啤酒吗?"

"我嘛,可以来一杯,"斯塔非说,"我已经习惯了。但,我的朋友嘛,"他转向威廉,继续说:"我的朋友嘛,我没法说。"

威廉回答:"来杯吧,我已经习惯了。"说完,他俩谁都没有笑出来。

斯塔格说:"好的。服务生,来两杯咖啡、三杯啤酒。"服务生取来账单,斯塔格照付。然后,斯塔格向这两个埃及人举起杯子,说道:"幸会!"

"幸会!"斯塔非说。

"幸会!"威廉说。

埃及人似乎听明白了,举起咖啡杯。"勤,"一个说。"谢谢你们,"另一个说。于是,就喝开了。

斯塔格放下杯子说:"来到你们国家,深感荣幸。"

"你喜欢?"

"是的,"斯塔格回答。"很不错的。"

音乐再次响起时,那两个穿银白色紧身装的胖女孩又表演一次。这次表演更令人着迷,无疑是所能看到的最奇特的肌肉控制表演:尽管摇摆屁股的仍然只是在摇摆屁股,但摇摆奶子的却如同橡树一般站在舞台中央,双臂举过头顶;她按顺时针方向转动左边的奶子,按逆时针方向转动右边的奶子,与此同时还摇摆屁股,而且所有的转动和摇摆都赶上了音乐的节奏;音乐节奏逐渐加快,音乐节奏越快,转动和摇摆得就越快。在台下,奶子的这种反向转动令一些埃及人十分着魔,他们的双手举到眼前,在空中画着圆圈,随着奶子的转动而挥舞着;大家跺着脚,兴高采烈地叫喊着。在台上,两个女孩铜黄色的脸上继续保持着那一成不变的微笑。

没过多大工夫,表演结束了,掌声也稀稀拉拉停了下来。

"太神奇啦,"斯塔格说。

"你喜欢?"

"嗯,真是神奇。"

"那些女孩子嘛,"镶金牙的说道,"很是特别的。"

威廉等不及了。他身体斜靠到桌上,说:"可以问你一个问题吗?"

"勤,"金牙说,"勤。"

"好吧,"威廉应道,"你认为你们国家的女人怎么样?喜欢这种……苗条的吗?"边说,边用双手演示,"或者,喜欢这种……肥胖的?"

他开口一个大笑,露出金牙,闪闪发亮。"我嘛,喜欢——喜欢这种……肥胖的。"同时,一双短粗的大手在空中画了一个大圆圈。

"你的朋友呢?"威廉问。

"我的朋友嘛,"他回答,"我没法说。"

"勤,"这位朋友说,"喜欢这样的。"他咧嘴一笑,随手在空中画出一个胖女孩的形状。

斯塔非问:"为什么你们喜欢的女人都是胖的啊?"

金牙想了想,说:"你们喜欢的女人都是很苗条的,对吗?"

"说吧,"斯塔非催促道,"我们喜欢苗条的。"

"为什么你们喜欢苗条的女人,你跟我说说。"

斯塔非用手掌蹭了蹭脖子的后部,问道:"威廉啊,为什么我们喜欢的女人都是苗条型的呢?"

"我嘛,"威廉回答,"已经习惯了。"

"我也一样的,"斯塔非说,"但是,为什么啊?"

威廉思索着。"我不知道,"他说,"我不知道为什么我们喜欢苗条的女人。"

"哈,瞧,"金牙说道,"你不知道吧。"边说,边倚着酒桌,偏向了威廉,得意洋洋地说:"问我嘛,我也不知道的。"

但这个回答并不令威廉满意,说道:"我这位斯塔格老兄说,以前埃及所有的富人都很肥胖,所有的穷人都很瘦弱。"

"错,"金牙回应道,"错、错、错。看看台上两个女孩,很胖吧,但很贫穷;看看埃及女王,就那个法丽达女王,很瘦却很富有。大错特错了你。"

第二章　事与愿违　第一节　《大兵"救美"》Madame Rosette

"你说的没错,但是多年以前呢?"威廉问。

"多年以前什么?"

威廉说,"噢,得啦。不谈这个啦。"

两个埃及人喝咖啡时发出的声响,听起来就像最后一滴水流出浴缸时发出的声音。喝完后,他俩起身要走。

"要走了吗?"斯塔格问道。

"勤,"金牙说。

威廉说:"谢谢你们。"斯塔非说:"勤。"另一个埃及人说:"勤。"斯塔格说:"谢谢你们。"相互握手之后,埃及人就告辞了。

"油滑型的。"威廉说。

"很油滑,"斯塔非说,"很是油滑的。"

他们三个人坐在那里开心地喝着。一直喝到午夜时分,服务生走过来对他们讲,要关门了,也没有酒了。当时,他们没有真正喝醉,因为喝得很慢,身体感觉也不错。

"服务生要赶我们走了。"

"走吧。去哪儿? 我们去哪儿呢,斯塔格?"

"我不知道啊。你想去哪儿?"

"去另一个像这样的地方吧。"威廉说,"这个地方不错。"

停顿了一会后,斯塔非用手拍了拍自己脖子的后部,慢条斯理地说,"斯塔格,我知道我应该去哪儿了。我要去罗塞特夫人那儿,把那儿所有女孩都救出来。"

"罗塞特夫人是谁啊?"威廉问道。

"她可了不得啊,"斯塔格说。

"她是个乌七八黑的老妓女,"斯塔非说。

"一个污秽不堪的老婊子,"斯塔格补充道。

"那走吧,"威廉说。"我们走。但,她是干什么的?"

他俩讲了她的所作所为,讲了打电话以及希金斯上校的事。威廉:"好的,我们走。我们把所有女孩子都救出来。"

他们起身离开。一到外头,他们才意识到,他们所在的地方是整个城镇相当偏僻的一个角落。

"我们必须得走一段了,"斯塔格说,"这儿打不着出租马车的。"

黑漆漆的夜没有月亮,但天空却繁星点点。街道狭窄,没有灯火。受开罗气味的影响,街道上也气味刺鼻。他们走着,四周静悄悄的。沿途不时会看到一两个男子,站在房子的暗处,倚着墙壁抽烟。

"我说啊,"威廉说,"油滑,什么来着?"

"很油滑,"斯塔非说,"很坏的类型。"

这三个人并肩齐行:个矮体阔的斯塔格,长着一头姜黄色的卷发;人高马大的斯塔非,头发黑黑;个头高挑的威廉年纪轻轻,光着头,因为他把帽子弄丢了。他们三个估摸着向镇中心走去,在那里他们能打到出租马车去罗塞特那儿。

斯塔非说:"哇,把那些女孩救出来,难道她们不会乐开了怀?"

"天啊,"斯塔格说,"应该开个派对庆贺的。"

"她真的把他们关起来吗?"威廉问。

"这,不会的,"斯塔格说,"这样说不准确,但是,如果我们现在救她们,今晚她们就不用再辛苦了。你看,她那儿的女孩只不过是普普通通的店员,白天仍然到商店上班。她们多少都犯了这样、那样的错,这些错不是她加上的,就是她发现的。于是,她就迫使她们晚上来提供性服务。可是,她们恨她,不想靠她过活。只要有机会,她们会把她的牙踢掉的。"

斯塔非说:"我们就给她们提供这样的机会。"

他们穿过了一条街道。威廉问:"斯塔格,那里会有多少个女孩呢?"

"我不清楚。我想,三十个或许有吧。"

"我的天啊,"威廉说,"这确实够开一个派对啦。她对待她们真的那么不好吗?"

斯塔格说,"三十三中队的人对我说,她不给她们工钱,每人一晚上约二十阿克,而每个客人她收取一百或二百阿克。一个晚上,每个女孩为罗塞特赚取五百到一千阿克不等。"

第二章　事与愿违　第一节　《大兵"救美"》Madame Rosette

"我的天啊,"威廉说,"一晚上一千皮亚斯特,而且有三十个女孩子,她一定是百万富婆了。"

"的确。有人算了一下,排除她外面的生意,她一周赚的钱相当于一千五百英镑啊。我算算啊,也就是说,一个月赚五千到六千英镑,一年就是六万啊。"

斯塔非缓过神来。"老天啊,"他说,"苍天大地啊,这个乌七八黑的老妓女。"

"这个污秽不堪的老婊子,"威廉骂道。

他们走到了城镇里更繁华的一个地段,但是连出租马车的影子也没有看到。

斯塔格说:"你听说过'玛丽之屋'吗?"

"玛丽之屋是什么?"威廉问。

"它是亚历山德里亚的一个地方。玛丽就是亚历山德里亚的罗塞特。"

"污秽不堪的老婊子,"威廉骂道。

"不是的,"斯塔格回应,"人们说她是一个好女人,但不管怎样,玛丽之屋上周被炸弹击中。海军当时在港里驻扎,此地全是上岸的水手,皇家海军的水手。"

"有炸死的吗?"

"很多水手炸死了。你知道发生什么事吗?张贴的告示说,他们在行动中阵亡。"

"舰长还是一位绅士,"斯塔非说。

"棒极了,"威廉说。

接着,他们看到一辆出租马车,喊住了。

斯塔非说:"我们不知道地址啊。"

"赶车的应该知道,"斯塔格说,"去罗塞特夫人那儿,"他吩咐赶车的。

赶车的咧嘴一笑,点了点头。威廉说:"我来赶车。师傅,把缰绳给我,坐到我边上,告诉我怎么走。"

师傅死活不干,但在威廉给了他十皮亚斯特后,就把缰绳给了威廉。威廉高高地坐在师傅的座位上,而师傅则坐在他旁边。斯塔格和斯塔非钻进车的后部。

"启程,"斯塔非说。威廉一声吆喝,马就飞奔起来。

"不好,"师傅尖叫,"不好,停下。"

"哪条路是去罗塞特的?"威廉大喊。

"停下,"师傅尖叫道。

威廉很是兴奋,"去罗塞特,"他喊,"走哪条路?"

赶车的心一横,认为阻止这个发疯的家伙唯一的办法就是把他送到目的地。于是,他尖叫道:"往这边,往左。"威廉使劲拉左缰绳,马就绕着拐角突然转向,可以看到当时马车只有一只轮子着地。

"倾斜得太厉害了,"斯塔非从后座喊道。

"现在往哪儿走?"威廉喊。

"左边,"师傅叫道。下一条街他们向左拐,另一条街向右拐,又左拐了两次,然后又向右拐去。突然,师傅喊道:"停。到了,这就是罗塞特。勤。"

威廉使劲拽缰绳,马被拽得头越仰越高,慢了下来,开始"哒哒哒"地小跑起来。

"在哪儿呢?"威廉问道。

"就这儿,"师傅说道,"勤。"他指着前面的一座房子,离他们不到二十米。威廉让马正好停在那所房子的前面。

"干得漂亮,威廉,"斯塔非称赞道。

"天呐,"斯塔格说。"简直太快了。"

"绝吧,"威廉说,"绝不绝啊?"他很开心。

汗水湿透了师傅的衣衫,他吓得不知道怎么发火了。

威廉问:"多少钱?"

"勤,二十皮亚斯特。"

威廉给了他四十,说道:"十分感谢。好马啊。"矮个子师傅拿到钱就跳上车,驱马而去。他迫不及待要离开啦。

第二章　事与愿违　第一节　《大兵"救美"》Madame Rosette

他们三人所在的街道同样狭窄、黑暗,但看得出,这里的房子很大,显得很繁荣。赶车师傅所指的、属于罗塞特的房子,又长又宽,有三层楼高,用灰色的混凝土建造。房子的前门敞开着,很大、很厚。往里走的时候,斯塔格说:"现在瞧我的吧,我都计划好了。"

一进去,就看见一个石头盖的灰色大厅,满是灰尘,感觉很冷;厅的顶棚吊了一盏电灯,没有灯罩。一个埃及男子站在大厅里,高高的,像一座山,块头很大,脸部扁平,两只耳朵好似被人打开了花。在他摔跤的生涯里,或许他被标榜为"杀手阿卜杜勒"或者"恶毒的帕夏"。但是眼下,他却穿着一件脏兮兮的白棉制服。

斯塔格说:"晚上好。罗塞特夫人在吗?"

阿卜杜勒仔细打量一下这三个飞行员,稍微犹豫一下,说道:"罗塞特夫人,顶楼。"

"谢谢,"斯塔格说,"十分感谢。"斯塔非注意到,斯塔格变得彬彬有礼起来。这样的转变,总会麻烦不断的。回想在中队那会儿,不管是领队飞行时,看到敌机时,还是要交火时,这位斯塔格老兄总是一下达命令就说"请听",一收到回话就说"谢谢"。这不是嘛,他正跟阿卜杜勒说"谢谢"呢。

他们踏着石头做成的楼梯上楼,楼梯上安装了铁栏杆。他们走过两个缓步台,发现这里像山洞一样光秃。第三段楼梯的顶部竟然没有缓步台,砌了一堵墙把里外分割开来,而楼梯径直通向一扇门。斯塔格按了门铃。过了一会儿,门上一块小面板向后滑动开启了,两只小小的黑眼睛向外探视。一个女子的声音传来,"你们几个小子有事吗?"斯塔格和斯塔非都听出来:这就是电话里的那个声音。斯塔格说,"我们想拜见罗塞特夫人。""夫人"一词,他用法语发音,这表明他是彬彬有礼的。

"你们都是当官的吗? 非官莫入。"那声音听起来就像木板破裂时的声音。

"是的,"斯塔格说,"我们是军官。"

"看起来可不像的。什么官儿呢?"

"皇家空军的。"

停顿一会儿。斯塔格知道她正在考虑呢——或许以前,飞行员给她惹过麻烦。他只希望她别看到威廉,还有威廉眼里跳跃的光芒,因为威廉现在的感觉还停留在刚才赶出租马车的兴奋劲上。突然,小面板合上,门打开了。

"来吧,进来吧,"他说。这个女人太贪心,对客人还是挑三拣四的。

他们走进去,一眼就看见了这个女人:个子不高,身穿一件宽松的黑绸缎衣服;人胖乎乎的、油光光的;几缕凌乱的黑发散搭在前额上;一张大脸,颜色如泥浆;一只大鼻子,又宽又阔;一张小鱼嘴,只有上嘴唇看出点黑胡须的痕迹。

"小子们,来办公室吧。"她边说,边摇摇摆摆地沿过道向左走去。过道又长又宽,长度不到五十米,宽有四米左右;过道正好穿过房子中央,与街道平行。如果从楼梯上去到办公室,就必须沿着过道向左拐,两边加起来约有八到十扇门;要是向右拐,就走到了过道的尽头,但是那里也有一扇门,他们三个往里走时听到那扇门后传出一阵乱哄哄女性的声音。斯塔格注意到,这是一间女性更衣室。

"小子们,这边走,"罗塞特说。她向左转去,沿着过道走了下去,离开那个发出声音的房间。三个人跟着她沿过道走下去,斯塔格在前,紧接着是斯塔非,威廉殿后。过道的地面铺了红地毯,一个个大大的粉红灯罩从天花板悬吊下来。他们沿过道走了约一半的距离时,身后的更衣室里传出一声喊叫。这时,罗塞特停下来,向四周看了看。

"小子们,"她说,"你们继续走,进办公室,左边最后一间就是。我随后就来。"她回转身,向更衣室走去。他们停下来,站在那里,看着她:她刚到门边,门就开了,里面冲出一个女孩。从站立的地方,他们可以看见那女孩的一头秀发遮住了面庞,穿了件看起来不整洁的晚装。看到罗塞特站在面前,她停了下来。他们听到她很生气地说了些什么,说得很快,而且还听见那女孩冲着她喊叫。这时,他们看到罗塞特抬起右手,在女孩脸的一侧扇了一巴掌,回过手来在同一个地方又是一巴掌,而且打得很重。女孩双手捂脸,"呜呜"哭了起来。罗塞特打开更衣室的门,把她推了进去。

"天啊,"斯塔格说,"她也太狠了,"威廉说:"看谁狠过谁。"斯塔非一声没吭。

罗塞特回到他们那儿,说道:"小子们,随我来。一点小麻烦而已,搞定了。"她带他们走到过道的尽头,进了左边最后一道门。这间屋子就是办公室了:房间中等大小,摆了两张红色的、长绒棉做的沙发,两三把红色的、长绒棉做的扶手椅;地面铺了一块红色的、厚厚的地毯;屋子的一角有一张小书桌,罗塞特就坐在桌后面,面对着整个屋子。

"坐下吧,小子们,"她说道。

斯塔格拖来一把扶手椅,斯塔非和威廉坐到沙发上。

"好吧,"她说,声音变得尖锐而急迫,"说正事吧。"

坐在椅子里的斯塔格,向前倾了倾身体。在鲜红色长绒棉的映衬下,他那短短的、姜黄色的头发,不知怎么的,看起来有点不对劲儿。"罗塞特夫人,"他开口说道,"见到您,很荣幸。对您我们早有耳闻。"这时,斯塔非看了眼斯塔格,心想:这家伙又彬彬有礼起来了。罗塞特也看了斯塔格一眼,她黑黑的小眼睛满是疑惑。"相信我,"斯塔格继续说,"我们一直盼望这一时刻,盼望好久了。"

他说得很令人愉快,而且很是客气,罗塞特信以为真了。

"小子们也太客气了,"她说,"在这儿,你们永远都会玩得开心,我是干这个的。现在,谈正事。"

威廉可再也等不及了。他慢条斯理地说:"斯塔格说你真了不起啊。"

"谢谢,小子们。"

斯塔非说:"斯塔格说你是一个污秽不堪的老妓女。"

威廉飞快说道:"斯塔格说你是一个乌七八黑的老婊子。"

"我清楚我说的是什么呀,"斯塔格说。

罗塞特一下子跳了起来。"这算什么事?"她尖叫道。她的脸也不再是泥浆色了,而变成了红黏土色。这几个小子一动不动,不微笑,也不大笑,就是坐在那儿一动不动,身体在座位上前倾,看着她。

罗塞特以前遇到过来找麻烦的,见识得太多了,她知道如何应对。可是,这次有些不同:这几个小子看起来没有喝醉,不是为了钱,也不是为了其中某一个女孩子,而是冲着她自己来的。这一点,她不喜欢。

"给我滚出去,"她大喊,"不想惹麻烦,就滚出去。"但是,他们几个一动不动。

暂停片刻后,她快速从书桌后面走出来,向门口奔去,可是斯塔格却抢先站到门口。就在她奔向斯塔格之际,斯塔非和威廉从后面一人抓住她一只胳膊。

"把她锁到屋里,"斯塔格说,"我们出去。"

接着,她可真正地大喊大骂起来了,骂的话简直无法写到纸面上,因为那字眼太污秽,简直不堪入目。那些骂人的话一股脑儿从她的小鱼嘴里喷出,如同奔腾的涧水,滔滔不绝,一路倾泻而下,还夹杂着阵阵吐沫星儿和口水。斯塔非和威廉扳着她的胳膊押着她回到屋里的一把大椅子那儿。她反抗着,喊叫着,如同一头大肥猪被拽扯着要屠宰一般。他俩把她弄到那把椅子跟前,使劲一推,她随即向后跌坐到椅子上。斯塔非疾步奔向她的书桌,一把扯断了电话线。斯塔格打开门,趁罗塞特还没有从椅子上站起来,他们三个奔出房间。斯塔格在屋子里的时候已经拿到了钥匙,所以一出屋就把门锁上了。出屋后,他们几个在过道里就站住了。

"天啊,"斯塔格说,"啥女人啊。"

"简直就是个疯婆子,"威廉说,"你听听。"

他们站在屋外的过道里,听着屋内的声音。他们听到她在喊叫,然后开始"砰砰"地锤门,可是喊叫始终没有中断。她的声音不再是一个女人发出的声音了,而是一头狂怒的、口齿伶俐的公牛的声音了。

第二章 事与愿违 第一节 《大兵"救美"》Madame Rosette

斯塔格催促道,"现在,我们要加快速度。还有那些女孩呢。跟紧我。从现在起,你们要严肃行动。切记行动要严肃。"

他顺着过道跑向更衣室,斯塔非和威廉紧随其后。在更衣室的外面,他停了下来,其他两位也跟着停了下来。他们仍然能听到罗塞特在办公室里喊叫。斯塔格说,"现在不要说话,切记行动要严肃。"说完,他打开门,走了进去。

屋子里约摸有十二个女孩。她们见状都抬起头,也不交谈了,都看着站在门道的斯塔格。斯塔格两只脚后跟向下"咔嚓"一声,说道:"军警在此。"这句话,他分别用英语和法语说了一遍,且面无表情,语调一本正经。说的时候,他头戴军帽,以立正姿势站在门口,而斯塔非和威廉则站在他后面。

"军警在此,"他又说了一遍,这次用的是英语。两个手指夹住身份证,出示给大家看。

女孩们谁也没有动地方,谁也没有说话。她们一动不动地待在原地,刚才说什么、做什么都停在半道儿,看起来就像一幅活人造型图,因为她们一动也不动地待在原地。其中一个女孩还是保持往上拉长筒袜的姿态:人坐在椅子上,一条腿笔直伸出,长筒袜套到了膝盖部位,双手握着长筒袜——她就保持着这个姿势。另一女孩在镜子前梳理头发,眼睛看着周围,但两手还放在头发上保持着梳头的姿势;还有一个女孩子一边要站立起来,一边涂抹唇膏——她抬眼看着斯塔格,但仍然举着唇膏放在嘴边;还有好几个女孩坐在普通的木头椅子上,无所事事,都抬起头向门口看去,但都保持着原先的坐姿。多数女孩穿着某种闪闪发光的晚装,有一两个女孩衣着不当,半遮半露,但多数女孩穿的衣服,或者绿的,或者蓝的,或者红的,或者金黄的,都闪闪发亮。她们转头看向斯塔格时,一动也不动的,好似一幅活人造型图。

斯塔格也停下来。随后,他说道:"我谨代表官方声明,打扰你们了。我也很抱歉,年轻的女士们。但是,你们必须随我们来登记一下,还有其他事宜要办。之后,你们就可以走了,这只是走一下形式,但你们必须跟我们来。请！我已经跟罗塞特夫人谈过了。"他用法语说"年轻的女士"。

斯塔格说完了，但是姑娘们还是没有动地方。

"请吧，"他说，"拿上你们的外衣。我们是军人。"他迈到一边，把住门，不让其关闭。突然之间，凝固的活人造型图溶解了：女孩子纷纷起身，迷惑之中小声地说着什么，其中有两三个女孩向门口挪去，其他女孩也先后效仿。穿着半遮半露的女孩飞快地套上晚装，用手拍拍头发，也跟上了。可是，没有一个穿外衣的。

"清点人数，"她们从房间鱼贯而出时，斯塔格这样吩咐斯塔非。于是，斯塔非大声点数，共有十四人。

"十四个，长官，"斯塔非报告。他尽量让自己的话听起来像一个军士长。

斯塔格说："完全正确。"随后，他转向在过道里挤作一团的女孩们说："现在，年轻的女士们。我从罗塞特夫人那里要到你们的名单，所以不要试图跑掉，也别担心。只是走一下军方形式而已。"

威廉出来了，随即打开通向楼梯那扇门，第一个跨了出去。女孩们紧跟其后，斯塔格和斯塔非殿后。女孩个个静悄悄的，她们有些疑惑和担心，还有一点点害怕，但是谁也不说话。除了一个高个子黑发女孩之外，没有一个人说话。她说，"我的天呐，走一下军方的形式。我的天呐，我的天呐。接下来呢?"也就说了这几句话而已，她们继续往下走。在前厅，他们遇到那个长着扁平脸孔和两只花椰菜耳朵的埃及人。就在那当儿，看起来有些不妙了，但斯塔格随后在埃及人面前晃了晃身份证说道："军警。"那家伙吃惊不小，没敢阻拦，随即放行了。

这样，他们就出来了，走在大街上。斯塔格说："还需要走一小段路，距离很近的。"然后，他们向右转。斯塔格带头沿人行道走，斯塔非殿后，威廉则跨到马路上保护队伍的侧翼。现在有一点月光了，可以看得相当清楚：威廉尽力跟上斯塔格的步伐，斯塔非尽量与威廉保持一致。他们三个仰起头、甩开胳膊前进，一副军人的姿态，这本身就很惹眼了。月光下,十四个女孩穿着闪闪发亮的晚装,沿着大街前进。斯塔格前面领队,威廉侧面护驾,斯塔非则断后。十四个女孩穿的衣服,或者绿的,或者蓝的,或者红的,或者金黄的,都闪闪发亮。景象真是壮观惹人眼啊。

女孩们开始喊喊喳喳交谈了。斯塔格尽管目不斜视,但却能听到他们的谈话。他行走在纵队的前头,遇到十字路口就向右拐去,其他人跟随着。沿着街区行走了不到五十米时,他们来到埃及一家咖啡馆前面。斯塔格看到咖啡馆遮上了窗帘,透出几缕光线。他转回头,喊道,"立——定。"女孩子停下脚步,但交谈依然不止,谁都看得出,队伍里有人不服从命令。毕竟,无法要求十四个脚穿高跟鞋、身着闪闪发光晚装的女孩子在夜晚一起跟着你走过城镇。就算走,也不能走很长时间,她们是走不了很长时间的,即使是走走军方的形式。斯塔格清楚这一点,现在他开始发话了。

"年轻的女士,"他说道,"听我说。"但是,队伍里有人不服从命令,只是说个不停。高个子的黑发女孩叫道:"我的天呐。这算什么事啊?不管以什么鬼名义,这是什么事啊?哎,我的天呐。"

"安静,"斯塔格命令道,"安静。"他喊完第二声的时候,交谈停了下来。

"年轻的女士,"他说。他现在变得有礼貌起来了,竭尽全力好好跟她们说话。一旦斯塔格彬彬有礼,就没有人不听他的了。真是奇妙啊!因为讲话时,他不用嘴唇去微笑,声音里就能露出某种微笑。他用声音微笑时,脸上却露出一副严肃的表情。这本身就很具说服力的,因为他给人的印象是:对大家友好,他是很认真严肃的。

"年轻的女士,"他一边说,一边用声音微笑着,"对军方而言,总会有一些拘泥于形式的东西,这是不可避免的。对此,我十分抱歉。但是,骑士风范也是有的。而且,你们必须了解的是,皇家空军具有很伟大的骑士风范。因此,现在你们要是进去,跟我们喝一杯啤酒的话,我们将不胜荣幸。这就是军人的骑士风范。"他向前跨出一步,打开咖啡馆的门说道:"看在上帝的份上,我们喝一杯吧。谁想喝一杯呢?"

女孩们突然间明白了一切,她们明白整个事件的来龙去脉了。这都是在一瞬间弄明白的。突然明白之后,她们吃惊不已。她们考虑了片刻,彼此看了看,又看了看斯塔格,又转身看了看斯塔非和威廉。看着后两位时,她们看到他俩的眼神,听到他俩发出的笑声。顿时,女孩们开始大笑起来,威廉和斯塔非也开始大笑起来,大家一起涌进咖啡馆。

高个子的黑发女孩拉着斯塔格的胳膊说道:"我的天呐,军警。我的天呐。噢,我的天呐。"她头向后一仰,大笑起来。斯塔格也随她大笑起来。威廉说:"这是军人的骑士风范。"大家都进了咖啡馆。

这地方很像之前他们去过的那家:什么都是木质的,而且地板上也有锯末,还有几个头戴红色无边圆塔帽的埃及人坐在那儿喝着咖啡。威廉和斯塔非把三张圆桌拼到一起,取来椅子,女孩子们随即坐了下来。其他几张桌子的埃及人放下手中的咖啡杯,从椅子上转过身来,张大嘴巴观瞧着。这些人像一条条胖胖的、浑身沾满泥巴的鱼,张大嘴巴继续观瞧着,其中有几个还变换了椅子的位置,正对着刚进来的这伙人,以获得更佳的观瞧视角。

一个服务生走上前来,斯塔格吩咐道:"十七杯啤酒。给我们上十七杯啤酒。"服务生说:"勤。"随即走开。

坐在那里,等着上啤酒的当儿,女孩们看了看三个飞行员,三个飞行员也看了看女孩们。威廉说:"这就是军人的骑士风范。"高个子的黑发女孩说:"我的天呐,你们真疯狂。噢,我的天呐。"

服务生上完啤酒。威廉举起杯子说:"为军人的骑士风范,喝。"黑发女孩说,"噢,我的天呐。"斯塔非什么也没说。他正忙着一个个打量着女孩们,估摸着哪一个女孩最合意,以便立即投入战斗。斯塔格微笑着。女孩们坐在那儿,身上穿着闪闪发光的晚装——或者绿的,或者蓝的,或者红的,或者金黄的。这景象几乎又构成一幅活人造型图。当然啦,这回是一幅画面:女孩坐在那儿,一小口、一小口喝着啤酒,看起来十分惬意,不再那么疑神疑鬼的了,因为对她们来说,

第二章　事与愿违　第一节　《大兵"救美"》Madame Rosette

整件事情现在看起来跟当初相差无几,她们也心知肚明了。

"天啊,"斯塔格说。他放下杯子,看了看周围。"噢,天啊。足够整个中队分配了。多么希望整个中队的人都在这里啊。"他又喝了一口,喝到半道,停了下来,快速放下杯子。"我知道了,"他说,"服务生。喂,服务生。"

"勤。"

"给我拿一大张纸来,还有一支铅笔。"

"勤。"服务生走开。返回时,拿来一张纸。他从耳朵后面摘下一支铅笔,递给斯塔格。斯塔格"砰"地一敲桌子,示意安静。

"年轻的女士,"他说道,"最后一次,需要走一个形式。再也没有其他形式要走了。"

"军方的,"威廉补充道。

"噢,我的天呐,"黑发女孩说道。

"也没什么,"斯塔格解释说。"就是要求你们在这张纸上写下你们的名字和电话号码,是为中队的那些朋友写的。之所以要写下来,就是要他们跟我们现在一样开心,却省去了今晚先前那些麻烦事。"斯塔格又用声音微笑了。看得出,女孩们喜欢他的声音。"若能写下来,他们将感激不尽,"他继续说,"因为他们也喜欢看到你们。他们将不胜荣幸。"

"好极了,"威廉说。

"疯了吧,"黑发女孩说道,但却把自己的名字和号码写到纸上,传给了下一个。斯塔格又点了一轮啤酒。女孩们穿着晚装坐在那儿,看起来当然很是滑稽可笑,却一一在纸上写下了名字。她们看起来惬意得很,威廉看起来更是惬意,而斯塔非看起来却是一脸的庄重,因为选择哪一个是个问题,分量太重了,心里也沉重起来。女孩们个个好模样,年轻、漂亮,各具特色,各有各的美,因为她们有的是希腊人,有的是叙利亚人,有的是法国人,有的是意大利人,有的稍微带有埃及和南斯拉夫血统以及诸如此类的特点,但是她们都漂亮,所有的女孩子都漂亮,都秀美端庄。

纸现在传回到斯塔格手里,名字都写上去了:十四个名字——十四种陌生的写法,还有十四个电话号码。斯塔格慢慢地拼读着。"将这贴到中队的告示板上,"他说,"那么,我将成为他们的大恩人啦。"

威廉说:"应当贴到总部去。刻蜡纸油印出来,发到所有中队,将极大鼓舞士气的。"

"噢,我的天呐,"黑发女孩说道,"你们太疯狂了。"

斯塔非慢慢站起来,拿起椅子,搬到桌子对面,挤放到两个女孩中间。"打扰了。坐这儿,你们介意吗?"他最终下了决心。现在,他转向右侧的女孩,不声不响地开始战斗了。这个女孩很漂亮,一头黑发,漂亮得很,体型也没的说。斯塔非开始跟她说话,对她的其他同伴完全不闻不问了。斯塔非一手托着头,转向这个女孩。看看斯塔非,就不难理解为什么他是整个中队最棒的飞行员了。这个斯塔非年轻有为,干什么都一个心思:他体格健壮,一路全神贯注地笔直奔跑,冲到自己的目的地;他坚定地走在蜿蜒曲折的路上,谨慎细心地变弯路为通衢,并快速通过,无可阻挡。他就是这样一种人。现在,他正跟这个漂亮女孩说话,但是谁也不知道他说了些什么。

与此同时,斯塔格在思考着,他在考虑下一步。就在大家第三杯啤酒要喝完之际,他又"砰"地一敲桌子,示意安静。

"年轻的女士们,"他说,"护送你们回家,我们将不胜荣幸。我送五个。"他都已经计算好了,"斯塔非送五个,娃娃脸威廉送四个。我们打三辆出租马车。你们五个坐我打的马车,到家一个,下一个。"

威廉说,"这就是军人的骑士风范。"

"斯塔非,"斯塔格喊,"斯塔非,这样安排可以吗?你送五个。谁最后下,你说了算。"

斯塔非看了看周围。"好,"他说,"噢,不错。很合我意。"

"威廉,你送四个。让她们一个一个下,你明白的。"

"妙极啦,"威廉说,"哇,太妙了。"

他们都起身向门口走去。高个子的黑发女孩拉起斯塔格的胳膊,问:"你送我吗?"

第二章　事与愿违　第二节　《小菜一碟》A Piece of Cake

"没错,"斯塔格回答,"我送你。"

"我最后一个下?"

"是啊,你最后一个下。"

"噢,我的天呐,"她说,"简直太好了。"

到了外面,他们打了三辆马车,然后就分头行事了。斯塔非行动迅速,他迅速把他要送的女孩弄上车,随后自己也钻了进去。斯塔格看到斯塔非的马车沿街驶去。接着,又看见威廉的马车离开了,但是那辆车出发时似乎猛地向前一冲,马就飞奔起来。斯塔格又看了一眼,这次他看到威廉高高地坐在赶车师傅的座位上,手握着缰绳。

斯塔格说:"我们走吧,"他送的五个女孩子就钻进了马车。车里有点挤压的感觉,好在大家都能坐进去。斯塔格一坐下来就感觉到座位上有一只胳膊抬了起来,从他的胳膊下方挽住了他。是那个高个子的黑发女孩的胳膊。他转身看着她。

"嗨,"他招呼道,"嗨,你好。"

"啊,好,"她轻声说道,"讨厌啊,你这人竟如此疯狂。"听完这话,斯塔格感到一股暖流在体内流淌,哼起了小曲。此时,出租马车正驶过黑暗的街道,发出"哒哒"的声响。

第二节　《小菜一碟》A Piece of Cake

罗尔德·达尔的《小菜一碟》(A Piece of Cake)收录在《罗尔德·达尔短篇故事集锦》(The Collected Short Stories of Roald Dahl)《向你飞跃》(Over to You)《五部畅销书集》(5 Bestsellers)以及《〈非凡亨利〉及另外六篇故事集》(The Wonderful Story of Henry Sugar and Six More)等书中。

这部小说中的部分情节,跟罗尔德·达尔某些作品的情节有些类似。感兴趣的读者可以进一步阅读《坠机余生》(Shot down over

Libya)①,或者《幸运开局》(Lucky Break)②。另外,本篇中关于飞机坠毁等情节的描述,存在某些争议③。

一、原作导读

在《〈非凡亨利〉及另外六篇故事集》这本书中,作者达尔在这部小说的开篇说:"这是我写的第一个故事,时间是 1942 年"(My first story—1942),而事实上,根据克里斯廷·霍华德(Kristine Howard)的观点,达尔的第一部小说应该是《坠机余生》,里面对坠机情节的描写跟本节中《小菜一碟》有着本质的区别④。如果说《坠机余生》是达尔颇有争议的坠机经历的"写实"版的话,那么本节所选的《小菜一碟》则是他坠机经历的"意识流"版,这一版中的艺术加工的痕迹尤其突出。

这篇小说完全是以第一人称"我"的视角展开的,但跟罗尔德·达尔其他很多作品中的"我"不同的是,这个叙述者"我"不是"隐身"的,而是"显身"的,或者说,是"显性"的,占据举足轻重的地位,其作用不仅是"纽带"或者"桥梁",而且是小说的主体。

"我"是战斗机驾驶员,坠机前的事情我记不太清楚了。我和同伴彼得在阿尔及利亚的富卡镇着陆、加油。油加满后,我们俩就准备分别起飞,飞往沙漠里的目的地。我总是能记起当时那个帮我拴上

---

① 具体可参阅克里斯廷·霍华德(Kristine Howard)创建并维护的网站"*Roald Dahl Fans.com*"(罗尔德·达尔粉丝网),网址为:http://www.roalddahlfans.com/,或者参阅《罗尔德·达尔短篇故事品读及汉译探索(第 1 卷)》第四章第二节。

② 具体可参阅"DAHL, R. *The Wonderful Story of Henry Sugar and Six More* [M]. England: Penguin Books Ltd., 2002",也可以参阅本书第四章。

③ 有关这方面的争议,读者可具体参阅《罗尔德·达尔短篇故事品读及汉译探索(第 1 卷)》第四章第二节。

④ 具体可参阅克里斯廷·霍华德(Kristine Howard)创建并维护的网站"*Roald Dahl Fans.com*"(罗尔德·达尔粉丝网),网址为:http://www.roalddahlfans.com/。

安全带的空勤人员的脸,还有他的那双眼睛:

　　……他那双眼睛极像我奶奶的眼睛,看上去好像一生的时间里都在帮飞行员拴安全带——拴好后,飞行员好像就一去不复返了。他站在机翼上,拉起我的安全带说:"要当心啊,粗心大意没有任何意义。"
　　"小菜一碟,"我回应。
　　"才不是呢。"
　　"真的,根本不算什么事儿,就是小菜一碟。"
　　... his eyes were like my grandmother's eyes, and he looked as though he had spent his life helping to strap in pilots who never came back. He stood on the wing pulling my straps and said, "Be careful. There isn't any sense not being careful."
　　"Piece of cake," I said.
　　"Like hell."
　　"Really. It isn't anything at all. It's a piece of cake."

　　可是,事实证明,事情并非"小菜一碟"——在沙漠上空战斗,我们遭遇了一连串的麻烦事儿。我飞得太低,无法跳伞逃生,结果飞机坠地,我昏了过去。醒来时,发现飞机起火,周围全是烟火。我奋力爬出驾驶舱,爬到了安全的地方。彼得在附近着陆,找到了我,并照看我,但我却失去了知觉。
　　故事的余下部分讲述的是"我"失去知觉后,意识之流不间断的流淌过程。
　　我"梦见"彼得跟其他几位伙计往机身上画一些好笑的图画,以便在空战中分散德军飞行员的注意力。战斗打响了,我在空中奋力驾机要突破德军飞机的重围。但是,德军战斗机驾驶员却跟我玩起了一种名叫"黄橙与柠檬"的儿童游戏,我机身上的图画一点儿也没有令他们发笑而分散注意力,我十分恼怒。我的身体和机身都被子弹击中,飞机变得无法控制,带着我旋转着向海面扎了下去——海面波涛汹涌,"白马"奔腾……

……我坐在一把大大的红色天鹅绒椅子上,当时已经到了晚上,身后有一阵风吹来。

"我在哪里?"我问。

"你失踪了,你失踪了,据传身亡。"

"那么,我一定得告诉我母亲。"

"不行,那部电话你用不了。"

"为什么用不了?"

"那部电话只能接通上帝。"

"你刚才说我怎么了?"

"失踪,据传身亡。"

. . . I was sitting in a great red chair made of velvet and it was evening. There was a wind blowing from behind.

"Where am I?" I said.

"You are missing. You are missing, believed killed."

"Then I must tell my mother."

"You can't. You can't use that phone."

"Why not?"

"It goes only to God."

"What did you say I was?"

"Missing, believed killed."

接着,我从红色椅子上起身,开始奔跑起来。我跑呀,跑呀,无法停下。奔跑中,我看到了母亲,母亲弯腰捡蘑菇,但我无法停下。我跑向一个悬崖,但还是无法停下,硬是冲下悬崖,落入无边的黑暗……

"我的脸怎么了?"

我听到她走到床边,感觉到她的一只手触摸到我的一只肩膀。

"你绝对不能再说话了,不允许你说话的,说话对你没有好处。你只需静静地躺着养病,不要担心,你很不错的。"

她穿过地板,我听到她的脚步声,还听到她打开门、又关上门的声音。

"护士,"我喊,"护士。"

但是,她已经走了。

"What's wrong with my face?"

I heard her coming up to the side of my bed and I felt her hand touching my shoulder.

"You mustn't talk any more. You're not allowed to talk. It's bad for you. Just lie still and don't worry. You're fine." I heard the sound of her footsteps as she walked across the floor and I heard her open the door and shut it again.

"Nurse," I said. "Nurse."

But she was gone.

二、原作释读

在这部小说中,作家罗尔德·达尔将现实与意识之流完美地融合起来,中间的转换可谓天衣无缝,这无疑令读者的阅读变得困难起来。阅读中,读者要分清每条"意识流"间的界线,思路要顺着"我"的一条条"支流"顺畅地"流淌"。

A Piece of Cake[①]

My first story—1942

---

① 本部小说原文出自"DAHL, R. *The Wonderful Story of Henry Sugar and Six More* [M]. England: Penguin Books Ltd., 2002"。

I do not remember much of it; not beforehand anyway; not until it happened.

There was the landing at Fouka①, where the Blenheim boys were helpful and gave us tea while we were being refuelled. I remember the quietness of the Blenheim boys, how they came into the mess②-tent to get some tea and sat down to drink it without saying anything; how they got up and went out when they had finished drinking and still they did not say anything. And I knew that each one was holding himself together because the going was not very good right then. They were having to go out too often, and there were no replacements③ coming along.

We thanked them for the tea and went out to see if they had finished refuelling our Gladiators. I remember that there was a wind blowing which made the wind-sock④ stand out straight, like a signpost⑤, and the sand was blowing up around our legs and making a rustling noise as it swished against the tents, and the tents flapped in the wind so that they were like canvas men clapping their hands.

"Bomber boys unhappy," Peter said.

"Not unhappy," I answered.

---

① Fouka: *Noun* Fouka is a town and commune in Tipaza Province in northern Algeria(阿尔及利亚)富卡

② mess: *Noun* a building or room in which members of the armed forces take their meals 军人食堂(e.g. the sergeants' mess 士官食堂)

③ replacement: *Noun* (Military) a sailor, soldier, or airman assigned to fill a vacancy in a military unit(军)补充兵员

④ windsock or wind-sock: *Noun* a light, flexible cylinder or cone mounted on a mast to show the direction and strength of the wind, especially at an airfield(尤指机场)风向袋;套筒风标

⑤ signpost: *Noun* a sign giving information such as the direction and distance to a nearby town, typically found at a road junction 路标;指向标;指示牌

"Well, they're browned off."

"No. They've had it, that's all. But they'll keep going. You can see they're trying to keep going."

Our two old Gladiators were standing beside each other in the sand and the airmen in their khaki shirts and shorts seemed still to be busy with refuelling. I was wearing a thin white cotton flying suit and Peter had on a blue one. It wasn't necessary to fly with anything warmer.

Peter said, "How far away is it?"

"Twenty-one miles beyond Charing Cross," I answered, "on the right side of the road." Charing Cross was where the desert road branched north to Mersah Matruh①. The Italian army was outside Mersah, and they were doing pretty well. It was about the only time, so far as I know, that the Italians have done pretty well. Their morale goes up and down like a sensitive altimeter, and right then it was at forty thousand because the Axis② was on top of the world. We hung around waiting for the refuelling to finish.

Peter said, "It's a piece of cake."

"Yes. It ought to be easy."

We separated and I climbed into my cockpit. I have always remembered the face of the airman who helped me to strap in. He was oldish, about forty, and bald except for a neat patch of golden hair at the back of his head. His face was all wrinkles, his eyes were like my grandmother's

---

① Mersa Matruh or Masah Matruh: *Noun* It is also spelled Marsa Matruh and Marsa Matrouh. It is a Mediterranean seaport and the capital of the Matrouh Governorate in Egypt. (埃及)马特鲁港

② Axis: *Noun* (the Axis) the alliance of Germany and Italy formed before and during the Second World War, later extended to include Japan and other countries(第二次世界大战期间德、意、日等国组成的)轴心国

eyes, and he looked as though he had spent his life helping to strap in pilots who never came back. He stood on the wing pulling my straps and said, "Be careful. There isn't any sense not being careful."

"Piece of cake," I said.

"Like hell①."

"Really. It isn't anything at all. It's a piece of cake."

I don't remember much about the next bit; I only remember about later on. I suppose we took off from Fouka and flew west towards Mersah, and I suppose we flew at about eight hundred feet. I suppose we saw the sea to starboard②, and I suppose—no, I am certain—that it was blue and that it was beautiful, especially where it rolled up on to the sand and made a long thick white line east and west as far as you could see. I suppose we flew over Charing Cross and flew on for twenty-one miles to where they had said it would be, but I do not know. I know only that there was trouble, lots and lots of trouble, and I know that we had turned and were coming back when the trouble got worse. The biggest trouble of all was that I was too low to bale out③, and it is from that point on that my memory comes back to me. I remember the dipping of the nose④ of the aircraft and I remember looking down the nose of the ma-

---

① like hell: (informal) used in ironic expressions of scorn or disagreement (非正式用法)（用讽刺口吻表示轻蔑或不同意）见鬼；决不；才不（e.g. Like hell, he thought. 才不呢,他想。）

② starboard: *Noun* the side of a ship or aircraft that is on the right when one is facing forward (The opposite of port)（船舶、飞机的）右舷；右边（port 的反义词）

③ bale out: to jump out of an aircraft with a parachute because the aircraft is going to have an accident（损坏的或失控的飞机上）跳伞

④ nose: *Noun* the front end of an aircraft, car, or other vehicle（飞机、轿车或其他车辆的）前端突出部

chine at the ground and seeing a little clump① of camel-thorn② growing there all by itself. I remember seeing some rocks lying in the sand beside the camel-thorn, and the camel-thorn and the sand and the rocks leapt out of the ground and came to me. I remember that very clearly.

Then there was a small gap of not-remembering. It might have been one second or it might have been thirty; I do not know. I have an idea that it was very short, a second perhaps, and next I heard a *crumph*③ on the right as the starboard wing tank caught fire, then another *crumph* on the left as the port tank did the same. To me that was not significant, and for a while I sat still, feeling comfortable, but a little drowsy. I couldn't see with my eyes, but that was not significant either. There was nothing to worry about. Nothing at all. Not until I felt the hotness around my legs. At first it was only a warmness and that was all right too, but all at once it was a hotness, a very stinging scorching hotness up and down the sides of each leg.

I knew that the hotness was unpleasant, but that was all I knew. I disliked it, so I curled my legs up under the seat and waited. I think there was something wrong with the telegraph system between the body and the brain. It did not seem to be working very well. Somehow it was a bit slow in telling the brain all about it and in asking for instructions. But I believe a message eventually got through, saying, "Down here there is

---

① clump: *Noun* a small group of trees or plants growing closely together 树丛;植物丛(e.g. a clump of ferns 一丛蕨类植物)

② camel thorn: *Noun* Alhagi camelorum (of the Middle East) and Acacia giraffae (of southern Africa), family Leguminosae(中东的)骆驼刺;(非洲南部的)吉腊夫氏相思树(豆科)

③ crump: *Noun* a loud thudding sound, especially one made by an exploding bomb or shell(炸弹或炮弹的)爆炸声

a great hotness. What shall we do? (Signed) Left Leg and Right Leg." For a long time there was no reply. The brain was figuring the matter out.

Then slowly, word by word, the answer was tapped over the wires. "The—plane—is—burning. Get—out—repeat—get—out—get—out." The order was relayed to the whole system, to all the muscles in the legs, arms and body, and the muscles went to work. They tried their best; they pushed a little and pulled a little, and they strained greatly, but it wasn't any good. Up went another telegram, "Can't get out. Something holding us in." The answer to this one took even longer in arriving, so I just sat there waiting for it to come, and all the time the hotness increased. Something was holding me down and it was up to the brain to find out what it was. Was it giants' hands pressing on my shoulders, or heavy stones or houses or steam rollers① or filing cabinets or gravity or was it ropes? Wait a minute. Ropes—ropes. The message was beginning to come through. It came very slowly. "Your—straps. Undo your—straps." My arms received the message and went to work. They tugged at the straps, but they wouldn't undo. They tugged again and again, a little feebly②, but as hard as they could, and it wasn't any use. Back went the message, "How do we undo the straps?"

This time I think that I sat there for three or four minutes waiting for the answer. It wasn't any use hurrying or getting impatient. That was the one thing of which I was sure. But what a long time it was all taking. I

---

① steam roller or steamroller: *Noun* a vehicle that moves forward on a large, heavy wheel in order to make a road surface flat 蒸汽压路机

② feeble: *Adjective* lacking physical strength, especially as a result of age or illness(尤指因年老或疾病而)虚弱的;衰弱的;乏力的(e.g. My legs are very feeble after the flu. 患了流感之后,我的腿虚弱乏力。)

said aloud, "Bugger① it. I'm going to be burnt. I'm..." but I was interrupted. The answer was coming—no, it wasn't—yes, it was, it was slowly coming through.

"Pull—out—the—quick—release—pin—you—bloody—fool—and—hurry."

Out came the pin and the straps were loosed. Now, let's get out. Let's get out, let's get out. But I couldn't do it. I simply couldn't lift myself out of the cockpit. Arms and legs tried their best but it wasn't any use. A last desperate message was flashed upwards and this time it was marked "Urgent".

"Something else is holding us down," it said. "Something else, something else, something heavy."

Still the arms and legs did not fight. They seemed to know instinctively that there was no point in using up their strength. They stayed quiet and waited for the answer, and oh what a time it took. Twenty, thirty, forty hot seconds. None of them really white hot yet, no sizzling of flesh or smell of burning meat, but that would come any moment now, because those old Gladiators aren't made of stressed steel like a Hurricane or a Spit. They have taut② canvas wings, covered with magnificently inflammable dope③, and underneath there are hundreds of small thin sticks,

---

① bugger: *Exclamation* used to express annoyance or anger 该死(用于表示烦恼或生气)

② taut: *Adjective* stretched or pulled tight; not slack 拉紧的(e.g. The fabric stays taut without adhesive. 不用黏合剂布料也能保持紧绷。)

③ dope: *Noun* a varnish applied to the fabric surface of model aircraft to strengthen them and keep them airtight(模型飞机表面织物为加固和密封而涂的)清漆

the kind you put under the logs for kindling①, only these are drier and thinner. If a clever man said, "I am going to build a big thing that will burn better and quicker than anything else in the world," and if he applied himself diligently to his task, he would probably finish up by building something very like a Gladiator. I sat still waiting.

Then suddenly the reply, beautiful in its briefness, but at the same time explaining everything. "Your—parachute—turn—the—buckle."

I turned the buckle, released the parachute harness② and with some effort hoisted myself up and tumbled over the side of the cockpit. Something seemed to be burning, so I rolled about a bit in the sand, then crawled away from the fire on all fours and lay down.

I heard some of my machine-gun ammunition going off in the heat and I heard some of the bullets thumping into the sand nearby. I did not worry about them; I merely heard them.

Things were beginning to hurt. My face hurt most. There was something wrong with my face. Something had happened to it. Slowly I put up a hand to feel it. It was sticky. My nose didn't seem to be there. I tried to feel my teeth, but I cannot remember whether I came to any conclusion about them. I think I dozed off.

All of a sudden there was Peter. I heard his voice and I heard him dancing around and yelling like a madman and shaking my hand and saying, "Jesus, I thought you were still inside. I came down half a mile away and ran like hell. Are you all right?"

---

① kindling: Noun [mass noun] small sticks or twigs used for lighting fires 引柴;引火之物

② harness: Noun an arrangement of straps for fastening something such as a parachute to a person's body or for restraining a young child 吊带(如降落伞上把人体系住或限制幼儿活动的吊带等)

第二章 事与愿违 第二节 《小菜一碟》A Piece of Cake

I said, "Peter, what has happened to my nose?"

I heard him striking a match in the dark. The night comes quickly in the desert. There was a pause.

"It actually doesn't seem to be there very much," he said. "Does it hurt?"

"Don't be a bloody fool, of course it hurts." He said he was going back to his machine to get some morphia① out of his emergency pack, but he came back again soon, saying he couldn't find his aircraft in the dark.

"Peter," I said, "I can't see anything."

"It's night," he answered. "I can't see either."

It was cold now. It was bitter cold, and Peter lay down close alongside so that we could both keep a little warmer. Every now and then he would say, "I've never seen a man without a nose before." I kept spewing② a lot of blood and every time I did it, Peter lit a match. Once he gave me a cigarette, but it got wet and I didn't want it anyway.

I do not know how long we stayed there and I remember only very little more. I remember that I kept telling Peter that there was a tin of sore throat tablets in my pocket, and that he should take one, otherwise he would catch my sore throat. I remember asking him where we were and him saying, "We're between the two armies," and then I remember English voices from an English patrol asking if we were Italians. Peter

---

① morphia: *Noun* old-fashioned term for morphine(过时用法)同"morphine"

morphine: *Noun* [mass noun] an analgesic and narcotic drug obtained from opium and used medicinally to relieve pain. Compare with heroin 吗啡

② spew: *Verb* [with obj.] expel large quantities of (something) rapidly and forcibly(大量)喷出;(快速)放出;涌出(e.g. Buses were spewing out black clouds of exhaust. 公共汽车排放出团团黑色的废气。)

said something to them; I cannot remember what he said. Later I remember hot thick soup and one spoonful making me sick①. And all the time the pleasant feeling that Peter was around, being wonderful, doing wonderful things and never going away. That is all that I can remember.

The men stood beside the aeroplane painting away and talking about the heat.

"Painting pictures on the aircraft," I said.

"Yes," said Peter. "It's a great idea. It's subtle."

"Why?" I said. "Just you tell me."

"They're funny pictures," he said. "The German pilots will all laugh when they see them; they'll shake so with their laughing that they won't be able to shoot straight."

"Oh baloney② baloney baloney."

"No, it's a great idea. It's fine. Come and have a look."

We ran towards the line of aircraft. "Hop, skip, jump," said Peter. "Hop skip jump, keep in time."

"Hop skip jump," I said, "Hop skip jump," and we danced along.

The painter on the first aeroplane had a straw hat on his head and a sad face. He was copying the drawing out of a magazine, and when Peter saw it he said, "Boy oh boy look at that picture," and he began to laugh. His laugh began with a rumble and grew quickly into a belly-roar and he slapped his thighs with his hands both at the same time and went on laughing with his body doubled up and his mouth wide open and his eyes shut. His silk top hat fell off his head on to the sand.

---

① sick: *Adjective* (informal) excellent(非正式用法)极好的

② baloney: *Noun* (informal) [mass noun] foolish or deceptive talk; nonsense. bologna(非正式用法)胡扯;废话

第二章 事与愿违 第二节 《小菜一碟》A Piece of Cake

"That's not funny," I said.

"Not funny!" he cried. "What d'you mean 'not funny'? Look at me. Look at me laughing. Laughing like this I couldn't hit anything. I couldn't hit a hay wagon or a house or a louse." And he capered① about on the sand, gurgling and shaking with laughter. Then he seized me by the arm and we danced over to the next aeroplane. "Hop skip jump," he said. "Hop skip jump."

There was a small man with a crumpled face writing a long story on the fuselage② with a red crayon. His straw hat was perched right on the back of his head and his face was shiny with sweat.

"Good morning," he said. "Good morning, good morning," and he swept his hat off his head in a very elegant way.

Peter said, "Shut up," and bent down and began to read what the little man had been writing. All the time Peter was spluttering③ and rumbling with laughter, and as he read he began to laugh afresh. He rocked from one side to the other and danced around on the sand slapping his thighs with his hands and bending his body. "Oh my, what a story, what a story, what a story. Look at me. Look at me laughing," and he hopped about on his toes, shaking his head and chortling④ like a madman. Then

---

① caper: *Verb* [no obj., with adverbial of direction] skip or dance about in a lively or playful way 蹦蹦跳跳;雀跃(e.g. Children were capering about the room. 孩子们在房间里蹦来跳去。)

② fuselage: *Noun* the main body of an aircraft(飞机的)机身

③ splutter: *Verb* [no obj.] make a series of short explosive spitting or choking sounds 作咳呛声(e.g. She coughed and spluttered, tears coursing down her face. 她又是咳又是呛,眼泪从脸上簌簌落下。)

④ chortle: *Verb* [no obj.] laugh in a breathy, gleeful way; chuckle 哈哈大笑;抿嘴轻笑(e.g. He chortled at his own execrable pun. 他对自己拙劣的双关语大笑了起来。)

suddenly I saw the joke and I began to laugh with him. I laughed so much that my stomach hurt and I fell down and rolled around on the sand and roared and roared because it was so funny that there was nothing else I could do.

"Peter, you're marvellous," I shouted. "But can all those German pilots read English?"

"Oh hell," he said. "Oh hell. Stop," he shouted. "Stop your work," and the painters all stopped their painting and turned round slowly and looked at Peter. They did a little caper on their toes and began to chant① in unison. "Rubbishy things—on all the wings, on all the wings, on all the wings," they chanted.

"Shut up," said Peter. "We're in a jam②. We must keep calm. Where's my top hat?"

"What?" I said.

"You can speak German," he said. "You must translate for us. He will translate for you," he shouted to the painters. "He will translate."

Then I saw his black top hat lying in the sand. I looked away, then I looked around and saw it again. It was a silk opera hat③ and it was lying there on its side in the sand.

"You're mad," I shouted. "You're madder than hell. You don't

---

① chant: *Verb* [with obj.] say or shout repeatedly in a sing-song tone 反复说；反复喊(e.g. Protesters were chanting slogans. 抗议者们一遍遍高喊着口号。)

② in a jam: (informal) an awkward situation or predicament(非正式用法)窘境；困境(e.g. I'm in a bit of a jam. Could you give me a lift to the train station? 我遇上一点小麻烦，你能让我搭你的车去火车站吗？)

③ opera hat: *Noun* a collapsible top hat 男用礼帽

know what you're doing. You'll get us all killed. You're absolutely plumb① crazy, do you know that? You're crazier than hell. My God, you're crazy."

"Goodness, what a noise you're making. You mustn't shout like that; it's not good for you." This was a woman's voice. "You've made youself② all hot," she said, and I felt someone wiping my forehead with a handkerchief. "You mustn't work yourself up like that."

Then she was gone and I saw only the sky, which was pale blue. There were no clouds and all around were the German fighters. They were above, below and on every side and there was no way I could go; there was nothing I could do. They took it in turns to come in to attack and they flew their aircraft carelessly, banking③ and looping and dancing in the air. But I was not frightened, because of the funny pictures on my wings. I was confident and I thought, "I am going to fight a hundred of them alone and I'll shoot them all down. I'll shoot them while they are laughing; that's what I'll do."

Then they flew closer. The whole sky was full of them. There were so many that I did not know which ones to watch and which ones to attack. There were so many that they made a black curtain over the sky and only here and there could I see a little of the blue showing through. But there was enough to patch a Dutchman's trousers, which was all that mattered. So long as there was enough to do that, then everything was all

---

① plum: *Adverb* (informal) exactly(非正式用法)正好地;准确地(e. g. trading opportunities plumb in the centre of central Europe 中欧正中心的贸易机会)

② 此处的"youself"若非临时造词,就是"yourself"之误。

③ bank: *Verb* (with reference to an aircraft vehicle) tilt or cause to tilt sideways in making a turn(飞机转弯时)倾侧(e. g. The plane banked as if to return to the airport. 飞机倾侧起来,似乎要飞回机场。)

right.

  Still they flew closer. They came nearer and nearer, right up in front of my face so that I saw only the black crosses which stood out brightly against the colour of the Messerschmitts① and against the blue of the sky; and as I turned my head quickly from one side to the other I saw more aircraft and more crosses and then I saw nothing but the arms of the crosses and the blue of the sky. The arms had hands and they joined together and made a circle and danced around my Gladiator, while the engines of the Messerschmitts sang joyfully in a deep voice. They were pla-

---

  ① Messerschmitt: *Noun* World War II fighter aircraft, notably the ME109, named after its chief designer, Willy Messerschmitt(第二次世界大战期间德国空军使用的)梅塞施米特式战斗机(尤指 ME109 型)

第二章 事与愿违 第二节 《小菜一碟》*A Piece of Cake*

ying Oranges and Lemons① and every now and then two would detach themselves and come out into the middle of the floor and make an attack and I knew then that it was Oranges and Lemons. They banked and swerved and danced upon their toes and they leant against the air first to one side, then to the other. "Oranges and Lemons said the bells of St Clement's," sang the engines.

But I was still confident. I could dance better than they and I had a better partner. She was the most beautiful girl in the world. I looked down and saw the curve of her neck and the gentle slope of her pale shoulders and I saw her slender arms, eager and outstretched.

Suddenly I saw some bullet holes in my starboard wing and I got angry and soared both at the same time; but mostly I got angry. Then I got

---

① Oranges and Lemons: "Oranges and Lemons" is an English nursery rhyme and singing game, which refers to the bells of several churches, all within or close to the City of London. 黄橙与柠檬（一种儿童韵体歌谣的唱歌游戏），其内容大致如下：

Oranges and lemons,
Say the bells of St. Clement's.
You owe me five farthings,
Say the bells of St. Martin's.
When will you pay me?
Say the bells of Old Bailey.
When I grow rich,
Say the bells of Shoreditch.
When will that be?
Say the bells of Stepney.
I do not know,
Says the great bell of Bow.
Here comes a candle to light you to bed,
And here comes a chopper to chop off your head!

confident and I said, "The German who did that had no sense of humour. There's always one man in a party who has no sense of humour. But there's nothing to worry about; there's nothing at all to worry about."

Then I saw more bullet holes and I got scared. I slid back the hood of the cockpit and stood up and shouted, "You fools, look at the funny pictures. Look at the one on my tail; look at the story on my fuselage. Please look at the story on my fuselage."

But they kept on coming. They tripped① into the middle of the floor in twos, shooting at me as they came. And the engines of the Messerschmitts sang loudly. "When will you pay me? said the bells of Old Bailey," sang the engines, and as they sang the black crosses danced and swayed to the rhythm of the music. There were more holes in my wings, in the engine cowling② and in the cockpit.

Then suddenly there were some in my body.

But there was no pain, even when I went into a spin③, when the wings of my plane went flip, flip, flip, faster and faster, when the blue sky and the black sea chased each other round and round until there was no longer any sky or sea but just the flashing of the sun as I turned. But the black crosses were following me down, still dancing and still holding hands and I could still hear the singing of their engines. "Here comes a

---

① trip: *Verb* [no obj., with adverbial] walk, run, or dance with quick light steps 轻快地走(或跑、跳舞)(e.g. They tripped up the terrace steps. 他们轻快地踏上了露天平台的台阶。)

② cowling: *Noun* the removable cover of a vehicle or aircraft engine(车辆的)引擎罩；(飞机的)整流罩

③ spin: *Noun* [usu. in sing.] a fast revolving motion of an aircraft as it descends rapidly(飞机急剧下降时的)急速旋转(e.g. He tried to stop the plane from going into a spin. 他努力阻止飞机在下降时旋转。)

第二章 事与愿违 第二节 《小菜一碟》A Piece of Cake

candle to light you to bed, here comes a chopper to chop off your head," sang the engines.

Still the wings went flip flip, flip, flip, and there was neither sky nor sea around me, but only the sun.

Then there was only the sea. I could see it below me and I could see the white horses①, and I said to myself, "Those are white horses riding a rough sea." I knew then that my brain was going well because of the white horses and because of the sea. I knew that there was not much time because the sea and the white horses were nearer, the white horses were bigger and the sea was like a sea and like water, not like a smooth place. Then there was only one white horse, rushing forward madly with his bit② in his teeth, foaming at the mouth, scattering the spray with his hooves③ and arching his neck as he ran. He galloped on madly over the sea, riderless and uncontrollable, and I could tell that we were going to crash.

After that it was warmer, and there were no black crosses and there was no sky. But it was only warm because it was not hot and it was not cold. I was sitting in a great red chair made of velvet and it was evening. There was a wind blowing from behind.

"Where am I?" I said.

"You are missing. You are missing, believed killed."

---

① white horse: Noun (plural noun) white-crested waves at sea 白浪
注：这里，作家达尔一语双关，"white horses"既指"白马"，又指"白浪"，玩了个文字游戏。

② bit: Noun a mouthpiece, typically made of metal, which is attached to a bridle and used to control a horse(马的)嚼子；衔铁

③ hoof: Noun the horny part of the foot of an ungulate animal, especially a horse(有蹄动物，尤指马的)蹄(e.g. There was a clatter of hoofs as a rider came up to them. 当一位骑手向他们骑来时，传来马蹄的得得声。)

"Then I must tell my mother."

"You can't. You can't use that phone."

"Why not?"

"It goes only to God."

"What did you say I was?"

"Missing, believed killed."

"That's not true. It's a lie. It's a lousy lie because here I am and I'm not missing. You're just trying to frighten me and you won't succeed. You won't succeed, I tell you, because I know it's a lie and I'm going back to my squadron. You can't stop me because I'll just go. I'm going, you see, I'm going."

I got up from the red chair and began to run.

"Let me see those X-rays again, nurse."

"They're here, doctor." This was the woman's voice again, and now it came closer. "You have been making a noise tonight, haven't you? Let me straighten your pillow for you, you're pushing it on to the floor." The voice was close and it was very soft and nice.

"Am I missing?"

"No, of course not. You're fine."

"They said I was missing."

"Don't be silly; you're fine."

Oh everyone's silly, silly, silly, but it was a lovely day, and I did not want to run but I couldn't stop. I kept on running across the grass and I couldn't stop because my legs were carrying me and I had no control over them. It was as if they did not belong to me, although when I looked down I saw that they were mine, that the shoes on the feet were mine and that the legs were joined to my body. But they would not do what I wanted; they just went on running across the field and I had to go with them. I ran and ran and ran, and although in some places the field was rough and bumpy, I never stumbled. I ran past trees and hedges and in one field there were some sheep which stopped their eating and scampered① off as I ran past them. Once I saw my mother in a pale grey dress bending down picking mushrooms, and as I ran past she looked up and said, "My basket's nearly full; shall we go home soon?" but my legs wouldn't stop and I had to go on.

Then I saw the cliff ahead and I saw how dark it was beyond the cliff. There was this great cliff and beyond it there was nothing but darkness, although the sun was shining in the field where I was running. The light of the sun stopped dead at the edge of the cliff and there was only darkness beyond. "That must be where the night begins," I thought, and once more I tried to stop but it was not any good. My legs began to go faster towards the cliff and they began to take longer strides, and I reached down with my hand and tried to stop them by clutching the cloth of my trousers, but it did not work; then I tried to fall down. But my legs were nimble②, and each time I threw myself I landed on my toes and went on running.

Now the cliff and the darkness were much nearer and I could see that unless I stopped quickly I should go over the edge. Once more I tried to throw myself to the ground and once more I landed on my toes and went on running.

---

① scamper: *Verb* [no obj., with adverbial of direction] (especially of a small animal or child) run with quick light steps, especially through fear or excitement(尤指小动物、小孩由于害怕或兴奋而)蹦跳；奔逃(e. g. He scampered in like an overgrown puppy. 他像一条长得超大的小狗一样蹦蹦跳跳地进来。)

② nimble: *Adjective* quick and light in movement or action; agile 灵活的；敏捷的(e. g. with a deft motion of her nimble fingers 随着她灵活的手指做出的一个熟练的动作)

I was going fast as I came to the edge and I went straight on over it into the darkness and began to fall.

At first it was not quite dark. I could see little trees growing out of the face of the cliff, and I grabbed at them with my hands as I went down. Several times I managed to catch hold of a branch, but it always broke off at once because I was so heavy and because I was falling so fast, and once I caught a thick branch with both hands and the tree leaned forward and I heard the snapping of the roots one by one until it came away from the cliff and I went on falling. Then it became darker because the sun and the day were in the fields far away at the top of the cliff, and as I fell I kept my eyes open and watched the darkness turn from grey-black to black, from black to jet black① and from jet black to pure liquid blackness which I could touch with my hands but which I could not see. But I went on falling, and it was so black that there was nothing anywhere and it was not any use doing anything or caring or thinking because of the blackness and because of the falling. It was not any use.

"You're better this morning. You're much better." It was the woman's voice again.

"Hallo."

"Hallo; we thought you were never going to get conscious."

"Where am I?"

"In Alexandria; in hospital."

"How long have I been here?"

"Four days."

"What time is it?"

"Seven o'clock in the morning."

---

① jet black: *Noun* a completely black colour 乌黑;深黑

"Why can't I see?"

I heard her walking a little closer.

"Oh, we've just put a bandage around your eyes for a bit."

"How long for?"

"Just for a while. Don't worry. You're fine. You were very lucky, you know."

I was feeling my face with my fingers but I couldn't feel it; I could only feel something else.

"What's wrong with my face?"

I heard her coming up to the side of my bed and I felt her hand touching my shoulder.

"You mustn't talk any more. You're not allowed to talk. It's bad for you. Just lie still and don't worry. You're fine." I heard the sound of her footsteps as she walked across the floor and I heard her open the door and shut it again.

"Nurse," I said. "Nurse."

But she was gone.

三、翻译探索

这篇小说中,作家达尔令主人公"我"的思绪如河流般蜿蜒流淌,"现实"与"意识"衔接自然,几乎不留任何痕迹。翻译中,也要注意这种风格的传达。翻译的难点就是对于某些文化层面东西的理解和翻译,如文中提到那些德军驾驶员故意跟我玩的那种"黄橙与柠檬"的儿童游戏,其译文要做到流畅自然、朗朗上口,确实值得探索一番。

小菜一碟

这是我写的第一个故事,时间是1942年。

这件事我记住的不太多。不管怎么说,事先发生的,我记住的不太多;事发之时的事情,我记住的也不太多。

当时,我们在阿尔及利亚的富卡镇着陆、加油,那里有一伙驾驶布雷尼单翼轰炸机的小子们很乐于助人,给我们茶水喝。我现在记得,那几个小子沉默寡言,走进充当食堂的帐篷里弄些茶水,然后坐下来一声不响地喝了起来,喝完后起身,走了出去,仍然一句话也没说。我知道,他们每个人都在竭力地控制着自己的情绪,因为当前情况不太好,他们得频繁出动,而且还没有兵员前来替换他们。

我们感谢他们提供茶水,然后出去看看我们的格斗士战机是否加满了油。我记得,当时一阵风吹来,把风向袋一下子横向拉直了,如同一个路标,沙子也被吹得在我们腿部周围扬起。风"嗖嗖"地吹向帐篷,吹得帐篷"唰啦、唰啦"作响,那些帐篷宛若穿着帆布装的男子在不断拍着手。

"开轰炸机那帮小子很不开心啊,"彼得说。

"不是不开心,"我回应。

"那么,他们感到枯燥乏味啦。"

"不是的。他们人疲马乏的,就这样,可他们还要挺下去。你看得出,他们咬紧牙关要挺下去。"

我们那两架陈旧的格斗士并排立在沙子里,穿黄卡其布衬衫和短裤的空勤人员似乎仍在忙活着给它们加油。我身穿一件薄薄的、棉质的白色飞行服,彼得穿的则是蓝色的,飞行时没有必要穿很保暖的衣服。

彼得问:"那距离有多远?"

"过了查灵岔口有将近三十四公里的距离,"我回答,"就在公路的右侧。"查灵岔口是沙漠公路的分叉处,自此向北延伸至马特鲁港。意大利军队驻扎在港口的外围,进展相当顺利。就我所知,这是意大利军队唯一一次进展如此顺利。在此之前,他们的士气一会儿上升,一会儿下降,就像飞机上升降无常的高度计。而此时,他们的士气上升到一万两千米,因为轴心国正处于世界之巅。我们在周围溜达着,等待着飞机加完油。

彼得说:"这是小菜一碟。"

第二章　事与愿违　第二节　《小菜一碟》A Piece of Cake

"是的,应该是易如反掌。"

我们分开行动,我爬进了驾驶舱。我总是记得帮我拴上安全带的那个空勤人员的脸,满是皱纹。他稍微上了点年纪,约有四十岁,除了脑袋后部整齐的一块金发区域外,整个脑袋就剩秃顶了。他那双眼睛极像我奶奶的眼睛,看上去好像一生的时间里都在帮飞行员拴安全带——拴好后,飞行员好像就一去不复返了。他站在机翼上,拉起我的安全带说:"要当心啊,粗心大意没有任何意义。"

"小菜一碟,"我回应。

"才不是呢。"

"真的,根本不算什么事儿,就是小菜一碟。"

接下来的事情,我记起的不是很多,我只记得后来的事情。我猜想,我们是从富卡起飞的,朝西飞向马特鲁港,我还猜想,我当时的飞行高度是二百四十米。我猜想,我们透过飞机的右舷看到了大海,因此我猜想呢——不,我敢肯定——大海蔚蓝、美丽,一浪一浪卷向沙滩,自东向西卷起一条长长的、宽宽的线条,一望无际。我猜想,我们在查灵岔口上方飞过,又继续飞行三十四公里,到达他们所说的预定地点,但是那只是我的猜想。我只知道,我们遇上了麻烦,层出不穷的麻烦,而且我知道,麻烦愈演愈烈之时,我们掉头往回飞。最大的麻烦在于,我飞得太低了,无法跳伞——就是从那一刻起,我的记忆力恢复过来了。我记得,飞机的前端向下沉去。我记得,顺着飞机前端向地面看去,看到地面生长着一丛丛的骆驼刺植物,彼此互不相干,那里的沙子和岩石纷纷跃出地表,向我冲来。那个场景,我记得十分清楚。

接下来,有一小段空隙我记不得了。那段空隙的间隔或许有一秒钟,或许有三十秒钟,我不得而知。我的一个意念就是,那段时间很短暂,或许是一秒钟,接下来,我就听到"嘭"的一声,右舷机翼的油箱就着起火来,然后又是"嘭"的一声,左舷机翼油箱也着起火来。对我来说,那不是至关重要的,我一动不动地坐了一会儿,感到舒适惬意,就是有点昏昏欲睡。我眼睛什么都看不见,但那也不是至关重要的,根本没有什么可担心的,丝毫的担心都不用。但是,我感觉两只腿的周围热起来,这时候不担心是不行的啦。一开始,只是一种暖烘烘的感觉,那也算是可以,但是突然间,一下子热了起来,两条腿的周围一股灼人的巨大热浪蹿了起来。

我知道,这种炎热不是那么令人好受的,但除此之外,我什么都不知道了。我不喜欢这种炎热,于是,我将双腿从座位下往上卷曲,等待着。我想,身体跟大脑之间的通信系统出了问题,这个系统的运转似乎不那么好。不知怎么的,这个系统在向大脑传递所有信息方面,速度慢了点,在获取大脑指令方面,也慢了点。但是,我相信,有一条信息最终还是传到了:"这下面有股巨大的热浪冒上来(叹息声),左腿和右腿该怎么办?"大脑正在核计该怎么办,好长一段时间没有回应。

接着,系统的线路上传来回音,缓慢地、一字一顿地传了过来:"本——机——在——燃——烧。跳——出——去,重——复,跳——出——去 跳——出——去。"命令传达到整个系统、腿部所有的肌肉、胳膊和身体。肌肉开始竭尽全能运转起来,推一推,拉一拉,全力绷紧,可是没有任何用处。另一条消息传了上去:"无法跳出去,有东西把我们固定住了。"对这条消息的回复,时间甚至更长一些,所以,我就坐在那儿等待回复。但是,热度始终在不断地增加。有什么东西将我扣住,这就得靠大脑查找原因所在了:是巨人的大手压在了我的双肩上了吗?还是沉重的石头、房子、蒸汽压路机,或者文件柜将我压住了呢?还是重力将我牵住,或者是绳子将我捆住?等会儿。绳子——对,绳子。回复的信息开始传来,传的速度很慢。"你——的——安全——带。解开——你的——安全——带。"我的胳膊收到了信息,开始运转。胳膊用力猛拉安全带,但就是解不开。于是,胳膊拉了一遍又一遍,尽管有点虚弱,但还是竭尽全力去拉,一点用处也没有。信息传向大脑:"我们怎么解安全带?"

我坐在那儿等待大脑的回复,我想,这一次我等了三四分钟的时间。除此之外,着急或者暴躁没有任何用处,我唯一能肯定的就是这

第二章 事与愿违 第二节 《小菜一碟》A Piece of Cake

一点。可是,所有的回复时间都很漫长。我大声喊:"真糟糕!我就要被烧焦了,我就要……"但话没说完就给打断了,回复传来——不,没有传来——是的,传来了,慢慢地传了过来:"拔出——快速——释放——栓——你——这个——蠢——货——赶快——跳。"

于是,释放栓拔下,安全带松开。现在,我们跳出去吧。我们跳出去,我们跳出去,但是,我却跳不了。怎么跳,我就是出不了驾驶舱。胳膊和腿都竭尽全力,但是毫无进展。绝望之中,最后一条信息飞速传向大脑,这一次还标上了"紧急"两个字。

"还有一个什么东西把我们压住了,"信息的内容是这样的。"某个别的东西,某个别的什么东西,某个很沉的东西。"

胳膊和腿也不再奋争了,它们似乎本能地知道,任凭气力用尽,也不会有什么意义。它们静静地原地不动,等待着回复。哇,等待的时间多么漫长!热乎乎之中,等待了二十秒、三十秒、四十秒。胳膊和腿都还没有变成白热化状态,肌肉没有发出"吡吡"的声音,也闻不到肉被烧焦的味道,但随时会有这样的危险出现,因为老式的格斗士战机不像飓风战机或者斯比特战机那样,是用高强度的钢制成的。格斗士的机翼是用绷紧的帆布做的,上面涂抹了极其不易燃烧的清漆。帆布之下铺的是成百上千的、短短的细杆,类似于放在木柴下用以引燃木柴的引柴,只不过这些短杆更干燥、更纤细。如果一个聪明之人说:"我要造一个大大的东西,这个东西要比世界上任何东西的燃烧性能都更好,燃烧速度都更快,"并且勤奋苦干的话,那么,他最终造出来的东西或许就极像格斗士战机。我一动不动地坐着,等待着。

接着,突然之间,回复信息传了过来,异常简短,同时却说明一切:"你的——降落伞——转动——伞的——搭扣。"

我转动搭扣,释放了降落伞的吊带,颇费气力将自己抬高,然后翻滚到驾驶舱的外侧。似乎有什么东西燃烧起来,于是,我在沙子里滚了一下,然后匍匐着离开火源,躺了下来。

我听到响声,那是我飞机上的机关枪弹药在燃烧中爆炸的声音,还有子弹"砰砰砰"射进附近沙子里的声音。对此,我并不担心,因为我只是听到了这些声音。

身体的各个部位开始疼痛起来,脸疼得最厉害。脸部有点不对劲儿,某些地方出了问题。于是,我慢慢抬起一只手抚摸着,摸起来黏糊糊的。我的鼻子似乎不在了,我尽量去摸牙齿,但是,我记不清当时到底摸没摸到牙齿。我想,我打了个盹儿。

突然间,彼得出现了。我听到他的声音,我听到他像疯了一样,蹦着、叫着、摇晃着我的手说:"天呐,我还以为你仍然困在里面呢。我在一里半开外的地方降落,拼命地跑过来。你还好吗?"

我说:"彼得,我的鼻子怎么了?"

沙漠里的夜晚降临得很快。我听到他在黑暗中擦燃一根火柴的声音,紧接着,停顿了一会儿。

"实际上,鼻子很大一部分似乎不在原位,"他说,"疼吗?"

"不要犯傻,当然疼了。"

他说,他要回自己飞机那儿从急救包里拿点吗啡来,但很快又回来了。他说,天太黑,找不到自己的飞机了。

"彼得,"我说,"我什么都看不见。"

"现在是晚上啊,"他回应,"我也什么都看不见。"

现在,天气开始冷起来,而且冷得厉害,彼得紧挨着我躺下,好使我们俩都感到更加暖和一点。他不时地会说上一句:"我以前从未看到过没有鼻子的人。"我一直大口地吐血,每吐一次,彼得就擦燃一根火柴。有一次,他递过来一支烟,但却给弄湿了,我也就不想再抽了。

我们在那儿待了多长时间,我不知道。我只知道,当时的事情我几乎不再记得什么了。我记得,我不断地对彼得说,我的兜子里有一个锡罐,里面装的是治嗓子疼的药片,我还告诉他,他应该服一片,否则他的嗓子就会像我的一样疼痛起来。我记得,我问过他我们在哪里,他说:"我们夹在敌我两军之间。"接着,我记得,从一只英国巡逻队里传来用英语说话的声音,问我们俩是不是意大利人。彼得对他们说了什么,但我记不得他说了什么。

第二章　事与愿违　第二节　《小菜一碟》A Piece of Cake

后来,我记得有浓稠的热汤,给我喝上一勺,感觉好极了。自始至终我有一种愉快的感觉,感觉彼得就在身边,他好极了,做得很棒,从不曾离开过。我能记得的,就只有这么多了。

伙计们站在飞机旁边,一边涂刷,一边谈论着炎热的天气。
"在机身上刷上图画,"我说。
"好的,"彼得应声说,"很棒的想法,很微妙的。"
"为什么?"我问,"你就跟我说说呗。"
"刷些很有趣儿的图案,"他说,"德国飞行员看到了,都会发笑。一笑,他们的身体就会抖动;一抖动,他们就不能够射中目标啦。"
"噢,胡扯、胡扯、胡扯啊。"
"不,想法很棒。好了,过来看一眼吧。"
我们向那排飞机跑去。"一跃、二蹦、三跳啊,"彼得说,"一跃二蹦三跳,踩上点儿啊。"
"一跃二蹦三跳,"我说,"一跃二蹦三跳。"奔跑中,我们舞蹈起来。

在第一架飞机上涂刷的那个伙计戴了顶草帽,露出一张伤感的面孔。他正在照着一本杂志往机身上涂呢。彼得看到他的画后,说道:"小子,噢,小子啊,看看那幅画。"说完,他就开始发笑。他的笑声开始还很低沉,接着很快就捧腹大笑起来,哈哈大笑。他一边笑,一边用双手猛劲拍打自己的大腿,拍打大腿的同时继续大笑不止,咧开了嘴、闭上了眼睛使劲儿笑,笑弯了身体,笑得他戴的那顶丝绸大礼帽从头顶掉落,落到沙子上。

"不好笑,"我说。
"还不好笑!"他叫道,"你说的'不好笑',是什么意思呢?看着我,看着我笑,笑成我这样,什么样的目标我也打不中的,哪怕是一辆装满干草的四轮车,或者是一座家用房屋,或者一所山中小屋都打不中的。"他在沙地里蹦来跳去,嘎嘎大笑,笑得浑身颤抖。紧接着,他抓起我的一只胳膊,我们跳着舞蹈奔向下一架飞机。"一跃二蹦三跳,"他说,"一跃二蹦三跳啊。"

一名小个头的男子板着一副面孔,正用一只红蜡笔往机身上写一则长篇故事呢。他戴的那顶草帽整个儿都扣到脑袋的后部,他的那张脸浸满了汗水,闪闪发亮。

"上午好,"他说,"上午好,上午好啊。"说完,他姿势优雅地将帽子从头上利索地摘掉。

彼得说:"闭嘴。"然后,他就弯下身体,开始阅读这位小个子伙计一直在写的内容。彼得始终嘟嘟囔囔、嘎嘎发笑。笑过后继续读,读几句又开始大笑。他将身体从一侧摇晃到另一侧,在沙地里转着圈儿舞蹈,还用双手拍着大腿,笑弯了腰。

"噢,天呐,故事真绝妙,故事真绝妙,故事真绝妙啊。看看我,看看我笑成啥样啦。"说完,他踮起脚尖,到处蹦跳,摇头晃脑,如疯子一般笑得前仰后合。接着,我突然间看到了那架飞机上写的笑话,就随同他一起大笑起来。我笑得太厉害,肚子都笑疼了,整个人跌倒在地,在沙子上转着圈儿、打起滚来。我狂笑不止,因为这故事太有意思了,以至于除了狂笑,没有其他任何事情可做。

"彼得,你真绝妙,"我喊道"可问题是,那些德国飞行员都懂英文吗?"

"哦,见鬼,"他说,"哦,见鬼,停下,"他喊道,"停下别干啦。"随即,所有涂刷的伙计都停了下来,慢慢转过身来,看着彼得。他们踮起脚尖,轻轻地雀跃,开始齐声反复吟唱:"破烂的东西,涂满机翼,涂满机翼,涂满机翼。"他们反复吟唱着。

"闭嘴,"彼得喊,"我们遇到麻烦了,我们必须保持镇定。我的大礼帽哪里去了?"

"什么?"我问。

"你会说德语,"他说,"你一定得帮我们翻译翻译。等着,他会为你们翻译的,"他冲着那几个涂刷的伙计喊道,"他会为你们翻译的。"

接下来,我看到他的那顶黑色的大礼帽躺在沙子上。我移开目光,接着又向周围看了看,又看见了那顶大礼帽。那是一顶丝绸做成的男式礼帽,侧躺在沙子上。

"你疯了,"我喊道,"你简直是疯狂透顶。你知不知道你在做些什么,你会让我们大家送命的。你是完全彻底、彻头彻尾地疯掉了,你知道吗?你疯狂透顶,我的天啊,你疯了。"

"天啊,你一直发出这样的噪音,不要再那样喊叫了,对你没有好处的。"这是一名女子说话的声音,"你已经搞得自己浑身发热啦,"她继续说。我感到有人正用手绢擦拭我的额头。"你一定不要像那样喊叫了,否则,你就会耗尽气力。"

接着,她走开了,我看到的只有灰蓝色的天空,一丝云彩都没有,周围尽是德国的战斗机:头上有,脚下有,身体各个侧面都有,我束手无策、无计可施,根本无法飞出去。它们轮番飞过来进攻,满不在乎地在空中飞来飞去,一会儿倾斜飞,一会儿翻跟头飞,一会儿上下舞蹈着飞。但是,由于我的机翼上有滑稽好笑的图片,我并不害怕。我想:"我要单枪匹马独斗一百架敌机,把它们统统击落。趁它们的飞行员大笑的当儿,我就射击。这就是我要做的。"

接下来,它们飞得越来越近,满天都是,弄得我不知道该瞄准哪一个,该射击哪一个。它们数量众多,在空中形成一面帘幕,只能透过星星点点的空间才能看见一点点蓝天,但是,透过来的蓝天面积足够缝补荷兰人穿的一条裤子了,那才是至关重要的。只要补丁足够,那么,一切都好办了。

它们还在靠近,越飞越近、越飞越近,简直就是飞到了我的面前,眼前看到的只有黑叉了。那些黑叉在梅塞施米特式战斗机的机身上凸显出来,耀眼醒目,与那些战斗机的机身颜色和天空的蓝色形成了鲜明的对比。我飞速地将头从一边转向另一边,看到更多的飞机、更多的叉形图案。很快,我能看到的只有黑叉的手臂,还有蓝蓝的天空。手臂上长出了手,这些手彼此牵在一起,形成一个圆圈,围绕着我驾驶的格斗士跳舞,梅塞施米特式战斗机的马达则用低沉的声音欢快地鸣唱。它们的驾驶员玩的是儿童游戏"黄橙与柠檬",每隔一会儿,其中的两架就会分离出来,跳到场地中央,展开一轮进攻。于是,我知道,这两位就是"黄橙"和"柠檬"啦。它们先倾斜飞行,再突然转弯,踮起脚尖舞蹈起来。然后,它们跃入空中,先向一边跳跃,再向另一边跳跃。"黄橙与柠檬,圣克莱门特教堂响起了钟声,"它们的引擎这样唱道。

但是,我仍然满怀信心,因为我比它们跳得更好,况且我还有一位技高一筹的舞伴,她是这个世界上最漂亮的女孩。我低头看了一眼,看到了她脖颈优美的曲线、缓缓下滑的、浅白双肩的皮肤表面,我还看到了她修长的双臂伸展开来,急切地等待着。

突然之间,我看到我驾驶的那架飞机的右舷机翼上面有几个弹孔,于是,我生气了,要将这两位一起吓跑,但是,我主要还是生气。接下来,我恢复了信心,说道:"留下弹孔那个德国人,一点儿幽默感都没有。每次聚会的时候,总会有那么一个人毫无幽默感而言,但没有什么可担心的,根本就没有什么可担心的。"

接下来,看到了更多的弹孔,我就害怕起来。我把驾驶舱盖滑开,站起身来喊道:"你们两个傻帽,看看滑稽好笑的图案吧。先看看飞机尾部的,再看看机身上的故事。拜托,看看机身上的故事。"

但是,梅塞施米特战机不断涌来。它们两个一组轻快地飞到场地中间,边飞边向我射击,同时,它们的引擎还高声鸣唱:"老城廓上的钟声启发,问你何时把钱给我支付?"引擎一边唱,黑叉一边舞,随着音乐的节奏摇摆。我驾驶的飞机的双翼上、引擎罩上、驾驶舱里,弹孔越来越多。

接下来,突然之间,我的身体上也有了几处弹孔。

但是,没有疼痛感,即使在下降中、处于旋转状态的我也没有疼痛感,即使我驾驶的飞机的机翼翻来转去、翻来转去、翻来转去的速度越来越快也没有疼痛感,即使蓝天和黑海在转呀、转呀地相互追逐着,直到看不见天空和大海而只能在我转身时看见一闪一闪的阳光的程度也没有疼痛感。但是,黑叉仍然跟着我一起下降,下降过程中,它们仍然手牵着手舞蹈,仍然能听得见它们引擎的鸣唱。"一只

第二章　事与愿违　第二节　《小菜一碟》*A Piece of Cake*

蜡烛在此点燃照你上床来,一把短斧在此举起砍掉你脑袋,"引擎唱道。

机翼仍然在翻来转去、翻来转去、翻来转去,我的四周没有了天空和大海,只剩下太阳。

接下来,只剩下大海了。我能够看到下方的大海,还能看到海面上如白马一般奔腾的浪花。于是,我对自己说:"那些都是大白马,骑着汹涌的浪花。"于是,我知道,由于白马和浪花的缘故,我的大脑运转良好。我知道,时间不太多了,因为浪花和白马越来越近,白马个头越来越大,浪花更像大海和海水,不像是静静开放的花朵。到了最后,只剩下一匹白马,疯狂地向前疾驰,牙齿卡在马嚼子上,嘴里喷着泡沫,马蹄子踏出飞沫,马头在奔跑中拱起。这匹马的马背上没有乘客,在大海上疯狂地向前狂奔,失去了控制。我可以断定,我们就要坠毁。

自那之后,越来越温暖,不见黑叉,也不见天空,但是,只有温暖,因为既不感到炎热难耐,也不感到寒冷刺骨。我坐在一把大大的红色天鹅绒椅子上,当时已经到了晚上,身后有一阵风吹来。

"我在哪里?"我问。

"你失踪了,你失踪了,据传身亡。"

"那么,我一定得告诉我母亲。"

"不行,那部电话你用不了。"

"为什么用不了?"

"那部电话只能接通上帝。"

"你刚才说我怎么了?"

"失踪,据传身亡。"

"那是说谎,不是事实。简直是弥天大谎,因为我人在这里好好的,没有失踪。你就是想要吓唬我,你不会得逞的。我对你说,你不会得逞的,因为我知道这是谎言,我要回我的飞行中队。你无法阻止我,因为我去意已决。我要走了,你看到的,我要走了。"

我从红色椅子上起身,开始奔跑起来。

"护士,让我再看看那几张 X 光片。"

"给你,医生。"又是那位女子的声音,但这次的声音离我更近了。"整个夜晚,你不断弄出声响,不是吗?我把你的枕头弄平整一点吧,你都快要把它推到地板上了。"声音离我很近,听起来很温柔、很美好。

"我失踪了吗?"

"没有,当然没有。你很不错的。"

"他们说,我失踪了。"

"不要犯傻,你很不错的。"

噢,大家都犯傻、犯傻、犯傻啦,可是,天气很不错,我也不想奔跑。问题是,我就是停不下来。我不停地奔跑,穿过了草地,无法停止,因为我的两条腿带着我跑,我无法控制它们,就好像它们不属于我似的。可是,我低头看去,发现它们长在我身上,跟我的身体相连,两只脚上的鞋也是我的,但是,他们就是不听我指挥,只是一味地穿越田野奔跑,我也不得不跟着它们。我就这样跟着它们跑呀、跑呀、跑呀,奇怪得很,有些地方的田野尽管高低不平、起伏不定,我却从来没有绊脚、摔倒。我跑过树林、树篱,跑到一块田野里,那里有一些羊正在吃草,看到我跑来,草也不吃了,惊慌地四下逃窜。有一次,我看到我母亲身穿浅灰色的衣服,弯着腰拣蘑菇,我奔跑经过她的身边,她抬起头,对我说:"篮子几乎拣满了,我们马上一起回家好吗?"可是,我的两条腿就是不肯停下来,于是,我继续奔跑下去。

接下来,我看到前方的悬崖,也看到悬崖以远的地方漆黑一片。这个大大的悬崖就横在眼前,尽管在我奔跑的田野里阳光明媚地照耀,但悬崖以远的地方除了黑漆漆的一片,什么都看不见。就在悬崖的边缘,太阳光戛然而止,不再照耀,只有黑漆漆的一片。"那里一定是黑夜开始的地方,"我这样想着。我再一次要努力停下,但是,一点用处都没有。我的两条腿开始向悬崖奔跑,速度越来越快,而且要开始大跨步前进。于是,我伸出一只手向下够去,紧紧抓住裤子,意欲止住双腿,但是没有效果。紧接着,我尽量让自己摔倒,但是,我的两

第二章 事与愿违 第二节 《小菜一碟》A Piece of Cake

条腿灵活得很,每次摔倒的尝试都被脚趾化解了。于是,我继续不停地奔跑。

现在,悬崖和黑暗离我越来越近了,我明白,要是不马上停下来,我就会跌入悬崖。我要尽力让自己再一次摔倒,但是,摔倒的尝试又被脚趾化解了。于是,我继续不停地奔跑。

到达悬崖边的时候,我的速度依然很快,直接越过边缘,奔入黑暗之中,开始跌落下去。

刚开始跌入的时候,还不算太黑,我能够看到一棵棵小树从悬崖表面长出。于是,我一边下落,一边抓向小树。有好几次,我设法抓住了树枝,但是每次我一抓住,树枝就立刻折断了,因为我太沉,而且下落速度又是那么快。有一次,我双手抓住了一根很粗的树枝,但是,树身却向下倾斜了,我听到"啪啪"的声响,树根竟然一根根断裂,最后,整棵树脱离了悬崖。于是,我继续跌落。接下来,越来越黑了,因为太阳和白天远在悬崖顶部的田野中。我一边下落,一边睁开眼睛看着黑漆漆的一片:从灰暗变成黑暗,从黑暗变成乌黑,从乌黑变成纯粹液态的黑暗,这种液态的黑暗,我用双手能够触摸得到,但是,眼睛却看不见。我还是继续跌落,四周黑得什么都不存在了。做什么、关心什么、想什么都没有任何的意义,因为除了黑暗,就是跌落,什么都失去了意义。

"今天早晨你好多了,好太多了。"又是那位女子的声音。

"嗨,你好。"

"嗨,你好。我们还以为,你永远不会恢复意识呢。"

"我在哪里?"

"在亚历山大港,在医院里。"

"我在这儿有多长时间了?"

"四天了。"

"现在几点了?"

"早晨七点钟。"

"为什么我什么都看不见?"

我听到她走得稍微靠近一些。

"哦,我们刚刚给你的眼睛缠了一圈绷带,就缠一会儿。"

"一会儿多长?"

"就一小段时间,不要担心。你很不错的,要知道,你很幸运。"

我用手指摸了摸脸,但却摸到了别的东西。

"我的脸怎么了?"

我听到她走到床边,感觉到她的一只手触摸到我的一只肩膀。

"你绝对不能再说话了,不允许你说话的,说话对你没有好处。你只需静静地躺着养病,不要担心,你很不错的。"

她穿过地板,我听到她的脚步声,还听到她打开门、又关上门的声音。

"护士,"我喊,"护士。"

但是,她已经走了。

第三章 生财之道

在这个世界上,作为个体的人若要生存下来,就得找到一个生财、聚财的门道,物质应是生存的第一要素,"所以虽是渊明先生,也还略略有些生财之道在,要不然,他老人家不但没有酒喝,而且没有饭吃,早已在东篱旁边饿死了①。"生财之道,可谓五花八门,但常言道:"君子爱财,取之有道,用之有度。"也就是说,要做到生财有道,即挣钱有合乎道义的办法,另外,生财还要讲究策略。《礼记·大学》里有这样的记载:

是故君子有大道,必忠信以得之,骄泰以失之。生财有大道。生之者众,食之者寡,为之者疾,用之者舒,则财恒足矣。仁者以财发身,不仁者以身发财。未有上好仁,而下不好义者也。未有好义,其事不终者也,未有府库财,非其财者也。

据《新京报(电子报)》2014年6月29日的一篇文章报道,"属于已故伊丽莎白王太后(伊丽莎白二世的母亲)的梅伊堡开始提供出租业务,只要花费5万英镑(约合53万人民币),就可以在王室城堡里

---

① 引自鲁迅《且介亭杂文二集·隐士》。

过周末了。梅伊堡是首个进行出租的王室城堡,该城堡不打广告,只向少数商界富豪和慈善家发邀请函①。"可见,生财之道古今中外皆有。

英国作家罗尔德·达尔短篇小说中有些主人公,也有生财之道,而且颇为"有道"。《管家之谋》中,乔治·克利弗夫妇花重金雇了一位法国厨师埃斯特拉贡先生,还雇了一位英国管家,名字叫提伯斯。可是,没有想到的是,这位管家生财有道,在克利弗先生款待客人的葡萄酒上开启了"生财之道"。《卖伞男子》中,一个上了年纪的小个子在雨天的生财之道更为奇特,竟在一位警惕性颇高的母亲面前"蒙混过关"。

第一节 《管家之谋》The Butler

罗尔德·达尔的《管家之谋》(The Butler)被收录在《罗尔德·达尔短篇故事集锦》(The Collected Short Stories of Roald Dahl)《完全出人意料故事集》(Completely Unexpected Tales)《更多出人意料故事集》(More Tales of the Unexpected)、《后续出人意料故事集》(Further Tales of the Unexpected)《〈伟大写手〉及其他故事集》(The Great Automatic Grammatizator and Other Stories)《〈宛若羔羊〉及其他故事集》(Lamb to the Slaughter and Other Stories)以及《〈卖伞男子〉及其他故事集》(The Umbrella Man and Other Stories)等书中。

一、原作导读

百万富翁乔治·克利弗先生是个典型的暴发户,他跟妻子很想跻身于英国的上流社会,于是他们不惜重金雇了一位法国大厨埃斯

---

① 引自《新京报(电子报)》,具体参见下列网址:http://epaper.bjnews.com.cn/html/2014-06/29/content_520737.htm? div = -1。

第三章 生财之道 第一节 《管家之谋》The Butler

特拉贡先生,还聘了一名管家提伯斯先生。

在这两位专业人士的扶持下,克利弗夫妇决心爬上社会的上层阶梯,于是开始以慷慨奢华的规模一周举行好几次晚宴聚会。

With the help of these two experts, the Cleavers set out to climb the social ladder and began to give dinner parties several times a week on a lavish scale.

但问题是,这些晚会的效果却不怎么太尽人意。这时,管家提伯斯先生提出意见说,原因在于克利弗先生用来招待客人的那些廉价的西班牙红酒上。

"那么,你这个蠢货,为什么不早告诉我?"克利弗先生大叫。"我不缺钱。如果他们想喝好酒,我会为他们提供这个世界上最上等的好酒!世界上最好的酒是什么?"

"Then why in heaven's name didn't you say so before, you twit?" cried Mr. Cleaver. "I'm not short of money. I'll give them the best flipping[①] wine in the world if that's what they want! What is the best wine in the world?"

在主人的授意下,管家设法买来一些 1929 年以及 1945 年产的法国葡萄酒,价格不菲,还传授给主人一些品酒方面的知识。但是,赴宴的客人并没有因此而热情高涨。对此,管家说,原因在于主人吩咐厨师埃斯特拉贡先生往色拉里放入了大量的醋,而主人并不赞同管家的说法,双方争执不下。

---

① flipping: Adjective [attrib.] (informal, chiefly Brit.) used for emphasis or to express mild annoyance(主要为英国英语非正式用法)该死的;讨厌的(用于加强语气或表示轻微恼怒)

在那天晚上举行的宴会上,克利弗先生一边称赞自己的葡萄酒,一边对管家大加嘲弄,这可惹怒了管家:

"先生,现在你喝的酒,"管家安静地说,"恰恰就是那种令人生厌的西班牙廉价红酒。"

克利弗先生看了看自己杯中的酒,又看了看管家。现在,血液涌向了他的脸部,皮肤开始变得猩红。"你撒谎,提伯斯!"他说。

"不,先生,我没有撒谎,"管家回答,"事实上,自我来到之日起,除了西班牙红酒,我从未给你上过任何别的酒。这种酒似乎很合你的口味。"

"The wine you are drinking, sir," the butler said quietly, "happens to be that cheap and rather odious Spanish red."

Mr. Cleaver looked at the wine in his glass, then at the butler. The blood was coming to his face now, his skin was turning scarlet. "You're lying, Tibbs!" he said.

"No sir, I'm not lying," the butler said. "As a matter of fact, I have never served you any other wine but Spanish red since I've been here. It seemed to suit you very well."

二、原作释读

罗尔德·达尔的这篇小说篇幅较短,情节也不复杂,阅读起来难度不大。值得注意的是,通过阅读,读者要体会好主人公乔治·克利弗先生的心态,也要体会好管家提伯斯的"把戏"。

The Butler[①]

---

① 本部小说原文出自"Roald Dahl. *The Collected Short Stories of Roald Dahl* [M]. England: Penguin Books Ltd., 1992"。

第三章 生财之道 第一节 《管家之谋》The Butler

As soon as George Cleaver had made his first million, he and Mrs. Cleaver moved out of their small suburban villa① into an elegant London house. They acquired a French chef called Monsieur② Estragon and an English butler called Tibbs, both wildly expensive. With the help of these two experts, the Cleavers set out to climb the social ladder and began to give dinner parties several times a week on a lavish③ scale.

But these dinners never seemed quite to come off. There was no animation④, no spark to set the conversation alight, no style at all. Yet the food was superb and the service faultless.

"What the heck's⑤ wrong with our parties, Tibbs?" Mr. Cleaver said to the butler. "Why don't nobody never loosen up and let themselves go?"

Tibbs inclined his head to one side and looked at the ceiling. "I hope, sir, you will not be offended if I offer a small suggestion."

"What is it?"

"It's the wine, sir."

"What about the wine?"

"Well, sir, Monsieur Estragon serves superb food. Superb food

---

① villa: *Noun* (especially in continental Europe) a large and luxurious country residence in its own grounds(尤指欧洲大陆)乡间别墅;度假别墅

② Monsieur: *Noun* used as a French courtesy title; equivalent to English "Mr."先生(法语中对男性的尊称)

③ lavish: *Adjective* (of a person) very generous or extravagant(人)慷慨的;奢侈的

④ animation: *Noun* [mass noun] the state of being full of life or vigour; liveliness 生气;活泼;热烈(e.g. They started talking with animation. 他们开始热烈交谈。)

⑤ heck: *Exclamation* (the heck) used for emphasis in questions and exclamations(用于加重语气)见鬼的

should be accompanied by superb wine. But you serve them a cheap and very odious① Spanish red."

"Then why in heaven's name didn't you say so before, you twit?" cried Mr. Cleaver. "I'm not short of money. I'll give them the best flipping② wine in the world if that's what they want! What is the best wine in the world?"

"Claret③, sir," the butler replied, "from the greatest chateaux④ in Bordeaux—Lafite, Latour, Haut-Brion, Margaux, Mouton-Rothschild and Cheval Blanc. And from only the very greatest vintage years, which are, in my opinion, 1906, 1914, 1929 and 1945. Cheval Blanc was also magnificent in 1895 and 1921, and Haut-Brion in 1906."

"Buy them all!" said Mr. Cleaver. "Fill the flipping cellar from top to bottom!"

"I can try, sir," the butler said. "But wines like these are extremely rare and cost a fortune."

"I don't give a hoot⑤ what they cost!" said Mr. Cleaver. "Just go out and get them!"

That was easier said than done. Nowhere in England or in France

---

① odious: *Adjective* extremely unpleasant; repulsive 可憎的;令人厌恶的

② flipping: *Adjective* [attrib.] (informal, chiefly Brit.) used for emphasis or to express mild annoyance(主要为英国英语非正式用法)该死的;讨厌的(用于加强语气或表示轻微恼怒)

③ claret: *Noun* [mass noun] a red wine from Bordeaux, or wine of a similar character made elsewhere 波尔多红葡萄酒;红葡萄酒;红酒

④ 此处的"chateaux"以及本段后面出现的"Bordeaux""Lafite""Latour" "Haut-Brion""Margaux""Mouton-Rothschild""Cheval Blanc"都是法国的葡萄酒产区或酒庄名字,以及相应的葡萄酒品牌。

⑤ not care (give) a hoot (two hoots): (informal) not care at all(非正式) 根本不在乎

could Tibbs find any wine from 1895, 1906, 1914 or 1921. But he did manage to get hold of some twenty-nines and forty-fives. The bills for these wines were astronomical①. They were in fact so huge that even Mr. Cleaver began to sit up and take notice. And his interest quickly turned into outright enthusiasm when the butler suggested to him that a knowledge of wine was a very considerable social asset. Mr. Cleaver bought books on the subject and read them from cover to cover. He also learned a great deal from Tibbs himself, who taught him, among other things, just how wine should be properly tasted. "First, sir, you sniff it long and deep, with your nose right inside the top of the glass, like this. Then you take a mouthful and you open your lips a tiny bit and suck in air, letting the air bubble through the wine. Watch me do it. Then you roll it vigorously around your mouth. And finally you swallow it."

In due course, Mr. Cleaver came to regard himself as an expert on wine, and inevitably he turned into a colossal bore. "Ladies and gentlemen," he would announce at dinner, holding up his glass, "this is a Margaux '29! The greatest year of the century! Fantastic bouquet②! Smells of cowslips③! And notice especially the after taste and how the ti-

---

① astronomical: *Adjective* (informal) (of an amount) extremely large(非正式用法)极大的;巨大的

② bouquet: *Noun* the characteristic scent of a wine or perfume(酒或香水的)香味;芬芳(e.g. The aperitif has a faint bouquet of almonds. 开胃酒有一股淡淡的杏仁香味。)

③ cowslip: *Noun* a European primula with clusters of drooping fragrant yellow flowers in spring, growing on dry grassy banks and in pasture 黄花九轮草;立金花;报春花

ny trace of tannin① gives it that glorious astringent② quality! Terrific, ain't it?'

The guests would nod and sip and mumble a few praises, but that was all.

"What's the matter with the silly twerps③?" Mr. Cleaver said to Tibbs after this had gone on for some time. "Don't none of them appreciate a great wine?"

The butler laid his head to one side and gazed upward. "I think they would appreciate it, sir," he said, "if they were able to taste it. But they can't."

"What the heck d'you mean, they can't taste it?"

"I believe, sir, that you have instructed Monsieur Estragon to put liberal④ quantities of vinegar in the salad-dressing."

"What's wrong with that? I like vinegar."

---

① tannin: *Noun* any of various complex phenolic substances of plant origin; used in tanning and in medicine 鞣酸;丹宁酸;单宁

注:单宁是葡萄酒的基本成分之一,是酒的结构、酒的口味和酒的陈化潜力的决定因素之一。只有红葡萄酒拥有单宁,因为单宁是从葡萄皮里的红色素(花色素)转换而来的。单宁不足的红酒要尽快喝掉,因为它经不起储藏,酒香会很快消散。单宁也使红酒具有了预防心脏病的特质。含单宁丰富的酒通常涩度高,我们说其具"收敛"性。如果一瓶红酒涩度过高,那通常是因为它年岁太小,最好等过了几年让酒体充分展开再喝。单宁在窖藏过程中会转换成酒香。

② astringent: *Adjective* (of taste or smell) sharp or bitter(味道或气味)涩的;辛辣的

③ twerp or twirp: *Noun* (informal) a silly or annoying person(非正式用法)笨蛋;讨厌的家伙

④ liberal: *Adjective* given, used, or occurring in generous amounts 大量的 (e.g. Liberal amounts of wine had been consumed. 已喝掉不少酒。)

第三章 生财之道 第一节 《管家之谋》The Butler

"Vinegar," the butler said, "is the enemy of wine. It destroys the palate①. The dressing should be made of pure olive oil and a little lemon juice. Nothing else."

"Hogwash②!" said Mr. Cleaver.

"As you wish, sir."

"I'll say it again, Tibbs. You're talking hogwash. The vinegar don't spoil my palate one bit."

"You are very fortunate, sir," the butler murmured, backing out of the room.

That night at dinner, the host began to mock his butler in front of the guests. "Mister Tibbs," he said, "has been trying to tell me I can't taste my wine if I put vinegar in the salad-dressing. Right, Tibbs?"

"Yes, sir," Tibbs replied gravely.

"And I told him hogwash. Didn't I, Tibbs?"

"Yes, sir."

"This wine," Mr. Cleaver went on, raising his glass, "tastes to me exactly like a Chateau Lafite '45, and what's more it is a Chateau Lafite '45."

Tibbs, the butler, stood very still and erect near the sideboard③, his face pale. "If you'll forgive me, sir," he said, "that is not a Lafite '45."

Mr. Cleaver swung round in his chair and stared at the butler.

---

① palate: *Noun* a person's sense of appreciation of taste and flavour, especially when sophisticated and discriminating(尤指能品味细微差别的)味觉

② hogwash: *Noun* [mass noun] (informal) nonsense(非正式用法)胡说；废话

③ sideboard: *Noun* a flat-topped piece of furniture with cupboards and drawers, used for storing crockery, glasses, and table linen 餐具柜

"What the heck d'you mean," he said. "There's the empty bottles beside you to prove it!"

These great clarets, being old and full of sediment①, were always decanted② by Tibbs before dinner. They were served in cut-glass③ decanters④, while the empty bottles, as is the custom, were placed on the sideboard. Right now, two empty bottles of Lafite '45 were standing on the sideboard for all to see.

"The wine you are drinking, sir," the butler said quietly, "happens to be that cheap and rather odious Spanish red."

Mr. Cleaver looked at the wine in his glass, then at the butler. The blood was coming to his face now, his skin was turning scarlet. "You're lying, Tibbs!" he said.

"No sir, I'm not lying," the butler said. "As a matter of fact, I have never served you any other wine but Spanish red since I've been here. It seemed to suit you very well."

"I don't believe him!" Mr. Cleaver cried out to his guests. "The man's gone mad."

"Great wines," the butler said, "should be treated with reverence. It is bad enough to destroy the palate with three or four cocktails before

---

① sediment: *Noun* [mass noun] matter that settles to the bottom of a liquid; dregs 沉淀物;渣滓

② decant: *Verb* [with obj.] gradually pour (wine, port, or another liquid) from one container into another, typically in order to separate the liquid from the sediment 慢慢倒出(酒等液体)(e.g. He decanted the rich red liquid into a pair of glasses. 他将醇红的酒慢慢倒入两个玻璃杯。)

③ cut-glass or cut glass: *Noun* [mass noun] glass that has been ornamented by having patterns cut into it by grinding and polishing 刻花玻璃

④ decanter: *Noun* a stoppered glass container into which wine or spirit is decanted 玻璃细颈酒瓶

dinner, as you people do, but when you slosh① vinegar over your food into the bargain②, then you might just as well be drinking dishwater."

Ten outraged faces around the table stared at the butler. He had caught them off balance③. They were speechless.

"This," the butler said, reaching out and touching one of the empty bottles lovingly with his fingers, "this is the last of the forty-fives. The twenty-nines have already been finished. But they were glorious wines. Monsieur Estragon and I enjoyed them immensely."

The butler bowed and walked quite slowly from the room. He crossed the hall and went out of the front door of the house into the street where Monsieur Estragon was already loading their suitcases into the boot of the small car which they owned together.

三、翻译探索

本篇小说的翻译中，除了一些有关葡萄酒品牌及产地方面的表达比较棘手之外，其他地方都比较容易处理。具体翻译中，可以在"雅"上以及风格的再现方面进行一番探索。

管家之谋

第一笔一百万一挣到手，乔治·克利弗就跟妻子克利弗太太一

---

① slosh: Verb [with obj. and adverbial of direction] pour (liquid) clumsily 笨拙地倒；泼溅；泼洒(e.g. She sloshed coffee into a cracked cup. 她笨手笨脚地把咖啡倒进了有裂纹的杯子。)

② into the bargain: in addition to what has been already mentioned or was expected 另外；而且还(e.g. I am now tired and extremely hungry—with a headache into the bargain. 我现在又累又饿，而且还头疼。)

③ catch/throw sb. off balance: make sb. surprised and no longer calm 使不知所措(e.g. The senator was clearly caught off balance by the unexpected question. 参议员显然被这个意想不到的问题弄得不知所措。)

起搬出郊区那座狭小的独立住宅,住进伦敦雅致考究的房子里。他们花重金雇了一位法国厨师埃斯特拉贡先生,还雇了一位英国管家,名字叫提伯斯。雇这两个人可是花了大价钱的。在这两位专业人士的扶持下,克利弗夫妇决心爬上社会的上层阶梯,于是开始以慷慨奢华的规模一周举行好几次晚宴聚会。

但是,这些晚会似乎从来都没有那么成功过,毫无生气,缺乏燃起交谈的火花,根本没有任何格调可言。然而,食品堪称一流,服务无懈可击。

"见鬼,提伯斯,我们的晚会问题出在什么地方?"克利弗先生问管家,"为什么从未有人无拘无束、畅所欲言过呢?"

提伯斯将头偏向一侧,眼睛看着天花板。"先生,我提一个小小的建议,希望你不会生气。"

"什么建议?"

"问题在酒,先生。"

"酒怎么了?"

"哦,先生,埃斯特拉贡先生做的食物堪称一流,一流的食品应该配上一流的葡萄酒,可是,你上的却是令人生厌的西班牙廉价红酒。"

"那么,你这个蠢货,为什么不早告诉我?"克利弗先生大叫。"我不缺钱。如果他们想喝好酒,我会为他们提供这个世界上最上等的好酒!世界上最好的酒是什么?"

"红葡萄酒,先生,"管家回答,"产自最伟大的波尔多地区的城堡酒庄——拉菲特酒庄、拉杜尔庄、奥比昂庄、玛歌庄、武当王庄以及白马庄,而且还得是在最大的年份生产的。依我看,是下列几个年份:1906、1914、1929 和 1945。白马庄 1895 年的和 1945 年的,以及奥比昂庄 1906 年的,也都很棒。"

"都买回来!"克利弗先生说。"把酒窖堆得满满的,从最底层堆到最顶层。"

"我可以试试,先生,"管家说。"可是,像这样的酒十分稀有,价格不菲。"

第三章 生财之道　第一节　《管家之谋》The Butler

"价格多少，我毫不在乎！"克利弗先生说，"只管去买回来就是！"

但是，这事儿说起来容易，做起来可就难了。全英国或者法国不论什么地方，提伯斯都找不到 1895 年、1906 年、1914 年或者 1921 年产的酒，但是，他还是设法买到了一些 1929 年以及 1945 年产的酒。即便是采购这样的酒，账单上的数字也是巨大的，以至于克利弗先生也端坐起来、开始关注了。管家向他建议说，了解点葡萄酒的知识是一笔很可观的社会财富。这时，他的兴趣才快速而彻底地转变成热情。克利弗先生买来一些有关这个主题的书，从头到尾读了起来。他也从提伯斯那儿学到了很多，而且最为重要的是，提伯斯教会他如何正确品酒。"先生，首先，将鼻子伸进杯子的顶部，长时间深深地吸入气味，就像这样。然后，喝一口，微微张开双唇，吸入空气，让空气冒着泡穿酒而过。看我是怎么做的。接着，让酒在嘴里使劲旋转，最后吞下。"

只要一有机会，克利弗先生就把自己当成了品酒专家，这样他也就不可避免地变成一个极其令人厌烦的人。"女士们、先生们，"晚宴上，他就会举起酒杯这样开场，"这是玛歌酒，1929 年的——本世纪最伟大的年份！芬芳四溢，美妙至极！闻起来有黄花九轮草的香气！特别注意其余味，还要注意一下微量丹宁酸所赋予那种美妙的苦涩品质！美妙无比，对吧？"

客人就会点头称是，小口品尝起来，嘟囔着赞扬几句，仅此而已。

"这些讨厌的蠢货是怎么回事儿？"一段时间过后，克利弗先生问提伯斯。"难道他们没有一个会赏识名酒的价值吗？"

管家将脑袋歪向一侧，眼睛盯向上方。"我想，他们会赏识到其价值的，先生，"他说，"那就必须具备这样的条件，使他们可以品尝到味道。但是，他们根本品尝不了。"

"他品尝不了？你说的到底是什么该死的意思？"

"先生，我相信你吩咐过埃斯特拉贡先生在色拉调味汁里放入了大量的醋。"

"这有什么不妥的吗？我喜欢吃醋。"

"醋，"管家说，"是酒的大敌，毁掉了味觉能力。调味汁应该用纯橄榄油加一点柠檬汁调制，其他的一概不需要。"

"胡诌八扯！"克利弗先生回应道。

"信不信由你，先生。"

"我再说一遍，提伯斯。你简直是胡诌八扯。醋一点儿都不会毁掉我的味觉能力。"

"你很幸运，先生，"管家低声说完就退出了房间。

那天晚上的宴会上，主人开始在客人面前嘲弄起管家来。"提比斯先生，"他说，"一直试图对我说，如果在色拉调味汁里放入醋，我就无法品尝葡萄酒了。对吗，提伯斯？"

"对的，先生，"提伯斯庄严地回答。

"而我却对他说，他简直是胡诌八扯。对吧，提伯斯？"

"对的，先生。"

"这种酒，"克利弗先生举起酒杯继续说，"对我而言，品尝起来极像拉斐特城堡酒庄1945年的酒，更进一步说，这种酒就是拉斐特城堡酒庄1945年的酒。"

身为管家的提伯斯一动不动地、笔直站在靠近餐具柜的地方，脸色苍白。"恕我冒昧，先生，"他说，"那酒不是1945年的拉斐特。"

克利弗从椅子上扭过身来，盯着管家。"你到底是何用意啊，"他说。"你旁边的那些空瓶子可以证明一切！"

这些很棒的红酒由于年份久而满是沉淀物，因而每次宴会开始前提伯斯总是先将它们倒入刻花玻璃高颈瓶以避开沉淀物。然后，用刻花玻璃高颈瓶给客人倒酒，而且一直的习惯是，空瓶子总是放到餐具柜上面。就在现在，两只1945年的拉斐特空瓶子竖立在餐具柜上，大家都能看得见。

"先生，现在你喝的酒，"管家安静地说，"恰恰就是那种令人生厌的西班牙廉价红酒。"

克利弗先生看了看自己杯中的酒，又看了看管家。现在，血液涌向了他的脸部,皮肤开始变得猩红。"你撒谎,提伯斯!"他说。

"不,先生,我没有撒谎,"管家回答。"事实上,自我来到之日起,除了西班牙红酒,我从未给你上过任何别的酒。这种酒似乎很合你的口味。"

"我不相信他说的话,"克利弗先生对着客人大声宣布。"这个家伙疯了。"

"出色的葡萄酒,"管家说,"应该受人敬重。晚宴前喝上三四杯鸡尾酒就足以将味觉功能毁掉,就像你们目前所做的一样。但是,更有甚者,要是蠢到将醋浇到食物表面的话,你们的酒喝起来跟洗碗水就没有什么差别了。"

餐桌四周十张愤慨的面孔盯着管家,他弄得大家不知所措,哑口无言。

"这种嘛,"管家说着,伸出手,手指深情地触摸着其中的一只空瓶子,"这种是1945年的最后一批了,1929年的早已喝完。它们都是值得称道的好酒,我跟埃斯特拉贡先生都喜欢喝,喜欢得不得了。"

管家鞠了一躬,十分缓慢地走出了房间。他穿过厅堂,走出房子的正门,来到大街上。在那儿,埃斯特拉贡先生已经将他们两个人的手提箱装进了那辆小车的行李箱。那辆小车是他们两个人共同出资购买的。

第二节 《卖伞男子》The Umbrella Man

罗尔德·达尔的《卖伞男子》(The Umbrella Man)被收录在《罗尔德·达尔短篇故事集锦》(The Collected Short Stories of Roald Dahl)《完全出人意料故事集》(Completely Unexpected Tales)《更多出人意料故事集》(More Tales of the Unexpected)《后续出人意料故事集》(Further Tales of the Unexpected)《〈伟大写手〉及其他故事集》(The Great Automatic Grammatizator and Other Stories)以及《〈卖伞男子〉及其他故

事集》(The Umbrella Man and Other Stories)等书中。此外,这部小说也被改编成电视系列剧——1980年5月10日播映的《出乎意料的故事集》(Tales of the Unexpected)第二部中的第11集(Episode 2.11),可见其影响力之大。

一、原作导读

这篇小说是以第一人称"我"(一个芳龄12岁的小女孩,姓名未交代)的视角展开的,但叙述者"我"是"隐身"的——地位是无足轻重的,属于"看热闹""围观"的类型,起到了"纽带"或者"桥梁"的作用。在这篇小说中,把"我"看成作家罗尔德·达尔本人的化身似乎很不合适,因为性别不一样,但可以把"我"看成是男扮女装的小达尔。这种"性别反串"也是很多中国古代男性诗人、词人惯用的"伎俩"——站在女性的角度写"闺怨"。

在伦敦,一位34岁的母亲领着自己12岁的女儿去看牙医,小女孩后牙漏了一个洞。补完牙洞,到咖啡店吃了点东西。走出咖啡店的时候大约是六点钟,天空下起雨来,但母女俩都没有带伞。她俩站在雨中,等待着出租车的到来。

就在这时,一名男子走上前来。他个子矮小,年龄相当大,或许有七十岁了,或许更大。他彬彬有礼地将帽子抬了抬,对母亲说:"请原谅,我真诚希望得到你的原谅……"

"嗯?"母亲问,显得很平静、很冷淡。

"我想知道,我能不能请求你帮我一个小忙,"他说,"只是一个小忙。"

Just then a man came up to us. He was a small man and he was pretty old, probably seventy or more. He raised his hat politely and said to my mother, "Excuse me, I do hope you will excuse me..."

"Yes?" my mother said, very cool and distant.

"I wonder if I could ask a small favour of you," he said. "It is only

第三章 生财之道 第二节 《卖伞男子》The Umbrella Man

a very small favour."

母亲生性多疑,警惕性很高,不轻易相信别人,特别是陌生人。小个子男子说,他把自己的钱包落家里了,要把自己那把伞(价值二十多英镑)给她,而她只需给他一英镑让他能够打车回家就可以了。母亲觉得这笔交易十分划算,而小女孩却说母亲"趁火打劫",于是,母亲决定不要雨伞而只给那名男子打车费,但那名男子死活不干。最终,母亲"如愿以偿",得到了雨伞,付给对方一英镑,可谓"皆大欢喜"。

母亲自豪地向自己的女儿炫耀自己判断好人、坏人的"智慧"是多么得高。小女儿一边听着,一边看着那名男子快速穿过大街,匆忙离开,不像是要打出租车的样子。

"他有什么事儿要去忙的,"母亲面无表情地说道。
"可是,忙什么事儿呢?"
"我不知道,"母亲气恼地说,"但是,我要弄个水落石出。跟我来。"她拉起我的胳膊,我们一起穿过了大街,然后向左拐。
"He's up to something," my mother said, stony-faced.
"But what?"
"I don't know," my mother snapped①. "But I'm going to find out. Come with me." She took my arm and we crossed the street together. Then we turned left.

母女俩跟踪那名男子,一直跟到了"红狮酒馆"。男子进了酒馆,母女俩则透过窗户向里观看:男子用卖伞而得到的一英镑买了一份威士忌,一饮而尽,然后就要离开酒馆。

---

① snap: *Verb* [reporting verb] say something quickly and irritably to someone 急促地说;怒声说

他慢慢地转身,离开了吧台,缓缓地挤过人群,移向他挂帽子和外衣的地方。随即,他戴上帽子,穿好外衣。然后,他镇定自若却又漫不经心地从那儿悬挂着很多雨伞的衣帽架上取下一把雨伞就离开了。他的这一举动,你几乎无法察觉得到。

Slowly, he turned away from the bar and edged his way back through the crowd to where his hat and coat were hanging. He put on his hat. He put on his coat. Then, in a manner so superbly cool and casual that you hardly noticed anything at all, he lifted from the coat-rack one of the many wet umbrellas hanging there, and off he went.

二、原作释读

这是一篇短小精悍、通俗流畅的小说,没有过多的词汇障碍,阅读起来比较通畅,给人一种淋漓尽致、一气呵成的感觉。

The Umbrella Man[①]

I'm going to tell you about a funny thing that happened to my mother and me yesterday evening. I am twelve years old and I'm a girl. My mother is thirty-four but I am nearly as tall as her already.

Yesterday afternoon, my mother took me up to London to see the dentist. He found one hole. It was in a back tooth and he filled it without hurting me too much. After that, we went to a café. I had a banana split[②] and my mother had a cup of coffee. By the time we got up to leave it was about six o'clock.

---

① 本部小说原文出自 "Roald Dahl. *The Collected Short Stories of Roald Dahl* [M]. England: Penguin Books Ltd., 1992"。

② split: a dessert of sliced fruit, ice cream, and toppings 水果片;冰淇淋

第三章 生财之道 第二节 《卖伞男子》The Umbrella Man

When we came out of the café it had started to rain. "We must get a taxi," my mother said. We were wearing ordinary hats and coats, and it was raining quite hard.

"Why don't we go back into the café and wait for it to stop?" I said. I wanted another of those banana splits. They were gorgeous.

"It isn't going to stop," my mother said. "We must get home."

We stood on the pavement in the rain, looking for a taxi. Lots of them came by but they all had passengers inside them. "I wish we had a car with a chauffeur①," my mother said.

Just then a man came up to us. He was a small man and he was pretty old, probably seventy or more. He raised his hat politely and said to my mother, "Excuse me, I do hope you will excuse me..." He had a fine white moustache and bushy white eyebrows and a wrinkly② pink face. He was sheltering under an umbrella which he held high over his head.

"Yes?" my mother said, very cool and distant.

"I wonder if I could ask a small favour of you," he said. "It is only a very small favour."

I saw my mother looking at him suspiciously. She is a suspicious person, my mother. She is especially suspicious of two things—strange men and boiled eggs. When she cuts the top off a boiled egg, she pokes around inside it with her spoon as though expecting to find a mouse or something. With strange men, she has a golden rule which says, "The nicer the man seems to be, the more suspicious you must become." This little old man was particularly nice. He was polite. He was well-spoken.

---

① chauffeur: *Noun* a person employed to drive a private or hired motor car 受雇于人的汽车司机

② wrinkly: *Adjective* having many lines or folds 皱的;有皱纹的

He was well-dressed. He was a real gentleman. The reason I knew he was a gentleman was because of his shoes. "You can always spot a gentleman by the shoes he wears," was another of my mother's favourite sayings. This man had beautiful brown shoes.

"The truth of the matter is," the little man was saying, "I've got myself into a bit of a scrape①. I need some help. Not much I assure you. It's almost nothing, in fact, but I do need it. You see, madam, old people like me often become terribly forgetful..."

My mother's chin was up and she was staring down at him along the full length of her nose. It was a fearsome thing, this frosty-nosed stare of my mother's. Most people go to pieces completely when she gives it to them. I once saw my own headmistress② begin to stammer③ and simper④ like an idiot when my mother gave her a really foul⑤ frosty-noser. But the

---

① scrape: Noun (informal) an embarrassing or difficult predicament caused by one's own unwise behaviour(非正式用法)窘境;困境(e.g. He'd been in worse scrapes than this before now. 他以前过得比现在更困难。)

② headmistress: Noun (chiefly Brit.) a woman who is the head teacher in a school(主要为英国英语用法)女校长

③ stammer: Verb [no obj.] speak with sudden involuntary pauses and a tendency to repeat the initial letters of words 结结巴巴地说话;结巴

④ simper: Verb [no obj.] smile or gesture in an affectedly coquettish, coy, or ingratiating manner 媚笑;假笑;忸怩作态(e.g. She simpered, looking pleased with herself. 她一脸假笑,看上去沾沾自喜。)

⑤ foul: Adjective (informal) very disagreeable or unpleasant(非正式用法) 非常不愉快的;讨厌的(e.g. The news had put Michelle in a foul mood. 这消息让米歇尔心情很坏。)

第三章 生财之道 第二节 《卖伞男子》The Umbrella Man

little man on the pavement with the umbrella over his head didn't bat① an eyelid. He gave a gentle smile and said, "I beg you to believe, madam, that I am not in the habit of stopping ladies in the street and telling them my troubles."

"I should hope not," my mother said.

I felt quite embarrassed by my mother's sharpness. I wanted to say to her, "Oh, mummy, for heaven's sake, he's a very very old man, and he's sweet and polite, and he's in some sort of trouble, so don't be so beastly② to him." But I didn't say anything.

The little man shifted his umbrella from one hand to the other. "I've never forgotten it before," he said.

"You've never forgotten what?" my mother asked sternly③.

"My wallet," he said. "I must have left it in my other jacket. Isn't that the silliest thing to do?"

"Are you asking me to give you money?" my mother said.

"Oh, good gracious me, no!" he cried. "Heaven forbid I should ever do that!"

"Then what *are* you asking?" my mother said. "Do hurry up. We're getting soaked to the skin here."

"I know you are," he said. "And that is why I'm offering you this umbrella of mine to protect you, and to keep forever, if... if only..."

---

① bat: *Verb* [with obj.] flutter (one's eyelashes), typically in a flirtatious manner(尤指轻浮地)眨(眼)(e.g. She batted her long dark eyelashes at him. 她冲着他扑闪着又长又黑的睫毛。)

② beastly: *Adjective* unkind; malicious 不友善的;险恶的;恶毒的

③ stern: *Adjective* (of a person or their manner) serious and unrelenting, especially in the assertion of authority and exercise of discipline(人或其态度)严厉的;认真的;不屈从的

"If only what?" my mother said.

"If only you would give me in return a pound for my taxi-fare just to get me home."

My mother was still suspicious. "If you had no money in the first place," she said, "then how did you get here?"

"I walked," he answered. "Every day I go for a lovely long walk and then I summon a taxi to take me home. I do it every day of the year."

"Why don't you walk home now?" my mother asked.

"Oh, I wish I could," he said. "I do wish I could. But I don't think I could manage it on these silly old legs of mine. I've gone too far already."

My mother stood there chewing her lower lip. She was beginning to melt① a bit, I could see that. And the idea of getting an umbrella to shelter under must have tempted her a good deal.

"It's a lovely umbrella," the little man said.

"So I've noticed," my mother said.

"It's silk," he said.

"I can see that."

"Then why don't you take it, madam," he said. "It cost me over twenty pounds, I promise you. But that's of no importance so long as I can get home and rest these old legs of mine."

I saw my mother's hand feeling for the clasp② of her purse. She saw

---

① melt: Verb become more tender or loving 心软化; 心柔化 (e.g. She was so beautiful that I melted. 她是如此美丽以致我心生柔情。)

② clasp: Noun a device with interlocking parts used for fastening things together 搭扣; 扣钩; 扣紧物 (e.g. a gold bracelet with a turquoise clasp 绿松石搭扣的金镯子)

第三章 生财之道 第二节 《卖伞男子》The Umbrella Man

me watching her. I was giving her one of my *own* frosty-nosed looks this time and she knew exactly what I was telling her. Now listen, mummy, I was telling her, you simply *mustn't* take advantage of a tired old man in this way. It's a rotten thing to do. My mother paused and looked back at me. Then she said to the little man, "I don't think it's quite right that I should take an umbrella from you worth twenty pounds. I think I'd better just *give* you the taxi-fare and be done with it."

"No, no no!" he cried. "It's out of the question! I wouldn't dream of it! Not in a million years! I would never accept money from you like that! Take the umbrella, dear lady, and keep the rain off your shoulders!"

My mother gave me a triumphant sideways look. There you are, she was telling me. You're wrong. He *wants* me to have it.

She fished into her purse and took out a pound note. She held it out to the little man. He took it and handed her the umbrella. He pocketed the pound, raised his hat, gave a quick bow from the waist, and said, "Thank you, madam, thank you." Then he was gone.

"Come under here and keep dry, darling," my mother said. "Aren't we lucky. I've never had a silk umbrella before. I couldn't afford it."

"Why were you so horrid to him in the beginning?" I asked.

"I wanted to satisfy① myself he wasn't a trickster②," she said. "And I did. He was a gentleman. I'm very pleased I was able to help him."

"Yes, mummy," I said.

---

① satisfy: *Verb* provide (someone) with adequate information or proof so that they are convinced about something 使确信;向……证实

② trickster: *Noun* a person who cheats or deceives people 骗子

"A *real* gentleman," she went on. "Wealthy, too, otherwise he wouldn't have had a silk umbrella. I shouldn't be surprised if he isn't a titled① person. Sir Harry Goldsworthy or something like that."

"Yes, mummy."

"This will be a good lesson to you," she went on. "Never rush things. Always take your time when you are summing someone up②. Then you'll never make mistakes."

"There he goes," I said. "Look."

"Where?"

"Over there. He's crossing the street. Goodness, mummy, what a hurry he's in."

We watched the little man as he dodged③ nimbly in and out of the traffic. When he reached the other side of the street, he turned left, walking very fast.

"He doesn't look very tired to me, does he to you, mummy?"

My mother didn't answer.

"He doesn't look as though he's trying to get a taxi, either," I said.

My mother was standing very still and stiff, staring across the street at the little man. We could see him clearly. He was in a terrific hurry.

---

① titled: *Adjective* having a title, especially a noble title 有头衔的;有爵位的

② sum sb./sth. up: (as sb./sth.) to decide or express what you think about sb./sth. 估量;判断(人或事物);视某人(或事物)为……(e.g. He had already summed her up as someone who hated to admit defeat. 他已经把她归为那种不愿认输的人。)

③ dodge: *Verb* [no obj., with adverbial of direction] move quickly to one side or out of the way 闪开;迅速让开(e.g. Adam dodged between the cars. 亚当在汽车间躲来闪去。)

第三章　生财之道　第二节　《卖伞男子》The Umbrella Man

He was bustling① along the pavement, sidestepping② the other pedestrians and swinging his arms like a soldier on the march.

"He's up to something," my mother said, stony-faced.

"But what?"

"I don't know," my mother snapped③. "But I'm going to find out. Come with me." She took my arm and we crossed the street together. Then we turned left.

"Can you see him?" my mother asked.

"Yes. There he is. He's turning right down the next street." We came to the corner and turned right. The little man was about twenty yards ahead of us. He was scuttling④ along like a rabbit and we had to walk very fast to keep up with him. The rain was pelting⑤ down harder than ever now and I could see it dripping from the brim of his hat on to

---

① bustle: Verb [no obj., with adverbial of direction] move in an energetic or noisy manner 匆匆忙忙地走;奔忙(e. g. People clutching clipboards bustled about. 手拿笔记板的人四处奔忙。)

② sidestep: Verb [with obj.] avoid (someone or something) by stepping sideways 侧步避开;横跨步避开(e. g. he sidestepped a defender and crossed the ball. 他横步避开防守队员,将球带过。)

③ snap: Verb [reporting verb] say something quickly and irritably to someone 急促地说;怒声说

④ scuttle: Verb [no obj., with adverbial of direction] run hurriedly or furtively with short quick steps 急赶;疾走(e. g. A mouse scuttled across the floor. 一只老鼠在地板上急溜溜地跑了过去。)

⑤ pelt: Verb [no obj.] (pelt down) (of rain, hail, or snow) fall quickly and very heavily(雨、冰雹或雪)下得很大;猛降

his shoulders. But we were snug① and dry under our lovely big silk umbrella.

"What *is* he up to?" my mother said.

"What if he turns round and sees us?" I asked.

"I don't care if he does," my mother said. "He lied to us. He said he was too tired to walk any further and he's practically running us off our feet! He's a barefaced② liar! He's a crook!"

"You mean he's *not* a titled gentleman?" I asked.

"Be quiet," she said.

At the next crossing, the little man turned right again.

Then he turned left.

Then right.

"I'm not giving up now," my mother said.

"He's disappeared!" I cried. "Where's he gone?"

"He went in that door!" my mother said. "I saw him! Into that house! Great heavens, it's a pub!"

It was a pub. In big letters right across the front it said THE RED LION.

"You're not going in are you, mummy?"

"No," she said. "We'll watch from outside."

There was a big plate-glass③ window along the front of the pub, and

---

① snug: *Adjective* comfortable, warm, and cosy; well protected from the weather or cold 温暖舒适的;不受天气(或寒冷)侵袭的(e.g. She was safe and snug in Ruth's arms. 她躺在罗斯的臂弯里,既安全,又温馨。)

② barefaced: *Adjective* shameless and undisguised 厚颜无耻的;公然露骨的

③ plate-glass or plate glass: *Noun* [mass noun] [often as modifier] thick fine-quality glass, typically used for shop windows and doors and originally cast in plates(尤指用于做橱窗和门的)平板玻璃

although it was a bit steamy on the inside, we could see through it very well if we went close.

We stood huddled together outside the pub window. I was clutching my mother's arm. The big raindrops were making a loud noise on our umbrella. "There he is," I said. "Over there."

The room we were looking into was full of people and cigarette smoke, and our little man was in the middle of it all. He was now without his hat and coat, and he was edging his way through the crowd towards the bar. When he reached it, he placed both hands on the bar itself and spoke to the barman. I saw his lips moving as he gave his order. The barman turned away from him for a few seconds and came back with a smallish tumbler① filled to the brim with light brown liquid. The little man placed a pound note on the counter.

"That's my pound!" my mother hissed②. "By golly③, he's got a nerve!"

"What's in the glass?" I asked.

"Whisky," my mother said. "Neat④ whisky."

The barman didn't give him any change from the pound.

---

① tumbler: *Noun* a drinking glass with straight sides and no handle or stem 平底酒杯(边面平直,无柄无脚)

② hiss: *Verb* [reporting verb] whisper something in an urgent or angry way (紧急或生气地)小声说

③ golly: *Exclamation* (informal, dated) used to express surprise or delight (非正式的古旧用法)啊;天呐(表示吃惊或高兴)

④ neat: *Adjective* (of liquid, especially spirits) not diluted or mixed with anything else(液体,尤指烈酒)纯的;清一的;净的(e.g. He drank neat Scotch. 他喝纯苏格兰威士忌。)

"That must be a treble① whisky," my mummy said.

"What's a treble?" I asked.

"Three times the normal measure," she answered.

The little man picked up the glass and put it to his lips. He tilted it gently. Then he tilted it higher... and higher... and higher... and very soon all the whisky had disappeared down his throat in one long pour.

"That's a jolly② expensive drink," I said.

"It's ridiculous!" my mummy said. "Fancy③ paying a pound for something to swallow in one go!"

"It cost him more than a pound," I said. "It cost him a twenty-pound silk umbrella."

"So it did," my mother said. "He must be mad."

The little man was standing by the bar with the empty glass in his hand. He was smiling now, and a sort of golden glow of pleasure was spreading over his round pink face. I saw his tongue come out to lick the white moustache, as though searching for one last drop of that precious whisky.

Slowly, he turned away from the bar and edged his way back through the crowd to where his hat and coat were hanging. He put on his hat. He put on his coat. Then, in a manner so superbly cool and casual

---

① treble: *Noun* a drink of spirits of three times the standard measure(一杯)三倍分量的酒

② jolly: *Adverb* [as submodifier] (Brit. informal) very; extremely(主要为英国英语非正式用法)非常;很;极

③ fancy: *Verb* [in imperative] used to express one's surprise at something(用以表示惊奇)居然(e.g. Fancy meeting all those television actors! 居然能见到那么多电视演员!)

第三章 生财之道 第二节 《卖伞男子》The Umbrella Man

that you hardly noticed anything at all, he lifted from the coat-rack one of the many wet umbrellas hanging there, and off he went.

"Did you see that!" my mother shrieked. "Did you see what he did!"

"Ssshh!" I whispered. "He's coming out!"

We lowered our umbrella to hide our faces, and peered out from under it.

Out he came. But he never looked in our direction. He opened his new umbrella over his head and scurried① off down the road the way he had come.

"So that's his little game!" my mother said.

"Neat②," I said. "Super."

We followed him back to the main street where we had first met him, and we watched him as he proceeded, with no trouble at all, to exchange his new umbrella for another pound note. This time it was with a tall thin fellow who didn't even have a coat or hat. And as soon as the transaction was completed, our little man trotted③ off down the street and was lost in the crowd. But this time he went in the opposite direction.

"You see how clever he is!" my mother said. "He never goes to the same pub twice!"

"He could go on doing this all night," I said.

---

① scurry: *Verb* [no obj., with adverbial of direction] (of a person or small animal) move hurriedly with short quick steps(人或小动物)小步快跑(e. g. Pedestrians scurried for cover. 行人小跑步寻找躲避之处。)

② neat: *Adjective* done with or demonstrating skill or efficiency 干净利落的(e. g. Hapgood's neat, precise tackling 哈普戈德干净利落、恰到好处的阻截)

③ trot: *Verb* [no obj., with adverbial of direction] (informal) go or walk briskly(非正式)快步走;轻快地走

"Yes," my mother said. "Of course. But I'll bet he prays like mad for rainy days."

三、翻译探索

本篇小说的翻译中,基本不会遇到什么难点,可以很顺畅地加以表达。具体翻译时,可以将注意力放到"忠实"和"通顺"这两点上,并在汉语的流畅性方面多做探索。

卖伞男子

我要跟你讲述一件有趣儿的事情,这件事儿昨晚就发生在我和我母亲身上。我是一个女孩,十二岁了。我母亲三十四岁,但是,我几乎已经和母亲一般高了。

昨天下午,我母亲带着我去伦敦市中心看牙医。牙医在我的后牙发现了一个洞。随后,他将洞填上,我没感觉太疼。补完牙,我们去了一家咖啡店,我要了一份香蕉冰淇淋,母亲要了一杯咖啡。起身离开的时候,大约是六点钟的光景。

我们一走出咖啡店,天就下起雨来。"我们必须得打辆出租车,"母亲说道。雨下得相当大,而我们穿戴的都是些普通的衣帽。

"我们俩为什么不返回咖啡店,等着雨停呢?"我问。我其实是想再吃一份香蕉冰淇淋,味道棒极了。

"雨不会停的,"母亲回答,"我们必须得赶回家。"

在雨中,我们俩站在人行道上,眼睛瞅着出租车。有很多出租车经过,但是,里面都有乘客。"我真希望,我们能拥有一辆专职司机开的小汽车,"母亲感叹道。

就在这时,一名男子走上前来。他个子矮小,年龄相当大,或许有七十岁了,或许更大。他彬彬有礼地将帽子抬了抬,对母亲说:"请原谅,我真诚希望得到您的原谅……"他留着整齐的白色胡须,白色的眉毛很是浓密,满是皱纹的脸呈粉红色。他将一把雨伞高高举过头顶,整个人站在伞下。

第三章 生财之道 第二节 《卖伞男子》The Umbrella Man

"嗯?"母亲问,显得很平静、很冷淡。

"我想知道,我能不能请求您帮我一个小忙,"他说,"只是一个小忙。"

我看见母亲用怀疑的眼神看着他。她是一个多疑的人,我是说我的母亲。她对两类人或事特别持有怀疑的态度——其中之一是陌生的男子,另外一个就是煮熟的鸡蛋。她将熟鸡蛋顶部切开,用勺子往里面戳,就好像期望从中找出老鼠之类的东西似的。对于陌生的男子,她坚守一条金科玉律,那就是:"男子看起来越友善,你就越要加以怀疑。"眼下,这位小个子的年迈男子特别友善,彬彬有礼。他说起话来文绉绉的,而且,穿戴讲究,真是具有绅士风度。我之所以说他具有绅士风度,是因为他脚上穿的那双鞋。"看男子脚上穿的鞋,你总是能够判断出他是不是一位绅士,"这是母亲最喜欢说的另一句话。这位男子脚上穿的是一双漂亮的棕色鞋子。

"事情是这样的,"小个子男子说道,"我自己陷入一种窘迫的境地,需要某种帮助。我向你保证,就一个小忙。事实上,这个忙小得几乎不算什么事儿,但是,我需要有人帮我这个小忙。您知道,尊贵的女士,像我这样上了年纪的人总是很健忘,甚至……"

我母亲的下巴撅了起来,眼睛顺着自己的鼻子看向这名男子。这是一件可怕的事情,我是指母亲顺着鼻子看人那种冷若冰霜的架势。这样的眼神盯人看,多数人当场就会完全崩溃的。有一次,母亲用这种冷若冰霜的眼神盯向我就读的那所学校的女校长,着实令人不快。当时我发现,校长说话开始结结巴巴,呆傻般痴笑起来。但是,头上举着一把雨伞站在人行道上的这位小个子男子,连眼皮也没动一下,只是轻柔一笑,说道:"尊贵的女士,我请求您相信,我并没有这样的习惯:在大街上拦住女士不放,向她倾诉自己的烦恼。"

"我希望不是,"母亲说。

对于母亲的尖刻态度,我颇感难为情,很想对她说:"哦,妈咪,看在老天的份上,他年纪很大、很大了,但友善又有礼貌。他遇到什么麻烦事儿了,不要对他如此不友善啦。"可是,我什么都没有说出来。

小个子男子将伞从一只手换到了另一只手。"这种东西,我以前从未忘记过,"他说。

"从未忘记过什么东西?"母亲厉声问道。

"我的钱包,"他说,"我一定是将钱包落在另一件短上衣里了。这事儿做得难道不是最为愚蠢的吗?"

"你是要冲我要钱吗?"母亲问。

"噢,老天哪,不!"他叫道,"我要是伸手要钱,苍天不容啊!"

"那么,你到底要什么?"母亲又问,"赶快说吧。我们在这儿站着,快要湿透了。"

"这个我知道,"他说,"所以嘛,我就为你们提供我自己的这把雨伞,使你们免受雨淋,雨伞你们就留着,如果……如果只需……"

"如果只需什么?"母亲问。

"作为回报,如果你只需付给我一英镑,我刚好可用来打出租车回家。"

母亲仍然心存疑虑。"首先,如果说你没有钱的话,"母亲说,"那么,你是怎么到这里的?"

"我走来的,"他回答,"每天我都步行很长一段距离,感觉很好,然后,我就招手打辆出租车回家。这一年中,我每天都是这样做的。"

"现在,你为什么不步行回家呢?"母亲问。

"噢,我希望我能走得动,"他说,"我多么希望我能走得动啊。可是,我想,我这两条不中用的老腿,恐怕是走不回去的。我已经走得太远了。"

我母亲站在原地,咬着自己的下嘴唇。她的心开始有点软化了,这一点,我看得出来。她很想得到一把伞用来遮雨,这个想法肯定对她有着极大的诱惑力。

"这把雨伞真不赖,"小个子男子说道。

"这我注意到了,"母亲回应。

"是*丝绸*的,"他说。

"我看得出来。"

第三章 生财之道 第二节 《卖伞男子》The Umbrella Man

"那么,尊贵的女士,为什么不买走呢?"他说,"我当时花了二十多英镑呢,这一点我向你保证。可是,只要我能回到家,让我这双老腿好好休息一下,那些钱就无关紧要了。"

我看见母亲的一只手往自己钱包的搭扣上摸去,她同时也看见我正看着她。这一次,我顺着自己的鼻子向母亲投以冷若冰霜的眼神,她十分清楚我要说的是什么。我似乎对她说:现在听着,妈咪,你千万不能这样利用一位疲乏的老人。这样做,就是腐化堕落的表现。于是,母亲停了一下,回看了我一眼。然后,她对老人说:"我想,要是买下你这把价值二十英镑的雨伞,我做得就不合适了。我想,我最好把打车费给你,就完事了。"

"不,不,不!"他叫道,"那是不可能的!我做梦也不想那样做!海枯石烂,我也不会那样做!我永远都不会像那样收下你的钱!拿走雨伞,亲爱的女士,别让雨淋湿你的双肩!"

母亲侧眼看了我一下,露出胜利的表情,似乎对我说:看到了吧,你错了,是他硬要我买的。

她将手伸进钱包,摸出一张一英镑的钞票,伸手递给了小个子男子。他接过钱,将伞递给她。然后,他将钱揣好,抬了抬帽子,身体快速从腰部向前一弯,鞠了一躬,说道:"谢谢您,尊贵的女士,谢谢您。"随后,他就走开了。

"亲爱的,到伞底下来,别再挨浇了,"母亲说,"我们太走运啦。我以前从未买过丝绸雨伞,买不起啊。"

"一开始,你对他为什么那么反感呢?"我问。

"我想证实,他不是一个骗子,"她回答,"我得到证实了,他是位正人君子。能帮上他,我很开心。"

"没错,妈咪,"我说。

"真是位正人君子,"她继续说,"也很有钱,否则,他就不会买丝绸雨伞了。就算他没有什么头衔——类似于哈里·戈兹沃西爵士这样的头衔,我也不会感到意外的。"

"没错,妈咪。"

"这件事也给你上了一堂示范课,"她继续说,"做什么事,永远都不要操之过急。判断一个人的好坏,总是要慢慢来。这样,你就永远不会犯错误。"

"他去那儿啦,"我说,"看啊。"

"哪儿?"

"就在那边。正穿过大街。我的天哪,妈咪,看他那匆匆忙忙的样子。"

我们看着那个小个子男子在车流中机敏地躲闪腾挪。到达大街对面后,他就向左转,飞快地走远。

"在我看来,他不是那么疲惫,妈咪,你看呢?"

母亲没有回答。

"看起来,他好像也不想打出租车了,"我说。

母亲一动不动,直挺挺地站立着,眼睛盯着大街对面的那位小个子男子。我们看得清清楚楚,他在匆忙地奔走。他沿着人行道匆匆而行,大步横跨避开其他行人。甩开双臂,如同士兵般迈步前进。

"他有什么事儿要去忙的,"母亲面无表情地说道。

"可是,忙什么事儿呢?"

"我不知道,"母亲气恼地说,"但是,我要弄个水落石出。跟我来。"她拉起我的胳膊,我们一起穿过了大街,然后向左拐。

"你看见他了吗?"母亲问。

"看见了,在那儿。他向右转,沿着下一条大街走了。"

我们来到街角,右转。小个子男子在我们前方不到二十米的地方,步履匆匆,走得很快,我们不得不加快脚步才能跟得上。雨下得很大,落得很急,比刚才大多了。我可以看见,雨水顺着他帽子的边缘滴落,落到他的双肩,然而,我们俩在这把大大的丝绸雨伞的庇护下,感到舒适无比、干爽自在。

"他要去忙什么?"母亲问。

"要是他转过身,看见我们,怎么办?"我问。

"看见了,我也不在乎,"母亲说,"谁叫他跟我们撒谎呢。他方才说自己太疲乏,走不动了,而实际上,他把我们俩的腿都要跑掉了。他厚颜无耻地撒谎!就是一个骗子!"

"你的意思是说,他不是一位有头衔的绅士吗?"我问。

"安静,"她说。

在下一个十字路口,小个子男子又向右转去。

接着,他转向左。

接着,向右转。

"现在,我不会放弃的,"母亲说。

"他消失不见啦!"我叫道,"他去哪儿了?"

"他从那扇门进去了!"母亲说,"我看到他了!进入了那所房子!老天哪,那是一家酒馆!"

那确实是一家酒馆。横跨房子的前脸,有几个大字:"红狮酒馆"。

"你不会进去吧,对吗,妈咪?"

"不进去,"她回答,"我们从外面观察。"

酒馆的前脸有一大块厚玻璃做成的窗户。尽管酒馆里面有点雾气,但是,只要靠近观看,里面的一切可以看得清清楚楚。

在窗户的外边,我们俩挤在一起站立着,我紧紧抓住母亲的一只胳膊。此时,大大的雨滴滴落到雨伞上,发出响亮的声音。"他在那儿,"我说,"就在那边。"

我们从外边往里看,屋子里挤满了人,弥漫着香烟的雾气。我们跟踪的那个小个子男子就在屋子的正中央。现在,他既没戴帽子,也没穿外衣,正穿过人群缓缓地往吧台那儿挤去。挤到吧台之后,他将双手放到台面上,冲着吧台男侍者说话。我看见他嘴唇动来动去,点着要喝的东西。男侍者随即转过身去离开,几秒钟后又返回,手里拿着一只体积稍小一点的平底玻璃杯,里面淡棕色的液体一直漫到杯子的边缘。小个子男子将一英镑纸币放到了柜台上。

"那是我的一英镑啊!"母亲放低声音说道,"天哪,他可真够大胆无耻的啦!"

"杯子里装的是什么?"我问。

"威士忌,"母亲回答,"不掺水的威士忌。"

男侍者收下一英镑,一点儿零钱也没有往回找。

"那一定是三倍量的威士忌,"母亲说。

"什么叫三倍量?"我问。

"正常一份威士忌三倍的量,"她回答。

小个子男子将酒杯端起,放到唇边,轻轻地倾斜酒杯。然后,他将酒杯更加倾斜地上仰……越仰越高……越仰越高……很快,整杯威士忌在他这一次性的不间断倾倒之下,顺着喉咙流下,消失不见了。

"那一杯可是价格不菲啊,"我说,"真是荒谬!"母亲说道,"居然将一英镑买的酒一口喝个精光!"

"他花掉的不止一英镑呢,"我说,"他花掉的是一把二十英镑的雨伞的钱。"

"的确如此,"母亲说,"他一定是疯啦。"

小个子男子站在吧台旁边,手里握着一只杯子,杯子里空空如也。现在,他微笑起来,整张粉红色的圆脸上闪现出一种喜悦的金色光芒。我看见,他将舌头伸了出来,舔了舔白色的胡须,好像是在寻找最后一滴残留下来的宝贵的威士忌。

他慢慢地转身,离开了吧台,缓缓地挤过人群,移向他挂帽子和外衣的地方。随即,他戴上帽子,穿好外衣。然后,他镇定自若却又漫不经心地从那儿悬挂着很多雨伞的衣帽架上取下一把雨伞就离开了。他的这一举动,你几乎无法察觉得到。

"你看到没有哪!"母亲尖声叫道,"你看到他的所作所为吧!"

"嘘!"我低声说,"他出来啦!"

我们将雨伞放低,遮住我们的脸,透过底边向外观瞧。

他跨出门来。可是,他根本没朝我们这边看。他打开新拿的雨伞,举过头顶,沿着马路快步而去,就像他来的时候走路的那个样子。

"这就是他的小把戏啦!"母亲说。

第三章 生财之道 第二节 《卖伞男子》The Umbrella Man

"干净利落,"我说,"超级漂亮。"

我们尾随着他回到了主大街我们最初相遇的地方。他一边行事,我们一边观察着:不费吹灰之力,他就将这把新伞又换成一英镑钞票。这次,他卖的对象是一个高个子的瘦家伙,这个家伙甚至连外衣都没穿,帽子也没戴。交易一结束,我们跟踪的这位小个子男子就加快脚步沿着大街走去,消失在人海之中。可是,这一次,他走的却是相反的方向。

"你看到了吧,他多么聪明啊!"母亲说。"同一家酒馆,他从不去第二次!"

"整个晚上,他可以一直做下去,"我说。

"没错,"母亲说,"当然没错的。可是,我敢打赌,他会发疯似地祈求下雨天的到来。"

第四章 人生之路

人生之路漫漫,功成名就难见。
还需努力进取,不负苦心一片。

现代汉语中,"功成名就"这一成语应该是演变自"功成名遂"。《墨子·修身》有语云:"名不徒生,而誉不自长,功成名遂,名誉不可虚假①。"功绩建立起来,名声也就随之而来,可谓水到渠成。看来,功与名是相辅相成的,"功成"则"名"自来,"名遂"或"名就"则在于"功成"。

人生之路漫漫,功名的取得不是一蹴而就的,也不是一朝一夕的事情,而是要经过一番艰苦的拼搏。其间,酸甜苦辣咸,五味杂陈,而功成名就者,当属最终尝到甜蜜滋味的人,正所谓"宝剑锋从磨砺出,梅花香自苦寒来"(古代无名氏《警世贤文·勤奋篇》)。这期间也不乏各种感慨:"三十功名尘与土,八千里路云和月"(宋代岳飞②《满江红·怒发冲冠》)"功名富贵若长在,汉水亦应西北流③"(唐代李白

---

① 转引自"商务印书馆辞书研究中心,2002:246"。
② 这首词是否系岳飞所作,存在争议。本书视之为岳飞所作。
③ 转引自《全唐诗》第166卷第003首。

《江上吟》)"功名富贵须待命,命若不来知奈何①"(唐代白居易《浩歌行》)"回首功名一梦中②"(宋代陆游《渔父·灯下读玄真子渔歌因怀山阴故隐追拟》)"鬓底青春留不住。功名薄似风前絮。何似瓮头春没数③"(宋代毛滂《渔家傲·鬓底青春留不住》)等。所以说,一生之中,还需努力进取,不负苦心一片。

英国作家罗尔德·达尔的人生之路,可谓曲折、坎坷,如同他某些短篇小说中的情节。然而,功夫不负有心人,达尔最终功成名就,也是经历了类似的过程,所不同的是,他有了一个"幸运开局"。在中国人常说的"万事开头难"的情况下,可以说,达尔开了个好头,可谓"Well-begun is half done",但是功成名就之前,他也走过一段艰辛之路。

那么,就让我们走进罗尔德·达尔的世界,去探寻人生之路的秘诀吧。

第一节 《幸运开局》(上部) Lucky Break (Part A)

罗尔德·达尔的《幸运开局》(Lucky Break)收录在《〈非凡亨利〉及另外六篇故事集》(The Wonderful Story of Henry Sugar and Six More)一书中④。这个故事开篇前,作者加上了一句类似于副标题的话:"我成为作家的前前后后"(How I Became a Writer),可见这不是

---

① 转引自《全唐诗》第435卷第003首。
② 转引自"中华诗库"网站,网址:http://www.shiku.org/。
③ 转引自"古诗文网",网址:http://so.gushiwen.org/。
④ 这部分信息以及本书以后此类部分中的资料都借鉴了克里斯廷·霍华德(Kristine Howard)创建并维护的网站"Roald Dahl Fans.com"(罗尔德·达尔粉丝网)中的部分信息,网址为:http://www.roalddahlfans.com/,由著者翻译整理。以后各章的此部分信息,若没特殊标明,其出处同此。

一篇"纯粹"的小说,而是达尔给读者提出的一些如何成为作家的意见和建议,此外还有达尔如何成为作家的一些个人的"奇闻轶事"以及他写过的小说中涉及的一些情节的"摘要"。可以说,《幸运开局》更像是一篇"意识流"式的、具有个人片段回忆的"传记"性的论说文。

一、原作导读

这篇故事中包含一些集锦性质的段落,散见于达尔某些短篇小说中,如《坠机余生》(*Shot down over Libya*)[①]《小菜一碟》(*A Piece of Cake*)[②]《公学遗恨》(*Galloping Foxley*)[③]等。其中,这篇故事中所涉及的英国公学里的体罚情节似乎取自他的传记《男孩时代》(*Boy*)。

达尔首先给那些立志要成为全职作家的人提出了一些意见,并列举了当作家应该具备的一些品质。接着,就像达尔许多小说中的结构一样,达尔的"意识"开始"流动"起来,先流淌到小时候上公学遭体罚的经历,而这些体罚的经历,在他的另一部短篇小说《公学遗恨》(*Galloping Foxley*)中有更为生动形象的描述,这里的描述也同样生动形象:

在过去那些日子里,监狱里要是有人被吊死的话,整座监狱就会静悄悄的,其他囚犯就会一声不响地坐在各自的牢房中,任由这样的行为开始、结束。学校里发生体罚行为时,情况跟监狱里的如出一辙:楼上的宿舍里,孩子们静悄悄地坐在床上,对被打者抱以同情之心。寂静中,从楼下的更衣室里传来"啪、啪……"抽打的声音。

---

① 关于这部小说,感兴趣的读者可以参阅《罗尔德·达尔短篇故事品读及汉译探索(第1卷)》第四章第二节。

② 关于这篇小说,感兴趣的读者可参阅本书第二章第二节。

③ 关于这部小说,感兴趣的读者可以参阅《罗尔德·达尔短篇故事品读及汉译探索(第5卷)》第一章第一节。

第四章 人生之路 第一节 《幸运开局》（上部）Lucky Break (Part A)

In the old days, when a man was about to be hanged, a silence would fall upon the whole prison and the other prisoners would sit very quietly in their cells until the deed had been done. Much the same thing happened at school when a beating was taking place. Upstairs in the dormitories, the boys would sit in silence on their beds in sympathy for the victim, and through the silence, from down below in the changing-room, would come the crack of each stroke as it was delivered.

在读公学这段经历中，达尔特别提到了那里的奥康纳太太。在临时照看达尔这样的小学生期间，奥康纳太太给他们讲述了整个英国文学史，可以算得上是达尔走上文学之路的领路人。正是因为奥康纳太太的引领，达尔开始如饥似渴地阅读文学作品，并最终成为一名作家。

但是，公学的期末成绩单发下来的时候，达尔的成绩并不理想。这样的成绩，怎么也不会让罗尔德·达尔想到，将来有一天自己会成为一名作家。

接下来，达尔讲述了他念完公学后的一部分成长经历。离开公学后，达尔踏上了职业之旅，首先"找到了一份工作，工作的部门当时被称作'壳牌石油公司东方员工培训部'"（I got a job with what was called the Eastern Staff of the Shell Oil Company）。

从此之后，达尔来到了异国他乡，开始了他人生之路新的冒险旅程——既新鲜、有趣，又刺激、危险，因为战争即将爆发。

二、原作释读

作家罗尔德·达尔在他的这篇作品中提到了很多作家及其作品（包括他自己的一些作品），个别作品的书写形式跟常见的形式略有差异，读者可以参照后面的探索性译文加以理解与辨别。同时，阅读中还要突破一些专有名词的障碍，特别是一些地名类的专有名词。

Lucky Break①

How I became a writer

A fiction writer is a person who invents stories.

But how does one start out on a job like this? How does one become a full-time professional fiction writer?

Charles Dickens② found it easy. At the age of twenty-four, he simply sat down and wrote *Pickwick Papers*, which became an immediate best-seller. But Dickens was a genius, and geniuses are different from the rest of us.

In this century (it was not always so in the last one), just about every single writer who has finally become successful in the world of fiction has started out in some other job—a schoolteacher, perhaps, or a doctor or a journalist or a lawyer. (*Alice in Wonderland* was written by a mathematician, and *The Wind in the Willows* by a civil servant③.) The first attempts at writing have therefore always had to be done in spare time, usually at night.

The reason for this is obvious. When you are adult, it is necessary to earn a living. To earn a living, you must get a job. You must if possible get a job that guarantees you so much money a week. But however much you may want to take up fiction writing as a career, it would be

---

① 本部小说原文出自"DAHL, R. *The Wonderful Story of Henry Sugar and Six More* [M]. London: Penguin Books Ltd., 2002"。

break: Noun a player's turn to make the opening shot of a game 开局

② Charles Dickens (1812—1870), English novelist 查尔斯·狄更斯 (1812—1870,英国小说家)。

③ civil servant: a member of the civil service 文职人员;公务员;公仆

第四章 人生之路 第一节 《幸运开局》(上部) Lucky Break (Part A)

pointless to go along to a publisher and say, "I want a job as a fiction writer." If you did that, he would tell you to buzz off① and write the book first. And even if you brought a finished book to him and he liked it well enough to publish it, he still wouldn't give you a job. He would give you an advance② of perhaps five hundred pounds, which he would get back again later by deducting it from your royalties③. (A royalty, by the way, is the money that a writer gets from the publisher for each copy of his book that is sold. The average royalty a writer gets is ten per cent of the price of the book itself in the book shop. Thus, for a book selling at four pounds, the writer would get forty pence. For a paperback selling at fifty pence, he would get five pence.)

It is very common for a hopeful fiction writer to spend two years of his spare time writing a book which no publisher will publish. For that he gets nothing at all except a sense of frustration.

If he is fortunate enough to have a book accepted by a publisher, the odds are that as a first novel it will in the end sell only about three thousand copies. That will earn him maybe a thousand pounds. Most novels take at least one year to write, and one thousand pounds a year is not enough to live on these days. So you can see why a budding fiction writer invariably has to start out in another job first of all. If he doesn't, he will almost certainly starve.

---

① buzz off: [often in imperative] (informal) go away(非正式用法)走开

② advance: an amount of money paid before it is due or for work only partly completed 预付款(e.g. The author was paid a £ 250,000 advance. 预付给作者25万英镑稿酬。)

③ royalty: *Noun* a sum paid to a patentee for the use of a patent or to an author or composer for each copy of a book sold or for each public performance of a work (专利权的)使用费;(著作的)版税;特许使用费

Here are some of the qualities you should possess or should try to acquire if you wish to become a fiction writer:

1. You should have a lively imagination.

2. You should be able to write well. By that I mean you should be able to make a scene come alive in the reader's mind. Not everybody has this ability. It is a gift, and you either have it or you don't.

3. You must have stamina①. In other words, you must be able to stick to what you are doing and never give up, for hour after hour, day after day, week after week and month after month.

4. You must be a perfectionist. That means you must never be satisfied with what you have written until you have rewritten it again and again, making it as good as you possibly can.

5. You must have strong self-discipline. You are working alone. No one is employing you. No one is around to give you the sack if you don't turn up for work, or to tick you off if you start slacking.

6. It helps a lot if you have a keen sense of humour. This is not essential when writing for grown-ups, but for children, it's vital.

7. You must have a degree of humility. The writer who thinks that his work is marvellous is heading for trouble.

Let me tell you how I myself slid in through the back door and found myself in the world of fiction.

At the age of eight, in 1924, I was sent away to boarding-school in a town called Weston-super-Mare, on the southwest coast of England.

---

① stamina: *Noun* [mass noun] the ability to sustain prolonged physical or mental effort 耐力;持久力(e.g. Their secret is stamina rather than speed. 他们的秘密是耐力而不是速度。)

第四章 人生之路 第一节 《幸运开局》(上部) Lucky Break (Part A)

Those were days of horror, of fierce discipline, of no talking in the dormitories, no running in the corridors, no untidiness of any sort, no this or that or the other, just rules and still more rules that had to be obeyed. And the fear of the dreaded cane hung over us like the fear of death all the time.

"The headmaster wants to see you in his study." Words of doom. They sent shivers over the skin of your stomach. But off you went, aged perhaps nine years old, down the long bleak corridors and through an archway that took you into the headmaster's private area where only horrible things happened and the smell of pipe tobacco hung in the air like incense. You stood outside the awful black door, not daring even to knock. You took deep breaths. If only your mother were here, you told yourself, she would not let this happen. She wasn't here. You were alone. You lifted a hand and knocked softly, once.

"Come in! Ah yes, it's Dahl. Well. Dahl, it's been reported to me that you were talking during prep① last night."

"Please sir, I broke my nib② and I was only asking Jenkins if he had another one to lend me."

"I will not tolerate talking in prep. You know that very well."

Already this giant of a man was crossing to the tall corner cupboard and reaching up to the top of it where he kept his canes.

"Boys who break rules have to be punished."

"Sir... I... I had a bust nib... I..."

---

① prep: *Noun* (informal) [mass noun] (Brit.) (especially in an independent school) school work that is set to be done outside lessons(英国非正式用法)(尤指私立学校的)课后作业;预习;家庭作业

② nib: *Noun* the pointed end part of a pen, which distributes the ink on the writing surface 笔尖

"That is no excuse. I am going to teach you that it does not pay to talk during prep. "

He took a cane down that was about three feet long with a little curved handle at one end. It was thin and white and very whippy①. "Bend over and touch your toes. Over there by the window. "

"But sir..."

"Don't argue with me, boy. Do as you're told. "

I bent over. Then I waited. He always kept you waiting for about ten seconds, and that was when your knees began to shake.

"Bend lower, boy! Touch your toes!"

I stared at the toecaps② of my black shoes and I told myself that any moment now this man was going to bash③ the cane into me so hard that the whole of my bottom would change colour. The welts④ were always very long, stretching right across both buttocks, blue-black with brilliant scarlet edges, and when you ran your fingers over them ever so gently afterwards, you could feel the corrugations⑤.

---

① whippy: *Adjective* flexible; springy 柔韧的;易弯曲的;有弹性的(e. g. new growths of whippy sapling twigs 新长出的柔软的嫩枝)

② toecap: *Noun* a piece of steel or leather constituting or fitted over the front part of a boot or shoe as protection or reinforcement(靴、鞋的)鞋头;鞋尖饰皮;外包头

③ bash: *Verb* [with obj.] (informal) strike hard and violently(非正式用法)重击;猛击

④ welt: *Verb* [no obj.] develop a raised scar 打出鞭痕(e. g. His lip was beginning to thicken and welt from the blow. 他的嘴唇正开始变肿,并显出被打的伤痕.)

注:这里的"welt"临时用作名词,意思为"鞭打的痕迹"。

⑤ corruption: *Noun* a wrinkle; fold; furrow; ridge 皱纹;皱折;波纹度;波状;沟纹;波形;槽形

第四章 人生之路 第一节 《幸运开局》(上部) Lucky Break (Part A)

Swish! . . . Crack!

Then came the pain. It was unbelievable, unbearable, excruciating①. It was as though someone had laid a white-hot poker across your backside② and pressed hard.

The second stroke would be coming soon and it was as much as you could do to stop putting your hands in the way to ward it off③. It was the instinctive reaction. But if you did that, it would break your fingers.

Swish! . . . Crack!

The second one landed right alongside the first and the white-hot poker was pressing deeper and deeper into the skin.

Swish! . . . Crack!

The third stroke was where the pain always reached its peak. It could go no further. There was no way it could get any worse. Any more strokes after that simply *prolonged* the agony. You tried not to cry out. Sometimes you couldn't help it. But whether you were able to remain silent or not, it was impossible to stop the tears. They poured down your cheeks in streams and dripped on to the carpet.

The important thing was never to flinch④ upwards or straighten up when you were hit. If you did that, you got an extra one.

---

① excruciate: *Verb* [with obj.] (rare) torment (someone) physically or mentally(罕)使受酷刑;折磨(e. g. I stand back, excruciated by the possibility. 我向后退了一步,为可能发生的事情烦躁不安。)

② backside: *Noun* (informal) a person's buttocks or anus(非正式用法)(人的)屁股;肛门

③ ward someone/something off: prevent from harming or affecting one 挡开 (e. g. She put up a hand as if to ward him off. 她举起一只手,好像要将他挡开。)

④ flinch: *Verb* [no obj.] make a quick, nervous movement of the face or body as an instinctive reaction to fear or pain(因害怕或疼痛而)退缩;畏缩(e. g. She flinched at the acidity in his voice. 他尖刻的话音令她畏缩。)

Slowly, deliberately, taking plenty of time, the headmaster delivered three more strokes, making six in all.

"You may go." The voice came from a cavern① miles away, and you straightened up slowly, agonizingly, and grabbed hold of your burning buttocks with both hands and held them as tight as you could and hopped out of the room on the very tips of your toes.

That cruel cane ruled our lives. We were caned for talking in the dormitory after lights out, for talking in class, for bad work, for carving our initials on the desk, for climbing over walls, for slovenly② appearance, for flicking③ paper-clips, for forgetting to change into house-shoes in the evenings, for not hanging up our games clothes, and above all for giving the slightest offence to any master. (They weren't called teachers in those days.) In other words, we were caned for doing everything that it was natural for small boys to do.

So we watched out words. And we watched our steps. My goodness, how we watched our steps. We became incredibly alert. Wherever we went, we walked carefully, with ears pricked for danger, like wild animals stepping softly through the woods.

Apart from the masters, there was another man in the school who frightened us considerably. This was Mr. Pople. Mr. Pople was a

---

① cavern: *Noun* a cave, or a chamber in a cave, typically a large one(尤指大的)洞穴;山洞;(洞穴的)深凹处;深处

② slovenly: *Adjective* (especially of a person or their appearance) untidy and dirty(尤指人或其外观)不整洁的;邋遢的(e.g. He was upbraided for his slovenly appearance. 他因为外表邋遢而被责骂。)

③ flick: *Verb* [with obj. and adverbial of direction] propel (something) with a sudden sharp movement, especially of the fingers(尤指用手指)弹开;拂去

第四章 人生之路 第一节 《幸运开局》(上部) Lucky Break (Part A)

paunchy①, crimson②-faced individual who acted as school-porter③, boiler superintendent④ and general handyman⑤. His power stemmed from the fact that he could (and he most certainly did) report us to the headmaster upon the slightest provocation⑥. Mr. Pople's moment of glory came each morning at seven-thirty precisely, when he would stand at the end of the long main corridor and "ring the bell". The bell was huge and made of brass, with a thick wooden handle, and Mr. Pople would swing it back and forth at arm's length in a special way of his own, so that it went *clangetty-clang-clang*, *clangetty-clang-clang*, *clangetty-clang-clang*. At the sound of the bell, all the boys in the school, one hundred and eighty of us, would move smartly to our positions in the corridor. We lined up against the walls on both sides and stood stiffly to attention, awaiting the headmaster's inspection.

But at least ten minutes would elapse before the headmaster arrived on the scene, and during this time, Mr. Pople would conduct a ceremony so extraordinary that to this day I find it hard to believe it ever took

---

① paunchy: *Adjective* having a protruding belly or abdomen 大肚子的

② crimson: *Noun* [mass noun] a rich deep red colour inclining to purple 深红色；绯红色

③ porter: *Noun* (Brit.) an employee in charge of the entrance of a hotel, block of flats, college, or other large building(英国用法)看门人；门房

④ superintendent: *Noun* a person who manages or superintends an organization or activity 负责人；主管人；指挥者

⑤ handyman: *Noun* a man who does odd jobs or various small tasks 受雇做杂事的人；做零活的人

⑥ provocation: *Noun* [mass noun] action or speech that makes someone annoyed or angry, especially deliberately(尤指蓄意)挑衅；激怒；刺激(e.g. You should remain calm and not respond to provocation. 你应该保持镇静，不要对挑衅作出反应。)

place. There were six lavatories in the school, numbered on their doors from one to six. Mr. Pople, standing at the end of the long corridor, would have in the palm of his hand six small brass discs, each with a number on it, one to six. There was absolute silence as he allowed his eye to travel down the two lines of stiffly-standing boys. Then he would bark out a name, "Arkle!"

Arkle would fall out① and step briskly down the corridor to where Mr. Pople stood. Mr. Pople would hand him a brass disc. Arkle would then march away towards the lavatories, and to reach them he would have to walk the entire length of the corridor, past all the stationary boys, and then turn left. As soon as he was out of sight, he was allowed to look at his disc and see which lavatory number he had been given.

"Highton!" barked Mr. Pople, and now Highton would fall out to receive his disc and march away.

"Angel!"...

"Williamson!"...

"Gaunt!"...

"Trice!"...

In this manner, six boys selected at Mr. Pople's whim were dispatched to the lavatories to do their duty. Nobody asked them if they might or might not be ready to move their bowels at seven-thirty in the morning before breakfast. They were simply ordered to do so. But we considered it a great privilege to be chosen because it meant that during the headmaster's inspection we would be sitting safely out of reach in blessed privacy.

In due course, the headmaster would emerge from his private quarters and take over from Mr. Pople. He walked slowly down one side of

---

① fall out: to leave a military formation 离队

第四章 人生之路 第一节 《幸运开局》(上部) Lucky Break (Part A)

the corridor, inspecting each boy with the utmost care, strapping his wristwatch on to his wrist as he went along. The morning inspection was an unnerving① experience. Every one of us was terrified of the two sharp brown eyes under their bushy eyebrows as they travelled slowly up and down the length of one's body.

"Go away and brush your hair properly. And don't let it happen again or you'll be sorry."

"Let me see your hands. You have ink on them. Why didn't you wash it off last night?"

"Your tie is crooked, boy. Fall out and tie it again. And do it properly this time."

"I can see mud on that shoe. Didn't I have to talk to you about that last week? Come and see me in my study after breakfast."

And so it went on, the ghastly② early-morning inspection. And by the end of it all, when the headmaster had gone away and Mr. Pople started marching us into the dining-room by forms, many of us had lost our appetites for the lumpy③ porridge that was to come.

I have still got all my school reports from those days more than fifty years ago, and I've gone through them one by one, trying to discover a hint of promise for a future fiction writer. The subject to look at was obviously English Composition. But all my prep-school reports under this

---

① unnerve: *Verb* [with obj.] make (someone) lose courage or confidence 使丧失勇气(或自信)

② ghastly: *Adjective* causing great horror or fear; frightful or macabre 可怕的;可怖的;令人毛骨悚然的

③ lumpy: *Adjective* full of or covered with lumps 多块的;高低不平的(e.g. He lay on the lumpy mattress. 他躺在凹凸不平的床垫上。)

heading were flat and non-committal①, excepting one. The one that took my eye was dated Christmas Term, 1928. I was then twelve, and my English teacher was Mr. Victor Corrado. I remember him vividly, a tall, handsome athlete with black wavy hair and a Roman nose②(who one night later on eloped③ with the matron④, Miss Davis, and we never saw either of them again). Anyway, it so happened that Mr. Corrado took us in boxing as well as in English Composition, and in this particular report it said under English, "See his report on boxing. Precisely the same remarks apply." So we look under Boxing, and there it says, "Too slow and ponderous⑤. His punches⑥ are not well-timed and are easily seen coming."

But just once a week at this school, every Saturday morning, every beautiful and blessed Saturday morning, all the shivering horrors would disappear and for two glorious hours I would experience something that came very close to ecstasy.

Unfortunately, this did not happen until one was ten years old. But no matter. Let me try to tell you what it was.

---

① non-committal: *Adjective* (of a person or a person's behaviour or manner) not expressing or revealing commitment to a definite opinion or course of action(人、行为或态度)不表态的;不明朗的(e.g. Her tone was non-committal, and her face gave nothing away. 她的语气不明朗,脸上也没表露出什么。)

② Roman nose: *Noun* a nose with a high bridge(高鼻梁型)鹰钩鼻

③ elope: *Verb* [no obj.] run away secretly in order to get married 私奔(e.g. Later he eloped with one of the housemaids. 后来他与一女佣私奔了。)

④ matron: *Noun* a woman in charge of domestic and medical arrangements at a boarding school or other establishment 女总管;女舍监

⑤ ponderous: *Adjective* slow and clumsy because of great weight 缓慢的;笨拙的(e.g. Her footsteps were heavy and ponderous. 她的脚步沉重而缓慢。)

⑥ punch: *Noun* a blow with the fist 一拳;一击

第四章　人生之路　第一节　《幸运开局》(上部) Lucky Break (Part A)

At exactly ten-thirty on Saturday mornings, Mr. Pople's infernal[①] bell would go *clangetty-clang-clang*. This was a signal for the following to take place:

First, all boys of nine and under (about seventy all told) would proceed at once to the large outdoor asphalt[②] playground behind the main building. Standing on the playground with legs apart and arms folded across her mountainous bosom was Miss Davis, the matron. If it was raining, the boys were expected to arrive in raincoats. If snowing or blowing a blizzard[③], then it was coats and scarves. And school caps, of course—grey with a red badge[④] on the front—had always to be worn. But no Act of God[⑤], neither tornado nor hurricane nor volcanic eruption was ever allowed to stop those ghastly two-hour Saturday morning walks that the seven-, eight- and nine-year-old little boys had to take along the windy esplanades[⑥] of Weston-super-Mare on Saturday mornings. They walked in

---

① infernal: *Adjective* [attrib.] (informal) irritating and tiresome (used for emphasis)(非正式)(用作强调)恼人的;烦人的;讨厌的(e.g. You're an infernal nuisance. 你是个讨厌鬼。)

② asphalt: *Noun* the pitch used in this mixture, sometimes found in natural deposits but usually made by the distillation of crude oil 沥青

③ blizzard: *Noun* a severe snowstorm with high winds 暴风雪

④ badge: *Noun* a small piece of metal, plastic, or cloth bearing a design or words, typically worn to show a person's name, rank, membership of an organization, or support for a particular cause 徽章;证章;奖章

⑤ Act of God: an instance of uncontrollable natural forces in operation (often used in insurance claims) (常用于保险索赔)不可抗力

⑥ esplanade: *Noun* a long, open, level area, typically beside the sea, along which people may walk for pleasure(尤指海滨供散步用的)长形空旷平地

crocodile① formation, two by two, with Miss Davis striding alongside in tweed② skirt and woollen stockings and a felt③ hat that must surely have been nibbled④ by rats.

The other thing that happened when Mr. Pople's bell rang out on Saturday mornings was that the rest of the boys, all those of ten and over (about one hundred all told) would go immediately to the main Assembly Hall and sit down. A junior master called S. K. Jopp would then poke his head around the door and shout at us with such ferocity⑤ that specks of spit would fly from his mouth like bullets and splash against the window panes across the room. "All right!" he shouted. "No talking! No moving! Eyes front and hands on desks!" Then out he would pop again.

We sat still and waited. We were waiting for the lovely time we knew would be coming soon. Outside in the driveway we heard the motor-cars being started up. All were ancient. All had to be cranked⑥ by hand. (The year, don't forget, was around 1927/28.) This was a Saturday morning ritual. There were five cars in all, and into them would pile

---

① crocodile: *Noun* (Brit. informal) a line of schoolchildren walking in pairs (英国英语非正式用法)(学生)两人一排的纵列

② tweed: *Noun* [mass noun] a rough-surfaced woollen cloth, typically of mixed flecked colours, originally produced in Scotland(原产于苏格兰的)粗花呢

③ felt: *Noun* [mass noun] a kind of cloth made by rolling and pressing wool or another suitable textile accompanied by the application of moisture or heat, which causes the constituent fibres to mat together to create a smooth surface 毛毡

④ nibble: *Verb* take small bites out of 啃;一点点地咬(或吃)

⑤ ferocity: *Noun* [mass noun] the state or quality of being ferocious 凶残;凶猛;狂暴(e.g. The ferocity of the storm caught them by surprise. 这场风暴来势凶猛,让他们大为吃惊。)

⑥ crank: *Verb* turn (a handle), typically in order to start an engine 转动(柄)(多为发动机器)

第四章 人生之路 第一节 《幸运开局》(上部) Lucky Break (Part A)

the entire staff of fourteen masters, including not only the headmaster himself but also the purple-faced Mr. Pople. Then off they would roar in a cloud of blue smoke and come to rest outside a pub called, if I remember rightly, "The Bewhiskered① Earl②". There they would remain until just before lunch, drinking pint③ after pint of strong brown ale④. And two and a half hours later, at one o'clock, we would watch them coming back, walking very carefully into the dining-room for lunch, holding on to things as they went.

So much for the masters. But what of us, the great mass of ten-, eleven- and twelve-year-olds left sitting in the Assembly Hall in a school that was suddenly without a single adult in the entire place? We knew, of course, exactly what was going to happen next. Within a minute of the departure of the masters, we would hear the front door opening, and footsteps outside, and then, with a flurry of loose clothes and jangling⑤ bracelets and flying hair, a woman would burst into the room shouting, "Hello, everybody! Cheer up! This isn't a burial service!" or words to

---

① bewhiskered: *Adjective* having hair or whiskers growing in the face 有络腮胡子的

② earl: *Noun* a British nobleman ranking above a viscount and below a marquess(英国的)伯爵(高于子爵,低于侯爵)

③ pint: *Noun* a unit of liquid or dry capacity equal to one eighth of a gallon, in Britain equal to 0.565 litre and in the US equal to 0.473 litre (for liquid measure) or 0.551 litre (for dry measure) 品脱(一种液量或干液单位,相当于1/8加仑,在英国相当于0.565升,在美国液量相当于0.473升,干量相当于0.551升。)

④ brown ale: [mass noun] (Brit.) dark, mild beer sold in bottles(英国英语)(瓶装)黑啤酒

⑤ jangle: *Verb* make or cause to make a ringing metallic sound, typically a discordant one(使)发出丁零当啷声(e.g. Ryan stood on the terrace jangling his keys. 赖安站在露台上把钥匙晃动得叮当作响。)

that effect①. And this was Mrs. O'Connor.

Blessed beautiful Mrs. O'Connor with her whacky② clothes and her grey hair flying in all directions. She was about fifty years old, with a horsey③ face and long yellow teeth, but to us she was beautiful. She was not on the staff. She was hired from somewhere in the town to come up on Saturday mornings and be a sort of babysitter, to keep us quiet for two and a half hours while the masters went off boozing④ at the pub.

But Mrs. O'Connor was no baby-sitter. She was nothing less than a great and gifted teacher, a scholar and a lover of English Literature. Each of us was with her every Saturday morning for three years (from the age of ten until we left the school) and during that time we spanned the entire history of English Literature from A. D. 597 to the early nineteenth century.

Newcomers to the class were given for keeps⑤ a slim blue book called simply *The Chronological Table*, and it contained only six pages. Those six pages were filled with a very long list in chronological order of

---

① to that effect: having that result, purpose, or meaning 以此为目的的;那样意思的(e.g. She thought it a foolish rule and put a notice to that effect in a newspaper. 她认为这是条愚蠢的规定,并在报纸上发表短评表达了这一观点。)

② wacky or whacky: *Adjective* (informal) funny or amusing in a slightly odd or peculiar way(非正式用法)滑稽古怪的;乖僻的;疯疯癫癫的(e.g. a wacky chase movie 一部滑稽古怪的追捕影片)

③ horsey or horsy: *Adjective* of or resembling a horse 马的;似马的(e.g. She had a long horsey face. 她长着一个马脸。)

④ booze: *Verb* [no obj.] drink alcohol, especially in large quantities 喝酒;(尤指)酗酒(e.g. Michael is trying to quit boozing. 迈克正试着戒去酗酒的毛病。)

⑤ for keeps: (informal) permanently; indefinitely(非正式用法)永远地;无限期地

all the great and not so great landmarks in English Literature, together with their dates. Exactly one hundred of these were chosen by Mrs. O'Connor and we marked them in our books and learned them by heart. Here are a few that I still remember:

A. D. 597 St Augustine lands in Thanet and brings Christianity to Britain
731 Bede's *Ecclesiastical*① *History*
1215 Signing of the Magna Carta②
1399 Langland's *Vision of Piers Plowman*
1476 Caxton sets up first printing press at Westminster
1478 Chaucer's *Canterbury Tales*
1485 Malory's *Morte d'Arthur*
1590 Spenser's *Faerie Queene*
1623 First Folio of Shakespeare
1667 Milton's *Paradise Lost*
1668 Dryden's *Essays*
1678 Bunyan's *Pilgrim's Progress*
1711 Addison's *Spectator*
1719 Defoe's *Robinson Crusoe*

---

① ecclesiastical: *Adjective* of or relating to the Christian Church or its clergy (与)基督教教会(有关)的;(与)基督教传教士(有关)的(e. g. the ecclesiastical hierarchy 教会的等级)

② Magna Carta: a charter of liberty and political rights obtained from King John of England by his rebellious barons at Runnymede in 1215, which came to be seen as the seminal document of English constitutional practice 大宪章(1215 年英格兰尼米德的反叛贵族迫使英王约翰签署的自由和政治权利文件,后来被视为开英国宪法先河的文件。)

1726 Swift's *Gulliver's Travels*
1733 Pope's *Essay on Man*
1755 Johnson's *Dictionary*
1791 Boswell's *Life of Johnson*
1833 Carlyle's *Sartor Resartus*
1859 Darwin's *Origin of Species*

Mrs. O'Connor would then take each item in turn and spend one entire Saturday morning of two and a half hours talking to us about it. Thus, at the end of three years, with approximately thirty-six Saturdays in each school year, she would have covered the one hundred items.

And what marvellous exciting fun it was! She had the great teacher's knack of making everything she spoke about come alive to us in that room. In two and a half hours, we grew to love Langland and his Piers Plowman. The next Saturday, it was Chaucer, and we loved him, too. Even rather difficult fellows like Milton and Dryden and Pope all became thrilling when Mrs. O'Connor told us about their lives and read parts of their work to us aloud. And the result of all this, for me at any rate, was that by the age of thirteen I had become intensely aware of the vast heritage of literature that had been built up in England over the centuries. I also became an avid① and insatiable reader of good writing.

Dear lovely Mrs. O'Connor! Perhaps it was worth going to that awful school simply to experience the joy of her Saturday mornings.

At thirteen I left prep school and was sent, again as a boarder, to one of our famous British public schools. They are not, of course, public

---

① avid: *Adjective* having or showing a keen interest in or enthusiasm for something 热心的;热衷的(e.g. an avid reader of science fiction 科幻小说的热心读者)

第四章 人生之路 第一节 《幸运开局》(上部) Lucky Break (Part A)

at all. They are extremely private and expensive. Mine was called Repton①, in Derbyshire②, and our headmaster at the time was the Reverend③ Geoffrey Fisher, who later became Bishop of Chester④, then Bishop of London, and finally Archbishop of Canterbury. In his last job, he crowned Queen Elizabeth II in Westminster Abbey⑤.

The clothes we had to wear at this school made us look like assistants in a funeral parlour⑥. The jacket was black, with a cutaway front and long tails hanging down behind that came below the backs of the knees. The trousers were black with thin grey stripes. The shoes were

---

① Repton: *Noun* Here, it refers to the Repton School. Repton School is a co-educational English independent school for both day and boarding pupils located in the village of Repton, Derbyshire, in the English Midlands. 这里的"Repton"指的是"雷普顿公学"。雷普顿公学是一所男女合校教育的独立学校,既招收走读生,又招收寄宿生。雷普顿公学位于英格兰中部地区德比郡的雷普顿村。

② Derbyshire: *Noun* a county of north central England; county town, Matlock 德比郡(英格兰中北部一郡,首府马特洛克。)

③ reverend: *Adjective* used as a title or form of address to members of the clergy 大人(对教士的尊称)

④ Chester: *Noun* a town in western England, the county town of Cheshire; pop. 115,000 (1991) 切斯特(英格兰西部城镇,柴郡首府,1991年人口115,000。)

⑤ Westminster Abbey: The collegiate church of St Peter in Westminster, originally the abbey church of a Benedictine monastery. Nearly all the kings and queens of England have been crowned in Westminster Abbey; it is also the burial place of many of England's monarchs and of some of the nation's leading figures. 威斯敏斯特教堂(位于威斯敏斯特的圣彼得大教堂,原先为本笃会僧侣的修道院,是几乎所有的英国国王和女王的加冕教堂,也是许多英国君主和一些名人的墓地。)

⑥ funeral parlour/parlor: a place where the dead are prepared for burial or cremation 殡仪馆

black. There was a black waistcoat① with eleven buttons to do up every morning. The tie was black. Then there was a stiff starched white butterfly collar and a white shirt.

To top it all off, the final ludicrous② touch was a straw hat that had to be worn at all times out of doors except when playing games. And because the hats got soggy③ in the rain, we carried umbrellas for bad weather.

You can imagine what I felt like in this fancy dress when my mother took me, at the age of thirteen, to the train in London at the beginning of my first term. She kissed me good-bye and off I went.

I naturally hoped that my long-suffering backside would be given a rest at my new and more adult school, but it was not to be. The beatings at Repton were more fierce and more frequent than anything I had yet experienced. And do not think for one moment that the future Archbishop of Canterbury objected to these squalid④ exercises. He rolled up his

---

① waistcoat: *Noun* (Brit.) a close-fitting waist-length garment, typically having no sleeves or collar and buttoning down the front, worn especially by men over a shirt and under a jacket(英国用法)背心；马甲

② ludicrous: *Adjective* so foolish, unreasonable, or out of place as to be amusing 滑稽有趣的；荒唐可笑的(e.g. It's ludicrous that I have been fined. 太荒唐了，我被罚了款。)

③ soggy: *Adjective* extremely wet and soft 极度湿软的(e.g. The pastry is a bit soggy. 面团过于湿软了一点儿。)

④ squalid: *Adjective* showing or involving a contemptible lack of moral standards 卑鄙的；恶劣的；道德败坏的(e.g. a squalid attempt to save themselves from electoral embarrassment 一个想使他们摆脱选举困窘的卑劣企图)

第四章 人生之路 第一节 《幸运开局》(上部) Lucky Break (Part A)

sleeves and joined in with gusto①. His were the bad ones, the really terrifying occasions. Some of the beatings administered by this Man of God②, this future Head of the Church of England③, were very brutal. To my certain knowledge he once had to produce a basin of water, a sponge and a towel so that the victim could wash the blood away afterwards.

No joke, that.

Shades of the Spanish Inquisition④.

But nastiest of all, I think, was the fact that prefects⑤ were allowed to beat their fellow pupils. This was a daily occurrence. The big boys

---

① gusto：Noun [mass noun] enjoyment or vigour in doing something; zest 津津有味；兴致勃勃；充沛的精力；热情 (e.g. She sang it with gusto. 她充满热情地演唱了这首歌曲。)

② Man of God：a clergyman 牧师；教士

③ Church of London：The English branch of the Western Christian Church, which combines Catholic and Protestant traditions, rejects the Pope's authority, and has the monarch as its titular head. The English Church was part of the Catholic Church until the Reformation of the 16th century; after Henry VIII failed to obtain a divorce from Catherine of Aragon he repudiated papal supremacy, bringing the Church under the control of the Crown. 英国国教会；英格兰圣公会（西方基督教英国分支；它结合天主教和新教传统，否认罗马教皇权威，认其君主为名义领袖；16世纪基督教改革运动前曾属天主教，亨利八世试图与阿拉贡的凯瑟琳离婚失败后，即否认罗马教皇拥有最高权力，将教会归入君王管辖。）

④ Spanish Inquisition：An ecclesiastical court established in 1478 and directed originally against converts from Judaism and Islam but later also against Protestants. It operated with great severity and was not suppressed until the early 19th century. 西班牙宗教法庭（1478年建立的天主教法庭，起先针对犹太教和伊斯兰教的皈依者，后来也反对新教徒；其手段残暴，直到19世纪早期才被废止。）

⑤ prefect：Noun (chiefly Brit.) a senior pupil in some schools authorized to enforce discipline（主要为英国英语用法）(英国某些公立学校、美国某些私立学校负责维持秩序的) 班长；级长

(aged 17 or 18) would flog① the smaller boys (aged 13, 14, 15) in a sadistic② ceremony that took place at night after you had gone up to the dormitory and got into your pyjamas.

"You're wanted down in the changing-room."

With heavy hands, you would put on your dressing-gown and slippers. Then you would stumble downstairs and enter the large wooden-floored room where the games clothes were hanging up around the walls. A single bare electric bulb hung from the ceiling. A prefect, pompous but very dangerous, was waiting for you in the centre of the room. In his hands, he held a long cane, and he was usually flexing it back and forth as you came in.

"I suppose you know why you're here," he would say.

"Well. I..."

"For the second day running you have burnt my toast!"

Let me explain this ludicrous remark. You were this particular prefect's fag③. That meant you were his servant, and one of your many duties was to make toast for him every day at teatime. For this, you used a long three-pronged toasting fork, and you stuck the bread on the end of it and held it up before an open fire, first one side, then the other. But the only fire where toasting was allowed was in the library, and as teatime

---

① flog: Verb [with obj.] beat (someone) with a whip or stick to punish or torture them 鞭打；棒打 (e.g. The executioner flogged the woman. 刽子手鞭打那女人。)

② sadistic: Adjective pertaining to or characterized by sadism; deriving pleasure or sexual gratification from extreme cruelty 有(性)虐待狂的

③ fag: Noun (Brit.) a junior pupil at a public school who works and runs errands for a senior pupil(英国用法)(英制公学里供高年级学生差遣的)低年级学生

第四章 人生之路 第一节 《幸运开局》(上部) Lucky Break (Part A)

approached, there were never less than a dozen wretched fags all jostling① for position in front of the tiny grate. I was no good at this. I usually held the bread too close and the toast got burnt. But as we were never allowed to ask for a second slice and start again, the only thing to do was to scrape the burnt bits off with a knife. You seldom got away with this. The prefects were expert at detecting scraped toast. You would see your own tormentor sitting up there at the top table, picking up his toast, turning it over, examining it closely as though it were a small and very valuable painting. Then he would frown and you knew you were for it.

So now it was night-time and you were down in the changing-room in your dressing-gown and pyjamas, and the one whose toast you had burnt was telling you about your crime.

"I don't like burnt toast."

"I held it too close. I'm sorry."

"Which do you want? Four with the dressing-gown on, or three with it off?"

"Four with it on," I said.

It was traditional to ask this question. The victim was always given a choice. But my own dressing-gown was made of thick brown camel-hair, and there was never any question in my mind that this was the better choice. To be beaten in pyjamas only was a very painful experience, and your skin nearly always got broken. But my dressing-gown stopped that from happening. The prefect knew, of course, all about this, and therefore whenever you chose to take an extra stroke and kept the dressing-gown on, he beat you with every ounce of his strength. Sometimes he

---

① jostle: Verb [no obj.] (jostle for) struggle or compete forcefully for 争夺;抢夺;为……而竞争(e.g. jumble of images jostled for attention 纷乱的图像令人目不暇接)

would take a little run, three or four neat steps on his toes, to gain momentum and thrust, but either way, it was a savage business.

In the old days, when a man was about to be hanged, a silence would fall upon the whole prison and the other prisoners would sit very quietly in their cells until the deed had been done. Much the same thing happened at school when a beating was taking place. Upstairs in the dormitories, the boys would sit in silence on their beds in sympathy for the victim, and through the silence, from down below in the changing-room, would come the crack of each stroke as it was delivered.

My end-of-term reports from this school are of some interest. Here are just four of them, copied out word for word from the original documents:

Summer Term, 1930 (*aged 14*). *English Composition*. "I have never met a boy who so persistently writes the exact opposite of what he means. He seems incapable of marshalling① his thoughts on paper."

Easter Term, 1931 (*aged 15*). *English Composition*. "A persistent muddler②. Vocabulary negligible③, sentences malconstructed. He reminds me of a camel."

Summer Term, 1932 (*aged 16*). *English Composition*. "This boy is

---

① marshal: *Verb* to arrange, place, or set in methodical order 整理; 排列 (e.g. He paused for a moment, as if marshalling his thoughts. 他停顿了一会儿,似乎在整理思路。)

② muddler: *Noun* a person who creates muddles, especially because of a disorganized method of thinking or working(因思想或工作无条理而)造成无序状态的人;造成混乱局面的人

③ negligible: *Adjective* so small or unimportant as to be not worth considering; insignificant 可忽略不计的;无关紧要的(e.g. He said that the risks were negligible. 他说风险可以忽略不计。)

an indolent① and illiterate member of the class."

Autumn Term, 1932 (*aged* 17). *English Composition*. "Consistently idle. Ideas limited." (And underneath this one, the future Archbishop of Canterbury had written in red ink, "He must correct the blemishes② on this sheet.")

Little wonder that it never entered my head to become a writer in those days.

When I left school at the age of eighteen, in 1934, I turned down my mother's offer (my father died when I was three) to go to university. Unless one was going to become a doctor, a lawyer, a scientist, an engineer or some other kind of professional person, I saw little point in wasting three or four years at Oxford or Cambridge, and I still hold this view. Instead, I had a passionate wish to go abroad, to travel, to see distant lands. There were almost no commercial aeroplanes in those days, and a journey to Africa or the Far East took several weeks.

So I got a job with what was called the Eastern Staff of the Shell Oil Company, where they promised me that after two or three years' training in England, I would be sent off to a foreign country.

"Which one?" I asked.

"Who knows?" the man answered. "It depends where there is a vacancy when you reach the top of the list. It could be Egypt or China or India or almost anywhere in the world."

That sounded like fun. It was. When my turn came to be posted abroad

---

① indolent: *Adjective* wanting to avoid activity or exertion; lazy 不积极的;懒惰的;懒散的

② blemish: *Noun* a small mark or flaw which spoils the appearance of something 瑕疵;污点(e.g. The merest blemish on a Rolls Royce might render it unsaleable. 劳斯莱斯汽车上只要有一点瑕疵,就可能无法出售。)

three years later, I was told it would be East Africa. Tropical suits were ordered and my mother helped me pack my trunk. My tour of duty was for three years in Africa, then I would be allowed home on leave for six months. I was now twenty-one years old and setting out for faraway places. I felt great. I boarded the ship at London Docks and off she sailed.

That journey took two and a half weeks. We went through the Bay of Biscay and called in at Gibraltar. We headed down the Mediterranean by way of Malta①, Naples② and Port Said③. We went through the Suez Canal④

---

① Malta: *Noun* an island country in the central Mediterranean, about 100 *km* (60 miles) south of Sicily; pop. 356,000 (est. 1991); official languages, Maltese and English; capital, Valletta 马耳他(地中海中部岛国,西西里岛以南约100公里,即60英里;1991年估计人口356,000;官方语言马耳他语和英语;首都瓦莱塔。)

② Naples: *Noun* a city and port on the west coast of Italy, capital of Campania region; pop. 1,206,000 (1990). It was formerly the capital of the kingdom of Naples and Sicily (1816—1860). Italian name Napoli. 那不勒斯(意大利西海岸港市,坎帕尼亚区首府,1990年人口1,206,000,曾是那不勒斯西西里王国1816—1860间的首都;意大利语名Napoli。)

③ Port Said: A city of northeast Egypt on the Mediterranean Sea at the northern entrance to the Suez Canal. It was founded in 1859 by the builders of the canal and was once an important coaling station. 塞得港(埃及东北部位于地中海的港市,是苏伊士运河的北部入口。塞得港由苏伊士运河的修造工人于1859年创建,曾是重要的煤运基地。)

④ Suez Canal: A shipping canal connecting the Mediterranean at Port Said with the Red Sea. It was constructed between 1859 and 1869 by Ferdinand de Lesseps. In 1875 it came under British control; its nationalization by Egypt in 1956 prompted the Suez crisis. 苏伊士运河(在赛德港处连接地中海与红海的航运运河,1859—1869年间由费迪南德·德·雷赛布开凿,1875年归英国控制,1956年被埃及收归国有,由此引发了苏伊士危机。)

第四章 人生之路 第一节 《幸运开局》(上部) Lucky Break (Part A)

and down the Red Sea①, stopping at Port Sudan②, then Aden③. It was tremendously exciting. For the first time, I saw great sandy deserts, and Arab soldiers mounted on camels, and palm trees with dates growing on them, and flying fish and thousands of other marvellous things. Finally we reached Mombasa④, in Kenya.

At Mombasa, a man from the Shell Company came on board and told me I must transfer to a small coastal vessel and go on to Dar-es-Salaam⑤,

---

① Red Sea: a long, narrow landlocked sea separating Africa from the Arabian peninsula. It is linked to the Indian Ocean in the south by the Gulf of Aden and to the Mediterranean in the north by the Suez Canal. 红海(分隔非洲和阿拉伯半岛的狭长陆围海,南部经亚丁湾与印度洋相连,北部经苏伊士运河与地中海相连。)

② Port Sudan: the chief port of Sudan, on the Red Sea 苏丹港(苏丹主要港市,位于红海。)

③ Aden: *Noun* A port in Yemen at the mouth of the Red Sea; pop. 400,800 (est. 1993). Aden was formerly under British rule, first as part of British India (from 1839), then from 1935 as a Crown Colony. It was capital of the former South Yemen from 1967 until 1990. 亚丁(也门在红海入海口一港市,1993 年估计人口 400,800;亚丁曾受英国统治,从 1839 年起是英属印度的一部分,后来自 1935 年起成为英国直辖殖民地;自 1967 年到 1990 年为前南也门首府。)

④ Mombasa: *Noun* a seaport and industrial city in SE Kenya, on the Indian Ocean; pop. 465,000 (est. 1989). It is the leading port and second-largest city of Kenya. 蒙巴萨(肯尼亚东南部海港和工业城市,临印度洋,1989 年估计人口 465,000;肯尼亚的主要港口和第二大城市。)

⑤ Dar-es-Salaam or Dar es Salaam: the chief port and former capital of Tanzania; pop. 1,360,850 (1988). It was founded in 1866 by the sultan of Zanzibar. Its Arabic name means "haven of peace". 达累斯萨拉姆(坦桑尼亚主要港口和前首都,1988 年人口 1,360,850;1866 年由桑给巴尔苏丹建立,其阿拉伯语名意为"和平港"。)

the capital of Tanganyika (now Tanzania①). And so to Dar-es-Salaam I went, stopping at Zanzibar② on the way.

For the next two years, I worked for Shell in Tanzania, with my headquarters in Dar-es-Salaam. It was a fantastic life. The heat was intense but who cared? Our dress was khaki③ shorts, an open shirt and a topee④ on the head. I learned to speak Swahili⑤. I drove up-country vis-

---

① Tanzania: *Noun* a country in East Africa with a coastline on the Indian Ocean; pop. 27,270,000 (est. 1991); official languages, Swahili and English; capital, Dodoma. 坦桑尼亚(东非的一个国家,临印度洋;1991年估计人口2,727万;官方语言为斯瓦希里语和英语;首都多多马。)

② Zanzibar: *Noun* An island off the coast of East Africa, part of Tanzania; pop. 640,580 (1988). Under Arab rule from the 17th century, Zanzibar was a prosperous trading port. It became a British protectorate in 1890 and an independent Commonwealth state in 1963, but in the following year the sultan was overthrown and the country became a republic, uniting with Tanganyika to form Tanzania. 桑给巴尔岛(东非海岸外的一个岛屿,系坦桑尼亚的一部分,1988年人口640,580;17世纪阿拉伯人统治时期为一繁荣的贸易港;1890年成为英国的保护国,1963年成为独立的英联邦国家,次年苏丹被推翻后成为共和国,与坦噶尼喀合并,称为坦桑尼亚。)

③ khaki: *Noun* a sturdy twilled cloth of a yellowish brown color used especially for military uniforms 黄卡其布

④ topee or topi: *Noun* a lightweight hat worn in tropical countries for protection from the sun 轻便遮阳帽

⑤ Swahili: *Noun* [mass noun] a Bantu language widely used as a lingua franca in East Africa and having official status in several countries. There are probably fewer than 2 million native speakers, but it is in everyday use by over 20 million. 斯瓦希里语(非洲东部作为通用语广泛使用的一种班图语,在几个国家都已成为官方语言;大概有不足200万本族语使用者,但日常使用者有2,000多万人。)

iting diamond mines, sisal① plantations, gold-mines and all the rest of it.

There were giraffes, elephants, zebras, lions and antelopes② all over the place, and snakes as well, including the Black Mamba③ which is the only snake in the world that will chase after you if it sees you. And if it catches you and bites you, you had better start saying your prayers. I learned to shake my mosquito boots upside down before putting them on in case there was a scorpion inside, and like everyone else, I got malaria④ and lay for three days with a temperature of one hundred and five point five.

(To be continued...)

三、翻译探索

在这部作品的翻译中,诸多专有名词可能是比较棘手的地方。其中,罗尔德·达尔在这部作品中"卖弄"了不少世界各个角落的地名,需要在翻译中一一查证、落实,特别是需要照顾到此类地名的一些常规性的译法,不可随意进行创造性的翻译。当然,对于一些小的地名,又查不到常规性译法,则可以根据读音进行创造性翻译了。

---

① sisal: *Noun* [mass noun] a Mexican agave with large fleshy leaves, cultivated for fibre production 剑麻;菠萝麻

② antelope: *Noun* a swift-running deer-like ruminant with smooth hair and upward-pointing horns, native to Africa and Asia, and including the gazelles, impala, gnus, and elands 羚羊

③ Black Mamba: a highly venomous slender olive-brown to dark grey snake that moves with great speed and agility. Native to eastern and southern Africa, it is the largest poisonous snake on the continent 非洲黑曼巴蛇

④ malaria: *Noun* [mass noun] an intermittent and remittent fever caused by a protozoan parasite which invades the red blood cells and is transmitted by mosquitoes in many tropical and subtropical regions 疟疾

幸运开局

我成为作家的前前后后

小说作家就是一个编造故事的人。

可问题是,一个人怎样才能开始从事这样一份工作呢?一个人怎样才能成为一名全职的专业小说作家呢?

查尔斯·狄更斯认为,这很容易做到。年仅二十四岁的时候,他就直接坐下来,写成了《匹克威克外传》,并立刻成为畅销书,但狄更斯是一位天才,而天才与我们其余的人并不一样。

在本世纪(这里指的是 20 世纪——译者注),几乎每一位最终在小说界获得成功的作家,刚起步的时候都是在做其他工作,像当学校老师,或者当医生、记者、律师什么的。例如,《爱丽丝漫游奇境》的作者起步时是一位数学家,《柳林风声》的作者起步时是一位文职人员。因此,写作的首次尝试都是在业余时间完成的,通常是在夜里完成的。但是,在上一世纪,情况却不总是如此。

在本世纪,情况之所以如此,其原因是显而易见的。长大成人后,你必须得谋生,而为了谋生,你就必须得工作。要是可能的话,你必须得找到这样一份工作,保证你一周能挣到足够的钱来维持生计。不管你有多么大的渴望要将小说写作当成一种职业生涯,下面的做法也只能是徒劳一场:走到一位出版商那里,对他说:"我想做一份当小说作家的工作。"倘若你真的那样去做了,那位出版商就会让你立马走人,回去先写出一本书来。即便你写完一本书拿给了他,他也喜欢得不得了要出版,但是,他仍然不会给你一份工作。充其量,他只能给你一笔预付款,或许会有五百英镑吧,但就算是这样一笔钱款,他日后也会从你的版税中扣除而再次取走的(顺便说一下,版税就是每卖出一本书,作者从出版商那里得到的钱。作者得到的平均版税就是他写的书在书店里销售价格的百分之十。这样算来,一本书要是卖四英镑的话,作者就会得到四十便士。一本平装书售价是五十便士的话,作者就只得五便士了)。

第四章 人生之路 第一节 《幸运开局》(上部) Lucky Break (Part A)

一名很有成功希望的小说作家花掉了两年的业余时间写完一本书,却没有一位出版商愿意给他出版,这样的事情司空见惯。在这种情况之下,除了失意、沮丧,他将一无所获。

要是好运当头,有哪个出版商同意为他出版,那么,极有可能出现的情况就是,作为一部处女作,这本小说最终只能卖出去约三千册。那样的话,他会挣到约一千英镑。要知道,多数小说至少需要一年的时间才能写成,一年就挣一千英镑是不足以过活的。所以嘛,你就会明白,为什么对于一位崭露头角的小说作家来说,起步之时他首先一定要做另外一份工作。否则的话,几乎可以肯定的是,他会因饥饿而死去。

如果你希望自己成为一名小说作家,你就应该具备或者应该获得下面这些品质中的某一些:

1. 你应该拥有一种活跃的想象力。

2. 你应该有能力将文章写好。我这样说的意思是,你应该有能力将一个场景在读者心中变得鲜活起来,使其栩栩如生。并非每一个人都具备这种能力,因为这是一种天赋。这种天赋,你或者具备,或者不具备。

3. 你必须有持久的耐力。换句话说,你必须坚持住手头的事情不放,要永不言弃,要一个小时、一个小时地坚持,要一天、一天地坚持,要一周、一周地坚持,要一个月、一个月地坚持。

4. 你必须精益求精、力求完美。这就等于说,你永远都不能满足于你已经写完的作品,你要一遍又一遍地反复修改,尽可能将其完善。

5. 你一定要有强大的自我约束力。记住,你是在独自耕耘,没有人雇你干活。要是你旷工,周围也没有人开除你。要是你懒散、懈怠,也没有人指责你。

6. 要是你的幽默感很是卓越,那将大有裨益。要是你写的内容针对成年读者,这一点倒不是那么至关重要,但是,要是写的内容针对的是儿童读者,这一点就至关重要了。

7. 你必须具有一定程度的谦恭性。认为自己的作品精彩绝妙的作家,势必会迈向险境。

我自己是如何一路上误打误撞,最后经由后门,滑落到小说世界中的,就让我跟你说说吧。

八岁的时候,也就是在 1924 年,我被送到一所寄宿学校去读书。这所学校坐落在一个叫作滨海韦斯顿的城镇里,这座城镇位于英格兰西南海岸。寄宿学校纪律严格,那些日子恐怖得很:宿舍里不许交谈,过道里不许奔跑,不允许有任何类型的不整洁行为,不许这个、不许那个,统统都不许。在这里,到处都是条条框框,到处都是必须遵守的规章制度。在这里,我们每时每刻都提心吊胆,害怕藤杖举过我们的头顶,那种害怕程度不亚于对于死亡的恐惧。

"校长要你到他的书房去。"听到这话,你就在劫难逃了。这样的话语会让你肚子表面的皮肤一阵阵地不寒而栗,但是,你还是得立即过去——当时约摸有九岁了吧,沿着阴冷的、长长的过道走过去,再穿过一道拱门,就进入校长的私人领地,那里只会有恐怖的事情发生,那里烟斗里烟草燃烧的气息在空中弥漫,犹如焚香一般。你就站在黑漆漆的房门外面,深深地吸气,甚至连门都不敢敲一下。你对自己说,要是母亲在这儿,那该有多好啊,她就不会让这一切发生了。但问题是,你孤立无援,你只得举起一只手,轻轻地那么一敲。

"进来!啊,没错,是达尔吧。那么,达尔,有人向我报告说,昨晚在做课后作业期间,你说话来着。"

"求求你,先生,我把笔尖弄断了,当时只是问詹金斯,还有没有笔尖借给我一个用。"

"我不会容忍做作业时说话,这一点你清楚得很。"

这个男性巨人奔向高高的角柜,伸手往柜子顶上够,那上面是他放置藤杖的地方。

"男孩子犯规就得受到惩罚。"

"先生……我……我的笔尖裂开……我……"

"那根本不是什么借口,我要教会你,让你知道,做作业期间说话

第四章 人生之路 第一节 《幸运开局》(上部) Lucky Break (Part A)

是得不偿失的。"

他将一根藤杖取了下来,那根藤杖有九十多厘米长,其中一头还带着一把弯曲的小手柄。藤杖是白色的,很细、很有柔韧性。"到窗户那儿去,腰弯下,手摸脚趾。"

"可是,先生……"

"不要跟我争辩,小子。让你怎么做,你就怎么做。"

于是,我弯下腰,然后等待着。他总是会让你等上约十秒钟的时间,十秒过后你的膝盖就招架不住,开始颤抖了。

"低一点儿,小子!摸到脚趾!"

我盯着自己脚上那双黑鞋的鞋头,对自己说,从现在起不一定什么时候,这个家伙就会挥动藤杖朝我猛击,非常用力,我整个屁股会改变颜色。藤杖抽打出的印记很长,横跨两个屁股蛋,青一块、紫一块的,边缘部分还渗出鲜红的血液。过后,要是你用手指在抽打后的表面轻轻摸一遍的话,就会有一种高高低低、起起伏伏的感觉。

"唰啦!……啪嚓!"

紧接着,疼痛就开始了。那种疼能把人折磨得要死,令人难以置信、无法忍受,就好像有人将一根白热的拨火棒横在你的屁股上,然后使劲往下压。

第二次抽打很快就会开始,你恨不得一下子伸出双手将这次抽打挡开,这也是一种本能的反应。可是,一旦你伸手去挡,你的手指就会一个个断掉。

"唰啦!……啪嚓!"

第二次抽打如期而至,紧挨着第一次抽打的痕迹落下,白色的拨火棒往皮肤里压得越来越深、越来越深。

"唰啦!……啪嚓!"

第三次抽打往往把疼痛推向了顶峰,简直就是登峰造极,比这次更厉害的抽打再也不会出现。自那之后,再多的抽打也只能延长一下这次的剧痛。你尽量不要哭出声来,可有时候就是无法忍住不哭。但问题是,不管忍得住忍不住你的哭声,眼泪是止不住的,它们会顺着脸颊如溪水般流淌下来,"啪啦啦"落到地毯上。

关键的事情是,抽打的时候,你永远也不要因为畏惧而挺身,或者直起腰来。要是那样做的话,会额外多抽打你一次。

接下来,校长慢慢地、从容地再抽打三次,耗时很长。这样,总共抽打的次数就是六次。

"你可以走了。"那声音仿佛从数公里外的一个深深的洞穴中传来。于是,你慢慢地直起腰,感到极度疼痛,双手一下子捂到燃烧的屁股上,竭尽全力紧紧捂住,踮起脚尖,蹦跳着走出屋子。

那根残忍的藤杖支配了我们的生活。宿舍熄灯后说话、课堂上讲话、在书桌上刻下名字的首字母、翻墙爬过去、外表邋遢、用手指弹回形针、晚上忘记换上便鞋、做游戏穿的服装没有挂起来,最主要的是,哪怕是最轻微地顶撞了一下哪位老爷(那些年月里,那里的老师不叫老师,而称呼为"老爷"),你就得遭受藤杖抽打。换句话说,我们被藤杖抽打的原因就是,我们做的一切都是小男孩自然而然要做的事情。

正因为如此,我们说话时得注意着点,走路时得注意着点。我的天啊,走路时,我们该怎么注意着点啊。结果,我们变得警惕异常、时刻提防。无论到哪里,我们走起路来都谨小慎微,时刻竖起耳朵听听是否有危险存在,就像野生动物轻手轻脚穿过树林一样。

除了那些老爷,学校里还有另外一个人令我们相当恐惧,这个人就是波普尔先生。波普尔这个人大腹便便,脸色深红。他是学校的门卫、锅炉看管人,还兼总务勤杂工。他的权利就是,哪怕有那么一点点的风吹草动,他就有可能(几乎可以肯定)去校长那儿报信,告发我们。波普尔先生的辉煌时刻就是在每天早晨正好七点半的时候。那时,他就会站在长长的主过道尽头"摇铃"。他摇的那只铃个头很大,是用黄铜做成的,上面安装了一个很粗的木柄。波普尔先生以他自己特殊的姿势,将胳膊完全伸展开来,前后摇晃起来,发出"当当啷——当当——当、当当啷——当当——当、当当啷——当当——当"的响声。一听到铃声,学校里所有的男孩子——共有一百八十

第四章 人生之路 第一节 《幸运开局》(上部) Lucky Break (Part A)

人——都麻利地奔向过道,各就各位,沿着墙壁两边排起长队,直挺挺地立正站好,等待着校长前来检阅。

但是,至少过去了十分钟,校长才到达现场。在校长到达前的那段时间里,波普尔先生会先主持一个仪式,这个仪式异乎寻常,至今我很难相信,这样的事情竟然会发生。学校里总共有六个厕所,厕所门上分别标有数字"一"至"六"。站在长长过道尽头的波普尔先生手掌心里握着六块黄铜做的小圆片,每块小圆片都标上了数字,数字从"一"到"六"不等。他任由自己的眼睛在两排直挺挺站立的男孩子中游移时,大家绝对不敢出半点儿声响。接着,他就一声大吼,喊出一个名字:"阿克尔!"

阿克尔就会脱离队列,沿着过道迅速奔向波普尔先生站立的地方。波普尔先生递过去一块黄铜做的圆片,阿克尔接过去后就直奔厕所而去:穿越整个过道,经过所有静静站立的同伴,然后向左转去。直到从众人的视线里消失,他才得空看一眼手中的圆片,看看给他的数字是多少。

"海顿!"波普尔先生大吼。现在,轮到海顿脱离队列,过来接圆片,然后匆忙离去。

"安杰尔!"……

"威廉森!"……

"冈特!"……

"普赖斯!"……

就这样,波普尔先生随意地、按自己的心愿,挑选出六名男生,派他们去厕所执勤。没有任何人问他们,是否在七点半吃早饭前做好了通大便的准备,他们只需遵守命令、照做不误就可以了。但是,我们却认为被选中算是享受一种尊贵的特权,因为那意味着在校长检阅期间,这几个离队的可以安稳无忧地待在厕所而免受折磨了。

时候一到,校长就从私人住处出来,接替了波普尔先生。只见他慢腾腾地沿着过道一侧走着,极其细心地审视每一个男孩子,一边走着,一边将自己手腕上佩戴的腕表收紧。早晨的检阅是一次令人胆战心惊的经历。他浓密的眉毛下长着一双尖锐的棕色眼睛,那双眼睛从上至下慢慢地扫视着每一个男孩子的身体,每每此时,我们每个人都惊恐万状。

"去,把头发好好洗一洗。下次要是还这样,你会后悔的。"
"让我看看你的两只手,上面有墨迹啊。昨晚为什么不洗掉?"
"小子,你的领结歪了。离队,重新系好,这次要好好地系上。"
"那只鞋上面,我看到了泥巴。关于这一点,难道上周我没有跟你谈过吗?早饭后,到书房来见我。"

一大清早,这种情形就这样持续着,真是令人恐惧的检阅。这一切都结束后,校长走开了,波普尔先生就开始带着我们,排着队形向食堂前进。此时,我们大家胃口全无,哪还有心思去吃随后端上来的、已经结成块的麦片粥呢。

五十多年过去了,我现在手头仍然有那些日子里保留下来的一些成绩单。我把它们一一翻了一遍,尽力想从中找出一丝线索,证明我将来有希望成为一名小说作家。很显然,我要查找这方面证据的科目就是英文写作。问题是,在这个科目之下,我所有学龄前成绩单上的成绩都平淡无奇,甚至一塌糊涂,但有一份成绩单除外。吸引我眼球的那份成绩单是1928年圣诞学期的。我当时十二岁,英文老师是维克托·科拉多。我至今对他还记忆犹新:他是一位英俊的高个子运动员,一头黑黑的波浪发,长了一只鹰钩鼻(后来的一天晚上,他与女舍监戴维斯小姐私奔了,我们再也没有看到过他们俩)。不管怎么说,事情巧就巧在,科拉多先生既教我们拳击,又教我们英文写作。就在这样吸引我眼球的成绩单上,英文写作成绩栏目下写着:"本科目成绩见拳击成绩栏,两者成绩完全相同。"所以,我们就看拳击成绩栏目,那下面是这样写的:"太缓慢、太笨拙。该生每一次出拳都不是很及时,很容易让人看到有拳头击打过来。"

但是,在这所学校里,一周只有一次的时间,也就是每个星期六的上午——每个美丽而愉悦的星期六的上午,所有胆战心惊的恐惧感都烟消云散。在长达两个小时的辉煌时间里,我所经历的可以算

第四章 人生之路 第一节 《幸运开局》(上部) Lucky Break (Part A)

得上是疯狂的喜悦。

不幸的是,年满十岁,才能遇到这样的狂喜之事,但也无关紧要,就让我跟你说说这是怎么一回事吧。

每个星期六的上午正好十点半的时候,波普尔那恼人的"当当唧——当当——当"的铃声就会响起。铃声一响就预示着下列事情会逐一发生:

首先,所有九岁以及九岁以下的男孩子(总共有七十人)立即奔向位于主楼后面的那个室外大沥青运动场。女舍监戴维斯小姐站在操场上,只见她双腿分开,胳膊交叉在胸前,她的胸部如高山一般高耸。要是赶上雨天,这些男孩子还得身穿雨衣赶到操场。如果赶上雪天或者暴风雪天,穿着外衣、戴上围巾也要赶来。当然啦,校帽总是要戴到头上的,帽子是灰色的,前面镶嵌了一枚红色的徽章。任何的不可抗力,不管是龙卷风也好,飓风也罢,还是什么火山喷发,都不能阻止星期六上午那两个小时讨厌的步行活动。这个活动,七岁、八岁、九岁的小男孩必须都参加。每个星期六的上午,这些小男孩必须沿着滨海韦斯顿地区空旷的平地步行,风从身边呼啸而过。他们排着鳄鱼队列行走,也就是两人一排纵向行走。戴维斯小姐大踏步走在队列旁边。她身穿粗花呢裙子,腿上套着羊毛长筒袜,头戴一顶毡帽,那顶毡帽肯定是被耗子啃过了。

星期六上午波普尔先生的铃声响起时,另一件发生的事情就是,其余的男孩子——所有那些十岁以及十岁以上的男孩子(总共约一百人),都要立即赶往主会馆坐好。一名地位低一些的老爷,名字叫S·K·约普,就会从门边伸出头来,冲着我们喊叫,喊的架势甚是凶猛,唾沫星像子弹一样从嘴里不断飞出,飞溅到屋子对面窗户的玻璃上。"好啦!"他大喊,"不许讲话! 不许动弹! 眼向前看,手放到书桌上!"随即,他会再次大喊一遍。

我们静静地坐着、等待着,等待美妙时刻的到来。我们知道,这一时刻很快就要到来。我们听到外面的机动车道上汽车发动的声音,都是些古老的车,都需要手摇柄来发动(不要忘了,当时可是在

1927年和1928年之间啊)。这就是星期六上午的仪式。总共有五辆汽车,而学校里总共十四位老爷都要塞进去——不仅包括校长本人,还包括紫色面孔的波普尔先生。接着,汽车拖着一股青烟,呼啸着飞驰而去,载着他们去校外的一个酒馆消遣。如果我没有记错的话,那个酒馆的名字叫"络腮胡伯爵"。他们坐在那个酒馆里,喝着浓浓的黑啤酒,喝完一大瓶又一大瓶,一直喝到快要吃午饭的时候才离开。两个半小时过后,也就是下午一点钟的时候,我们就会看到他们赶了回来,小心翼翼地走进食堂吃午饭,一边走还一边扶着周围的东西。

关于这些老爷,就说到这儿。问题是,我们这一大批十岁、十一岁、十二岁的男孩子留在原地,坐在学校偌大的会馆里,突然之间没有一个成年人看管,我们会怎样?当然,接下来会发生什么,我们再也清楚不过啦。这些老爷离开还不到一分钟的时间,我们就听见大门开了,外面响起了脚步声。接着,有人走进来,宽松衣服发出一阵响动,手镯叮当作响,头发飞舞起来。此时,一名妇女闪进屋子喊道:"嗨,大家好!高兴起来吧!这可不是什么葬礼仪式啊!"或者说些类似的话。这位就是奥康纳太太。

漂亮的奥康纳太太令人愉悦,她的服饰滑稽、古怪,灰色的头发披散开来、到处飞舞。她大约五十岁的样子,长着一副马面,牙齿又长又黄。但是,对我们来说,她很是漂亮。她不是学校的员工,是从城里某个地方雇来的,专门在星期六的上午照顾我们,相当于保姆的角色,好让我们安安静静地度过两个半小时。其间,学校的老爷都离开,去酒馆痛饮一番了。

可是,奥康纳太太绝不是什么保姆。她的作用绝不亚于一位伟大而有天赋的教师,她是一位学者,酷爱英国文学。我们中的每个人每个星期六上午都跟她待在一起,一待就是三年(从十岁开始,一直到离开学校那年)。三年期间,我们涉猎了整个英国文学史——从公元597年一直到19世纪早期。

对于新加入这门课程学习的孩子,每人发给一本薄薄的蓝皮小

第四章 人生之路 第一节 《幸运开局》(上部) Lucky Break (Part A)

册子，总共才六页，名称是《文学编年表》，供他们永久保存。那本六页的小册子按照年代的顺序列出长长的清单，包括年代以及每个年代在英国文学史上所发生的重大的，或者不怎么重大的里程碑式的事件。奥康纳太太正好选出一百个此类事件，我们将这些事件在课本上做上标记，并铭记在心。我仍然能记忆起其中的一些：

公元597年　圣奥古斯丁登陆萨尼特岛，并将基督教带到不列颠群岛
731年　比德编写《基督教会史》
1215年　《大宪章》签署
1399年　朗格兰发表长诗《耕农皮尔斯的梦幻》
1476年　卡克斯顿在威斯敏斯特设立了第一家印刷厂
1478年　乔叟完成《坎特伯雷故事集》
1485年　马洛礼完成《亚瑟王之死》
1590年　斯宾塞发表长诗《仙后》
1623年　莎士比亚的《第一对开本》刊印
1667年　米尔顿的史诗《失乐园》发表
1668年　德莱顿的《论文集》刊印
1678年　班扬完成《天路历程》
1711年　阿狄森发表《旁观者》
1719年　笛福完成《鲁宾逊漂流记》
1726年　斯威夫特完成《格列佛游记》
1733年　蒲柏写成《论人》
1755年　约翰逊编撰完成《英语辞典》
1791年　鲍斯韦尔完成《约翰逊传记》
1833年　卡莱尔写成《萨特·雷萨特》
1859年　达尔文发表《物种起源》

奥康纳太太轮流讲解这些条目，整个一个星期六上午的两个半小时的时间里，她拿出其中一个条目讲给我们听。这样，三年时间结

束的时候(每学年约有三十六个星期六),她就会将一百个条目全部讲完了。

这其中真是乐趣多多、内容绝妙,令人兴奋无比!她具备伟大教师的才能,在那间屋子里,她能够将自己所讲的内容活灵活现地呈现在我们面前。在那两个半小时的时间里,我们渐渐地爱上了朗格兰和他笔下的耕农皮尔斯。下一个星期六,她讲乔叟,我们喜爱上了乔叟。即便是一个有点相当难懂的家伙,像弥尔顿、德莱顿、蒲柏之类的作家,只要奥康纳太太一跟我们朗读他们的生平以及作品的一部分内容,我们大家都会兴奋不已。对我而言,不管从哪方面来说,这一切带来的结果就是,我十三岁时就已经强烈地意识到,这笔巨大的文学遗产是好几个世纪以来,英国人积累下来的财富。对于优秀的作品,我渴望去阅读,读起来就"贪得无厌"。

和蔼的奥康纳太太是多么可爱啊!或许,去那所糟糕透顶的学校是值得的,就是因为在那里可以体验到每个星期六上午的快乐。

十三岁的时候,我离开了学龄前学校,却又被送入其中一所有名的英国公立学校,又成了一名寄宿生。当然,公立学校并不是公家的,都是私有性质的,而且费用很贵。我就读的那所学校名为雷普顿公学,位于德比郡。当时,我们学校的校长是杰弗里·费希尔牧师,他后来当上了切斯特主教,接着又当上了伦敦主教,最后成为坎特伯雷大主教。他一生中做过的最后一件事情就是,在威斯敏斯特教堂,为伊丽莎白女王二世加冕。

在这所学校,我们必须得穿一种衣服,这种衣服让我们看起来就像是殡仪馆里的助手:上衣是黑色的,前部切掉了一部分,后部垂下长长的尾巴,一直垂到膝盖后面以下的部位;裤子是黑色的,上面带有细细的、灰色的条纹,鞋是黑色的;马甲是黑色的,每天早晨还得把上面的十一枚纽扣一一扣好;领带是黑色的;还有一条直挺挺的、经过淀粉浆洗后变得硬邦邦的蝴蝶形衣领,再加上一件白色的衬衫。

更有甚者,最后一个滑稽、荒唐的服饰是一顶草帽——走出屋子就必须一直戴着,只有做游戏时才可以摘掉。帽子遇雨就会因被淋

第四章 人生之路 第一节 《幸运开局》(上部) Lucky Break (Part A)

湿而变软。因此,若碰上下雨之类的坏天气,我们都得带把雨伞。

十三岁那年第一学期开始的时候,我就这身奇特的打扮跟着母亲去伦敦坐火车,我当时的感受你是可想而知的。她吻我告别,我随即启程。

我自然而然地希望,在这所崭新的、更加适宜成年人的学校里,我那长期遭受折磨的屁股不会再受罪了,但是,情况并非如此。雷普顿公学的体罚行为比我经历的任何东西都要激烈得多、频繁得多。任何时候都不要天真地认为,未来的坎特伯雷大主教会反对这些卑劣的行径。他卷起袖子,也加入到体罚的行列,而且乐此不疲。他打起人来很是凶狠,那场景真是令人胆战心惊。作为一位神职人员——英国国教会未来的领袖,他的一些打人行为极其残忍。我十分清楚地记得,有一次他打完人之后,不得不端来一盆水,拿来一块海绵和一条毛巾,好让被打者随后能将身上流淌出来的血液擦掉。

这,绝不是什么玩笑。

简直就是西班牙宗教法庭迫害异教徒的卑劣行径。

但是,这个学校所有的卑劣行径中,我认为最为卑劣的就是学长得到允许,可以去打其他同学,这样的事每天都有。大男孩(年纪十七或者十八)会抽打小一些的男孩(年纪十三、十四或十五),如虐待狂一般,通常在晚上你上楼回到宿舍,套上宽松的睡衣、睡裤后开始进行。

"要你到楼下的更衣室去一趟。"

尽管双手发沉,你还是得套上浴袍、穿上拖鞋,然后跌跌撞撞地下楼,进入那间大大的、铺上了木制地板的房间。那里的四壁挂满了做游戏用的服装,天花板上垂下一只没有灯罩的电灯泡。一名学长在屋子中央等着你,一副耀武扬威、杀气腾腾的样子,双手握着一根长长的藤条。你进来的时候,他通常都是在弯来弯去地摆弄着手里的那根藤条。

"我想,你知道来这儿的原因吧,"他会这样说。

"哦,我……"

"一连两天啦,你都把我的面包烤煳了。"

我得解释一下,他为什么冷不丁冒出这样一句荒唐可笑的话。你是低年级学生,要受眼前这位学长的差遣,那就意味着,你是他的仆人,要伺候他。差事很多,但其中一个就是在每天下午的茶点时间为他烤面包。你要使用一根长长的、带有三个尖齿的烤叉,用叉齿将面包叉住,然后举到明火前,烤完一面,再烤另一面。但问题是,唯一允许烤面包的火源在图书馆里面,而且随着午后茶点时间的临近,那里聚拢的命运悲惨的低年级学生不下十二人,大家你推我搡、你争我夺,都想在那个微小的烤架前占有一席之地。我不谙此道,总是将面包举得太近,结果就烤煳了。但是,重新再烤一块面包是绝对不可能的,因此,我们唯一能做的,就是用一把小刀将烤煳的部分刮掉。只要用刀一刮,就逃不出学长的眼睛,学长个个都是行家里手,擅长探测被刮过的面包。你会看到这个让你的身体吃尽苦头的家伙端坐在上座的位置上,拿起那块面包,翻来覆去地仔细查看,仿佛在检验一小幅价值不菲的画作。随后,他就会眉头一皱,你也就知道在劫难逃了。

所以嘛,现在到了晚上,你就得穿着睡衣、睡裤,披上浴袍,下楼到更衣室去。那个学长,也就是面包被你烤煳的那个,就会对你的罪行数落一番。

"我不喜欢吃烤煳的面包。"

"我举得太近了,很抱歉。"

"你选哪一个?浴袍不脱掉,打四下,还是脱掉后,打三下?"

"不脱掉,打四下吧。"我回答。

问这样的问题,已经成为惯例,总会让被打者去选择。我自己穿的浴袍是用浓密的棕色骆驼毛制成的,所以我的心里从来都是毫不含糊地做出这样一个更好的选择。穿着睡衣、睡裤挨打,只能是一场痛苦的经历,你的皮肤几乎总是会被打得裂开,但是,我的浴袍可以避免此类事情发生。当然,这位学长对这一切清楚得很,因此呢,不管是什么时候,只要你选择了宁愿被多打一下而不脱掉浴袍的话,他

第四章 人生之路 第一节 《幸运开局》(上部) Lucky Break (Part A)

就会使出浑身力气拼命地抽打。有时候,他会助跑一小段距离,踮起脚尖,从三四步远的距离,大力冲过来,以便获得更多的冲刺力和抽打力。不管以何种方式抽打,这都是一种粗野的行径。

在过去那些日子里,监狱里要是有人被吊死的话,整座监狱就会静悄悄的,其他囚犯就会一声不响地坐在各自的牢房中,任由这样的行为开始、结束。学校里发生体罚行为时,情况跟监狱里的如出一辙:楼上的宿舍里,孩子们静悄悄地坐在床上,对被打者抱以同情之心。寂静中,从楼下的更衣室里传来"啪,啪……"抽打的声音。

在这所学校里,我的期末成绩单很有意思,下面是其中的四份,是我从原始成绩单上一字不差抄下来的:

1930年夏季学期(十四岁时),英文写作。

"我还从来没有遇到这样一个男孩子,每次写出来的跟心里想的完全相反。他似乎不具备将思想表述到纸面上的能力。"

1931年复活节假期(十五岁时),英文写作。

"每次都写得混乱不堪,词汇量寥寥无几,句子结构支离破碎。他倒是让我想起了骆驼。"

1932年夏季学期(十六岁时),英文写作。

"这个男孩子是班级里一名迟缓呆滞、不懂读写的学生。"

1932年秋季学期(十七岁时),英文写作。

"每次都吊儿郎当,思维受限。"(在这份成绩单的下方,未来的坎特伯雷大主教还用红笔写着:"他必须改正这张纸上面的缺陷。")

那些日子里,当一位作家的念头从来没有进过我的大脑,也就不足为奇了。

1934年,我十八岁。离开学校时,母亲提出要我上大学,我没加理会(我三岁时,父亲去世了)。一个人要是不想当医生、律师、科学家、工程师,或者类似其他方面的专业人员的话,我看不出浪费三四年的时间上牛津、剑桥这样的大学有什么意义,我至今还是这样看的。与上大学相反的是,我怀有一种热切的希望要出国,要去旅行,要看看遥远的地方。那些岁月里,几乎没有什么商业化的飞机投入运营,去非洲或者远东的旅程要花上好几周的时间。

所以,我找到了一份工作,工作的部门当时被称作"壳牌石油公司东方员工培训部"。那里的人向我许诺,在英国接受两三年的培训后,就会把我派往国外。

"哪个国家?"我问。

"谁知道呢?"这名男子回答,"这取决于,当你的名字排到榜首时,哪个地方有空缺啦,可能是埃及、中国、印度,也可能是世界上任何一个国家。"

那话听起来很有意思,却也的确如此。三年后,轮到我的名字被列入出国人员名单时,我被告知,要去的地方是东非。订购了去热带穿的服装后,母亲帮我收拾衣箱。我这次到非洲,一去就是三年时间,然后才允许我回家度假六个月。我已经二十一岁,就要出发,到遥远的地方,感觉棒极了。我在伦敦码头登船,驶离了家乡。

那次旅程用了两周半的时间。我们穿过比斯开湾,短暂停靠在直布罗陀,接下来,取道马耳他、那不勒斯、塞得港,驶向地中海。我们穿过苏伊士运河,沿红海行驶,停靠在苏丹港,再驶向亚丁。整个旅程相当令人兴奋。我第一次看到了满眼尽是沙粒的大沙漠,看到了阿拉伯士兵骑在骆驼上,看到了结满枣子的椰枣树,看到了飞鱼,还看到了其他成百上千的奇妙的事物。最后,我们到达了肯尼亚的蒙巴萨市。

在蒙巴萨,来自壳牌石油公司的一名男子登上船,对我说,我必须转乘一艘小型海船,继续前行,赶往坦噶尼喀(现在的坦桑尼亚)的首都达累斯萨拉姆。就这样,我去了达累斯萨拉姆,途中在桑给巴尔岛稍作停留。

随后的两年时间里,我在坦桑尼亚壳牌公司设在达累斯萨拉姆的总部工作。那段时间的生活奇妙无比,热得要命又有谁会在意呢?我们的装束就是黄卡其布的短裤、敞开式衬衫,还有一顶软遮阳帽。我学会说斯瓦希里语,开车到内地去看钻石矿、剑麻种植园以及金矿等等地方。

这个地方遍地都是长颈鹿、大象、斑马、狮子、羚羊,还有各种蛇,包括非洲黑曼巴蛇——世界上唯一的一种看到你就会追逐你的蛇。要是它追上你、咬你一口的话,你最好就开始祷告吧。我学会将防蚊靴倒过来摇晃几下再穿上,以防里面爬进蝎子。跟其他人一样,我也得过疟疾,卧床三天,高烧40.8℃。

(待续……)

第二节 《幸运开局》(下部) Lucky Break (Part B)

如第一节所述,罗尔德·达尔的《幸运开局》(Lucky Break)收录在《〈非凡亨利〉及另外六篇故事集》(The Wonderful Story of Henry Sugar and Six More)一书中。这个故事开篇前,作者加上了一句类似于副标题的话:"我成为作家的前前后后"(How I Became a Writer),可见这不是一篇"纯粹"的小说,而是达尔给读者提出的一些如何成为作家的意见和建议,此外还有达尔如何成为作家的一些个人的"奇闻轶事"以及他写过的小说中涉及的一些情节的"摘要"。可以说,《幸运开局》更像是一篇"意识流"式的、具有个人片段回忆的"传记"性的论说文。

一、原作导读

时光流转,转眼之间,1939年的9月到来了。

1939年9月,显而易见的是,以希特勒为首的德国就要爆发一场战争了。

In September 1939, it became obvious that there was going to be a war with Hitler's Germany.

接下来,达尔讲述了战争(第二次世界大战)期间以及战后他的部分经历,包括他的那次颇有争议性的坠机经历①。正因为这次经历,他被派往美国首都华盛顿,为英国大使馆工作,这样他才有机会幸运地见到了美国作家 C·S·福雷斯特,还成为美国总统富兰克林·罗斯福的座上客。

当时,福雷斯特为一本杂志的约稿伤透了脑筋,怎么都写不出来。他听说达尔有战争这方面的经历,就去找达尔交谈,想找点灵感。就餐期间,不善言谈的达尔提出了自己的想法:

"这样吧,"我提议道,"如果您觉得可以的话,我尽量把发生的事情写到纸上,寄给您。然后,您就可以花点时间适当改正一下。这样做,是不是更容易些?我今晚就可以写出来。"

尽管当时我不得而知,但那一刻我的提议却改变了我的人生。

"你的提议绝妙得很,"福雷斯特说,"那样的话,我就可以把这个无用的记事本挪开,我们可以好好享受午餐了。你真的愿意为我那样去做吗?"

"我乐意之至,"我说,"可是,你一定不要期望我会写得会有多好,我只能将事实付诸纸面。"

"Look," I said. "If you like, I'll try to write down on paper what happened and send it to you. Then you can rewrite it properly yourself in your own time. Wouldn't that be easier? I could do it tonight."

That, though I didn't know it at the time, was the moment that changed my life.

---

① 关于这一点,读者可以参阅《罗尔德·达尔短篇故事品读及汉译探索(第1卷)》第四章第二节的开头部分的叙述。

第四章 人生之路 第二节 《幸运开局》(下部) Lucky Break (Part B)

"A splendid idea," Forester said. "Then I can put this silly notebook away and we can enjoy our lunch. Would you really mind doing that for me?"

"I don't mind a bit," I said. "But you mustn't expect it to be any good. I'll just put down the facts."

两周过后,达尔接到了福雷斯特的亲笔信,信中福雷斯特高度赞扬了达尔所写的文章,认为达尔是"一位才华横溢的作家"(a gifted writer),并原封不动发表了达尔写的那篇文章,也就是上面提到的《小菜一碟》,这奠定了达尔的作家之路,达尔的写作生涯因此而变得一发不可收。

你瞧,事情就是这个样子,这就是我成为作家的前前后后。要不是我有幸遇上福雷斯特先生,这一切或许从来就不会发生。

So there you are. That's how I became a writer. Had I not been lucky enough to meet Mr. Forester, it would probably never have happened.

二、原作释读

作家罗尔德·达尔在他的这篇作品中提到了很多作家及其作品(包括他自己的一些作品),个别作品的书写形式跟常见的形式略有差异,读者可以参照后面的探索性译文加以理解与辨别。同时,阅读中还要突破一些专有名词的障碍,特别是一些地名类的专有名词。

Lucky Break

(Continued from the above)

In September 1939, it became obvious that there was going to be a war with Hitler's Germany. Tanganyika, which only twenty years before had been called German East Africa, was still full of Germans. They were everywhere. They owned shops and mines and plantations all over the country. The moment war broke out, they would have to be rounded up. But we had no army to speak of in Tanganyika, only a few native soldiers, known as Askaris①, and a handful of officers. So all of us civilian men were made Special Reservists②. I was given an armband and put in charge of twenty Askaris. My little troop and I were ordered to block the road that led south out of Tanganyika into neutral Portuguese East Africa. This was an important job, for it was along that road most of the Germans would try to escape when war was declared.

I took my happy gang with their rifles and one machine-gun and set up a road-block in a place where the road passed through dense jungle, about ten miles outside the town. We had a field telephone to headquarters which would tell us at once when war was declared. We settled down to wait. For three days we waited. And during the nights, from all around us in the jungle, came the sound of native drums beating weird hypnotic③ rhythms. Once, I wandered into the jungle in the dark and came across about fifty natives squatting in a circle around a fire. One man only was beating the drum. Some were dancing round the fire. The remainder were drinking something out of coconut shells. They welcomed me into their circle. They were lovely people. I could talk to them in their language. They gave me a shell filled with a thick grey intoxicating

---

① askari: *Noun* (in East Africa) a soldier or police officer (东非) 士兵;警察

② reservist: *Noun* a member of the military reserve forces 预备役军人

③ hypnotic: *Adjective* of, producing, or relating to hypnosis (与) 催眠 (有关) 的 (e.g. a hypnotic state 催眠状态)

第四章 人生之路 第二节 《幸运开局》(下部) Lucky Break (Part B)

fluid made of fermented① maize. It was called, if I remember rightly, Pomba②. I drank it. It was horrible.

The next afternoon, the field telephone rang and a voice said, "We are at war with Germany." Within minutes, far away in the distance, I saw a line of cars throwing up clouds of dust, heading our way, beating it for the neutral territory of Portuguese East Africa as fast as they could go.

Ho ho, I thought. We are going to have a little battle, and I called out to my twenty Askaris to prepare themselves. But there was no battle. The Germans, who were after all only civilian townspeople, saw our machine-gun and our rifles and quickly gave themselves up. Within an hour, we had a couple of hundred of them on our hands. I felt rather sorry for them. Many I knew personally, like Willy Hink the watchmaker and Herman Schneider who owned the soda-water factory. Their only crime had been that they were German. But this was war, and in the cool of the evening, we marched them all back to Dar-es-Salaam where they were put into a huge camp surrounded by barbed wire③.

① ferment: Verb [no obj.] (of a substance) undergo fermentation 发酵 (e.g. The drink had fermented, turning some of the juice into alcohol. 饮料发酵了, 把一些果汁变成了酒精。)

② pombe: Noun [mass noun] (in Central and East Africa) a fermented drink made from various kinds of grain and fruit(中非和东非用各种谷物和果子做的)非洲酒

③ barbed wire: Noun [mass noun] wire with clusters of short, sharp spikes set at short intervals along it, used to make fences or in warfare as an obstruction(用于制围栏或战场障碍物的)带刺铁丝

· 285 ·

The next day, I got into my old car and drove north, heading for Nairobi①, in Kenya, to join the R. A. F.② It was a rough trip and it took me four days. Bumpy jungle roads, wide rivers where the car had to be put on to a raft and pulled across by a ferryman hauling on a rope, long green snakes sliding across the road in front of the car. (N. B. Never try to run over a snake because it can be thrown up into the air and may land inside your open car. It's happened many times.) I slept at night in the car. I passed below the beautiful Mount Kilimanjaro③, which had a hat of snow on its head. I drove through the Masai country where the men drank cows' blood and every one of them seemed to be seven feet tall. I nearly collided with a giraffe on the Serengeti Plain④. But I came safely to Nairobi at last and reported to R. A. F. headquarters at the airport.

For six months, they trained us in small aeroplanes called Tiger Moths, and those days were also glorious. We skimmed all over Kenya in

---

① Nairobi: *Noun* the capital of Kenya; pop. 1,346,000 (est. 1989). It is situated on the central Kenyan plateau at an altitude of 1,680 m (5,500 ft). 内罗毕（肯尼亚首都，1989年估计人口 1,346,000，位于肯尼亚高原中部，海拔 1,680 米，即 5,500 英尺）。

② R. A. F. or RAF: *Abbreviation* Royal Air Force 英国皇家空军

③ Mount Kilimanjaro: *Noun* The highest mountain in Africa, in northeast Tanzania near the Kenya border, rising in two snow-capped peaks to 5,898.7 m (19,340 ft). 乞力马扎山（非洲最高山，位于坦桑尼亚东北部，靠近肯尼亚边境，有两座白雪皑皑的主峰拔地而起，高度为 5,898.5 米，相当于 19,340 英尺）。

④ Serengeti Plain: a vast plain in Tanzania, to the west of the Great Rift Valley. In 1951 the Serengeti National Park was created to protect the area's large numbers of wildebeest, zebra, and Thomson's gazelle 塞伦盖蒂大平原（坦桑尼亚大平原，位于东非大裂谷以西；1951 年建立塞伦盖蒂国家公园以保护该区域大量的角马、斑马和汤姆森羚羊）。

our little Tiger Moths①. We saw great herds of elephants. We saw the pink flamingoes② on Lake Nakuru③. We saw everything there was to see in that magnificent country. And often, before we could take off, we had to chase the zebras off the flying-field. There were twenty of us training to be pilots out there in Nairobi. Seventeen of those twenty were killed during the war.

From Nairobi, they sent us up to Iraq, to a desolate airforce base near Baghdad④ to finish our training. The place was called Habbaniyih, and in the afternoons it got so hot (130 degrees in the shade) that we were not allowed out of our huts. We just lay on the bunks⑤ and sweated. The unlucky ones got heat-stroke and were taken to hospital and

---

① tiger moth: a stout moth which has boldly spotted and streaked wings and a hairy caterpillar (woolly bear) 桔灯蛾;虎蛾

注:这里大写,指的是一种战斗机。

② flamingo: *Noun* a tall wading bird with mainly pink or scarlet plumage and long legs and neck. It has a heavy bent bill that is held upside down in the water in order to filter-feed on small organisms 红鹳;火烈鸟

③ Nakuru: *Noun* an industrial city in western Kenya; pop. 162,800 (1989). Nearby is Lake Nakuru, famous for its spectacular flocks of flamingos. 纳库鲁(肯尼亚西部工业城市,1989年人口162,800,附近有闻名的火烈鸟栖息地纳库鲁湖。)

④ Baghdad: *Noun* The capital of Iraq, on the River Tigris; pop. 648,600 (est. 1985). A thriving city under the Abbasid caliphs in the 8th and 9th centuries, it was taken by the Ottoman sultan Suleiman in 1534 and remained under Ottoman rule until the First World War. In 1920 it became the capital of the newly created state of Iraq. 巴格达(伊拉克首都,位于底格里斯河畔,1985年估计人口648,600,公元8~9世纪阿拔斯王朝哈里发统治时很繁盛,1534年被奥斯曼帝国苏丹苏莱曼占领,直至第一次世界大战,1920年成为新建立的伊拉克国首都。)

⑤ bunk: *Noun* a narrow shelf-like bed, typically one of two or more arranged one on top of the other 架子床(尤指多层床之一层)

packed in ice for several days. This either killed them or saved them. It was a fifty-fifty chance.

At Habbaniyih, they taught us to fly more powerful aeroplanes with guns in them, and we practised shooting at drogues①(targets in the air pulled behind other planes) and at objects on the ground.

Finally, our training was finished, and we were sent to Egypt to fight against the Italians in the Western Desert of Libya. I joined 80 Squadron, which flew fighters, and at first we had only ancient single-seater bi-planes called Gloster Gladiators. The two machine-guns on a Gladiator were mounted one on either side of the engine, and they fired their bullets, believe it or not, *through* the propeller. The guns were somehow synchronized② with the propeller shaft③ so that in theory the bullets missed the whirling propeller blades. But as you might guess, this complicated mechanism often went wrong and the poor pilot, who was trying to shoot down the enemy, shot off his own propeller instead.

I myself was shot down in a Gladiator which crashed far out in the Libyan desert between the enemy lines. The plane burst into flames, but I managed to get out and was finally rescued and carried back to safety by our own soldiers who crawled out across the sand under cover of darkness.

---

① drogue: *Noun* a funnel-shaped or cone-shaped device towed behind an aircraft as a target or as a windsock 锥形拖靶;风(向)袋

② synchronize or synchronise: *Verb* [with obj.] cause to occur or operate at the same time or rate 使同步发生(或运转)

③ shaft: *Noun* a long cylindrical rotating rod for the transmission of motive power in a machine(机器的)轴

第四章 人生之路 第二节 《幸运开局》(下部) Lucky Break (Part B)

That crash sent me to hospital in Alexandria① for six months with a fractured skull and a lot of burns. When I came out, in April 1941, my squadron had been moved to Greece to fight the Germans who were invading from the north. I was given a Hurricane and told to fly it from Egypt to Greece and join the squadron. Now, a Hurricane fighter was not at all like the old Gladiator. It had eight Browning machine-guns, four in each wing, and all eight of them fired simultaneously when you pressed the small button on your joy-stick②. It was a magnificent plane, but it had a range of only two hours' flying-time. The journey to Greece, non-stop, would take nearly five hours, always over the water. They put extra fuel tanks on the wings. They said I would make it. In the end, I did. But only just. When you are six feet six inches tall, as I am, it is no joke to be sitting crunched up in a tiny cockpit③ for five hours.

In Greece, the R.A.F. had a total of about eighteen Hurricanes. The Germans had at least one thousand aeroplanes to operate with. We had a hard time. We were driven from our aerodrome④ outside Athens (Elevis), and flew for a while from a small secret landing strip further west (Menidi). The Germans soon found that one and bashed it to bits,

---

① Alexandria: *Noun* the chief port of Egypt; pop. 3,170,000 (est. 1990). Alexandria was a major centre of Hellenistic culture 亚历山大(埃及主要港口,1990年估计人口3,170,000;曾是希腊文化的重要中心。)

② joy-stick or joystick: (informal) the control column of an aircraft (非正式)(飞机的)操纵杆

③ cockpit: *Noun* a compartment for the pilot, and sometimes also the crew, in an aircraft or spacecraft(飞机或航天器的)飞行员座舱(或机组人员座舱)

④ aerodrome: *Noun* (Brit.) a small airport or airfield(英)小型飞机(降落)场

so with the few planes we had left, we flew off to a tiny field (Argos①) right down in the south of Greece, where we hid our Hurricanes under the olive trees when we weren't flying.

But this couldn't last long. Soon, we had only five Hurricanes left, and not many pilots still alive. Those five planes were flown to the island of Crete②. The Germans captured Crete. Some of us escaped. I was one of the lucky ones. I finished up back in Egypt. The squadron was re-formed and re-equipped with Hurricanes. We were sent off to Haifa③, which was then in Palestine (now Israel), where we fought the Germans

---

① Argos: *Noun* a city in the NE Peloponnese of Greece; pop. 20,702 (1981). One of the oldest cities of ancient Greece, it dominated the Peloponnese and the western Aegean in the 7th century B.C. 阿尔戈斯城(希腊伯罗奔尼撒半岛东北部一城市,1981年人口20,702,古希腊最古老城市之一,公元前7世纪时曾控制了伯罗奔尼撒半岛和爱琴海西部海域。)

② Crete: a Greek island in the eastern Mediterranean; pop. 536,980 (1991); capital, Heraklion. It is noted for the remains of the Minoan civilization which flourished there in the 2nd millennium B.C. It fell to Rome in 67 B.C. and was subsequently ruled by Byzantines, Venetians, and Turks. Crete played an important role in the Greek struggle for independence from the Turks in the late 19th and early 20th centuries, becoming administratively part of an independent Greece in 1913. Greek name Kríti. 克里特岛(地中海东部一希腊岛屿,1991年人口536,980,首都伊拉克利翁,因公元前两千年繁荣的弥诺斯文化遗产闻名;公元前67年向罗马称臣,后相继被拜占庭人、威尼斯人和土耳其人统治;克里特岛在19世纪末和20世纪初希腊为争取独立而与土耳其进行的斗争中起了重要作用,1913年成为希腊的独立的一个行政区,希腊语名"Kríti"。)

③ Haifa: *Noun* The chief port of Israel, in the north-west of the country on the Mediterranean coast; pop. 248,200 (est. 1993) 海法(以色列西北部主要港口,位于地中海沿岸,1993年估计人口248,200。)

第四章　人生之路　第二节　《幸运开局》(下部) *Lucky Break* (*Part B*)

again and the Vichy French① in Lebanon② and Syria③.

At that point, my old head injuries caught up with me. Severe headaches compelled me to stop flying. I was invalided④ back to England and

---

① Vichy France: *Noun* the Vichy Regime, the Vichy Government, or simply Vichy are common terms used to describe the government of France which collaborated with the Axis powers during the Second World War 维希法国傀儡政权(政府或军队),指的是第二次世界大战期间与轴心国勾结的那部分法国政权。
注:这里的"Vichy French"指的是法国傀儡政权下的那批军队。
② Lebanon: *Noun* a country in the Middle East with a coastline on the Mediterranean Sea; pop. 2,700,000 (est. 1990); official language, Arabic; capital, Beirut 黎巴嫩(中东地中海沿岸国家;1990年估计人口2,700,000,官方语言阿拉伯语;首都贝鲁特。)
③ Syria: *Noun* a country in the Middle East with a coastline on the eastern Mediterranean Sea; pop. 12,824,000 (est. 1991); official language, Arabic; capital, Damascus 叙利亚(中东国家,位于地中海东岸;1991年估计人口12,824,000;官方语言是阿拉伯语;首都大马士革。)
④ invalid: *Verb* [with obj.] (usu. be invalided) remove (someone) from active service in the armed forces because of injury or illness 使(因伤或病)退役(e.g. He was badly wounded and invalided out of the infantry. 他受伤严重从步兵团退役了。)

sailed on a troopship from Suez to Durban① to Capetown② to Lagos③ to Liverpool④, chased by German submarines in the Atlantic and bombed by long-range Focke-Wulf⑤ aircraft every day for the last week of the voyage.

I had been away from home for four years. My mother, bombed out of her own house in Kent⑥ during the Battle of Britain and now living in a

---

① Durban: *Noun* a seaport and resort in South Africa, on the coast of Kwa-Zulu/Natal; pop. 1,137,380 (1991). Former name (until 1835) Port Natal 德班（南非港市及旅游胜地,位于夸祖卢/纳塔尔海滨,1991年人口1,137,380;1835年前名称为"Port Natal"。)

② Capetown or Cape Town: the legislative capital of South Africa and administrative capital of the province of Western Cape; pop. 776,600 (1985) 开普敦（南非立法机构所在地的首都,西开普省行政首府;1985年人口776,600。)

③ Lagos: *Noun* the chief city of Nigeria, a port on the Gulf of Guinea; pop. 1,347,000 (1992). Originally a centre of the slave trade, it became capital of the newly independent Nigeria in 1960. It was replaced as capital by Abuja in 1991. 拉各斯（尼日利亚主要城市,几内亚湾港口;1992年人口1,347,000;原为奴隶贸易中心,1960年独立后尼日利亚首都,1991年被新首都阿布贾取代。)

④ Liverpool: *Noun* a city and seaport in NW England, situated at the east side of the mouth of the River Mersey; pop. 448,300 (1991). Liverpool developed as a port in the 17th century with the import of cotton from America and the export of textiles produced in Lancashire and Yorkshire, and in the 18th century became an important centre of shipbuilding and engineering 利物浦（英格兰西北城市及港口,位于默西河口东侧,1991年人口448,300,17世纪随着从美国进口棉花,出口兰开夏郡和约克郡生产的织物而发展成港口,18世纪成为重要的造船和工程中心。)

⑤ 这里的是"Focke-Wulf",指的是德国的福克沃尔夫战机,为单座位单引擎战斗机,被视为二战期间最优秀的战斗机之一。

⑥ Kent: *Noun* a county on the SE coast of England; county town, Maidstone 肯特（英格兰东南海岸一郡;首府梅德斯通。)

small thatched cottage in Buckinghamshire①, was happy to see me. So were my four sisters and my brother. I was given a month's leave. Then suddenly I was told I was being sent to Washington D. C. in the United States of America as Assistant Air Attaché. This was January 1942, and one month earlier the Japanese had bombed the American fleet in Pearl Harbor. So the United States was now in the war as well.

I was twenty-six years old when I arrived in Washington, and I still had no thoughts of becoming a writer.

During the morning of my third day, I was sitting in my new office at the British Embassy② and wondering what on earth I was meant to be doing, when there was a knock on my door. "Come in."

A very small man with thick steel-rimmed spectacles shuffled③ shyly into the room. "Forgive me for bothering you," he said.

"You aren't bothering me at all," I answered. "I'm not doing a thing."

He stood before me looking very uncomfortable and out of place. I thought perhaps he was going to ask for a job.

---

① Buckinghamshire: *Noun* a county of central England; county town, Aylesbury 白金汉郡(英格兰中部一郡,首府艾尔斯伯里。)

② embassy: *Noun* the official residence or offices of an ambassador 大使馆; 大使官邸(或办事处)

③ shuffle: *Verb* [no obj., with adverbial] walk by dragging one's feet along or without lifting them fully from the ground 拖着脚走(e.g. I stepped into my skis and shuffled to the edge of the steep slope. 我穿上雪屐,拖着脚走到陡峭的山坡边。)

"My name," he said, "is Forester. C. S. Forester①."

I nearly fell out of my chair. "Are you joking?" I said.

"No," he said, smiling. "That's me."

And it was. It was the great writer himself, the inventor of Captain Hornblower and the best teller of tales about the sea since Joseph Conrad②. I asked him to take a seat.

"Look," he said. "I'm too old for the war. I live over here now. The only thing I can do to help is to write things about Britain for the American papers and magazines. We need all the help America can give us. A magazine called the *Saturday Evening Post* will publish any story I write. I have a contract with them. And I have come to you because I think you might have a good story to tell. I mean about flying."

"No more than thousands of others," I said. "There are lots of pilots who have shot down many more planes than me."

"That's not the point," Forester said. "You are now in America, and because you have, as they say over here, 'been in combat', you

---

① C. S. Forester (1899—1966), English novelist; pseudonym of Cecil Lewis Troughton Smith. He is remembered for his seafaring novels set during the Napoleonic Wars, featuring Captain Horatio Hornblower. C·S·福雷斯特(1899—1966,英国小说家,塞西尔·路易斯·特劳顿·史密斯的笔名,以航海小说著称,常以拿破仑时代战争为背景,主人公是霍雷肖·霍恩布洛船长。)

② Joseph Conrad (1857—1924), Polish-born British novelist; born Józef Teodor Konrad Korzeniowski. Much of his work, including his story Heart of Darkness (1902) and the novel Nostromo (1904), explores the darkness within human nature 约瑟夫·康拉德(1857—1924,波兰出生的英国小说家,出生名约瑟夫·西奥多·康拉德·柯日涅夫斯基;他的许多作品,包括小说《黑暗之心》[1902]和长篇小说《诺斯特罗莫》[1904],都探讨了人性的黑暗面。)

are a rare bird① on this side of the Atlantic. Don't forget they have only just entered the war."

"What do you want me to do?" I asked.

"Come and have lunch with me," he said. "And while we're eating, you can tell me all about it. Tell me your most exciting adventure and I'll write it up for the *Saturday Evening Post*. Every little bit helps."

I was thrilled. I had never met a famous writer before. I examined him closely as he sat in my office. What astonished me was that he looked so ordinary. There was nothing in the least unusual about him. His face, his conversation, his eyes behind the spectacles, even his clothes were all exceedingly normal. And yet here was a writer of stories who was famous the world over. His books had been read by millions of people. I expected sparks to be shooting out of his head, or at the very least, he should have been wearing a long green cloak and a floppy hat with a wide brim.

But no. And it was then I began to realize for the first time that there are two distinct sides to a writer of fiction. First, there is the side he displays to the public, that of an ordinary person like anyone else, a person who does ordinary things and speaks an ordinary language. Second, there is the secret side which comes out in him only after he has closed the door of his workroom and is completely alone. It is then that he slips into another world altogether, a world where his imagination takes over and he finds himself actually *living* in the places he is writing about at that moment. I myself, if you want to know, fall into a kind of trance and everything around me disappears. I see only the point of my

---

① rare bird: an exceptional person or thing; a rarity 不寻常的人(或物); 罕见的人(或物)(e.g. The style is a rare bird in Brazilian music. 这一风格在巴西音乐中颇为罕见。)

pencil moving over the paper, and quite often two hours go by as though they were a couple of seconds.

"Come along," C S. Forester said to me. "Let's go to lunch. You don't seem to have anything else to do."

As I walked out of the Embassy side by side with the great man, I was churning① with excitement. I had read all the Hornblowers and just about everything else he had written. I had, and still have, a great love for books about the sea. I had read all of Conrad and all of that other splendid sea-writer, Captain Marryat② (*Mr. Midshipman Easy*, *From Powder Monkey③ to Admiral*④, etc.), and now here I was about to have lunch with somebody who, to my mind, was also pretty terrific.

He took me to a small expensive French restaurant somewhere near the Mayflower Hotel in Washington. He ordered a sumptuous⑤ lunch, then he produced a notebook and a pencil (ballpoint pens had not been invented in 1942) and laid them on the tablecloth. "Now," he said,

---

① churn: *Verb* [no obj.] (of liquid) move about vigorously(液体)翻腾

② Frederick Marryat (1792—1848), English novelist and naval officer; known as Captain Marryat. Notable works: Peter Simple (1833), Mr. Midshipman Easy (1836), The Children of the New Forest (1847) 弗雷德里克·马里亚特(1792—1848,英国小说家和海军军官;通称马里亚特船长;代表作品:《傻子彼得》[1833],《海军军官候补生伊齐先生》[1836],《新福利斯特的孩子们》[1847]。)

③ powder monkey: (historical) a boy employed on a sailing warship to carry powder to the guns(历史上的用法)(军舰上雇佣的)弹药搬运工

④ admiral: *Noun* (Admiral) a naval officer of the second most senior rank, above vice admiral and below(e. g. Admiral of the Fleet or Fleet Admiral 海军上将)

⑤ sumptuous: *Adjective* splendid and expensive-looking 华丽的;豪华的(e. g. The banquet was a sumptuous, luxurious meal. 这宴会是一次豪华、奢侈的聚餐。)

第四章 人生之路 第二节 《幸运开局》(下部) Lucky Break (Part B)

"tell me about the most exciting or frightening or dangerous thing that happened to you when you were flying fighter planes."

I tried to get going. I started telling him about the time I was shot down in the Western Desert and the plane had burst into flames.

The waitress brought two plates of smoked salmon.

While we tried to eat it, I was trying to talk and Forester was trying to take notes.

The main course was roast duck with vegetables and potatoes and a thick rich gravy①. This was a dish that required one's full attention as well as two hands. My narrative began to flounder②. Forester kept putting down the pencil and picking up the fork, and vice versa. Things weren't going well. And apart from that, I have never been much good at telling stories aloud.

"Look," I said. "If you like, I'll try to write down on paper what happened and send it to you. Then you can rewrite it properly yourself in your own time. Wouldn't that be easier? I could do it tonight."

That, though I didn't know it at the time, was the moment that changed my life.

"A splendid idea," Forester said. "Then I can put this silly notebook away and we can enjoy our lunch. Would you really mind doing that for me?"

"I don't mind a bit," I said. "But you mustn't expect it to be any good. I'll just put down the facts."

---

① gravy: Noun [mass noun] the fat and juices exuding from meat during cooking 肉汁

② flounder: Verb (figurative) struggle mentally; show or feel great confusion (比喻用法)思路紊乱;心乱如麻(e. g. He floundered, not knowing quite what to say. 他的心好乱,不知该说什么才好。)

"Don't worry," he said, "So long as the facts are there, I can write the story. But please," he added, "let me have plenty of detail. That's what counts in our business, tiny little details, like you had a broken shoelace on your left shoe, or a fly settled on the rim of your glass at lunch, or the man you were talking to had a broken front tooth. Try to think back and remember everything."

"I'll do my best," I said.

He gave me an address where I could send the story, and then we forgot all about it and finished our lunch at leisure. But Mr. Forester was not a great talker. He certainly couldn't talk as well as he wrote, and although he was kind and gentle, no sparks ever flew out of his head and I might just as well have been talking to an intelligent stockbroker or lawyer.

That night, in the small house I lived in alone in a suburb of Washington, I sat down and wrote my story. I started at about seven o'clock and finished at midnight. I remember I had a glass of Portuguese brandy to keep me going. For the first time in my life, I became totally absorbed in what I was doing. I floated back in time and once again I was in the sizzling hot desert of Libya, with white sand underfoot, climbing up into the cockpit of the old Gladiator, strapping myself in, adjusting my helmet, starting the motor and taxiing① out for take-off. It was astonishing how everything came back to me with absolute clarity. Writing it down on paper was not difficult. The story seemed to be telling itself, and the hand that held the pencil moved rapidly back and forth across each page. Just for fun, when it was finished, I gave it a title. I called it "A Piece

---

① taxi: Verb [no obj., with adverbial of direction] (of an aircraft) move slowly along the ground before take-off or after landing(飞机缓慢滑行(e.g. The plane taxis up to a waiting limousine. 飞机缓缓滑向一辆等在那里的豪华轿车。)

第四章 人生之路 第二节 《幸运开局》(下部) Lucky Break (Part B)

of Cake".

The next day, somebody in the Embassy typed it out for me and I sent it off to Mr. Forester. Then I forgot all about it.

Exactly two weeks later, I received a reply from the great man. It said:

Dear RD, *You were meant to give me notes, not a finished story. I'm bowled over*[①]*. Your piece is marvellous. It is the work of a gifted writer. I didn't touch a word of it. 1 sent it at once under your name to my agent, Harold Matson, asking him to offer it to the* Saturday Evening Post *with my personal recommendation. You will be happy to hear that the* Post *accepted it immediately and have paid one thousand dollars. Mr. Matson's commission is ten per cent. I enclose his check for nine hundred dollars. It's all yours. As you will see from Mr. Matson's letter, which 1 also enclose, the* Post *is asking if you will write more stories for them. I do hope you will. Did you know you were a writer? With my very best wishes and congratulations, C. S. Forester.*

"A Piece of Cake" is printed at the end of this book.

Well! I thought. My goodness me! Nine hundred dollars! And they're going to print it! But surely it can't be as easy as all that? Oddly enough, it was.

The next story I wrote was fiction. I made it up. Don't ask me why. And Mr. Matson sold that one, too. Out there in Washington in the eve-

---

① bowl someone over: (usu. be bowled over) (informal) completely overwhelm or astonish someone, for example by one's good qualities or looks(非正式)使大吃一惊;使惊呆(e. g. When he met Angela he was just bowled over by her. 遇到安吉拉时他都惊呆了。)

nings over the next two years, I wrote eleven short stories. All were sold to American magazines, and later they were published in a little book called *Over to You*.

Early on in this period, I also had a go at a story for children. It was called "The Gremlins①", and this I believe was the first time the word had been used. In my story, Gremlins were tiny men who lived on R. A. F. fighter-planes and bombers, and it was the Gremlins, not the enemy, who were responsible for all the bullet-holes and burning engines and crashes that took place during combat. The Gremlins had wives called Fifinellas, and children called Widgets, and although the story itself was clearly the work of an inexperienced writer, it was bought by Walt Disney② who decided he was going to make it into a full-length③ animated film. But first it was published in *Cosmopolitan Magazine* with

---

① gremlin：*Noun*（informal）an imaginary mischievous sprite regarded as responsible for an unexplained problem or fault, especially a mechanical or electronic one(非正式)（被认为导致出现原因不明的机械或电子等故障或差错的）小妖精（e.g. A gremlin in my computer omitted a line. 我电脑里的小精灵使文档漏掉了一行。)

② Walt Disney（1901—1966）, American animator and film producer; full name Walter Elias Disney. He made his name with the creation of cartoon characters such as Mickey Mouse, Donald Duck, Goofy, and Pluto. Snow White and the Seven Dwarfs（1937）was the first full-length cartoon feature film with sound and colour. Other notable films：Pinocchio（1940）, Dumbo（1941）, and Bambi（1942）沃尔特·迪斯尼(1901—1966,美国漫画家和电影制片人,全名沃尔特·伊莱亚斯·迪斯尼,因创作米老鼠、唐老鸭、古菲狗和布鲁托等卡通人物而出名;《白雪公主和七个小矮人》[1937]是第一部彩色有声卡通长片;其他代表作品:《木偶奇遇记》[1940]《小飞象丹波》[1941]和《小鹿斑比》[1942]。)

③ full-length：*Adjective* of the standard length 标准长度的（e. g. a full-length Disney cartoon 标准长度的迪斯尼卡通片)

第四章 人生之路 第二节 《幸运开局》(下部) Lucky Break (Part B)

Disney's coloured illustrations (December 1942), and from then on, news of the Gremlins spread rapidly through the whole of the R. A. F. and the United States Air Force, and they became something of a legend.

Because of the Gremlins, I was given three weeks' leave from my duties at the Embassy in Washington and whisked① out to Hollywood②. There, I was put up at Disney's expense in a luxurious Beverly Hills③ hotel and given a huge shiny car to drive about in. Each day, I worked with the great Disney at his studios in Burbank④, roughing⑤ out the story-line for the forthcoming film. I had a ball. I was still only twenty-six. I atten-

---

① whisk: *Verb* [with obj. and adverbial of direction] take or move (someone or something) in a particular direction suddenly and quickly 迅速移动；飞快带走；急忙运送(e. g. His jacket was whisked away for dry-cleaning. 他的外套被匆匆送去干洗了。)

② Hollywood: *Noun* a district of Los Angeles, the principal centre of the American film industry 好莱坞(洛杉矶一区，美国电影业中心。)

③ Beverly Hills: a largely residential city in California, on the NW side of the Los Angeles conurbation; pop. 31,970 (1990). It is famous as the home of many film stars 贝弗利山(加利福尼亚州一居住型城市，位于洛杉矶市西北,1990年人口31,970；作为很多电影明星的居住地而闻名。)
注：这里的"Beverly Hills"是一座位于美国加州洛杉矶县西边的城市，是典型的富人区，里面有高级住宅。一般译作"贝弗利山"，中国大陆又译作"贝弗利希尔斯"，台湾译作"比佛利山"，香港译作"比华利山"。本书采用的是"贝弗利山"这一译法。

④ Burbank: *Noun* a city in southern California, on the north side of the Los Angeles conurbation; pop. 93,640 (1990). It is a centre of the film and television industries 伯班克(加利福尼亚州南部城市，位于洛杉矶大都市北部；1990年人口93,640,是影视业的中心。)

⑤ rough: *Verb* (rough something out) produce a preliminary and unfinished sketch or version of something 草拟；画……的轮廓；拟出……的梗概(e. g. The engineer roughed out a diagram on his notepad. 工程师在笔记本上草拟了个图表。)

ded story-conferences in Disney's enormous office where every word spoken, every suggestion made, was taken down by a stenographer① and typed out afterwards. I mooched② around the rooms where the gifted and obstreperous③ animators worked, the men who had already created *Snow White*, *Dumbo*, *Bambi* and other marvellous films, and in those days, so long as these crazy artists did their work, Disney didn't care when they turned up at the studio or how they behaved.

When my time was up, I went back to Washington and left them to it.

My Gremlin story was published as a children's book in New York and London, full of Disney's colour illustrations, and it was called of course *The Gremlins*. Copies are very scarce now and hard to come by. I myself have only one. The film, also, was never finished. I have a feeling that Disney was not really very comfortable with this particular fantasy. Out there in Hollywood, he was a long way away from the great war in the air that was going on in Europe. Furthermore, it was a story about the Royal Air Force and not about his own countrymen, and that, I think, added to his sense of bewilderment. So in the end, he lost interest and dropped the whole idea.

---

① stenographer: *Noun* a person skilled in the use of shorthand and in typing; a person with these skills whose job it is to record verbatim everything that is said during a court case 速记员; 庭审速记员 (e.g. The police stenographer recorded the man's confession word by word. 警察局速记员逐字记下了那个人的供词。)

② mooch: *Verb*（informal）[no obj.]（mooch about/around）（Brit.）loiter in a bored or listless manner(英国英语非正式用法)无聊闲逛; 漫步(e.g. He just mooched about his bedsit. 他只是在卧室兼起居室里随意走走。)

③ obstreperous: *Adjective* noisy and difficult to control 喧嚣的; 喧闹的; 狂放的; 难控制(e.g. The boy is cocky and obstreperous. 那男孩自以为是而又不服管束。)

第四章　人生之路　第二节　《幸运开局》(下部) Lucky Break (Part B)

  My little Gremlin book caused something else quite extraordinary to happen to me in those wartime Washington days. Eleanor Roosevelt① read it to her grandchildren in the White House and was apparently much taken with it. I was invited to dinner with her and the President. I went, shaking with excitement. We had a splendid time and I was invited again. Then Mrs. Roosevelt began asking me for week-ends to Hyde Park, the President's country house. Up there, believe it or not, I spent a good deal of time alone with Franklin Roosevelt② during his relaxing hours. I would sit with him while he mixed the martinis③ before Sunday lunch, and he would say things like, "I've just had an interesting cable④

---

  ① Anna Eleanor Roosevelt (1884—1962), American humanitarian and diplomat. She was the niece of Theodore Roosevelt, and married Franklin D. Roosevelt in 1905. She was involved in a wide range of liberal causes; as chair of the UN Commission on Human Rights she helped draft the Declaration of Human Rights (1948) 安娜·埃莉诺·罗斯福(1884—1962,美国人道主义者和外交家,西奥多·罗斯福的侄女,1905年和富兰克林·D·罗斯福结婚;她广泛参加各种开明的政治和社会活动,作为联合国人权委员会主席,她帮助起草了《人权宣言》[1948]。)

  ② Franklin D. Roosevelt (1882—1945), American Democratic statesman, 32nd President of the US 1933—1945; full name Franklin Delano Roosevelt; known as FDR. His New Deal of 1933 helped to lift the US out of the Great Depression, and he played an important part in Allied policy during the Second World War. He was the only American President to be elected for a third term in office. 富兰克林·D·罗斯福(1882—1945,美国民主党政治家,美国第32任总统［1933—1945］,全名富兰克林·德拉诺·罗斯福,通称"FDR";他1933年实行的"新政"帮助美国摆脱了"大萧条",在第二次世界大战中他对同盟国的政策起了重要作用。他是唯一蝉联三届的美国总统。)

  ③ Martini: Noun a type of vermouth produced in Italy(意大利产)马提尼酒,也有人译作"马丁尼酒"。本书采用前一个翻译。

  ④ cable: Noun a cablegram 海底电报;电报

from Mr. Churchill①." Then he would tell me what it said, something perhaps about new plans for the bombing of Germany or the sinking of U-Boats②, and I would do my best to appear calm and chatty, though actually I was trembling at the realization that the most powerful man in the world was telling me these mighty secrets. Sometimes he drove me around the estate in his car, an old Ford I think it was, that had been specially adapted for his paralysed legs. It had no pedals. All the controls were worked by his hands. His secret-service men would lift him out of his wheel-chair into the driver's seat, then he would wave them away and off we would go, driving at terrific speeds along the narrow roads.

One Sunday during lunch at Hyde Park, Franklin Roosevelt told a story that shook the assembled guests. There were about fourteen of us sitting on both sides of the long dining-room table, including Princess Martha of Norway and several members of the Cabinet③. We were eating a rather insipid④ white fish covered with a thick grey sauce. Suddenly the President pointed a finger at me and said, "We have an Englishman here. Let me tell you what happened to another Englishman, a representative of the King, who was in Washington in the year 1827." He gave

---

① Sir Winston Leonard Spencer Churchill (1874—1965), British Conservative statesman, Prime Minister 1940—1945 and 1951—1955. 温斯顿·伦纳德·斯潘塞·丘吉尔爵士(1874—1965,英国保守党政治家,于 1940—1945 年,1951—1955 年任首相。)

② U-boat: *Noun* a German submarine used in the First or Second World War (两次世界大战中的)德国潜艇

③ Cabinet: *Noun* (in the UK, Canada, and other Commonwealth countries) the committee of senior ministers responsible for controlling government policy(英国、加拿大及其他英联邦国家的)内阁

④ insipid: *Adjective* lacking flavour 没有味道的(e.g. mugs of insipid coffee 一杯杯淡而无味的咖啡)

第四章 人生之路 第二节 《幸运开局》(下部) Lucky Break (Part B)

the man's name, but I've forgotten it. Then he went on, "While he was over here, this fellow died, and the British for some reason insisted that his body be sent home to England for burial. Now the only way to do that in those days was to pickle it in alcohol. So the body was put into a barrel of rum①. The barrel was lashed② to the mast of a schooner③ and the ship sailed for home. After about four weeks at sea, the captain of the schooner noticed a most frightful stench④ coming from the barrel. And in the end, the smell became so appalling they had to cut the barrel loose and roll it overboard. But do you know why it stank⑤ so badly?" the President asked, beaming at the guests with that famous wide smile of his. "I will tell you exactly why. Some of the sailors had drilled a hole in the bottom of the barrel and had inserted a bung⑥. Then every night they had been helping themselves to the rum. And when they had drunk it all, that's when the trouble started." Franklin Roosevelt let out a great roar of laughter. Several females at the table turned very pale and I saw them pushing their plates of boiled white fish gently away.

All the stories I wrote in those early days were fiction, except for that first one I did with C S. Forester. Nonfiction, which means writing

---

① rum: *Noun* [mass noun] an alcoholic spirit distilled from sugar-cane residues or molasses 朗姆酒(由甘蔗残渣或糖蜜制成的蒸馏酒)

② lash: *Verb* [with obj. and adverbial] fasten (something) securely with a cord or rope 系紧;拴牢

③ schooner: *Noun* a sailing ship with two or more masts, typically with the foremast smaller than the mainmast(二帆或二帆以上,尤指其前桅小于其主桅的)纵桅船

④ stench: *Noun* a strong and very unpleasant smell 恶臭

⑤ stink: *Verb* [no obj.] have a strong unpleasant smell 发恶臭;有恶臭;有异味(e. g. The place stank like a sewer. 那地方就像阴沟一样发出恶臭。)

⑥ bung: *Noun* a stopper for closing a hole in a container 塞子

about things that have actually taken place, doesn't interest me. I enjoy least of all writing about my own experiences. And that explains why this story is so lacking in detail. I could quite easily have described what it was like to be in a dog-fight with German fighters fifteen thousand feet above the Parthenon① in Athens②, or the thrill of chasing a Junkers③ 88 in and out the mountain peaks in Northern Greece, but I don't want to do it. For me, the pleasure of writing comes with inventing stories.

Apart from the Forester story, I think I have only written one other non-fiction piece in my life, and I did this only because the subject was so enthralling④ I couldn't resist it. The story is called "The Mildenhall Treasure", and it's in this book.

So there you are. That's how I became a writer. Had I not been lucky enough to meet Mr. Forester, it would probably never have hap-

---

① Parthenon: *Noun* the temple of Athene Parthenos, built on the Acropolis in 447—432 bc by Pericles to honour Athens' patron goddess and to commemorate the recent Greek victory over the Persians. It was designed by Ictinus and Callicrates with sculptures by Phidias. 帕台农神庙(雅典娜主神庙,公元前472—432年由伯里克利建于雅典卫城上,以祭奉雅典的守护女神雅典娜,纪念当时希腊战胜波斯,由伊克蒂诺和卡利克拉特设计,菲迪亚斯雕塑。)

② Athens: *Noun* the capital of Greece; pop. 3,096,775 (1991). Greek name athínai 雅典(希腊首都,1991年人口3,096,775,希腊语名"athínai"。)

③ Junkers or Ju: It was a major German aircraft manufacturer. It produced some of the world's most innovative and best-known airplanes over the course of its fifty-plus year history in Dessau, Germany. "Ju"是"Junkers"的简写形式,原指德国的一家著名的飞机制造公司,本文中指的是德国的容克斯战机。它是第二次世界大战时纳粹德国空军(Luftwaffe)所使用的双活塞式引擎中型军用机,从1939年开始服役到1945年。于20世纪30年代中期由容克斯飞机与发动机制造厂的总设计师雨果·容克斯(Hugo Junkers)亲手设计出来。

④ enthralling: *Adjective* capturing interest as if by a spell 迷人的

第四章 人生之路 第二节 《幸运开局》(下部) Lucky Break (Part B)

pened.

Now, more than thirty years later. I'm still slogging① away. To me, the most important and difficult thing about writing fiction is to find the plot. Good original plots are very hard to come by. You never know when a lovely idea is going to flit② suddenly into your mind, but by golly③, when it does come along, you grab it with both hands and hang on to it tight. The trick is to write it down at once, otherwise you'll forget it. A good plot is like a dream. If you don't write down your dream on paper the moment you wake up, the chances are you'll forget it and it'll be gone for ever.

So when an idea for a story comes popping into my mind, I rush for a pencil, a crayon, a lipstick, anything that will write, and scribble a few words that will later remind me of the idea. Often, one word is enough. I was once driving alone on a country road and an idea came for a story about someone getting stuck in an elevator between two floors in an empty house. I had nothing to write with in the car. So I stopped and got out. The back of the car was covered with dust. With one finger I wrote in the dust the single word ELEVATOR. That was enough. As soon as I got home, I went straight to my work-room and wrote the idea down in an old red-covered school exercise-book which is simply labelled "Short Sto-

---

① slog: *Verb* [no obj.] work hard over a period of time(一段时间)艰苦地干;努力苦干(e.g. They were slogging away to meet a deadline. 他们在截止日期前拼命干。)

② flit: *Verb* [no obj., with adverbial of direction] move swiftly and lightly 轻快地移动(e.g. Small birds flitted about in the branches. 小鸟在树枝间轻快跳跃。)

③ golly: *Exclamation* (informal, dated) used to express surprise or delight (非正式的古旧用法)啊;天呐(表示吃惊或高兴)

ries".

I have had this book ever since I started trying to write seriously. There are ninety-eight pages in the book. I've counted them. And just about every one of those pages is filled up on both sides with these so-called story ideas. Many are no good. But just about every story and every children's book I have ever written has started out as a three- or four-line note in this little, much-worn red-covered volume. For example:

What about a chocolate factory That makes fantastic and marvellous Things — with a crazy man running it?

This became *Charlie and the Chocolate Factory*.

A story about Mr. Fox who has a whole network of underground Tunnels leading to all the shops in the village. At night, he goes up through the floorboards and helps himself.

Fantastic Mr. Fox.

第四章 人生之路 第二节 《幸运开局》(下部) Lucky Break (Part B)

> *Jamaica and The small boy who saw a giant Turtle captured by native fishermen. Boy pleads with his father to buy Turtle and release it. Becomes hysterical. Father buys it. Then what? Perhaps boy goes with or joins Turtle.*

"The Boy Who Talked with Animals".

> *A man acquires the ability to see through playing-cards. He makes millions at casinos.*

This becomes "Henry Sugar".

Sometimes, these little scribbles will stay unused in the notebook for five or even ten years. But the promising ones are always used in the end. And if they show nothing else, they do, I think, demonstrate from what slender① threads a children's book or a short story must ultimately be woven. The story builds and expands while you are writing it. All the best stuff comes at the desk. But you can't even start to write that story unless you have the beginnings of a plot. Without my little notebook, I would be quite helpless.

---

① slender: *Adjective* (especially of a rod or stem) of small girth or breadth (尤指竿或茎)细长的(e.g. slender iron railings 细长的铁栏杆)

(The end)

三、翻译探索

在这部作品的翻译中，诸多专有名词可能是比较棘手的地方。其中，罗尔德·达尔在这部作品中"卖弄"了不少世界各个角落的地名，需要在翻译中一一查证、落实，特别是需要照顾到此类地名的一些常规性的译法，不可随意进行创造性的翻译。当然，对于一些小的地名，又查不到常规性译法，则可以根据读音进行创造性翻译了。

幸运开局

（接上）

1939年9月，显而易见的是，以希特勒为首的德国就要爆发一场战争了。早在二十年前就被称为"德国的东非"的坦噶尼喀，德国人仍然到处可见：他们遍布各处，他们的店铺、矿厂、种植园在这个国家随处可见。战争刚爆发那会儿，他们必须得召集一下，才能聚拢到一块儿。但是，我们则根本没有什么像样的军队，只有少量的本地士兵和几名军官，这样的士兵被称作"东非土著兵"。所以，我们所有这些平民百姓都被征集起来，变成"特殊预备役军人"，还发给我一个袖章，让我掌管二十名东非土著兵。我和我带领的这小股部队得到命令，要求我们封锁住北部的那条公路，该条公路从坦噶尼喀通往保持中立的"葡萄牙的东非"。这项任务很重要，因为一旦开战，多数的德国人会沿着这条公路逃走。

我带领我这帮家伙端着步枪，还有一挺机关枪，奉命前往，并在公路上的一个地方设置了路障。这个地方离城镇约十六公里远，从茂密的丛林穿过。我们有一部野战电话，用以跟总部联络，一旦开战，就能立刻从总部那里得到消息。我们安顿下来等待着，一连等了三天。夜间，我们听到四周的丛林里传来当地人敲鼓的声音，节奏十分的怪异，具有催眠的功效。有一次，我在黑暗中漫无目的地走进丛林，撞见大约五十名当地人，他们围绕一堆火蹲坐在那儿。一个人专

第四章 人生之路 第二节 《幸运开局》(下部) Lucky Break (Part B)

门负责敲鼓,一些人绕着火堆跳舞,其余的人端着椰果壳喝着什么东西。见我到来,他们欢迎我加入他们的圈子。他们都是些可爱的人,我能够用他们的语言跟他们交谈。他们递给我一个椰果壳,里面盛满了一种浓稠的、醉人的灰色液体,是用发酵的玉米做成的。如果我没记错的话,这种东西被称为"泡姆巴"。我喝了下去,味道差极了。

接下来一天的下午,野战电话响起,一个声音说道:"我们与德国开战了。"没过几分钟,我看见远远的有一排小汽车,扬起一股股烟尘向我们这个方向驶来,全速驶向中立领地——葡萄牙的东非。

呵呵,我想,我们就要进行一场小小的战斗了。于是,我招呼我手下的二十名东非土著兵各自做好战斗准备。但是,实际并没有什么战斗可言,那些德国人只不过都是一些城里的平民百姓,看到机关枪和步枪马上就放弃了逃跑的念头。一个小时的工夫,我们手里就控制住了好几百名这样的德国人。我对他们深感愧疚,他们中很多人我还认识,像制作手表的维利·欣克,还有苏打水厂的厂主赫尔曼·施奈德。他们唯一的罪行就是,他们是德国人。可这是战争时期,到了晚上凉爽的时候,我们将他们押回达累斯萨拉姆,投进一座大型的集中营,集中营四周用带刺的铁丝网围住。

第二天,我跳进我那辆老旧的小汽车向北开去,驶向肯尼亚的内罗毕,要加入那里的英国皇家空军。这次旅途崎岖坎坷,用了四天的时间。一会儿是颠簸的丛林公路,车前有长长的绿蛇横过马路(特别注意:永远也不要试图从蛇身上压过去,因为那样的话,蛇就会被甩到空中,或许会落入敞开的车内。这样的事发生很多次了),一会儿是宽阔的河流——小汽车必须得放到木筏上,由摆渡工牵引着渡过。夜晚,我是睡在车里度过的。我从乞力马扎罗山底部经过,山峰戴上了一顶雪帽。我驱车穿过马赛地区,那里的男人喝奶牛的血液,每人似乎都有两米一还高的个头。在塞伦盖蒂大草原上,我险些撞上一头长颈鹿,但是,我最终还是安全地抵达内罗毕,到位于机场的皇家空军总部报到。

在那里长达六个月的时间里,他们用被称为"虎蛾"的小型飞机来训练我们,那是一些充满荣耀的日子。我们驾驶小虎蛾掠遍肯尼亚所有的天空,看到大群的大象家族,看到了纳库鲁湖上粉色的火烈鸟,看到了这个壮丽的国度里能够看到的一切。每次为了能够起飞,我们不得不经常将机场里的斑马先驱赶走。在内罗毕,我们一共有二十人接受培训成为飞行员,其中的十七人死于战场。

内罗毕培训结束后,我们被送往伊拉克靠近巴格达的一个人迹罕至的空军基地完成余下的培训任务。那个地方叫哈巴尼伊,午后热得很(阴影下温度为54℃),我们是不允许走出营房小屋的,只有躺在架子床上任凭汗水流出。不走运的会因为中暑而被送进医院,用冰包裹几天的时间。这样做会要他们的命,也会救他们的命,机会各占一半。

在哈巴尼伊这个地方,他们教我们驾驶更大功率的、装备枪炮的飞机,我们练习射击锥形拖靶(其他飞机后面拖着的空中靶)以及地面目标。

最后,培训结束,我们被派往埃及与利比亚大沙漠里的意大利军队作战。在那里,我加入了80飞行中队,开的是战斗机。开始的时候,我们驾驶的只是古老的单座双翼飞机,这种飞机被称为"格洛斯特格斗士",两挺机关枪分别安装在引擎的两端。不管你相信还是不相信,机关枪的子弹是通过螺旋桨射出的。机关枪以某种方式跟螺旋桨轴杆同步运转,这样从理论上来说,子弹就不会射中旋转的螺旋桨叶片。但是,或许你也会猜得出,这种复杂的运转机制经常会出差错,可怜的飞行员本打算要将敌机击落,却不幸射中了自己飞机的螺旋桨。

驾驶格斗士时,我自己曾被击落,飞机在利比亚沙漠深处、敌军的防线之间坠毁。当时,坠落后飞机起火,我则设法爬了出来,最终获救——是我们自己的战友,在夜色的掩护下,爬着穿过了沙漠,把我抬回去的。

这次飞机坠落后,我颅骨断裂,身体多处烧伤,被送到亚历山大的一所医院,一住就是六个月。1941年4月我出院时,我的飞行中队

第四章 人生之路 第二节 《幸运开局》（下部）Lucky Break（Part B）

已经转移到希腊与德军作战，德军当时从北部入侵希腊。于是，给了我一架飓风式战斗驱逐机，让我从埃及飞往希腊，加入我的飞行中队行列。现在，飓风战斗机跟老式的格斗士飞机有着天壤之别。飓风上有八挺机关枪，每只机翼各有四挺。只需按一下操纵杆上的小按钮，八挺机关枪就会同时射击。这种飞机虽然非同凡响，飞行时间却只有两个小时，而去往希腊的旅程，即使不停地飞，也要将近五个小时的时间，而且总是在水面上方飞行。因此，他们给这架飞机安装了几个备用油箱，并交代说，我会成功抵达的。最终证明，我的确成功抵达，但却是勉勉强强做到的。要是你的个头接近两米——我就这个身高，嘎吱作响地坐在窄小的飞行员座舱里，还连续飞上五个小时，那绝不是在开玩笑啊。

在希腊，英国皇家空军总共大约有十八架飓风战斗机，而德军至少有一百架飞机可投入战斗。时机对我们很不利。我们从位于雅典外围的小型机场（埃利维斯）被驱逐出去后，有一段时间，我们从更往西一些的一个小型的秘密起落跑道（梅尼迪）起飞，但是，德军很快就发现了这个跑道，随之将其炸成碎块。因此呢，我们驾驶剩下的几架飞机飞到位于希腊正南部的一个微型机场（阿尔戈斯）。在那里没有飞行任务时，我们就将飓风战斗机藏到橄榄树下面。

但是，这种情况也不可能持续太久。很快，我们只剩下五架飞机了，活下来的飞行员也不是很多。于是，我们驾驶这五架飞机飞到克里特岛。德军攻占了克里特岛，我们中有一些幸运的逃了出来，我是其中的一个。最终，我返回埃及。在那里飞行中队重新组建起来，重新配备了飓风战斗机。然后，我们被派往海法，海法当时归巴勒斯坦（现在的以色列）所有，在那里我们又与德军作战，还与盘踞在黎巴嫩和叙利亚的维希法国兵交火。

那时候，我头部的旧伤让我吃尽了苦头。由于头疼得厉害，我被迫中止飞行。我因伤病退役，要回到英国。当时，我乘军队运兵船从苏伊士出发，先后经过德班、开普敦、拉各斯，最后到达利物浦。一路上，德军潜艇在大西洋紧追不放，航海的最后一周时间里，每天都有远程福克沃尔夫战斗机前来轰炸。

我离家已经有四年时间了,母亲看见我很高兴。不列颠战役期间,飞机狂轰滥炸,她离开了自己在肯特郡的家,现在居住在白金汉郡的一个茅舍中。我的四个姐妹和一个兄弟见到我,也都很高兴。我的假期是一个月,接着突然之间,告诉我说,要派我到美利坚合众国的华盛顿特区当空军大使馆助理专员。宣布这个消息的时间是1942年1月,就在一个月前,日本轰炸了美国珍珠港舰队。因此,美国现在也卷入了这场战争。

到达华盛顿的时候,我二十六岁,仍然没有想当作家的念头。

第三天上午,我坐在英国大使馆给我分配的新办公室里,思绪飞扬,开始猜测到底要我做些什么。突然,有人敲门。"进来。"

一名戴着厚厚的、钢质镜框眼镜的小个子男子拖着脚步,不太好意思地走了进来。"打扰你了,请原谅,"他说。

"你根本没有打扰我,"我回答。"我正闲着呢。"

他站在我的面前,显得很不舒适、很不自在。我就想,他或许想要谋一份差事吧。

"我名叫福雷斯特,"他介绍道,"C·S·福雷斯特。"

我差点从椅子上跌落到地上。"你是开玩笑吗?"我说。

"没有,"他微笑着说道。"那个人就是我。"

的确,他就是大名鼎鼎的福雷斯特,一位伟大的作家。他塑造了霍恩布洛船长,是继约瑟夫·康拉德之后最优秀的故事家。我请他坐下。

"听着,"他说。"我年纪太大了,无法参战。现在,我就住在离这不远的地方。我唯一能做的,就是帮忙为美国的报章杂志写一些关于英国在战争方面的事情,而且我们需要美国能提供给我们全面的帮助。一家名为《星期六晚邮报》的杂志愿意刊登我写的故事,我跟他们签订了合同。我之所以到这里来,就是因为我想,你会有好的故事可以讲一讲,我是指飞行方面的故事。"

"我跟其他成千上万的飞行员没什么两样,"我说。"击落的敌

第四章　人生之路　第二节　《幸运开局》(下部) Lucky Break (Part B)

机比我多得多的飞行员有的是啊。"

"那不是问题的关键，"福雷斯特说。"现在你人在美国，就像这里的那些人说的那样，你'参过战'，在大西洋的这边，你简直就成了稀世珍宝。不要忘了，这儿的那些人才刚刚介入战争。"

"你想要我做些什么？"我问。

"跟我来吃午饭吧，"他说。"我们一边吃，你一边跟我讲述所有这一切，跟我讲你最为兴奋的冒险经历，我就写下来，发表到《星期六晚邮报》上。任何细枝末叶都会大有裨益的。"

我感觉激动不已，以前还从来没有遇到过著名的作家呢。趁他坐在我办公室的当儿，我仔细地打量着他，可是，令我大吃一惊的是，他相貌平平，一点儿也没有任何出奇的地方。他的面孔、谈吐、眼镜后面那双眼睛，甚至他的衣着打扮都平常得不能再平常了。然而，眼前的这个人却是一位世界知名的故事作家，有数以百万计的人读过他的作品。此时此刻，我期望他的脑袋里能迸射出火花来，抑或至少他也应该身披一件长长的绿色斗篷，头戴一顶宽边软帽。

但是，什么都没有。就是在那时，我平生第一次开始意识到，一个作家所具有的截然不同的两面。首先，是他向公众展示的那一面，也就是跟其他任何人都一样的、普普通通的一面：做普通人做的事，说普通人说的话。其次，是他隐秘的那一面，这一面只有在他关上工作间的门、一个人独处而不受打扰的时候，才会展现出来。就是在那个时候，他完完全全滑入另外一个世界。在那个世界里，他的想象力自由驰骋，甚至发现自己就生活在自己写作时所创造的世界里。要是你想知道的话，我自己就进入一种恍惚入迷的状态，周围的一切都消失不见，只看见自己的铅笔尖在纸面上移动。每每此时，虽然两个小时已过，却好似只有两三秒钟的时间。

"随我来吧，"C·S·福雷斯特对我说道。"我们一起去吃午饭吧。你似乎也没有其他什么事情要做。"

跟这位了不起的人肩并肩步行走出大使馆，我内心的激动和兴奋始终难以平静下来。我已经读过他的所有关于霍恩布洛船长的故事,还读完了几乎他所有的其他作品。对于航海方面的书籍,无论过去还是现在,我始终怀有一种伟大的爱,我已经读完康拉德所有的作品,还读过另外一位杰出的航海作家的所有作品,他被称为"马里亚特船长"(作品有《海军军官候补生伊齐先生》《从弹药搬运工到舰队司令》等)。现在,就在此时此地,我就要跟其中的一位共进午餐,而在我的心目中,这一位跟他们并驾齐驱、不分伯仲。

他带着我去了一家小型的、但却很昂贵的法国餐馆,这家餐馆位于华盛顿的五月花酒店附件的一个地方。他点完一顿奢华的午餐后,拿出一个记事本和一支铅笔(1942年的时候,圆珠笔还没有发明出来),放到桌布上。"现在,"他说,"跟我讲讲,你驾驶战斗机飞行期间所发生的极其令人兴奋,或者极其令人恐惧,或者极其危险的事情吧。"

我竭尽全力讲了起来,从利比亚大沙漠里我的飞机被击中、坠落、燃烧的时候讲起。

女服务员送来两盘熏鲑鱼。接下来,我们使劲吃着鲑鱼的同时,我使劲地去讲,福雷斯特则使劲地去记。

主菜是烤鸭,再配上蔬菜、土豆和一份浓稠、油腻的肉汁。吃这道菜不能走神,还要用上两只手。这时,我的叙述思路开始紊乱,福雷斯特则不断地放下铅笔、拿起叉子,然后再放下叉子、拿起铅笔,如此循环往复,事情进行得并不顺利。况且,我从来就不很擅长大声讲故事。

"这样吧,"我提议道。"如果你觉得可以的话,我尽量把发生的事情写到纸上,寄给你。然后,你就可以花点时间适当改正一下。那样做,是不是更容易些?我今晚就可以写出来。"

尽管当时我不得而知,但那一刻我的提议却改变了我的人生。

"你的提议绝妙得很,"福雷斯特说。"那样的话,我就可以把这个无用的记事本挪开,我们可以好好享受午餐了。你真的愿意为我那样去做吗?"

"我乐意之至,"我说。"可是,你一定不要期望我会写得怎么样

第四章 人生之路 第二节 《幸运开局》(下部) Lucky Break (Part B)

的好,我只能将事实付诸纸面。"

"不用担心,"他安慰说。"只要有事实在,我就能写出故事来,那就拜托你啦,"他补充道,"给我多写些细节出来。在我们这一行里,细节至关重要,越细微、琐碎的细节越好,像你左脚的鞋带断了,或者午饭时一只苍蝇落到你的杯子边上啦,或者跟你说话的那名男子门牙残缺不全啦,等等。尽量去回忆,把这一切都想出来啊。"

"我会尽力的,"我回应。

他给我一个地址,以便我可以把故事寄过去。接下来,我们抛开一切,在无比的惬意和享受中吃完了午餐。话说回来了,福雷斯特先生不是很擅长言谈,当然啦,他说的没有他写得好。尽管他很友好、和蔼,但说话时,头脑中并没有强烈的、愉悦的情感火花迸发出来。我跟他谈话,就如同跟一位高明的股票经纪人或者律师在交谈。

那天夜晚,在华盛顿郊区我独自一人居住的小房子里,我坐了下来,开始写我自己的故事。我大约是从晚上七点钟开始写的,半夜的时候写完了。我现在还记得,我喝了一杯葡萄牙白兰地酒,支撑着我写下去。全身心投入手头所做的事情,这是我人生中的第一次。我穿越时间,漂移到过去,于是,我又置身于炙热的利比亚大沙漠,脚下是白色的沙子。我爬进旧式格斗士战机的驾驶舱,系好安全带,调整好头盔,发动引擎,将飞机缓慢滑行到起飞的位置。令我震惊的是,这一切又回到眼前,那么清晰、明确,写到纸上也不是什么困难的事情。这个故事似乎是自己自动讲出来的,我的手只是握紧铅笔在纸上前前后后迅速移动,然后翻过一页继续移动,如此而已。写完后,我就给它取了个题目,就是为了好玩,题目是《小菜一碟》。

第二天,大使馆里有人帮我打印出来,我就寄给福雷斯特先生,然后就忘得一干二净啦。

正好两周过后,我收到了这位伟人的回信,信上说:

亲爱的小罗,本来让你给我写个笔记式的草稿,未曾想你却写了个故事的成稿给我。你写的棒极了,我惊呆了:这就是一位才华横溢的作家写的啊。于是,我一字未动,立即以你的名字发给我的经纪人哈罗德·马特森,请求他在我个人推荐的基础上将稿件提供给《星期六晚邮报》。这份杂志接受了稿件,支付了一千美元。听到这个消息,你一定很开心。马特森先生收百分之十的经纪费,所以这封信里我附上一张九百美元的支票,这些钱都是你的。这封信里我也附上了马特森先生的信件,从中你也能看到,这份杂志问你是否愿意为他们写更多的故事,我真心希望你能多写一些。你是一位作家了,你知道吗?请接受我最好的祝愿和衷心的祝贺!C. S. 福雷斯特敬上。

本书的最后部分印上的就是《小菜一碟》这篇故事。

我想,哇!我的天哪!给了我九百美元!他们还要印刷出版呢!但是,事情肯定都会像这样易如反掌吗?

虽然非常奇怪,但的确如此。

我写的下一篇故事是虚构的,也就是我编造出来的,不要问我为什么。马特森先生也将那个故事推销出去发表了。随后的两年,远在华盛顿,在夜晚的时间里,我写出了十一部短篇小说,所有这些都推销给美国的杂志发表了。后来,这些故事集结成一本小册子出版,书名为《向你飞跃》。

这一时期的早些时候,我也做了一次尝试,写了一篇儿童故事,叫作《小魔精》,而且我相信,这是首次使用"小魔精"这个词。在我的这篇故事里,小魔精就是一些微型的小人,他们居住在英国皇家空军的战斗机里、炸弹里。战役中产生的所有的弹孔、燃烧的引擎和坠毁的飞机都是这些小魔精捣的鬼,而不是敌人造成的。小魔精都有老婆,名叫菲菲内拉,他们的孩子名叫威杰特。尽管从这个故事本身可以很明显地看出,它是出自一个毫无经验的作家之手,却被沃尔特·迪斯尼买了去,他决定将这个故事制作成一部标准长度的卡通片。但在此之前,《世界女性时尚杂志》刊登了这篇故事(1942年12月),里面还配有迪斯尼的彩色插图。从那时起,小魔精的消息不胫而走,很快传遍整个英国皇家空军以及美国空军,这些小魔精也随之变成

第四章　人生之路　第二节　《幸运开局》(下部) Lucky Break (Part B)

了某种传奇之物。

由于小魔精的缘故，驻华盛顿大使馆给了我三周的假期，我火速赶往好莱坞。在那里，迪斯尼出钱，让我住进贝弗利山的一家豪华酒店，还提供给我一辆大大的、闪亮的轿车，让我开着到处兜风。每天，我都与这位了不起的迪斯尼一道，在他的位于伯班克的工作室里，草拟即将制作的卡通片的故事情节。我开心得不得了，我当时年仅二十六岁啊。在迪斯尼巨大办公室举行的剧情商谈会，我参加了，会上说的每个字、提的每条建议都被速记员记录下来，日后再打印出来。我在这里的个个房间随意地走动，里面工作的尽是些才华横溢、不拘一格的动画制作大师，他们已经创造出《白雪公主》《小飞象丹波》《小鹿斑比》等美妙绝伦的影片。在那些日子里，只要这些狂热的艺术家真正地在做事，那么，他们何时到场、举止规范与否，迪斯尼根本不去在意。

假期结束之际，我返回华盛顿，事情就留给他们去做了。

我写的小魔精的故事作为儿童读物分别在纽约和伦敦出版，里面满是迪斯尼的彩色插图，当然啦，题目都叫《小魔精》。这些版本现在很稀有，很难搞到手，连我本人也只有一册在手。筹拍的电影也从未完成，我有一种感觉，认为迪斯尼不是真正地热衷于这个特定的奇幻故事。在好莱坞那个地方待着，他也就远离了在欧洲的天空进行的那场大战。况且，这个故事是关于英国皇家空军的，而与他的同胞无关，这更令他茫然若失。所以嘛，到了最后，他失去了兴趣，全部的制作念头就此放弃。

战争期间在华盛顿度过的那些日子里，我写的那本小魔精的薄册子给我带来了某种异乎寻常的意外收获。在白宫，埃莉诺·罗斯福将这个故事读给她的孙辈孩子们听，很显然，她十分喜爱这个故事。因此，我应邀跟她以及总统共进晚餐。我去了，因激动、兴奋而浑身颤抖。我跟他们在那儿共度了美妙的时光，并再一次得到了邀请。接下来，罗斯福太太开始请我到总统乡下的宅邸——海德帕克——过周末。不管你相信与否，在那里，在富兰克林·罗斯福休闲期间,大部分时间我跟他单独待在一起。星期天吃午饭前,我跟他坐在一起,看着他调马提尼酒,边调酒边说着诸如此类的话:"我刚刚接到丘吉尔先生发来的一封有趣儿的电报。"接着,他就会告诉我电报的内容,或许是关于轰炸德国的新的作战计划,或者是关于炸沉德国U型潜艇的新的作战计划。每每此时,我就尽量使自己看起来轻松、镇定,尽管实际上我浑身颤抖,因为我意识到,这位世界上拥有至高无上权利的人正在跟我透露一些天大的机密。有的时候,他开车载着我到庄园周围转悠。我想,他开的是辆老款式的福特车,并为他残疾的双腿做了改造:没有踩踏板,所有的控制都由手来完成。他的特工人员把他从轮椅上抬下来,抬到驾驶座位上,他就一挥手示意他们离开,然后我们就出发了,沿着窄窄的马路飞速行驶。

有一天,在海德帕克吃午饭期间,富兰克林·罗斯福讲了一个故事,把在场聚会的客人都震住了。我们分坐在餐厅里长长的桌子两边,总共约十四个人,包括挪威公主玛莎以及几位内阁成员。我们当时吃的是一种很是淡而无味的白色的鱼,上面浇上一层浓稠的灰色汤汁。突然之间,总统用一根手指指向我,说道:"我们这儿有一位英国人,就让我给你们讲讲另外一位英国人的故事吧。他是国王的代表,于1827年来到华盛顿。"他说出了那个人的名字,但是我没有记住。接着,他继续说:"待在这儿期间,这个人死了。出于某种考虑,英国坚持要将他的尸体运回英格兰埋葬,但那个年头儿保存尸体唯一的途径就是用酒精浸泡。所以,尸体被放进一桶朗姆酒里,酒桶则被牢牢地绑在纵桅船的桅杆上,船扬帆起航,踏上回家的旅程。在大海上航行了约四周之后,船长就注意到,酒桶里发出一股极其可怕的恶臭。到了最后,臭气实在太熏人了,他们就将绳子砍断,让酒桶滚到甲板上。可问题是,你们知道为什么酒桶会发出恶臭吗?"总统问道,冲着客人,面露灿烂的笑容,也就是他那有名的咧嘴微笑。"我就告诉你们其中的缘由吧。有几个水手在桶底钻了一个洞,并用塞子堵住。然后呢,每天晚上,他们都来随意地放酒喝,酒喝完,麻烦也就开始了。"富兰克林·罗斯福"嘎"的一声大笑,但桌旁有几位女士脸

第四章 人生之路 第二节 《幸运开局》(下部) Lucky Break (Part B)

色变得苍白,我看到她们将手边盛着白色炖鱼的碟子轻轻推开了。

早年写的那些故事都是虚构的,答应 C. S. 福雷斯特写的那篇除外。我对非虚构的作品——写实际发生的事情——不感兴趣,我最不喜欢写的就是有关我个人的经历,这也说明,为什么本篇故事缺乏细节。在雅典的帕台农神庙四千五百多米的上空跟德国的战斗机进行一番大混战是怎样的一种真情实景,在北部希腊的山峰间跟一架德国容克斯 88 型战斗机追来追去是怎样的一种惊心动魄,这些场面我都能轻易地描写出来,但是,我不愿意那样去做。对我来说,写作的快乐来自故事的编写。

除了给福勒斯特的那篇故事,我想我的一生中,我还写了另外一篇非虚构的作品,这部作品之所以没有虚构仅仅是因为故事的主题太吸引我,令我无法抗拒。这篇故事的题目是《宝藏风波》,也收录在这本书中。

你瞧,事情就是这个样子,这就是我成为作家的前前后后。要不是我有幸遇上福雷斯特先生,这一切或许从来就不会发生。

现在,三十多年过去了,我仍然在艰苦地跋涉。对我来说,写虚构的作品最为重要、最为困难的地方就是要找到情节,但是,原创性的优秀情节很难到手。你永远都不会知道,一个可爱的想法什么时候会突然跃入你的头脑。可是,老天啊,要是这样一个想法实实在在地出现在你的眼前,你就立即伸出双手抓住,而且要紧紧地抓住不放。这其中的窍门就是,将其立刻写出来,否则你就会忘掉。优秀的情节就像是一场梦,要是你醒来的那一刻不把梦记到纸上,你就很有可能忘掉,永远再找不到。

所以呢,要是关于一个故事的想法一下子跳入我的头脑,我就会匆忙拿起一支铅笔,或者一根蜡笔,或者一支口红笔,或者任何能写出字迹的东西,潦草地写上几笔,这样日后就会让我想起这样的想法。经常发生的情况是,一个词就足以起到提醒的作用了。有一次,我独自驾车行驶在乡间公路上,关于一个故事的想法出现了:一座空空的房子里,有人卡在两层楼之间的电梯里。当时,车里没有任何能够写出字来的东西,所以我就停下来,下了车。车的后盖部位全是尘土,于是,我就用一根手指在尘土上面写下一个词"电梯",这就足矣。一到家,我就径直奔向写作室,在一个陈旧的、学校用的练习本上写下了这个想法,本子的封皮是红色的,上面就简单地标上四个字"短篇故事"。

这个本子自从我正式开始写作的时候就有了,共有九十八页,我早就数过了。几乎每一页的正反两面都写满了所谓的故事想法,不是每一条想法都用得上。但是,在这个薄薄的、不知被翻过多少遍的红色封皮的小册子里,能够找到我写出来的几乎每一篇故事以及儿童小说的、简短的想法记录,每条记录就三四行的样子。例如:

> What about a chocolate factory
> That makes fantastic and marvellous
> Things — with a crazy man running it?

(手写体的译文:建一座巧克力工厂如何?工厂制作出奇异、美妙的东西来,还有一位疯狂的家伙在里面经营、管理。)

上面的想法成就了《查利与巧克力工厂》。

> A story about Mr. Fox who has a
> whole network of underground Tunnels
> leading to all the shops in the village.
> At night, he goes up through the
> floorboards and helps himself.

(手写体的译文:关于一只狐狸的故事,这只狐狸拥有一整套地下通道网络,通向村里所有的店铺。夜晚降临,他就通过地板上来,

第四章 人生之路 第二节 《幸运开局》(下部) Lucky Break (Part B)

喜欢什么就要什么。)

这是《了不起的狐狸爸爸》的想法。

> Jamaica and the small boy who saw a giant Turtle captured by native fishermen. Boy pleads with his father to buy Turtle and release it. Becomes hysterical. Father buys it. Then what? Perhaps boy goes with or joins Turtle.

(手写体的译文:牙买加,一个小男孩救了一只被当地渔夫捕获的大海龟。孩子请求父亲买下海龟放生,心情急切得很。父亲花钱买下,接着如何?或许孩子跟海龟走,成为其中的一员。)

这是《海龟奇事》的想法。

> A man acquires the ability to see through playing-cards. He makes millions at casinos.

(手写体的译文:一名男子获得了看穿纸牌的能力,在赌场赢了数百元。)

这个想法成就了《非凡亨利》。

有的时候,这些短短的潦草记录在小册子里一待就是五年,甚至是十年,也派不上用场,可是,看起来有价值的记录最终总是得到了利用。我想,就算是有些记录也看不出有什么价值,它们的存在也确确实实证明:一本儿童小说或者一个短篇故事最终编织出来,当初使用的是一根根什么样的线,而且是那么纤细。然后,随着写作的进行,故事体积开始增大、扩展,所有最好的材料源源不断涌向案头。可是,如果开始的时候没有情节这根线头的话,你甚至无法动笔去写。要是没有这本小小的记录册子的话,我就会束手无策。

(终结)

参考文献

[1] DAHL, R. The Wonderful Story of Henry Sugar and Six More [M]. London: Penguin Books Ltd., 2002.

[2] DAHL, R. The Best of Roald Dahl [M]. London: Penguin Books Ltd., 2006.

[3] DAHL, R. The Collected Short Stories of Roald Dahl [M]. London: Penguin Books Ltd., 1992.

[4] Dictionary.com LLC's. Dictionary.com [DB/OL]. Oakland, CA: Dictionary.com LLC's Online, http://dictionary.reference.com/.

[5] Farlex, Inc. The Free Online Dictionary [DB/OL]. Huntingdon Valley, PA: The Free Online Dictionary by Farlex, Inc. http://www.thefreedictionary.com/.

[6] HOWARD, K. Roald Dahl Fans [Z/OL]. Sydney. http://www.roalddahlfans.com/ (1996 – 2013).

[7] Merriam-Webster, Incorporated. Merriam-Webster [DB/OL]. Springfield, MA: Merriam-Webster Online. http://www.merriam-webster.com/.

[8] Oxford University Press. Oxford Dictionaries [DB/OL]. Oxford: Oxford Dictionaries Online, http://www.oxforddictionaries.com/.

[9] Wikimedia Foundation, Inc. Wikipedia[DB/OL]. http://en.wikipedia.org/.

[10] 陈钰. 畸形精神世界的工笔画家——谈罗尔德·达尔的小说创作特色[J]. 武汉：外国文学研究, 1985(4): 66-69.

[11] 金山软件. 金山词霸2009牛津版[CP]. 北京：北京金山软件有限公司, 2008.

[12] 单畅, 王永胜. 唐代五绝品读及英译探索(上册)[M]. 长春：吉林大学出版社, 2013.

[13] 商务印书馆辞书研究中心. 新华成语词典[M]. 北京：商务印书馆, 2002.

[14] 新华社译名室. 世界人名翻译大辞典[M]. 北京：中国对外翻译出版公司, 2007.

[15] 周定国. 世界地名翻译大辞典[M]. 北京：中国出版集团, 中国对外翻译出版公司, 2008.

附　　录

附录1

生平时间轴

In 1911, Harald Dahl (Roald's father) marries Sofie Magdalene Hesselberg and they move to Llandaff, South Wales.

1911年,罗尔德·达尔的父亲哈拉尔德·达尔与索菲耶·玛德琳·赫赛尔贝里结婚,搬到南威尔士兰达夫居住[①]。

罗尔德·达尔生平时间轴(包括小说、电影、电视电影、电视节目以及他所参与的戏剧作品等)

1916　Roald Dahl is born September 13, 1916 in Llandaff, Glamorgan, U.K.
　　　9月13日,罗尔德·达尔出生在英国格拉摩根郡兰达夫。
1920　Sister Astri dies of appendicitis at the age of seven. A few months later Dahl's father, Harald Dahl, dies.

---

① 本书附录中的资料出自克里斯廷·霍华德(Kristine Howard)创建并维护的网站"*Roald Dahl Fans.com*"(罗尔德·达尔粉丝网),但有所增删和更改,网址为:http://www.roalddahlfans.com/,由著者翻译整理。

达尔的姐姐阿斯特里死于阑尾炎,年仅 7 岁。几个月后,达尔的父亲哈拉尔德·达尔去世。

1923　Enters Llandaff Cathedral School.
就读于兰达夫教堂学校。

1925　Enters St. Peter's School in Weston-Super-Mare.
就读于滨海韦斯顿圣彼得学校。

1929　Enters Repton Public School in Derby.
就读于德比郡雷普顿公学。

1934　Graduates from Repton. Accepts position with Shell Oil Company in London.
毕业于雷普顿公学,并在伦敦壳牌公司谋到了职位。

1938　Begins working in Shell's branch office in East Africa.
就职于壳牌公司东非分公司办公室。

1939　Joins Royal Air Force. Learns to fly fighter plane in Nairobi, Kenya.
加入皇家空军,开始在肯尼亚内罗毕学习驾驶战斗机。

1940　Suffers serious injuries as result of plane crash in Libya. Spends several months in military hospital in Alexandria, Egypt.
达尔驾驶的飞机在利比亚坠毁,达尔身受重伤,在埃及亚历山大港的军医院养病数月。

1941　Rejoins his squadron, then stationed in Greece.
回到原来的飞行中队,驻扎在希腊。

1942　Begins working at British Embassy in Washington. "Shot Down Over Libya" appears in *Saturday Evening Post* in August.
就职于英国驻华盛顿大使馆;《坠机余生》在 8 月的《星期六晚邮报》刊登。

1943　*The Gremlins*, the first published book.

第一本书《小魔精》出版。

1944　Dahl secures literary agent, Ann Watkins, and short stories begin to be published in American magazines.
达尔物色到文学出版经纪人安·沃特金斯,随后开始陆续在美国一些杂志发表短篇小说。

1945　Moves back to Amersham, England to be near mother Sofie.
搬回英格兰阿默舍姆镇居住,以便照顾母亲索菲耶。

1946　Over to You.
《向你飞跃》出版。

1948　Some Time Never: A Fable for Supermen. Begins dividing his time between England and New York City.
《某些时间一去永不返:一篇超人寓言》出版;奔波于英格兰和纽约市之间。

1951　Meets future wife, actress Patricia Neal.
遇见未来的妻子——女演员帕特里夏·尼尔。

1953　Marries Patricia Neal on July 2. Someone Like You.
7月2日与帕特里夏·尼尔成婚;《如你之人》出版。

1954　Purchases "Little Whitefield" farmhouse (later renamed "Gipsy House") in Great Missenden, England.
买下英格兰大米森登镇的"小怀特菲尔德"农舍,后来将其改名为"吉卜赛房舍"。

1955　"The Honeys". Daughter Olivia Twenty is born April 20.
戏剧《甜蜜爱人》演出;4月20日,女儿奥利维娅出生。

1957　Daughter Chantal Sophia (renamed Tessa to avoid the rhyme) is born April 11.
4月11日,女儿尚塔尔·索菲娅出生,后来改名为特莎,以避免与大女儿的名字同韵。

1958　Alfred Hitchcock Presents including 6 of Dahl's short stories: "Lamb to the Slaughter" "Dip in the Pool" "Man from the

South" "*Mrs. Bixby and the Colonel's Coat*" and "*The Landlady*".

电视节目《阿尔弗雷德·希区柯克出品短剧选》开播,达尔 6 篇短篇小说入选,包括《宛若羔羊》《赌海沉溺》《南方来客》《貂皮大衣》以及《神秘房东》。

1959　*Kiss Kiss.*

《吻了又吻》出版。

1960　Son, Theo Matthew Roald, is born July 30. Later baby's carriage is hit by taxicab in New York City, causing massive head injuries.

7 月 30 日,儿子西奥·马修·罗尔德出生;没过多久,婴儿车在纽约市被出租车撞上,儿子头部大面积受伤。

1961　Hosts *Way Out*. *James and the Giant Peach*.

主持《脱险记》节目;《詹姆斯与大仙桃》出版。

1962　Daughter Olivia dies of measles encephalitis on November 17.

11 月 17 日,女儿奥利维娅死于麻疹脑炎。

1964　*Charlie and the Chocolate Factory*. Daughter Ophelia Magdalena is born May 12. 36 Hours.

《查利与巧克力工厂》出版;5 月 12 日,女儿奥菲利娅出生;电影《三十六小时》上映。

1965　Patricia Neal suffers three massive strokes on February 17 and returns home three months later. Daughter Lucy Neal is born August 4. *Parson's Pleasure*.

2 月 17 日,妻子帕特里夏·尼尔患大中风三次,三个月后回国;8 月 4 日,女儿露西·尼尔出生;电视电影《虚欢一场》播映。

1966　*The Magic Finger*.

《魔法手指》出版。

1967　Dahl's mother Sofie dies on November 17. *You Only Live*

Twice.

11月17日，达尔母亲索菲耶去世；电影《雷霆谷》上映。

1968　Selected Stories of Roald Dahl. Chitty Chitty Bang Bang.
《罗尔德·达尔小说选》出版；电影《飞天万能车》上映。

1969　Twenty Nine Kisses from Roald Dahl.
《罗尔德·达尔二十九篇成人故事集》出版。

1970　Fantastic Mr. Fox.
《了不起的狐狸爸爸》出版。

1971　Willy Wonka and the Chocolate Factory and The Night Digger.
电影《欢乐糖果屋》上映；电影《黑夜挖掘人》上映。

1972　Charlie and the Great Glass Elevator.
《查利与大玻璃升降机》出版。

1974　Switch Bitch.
《迷情乱性》出版。

1975　Danny the Champion of the World.
《世界冠军丹尼》出版。

1977　The Wonderful Story of Henry Sugar and Six More.
《〈非凡亨利〉及另外六篇故事集》出版。

1978　The Enormous Crocodile and The Best of Roald Dahl.
《大大个头的鳄鱼》和《罗尔德·达尔小说精品集》出版。

1979　My Uncle Oswald, Tales of the Unexpected, and Taste and Other Tales. Hosts "Tales of the Unexpected". Separates from Patricia Neal.
《我的叔叔奥斯瓦尔德》《出乎意料的故事集》以及《〈品酒"大师"〉及另外六篇故事集》出版；主持电视剧《出乎意料的故事集》；与妻子帕特里夏·尼尔分居。

1980　The Twits, More Tales of the Unexpected, and A Roald Dahl Selection: Nine Short Stories.

《特威特夫妇》《更多出人意料故事集》以及《罗尔德·达尔作品精选:九部短篇小说集》出版。

1981　The Patricia Neal Story. George's Marvelous Medicine and Further Tales of the Unexpected.
电视电影《帕特里夏·尼尔的故事》播映;《小乔治的灵丹妙药》和《后续出人意料故事集》出版。

1982　The BFG and Revolting Rhymes.
《好心眼儿的巨人》和《反叛性童话集》出版。

1983　The Witches, Dirty Beasts, and Roald Dahl's Book of Ghost Stories. Divorces Patricia Neal on November 17 and marries Felicity Crosland.
《女巫》和《脏兮兮的野兽故事集》出版;达尔编辑的《罗尔德·达尔倾心的鬼怪故事集》出版;11月17日,与帕特里夏·尼尔离婚;与弗利西蒂·克罗斯兰结婚。

1984　Boy: Tales of Childhood.
传记《男孩时代:儿时故事》出版。

1985　The Giraffe and the Pelly and Me.
《我与长颈鹿和小鹈鹕》出版。

1986　Going Solo, Completely Unexpected Tales, Two Fables, and The Roald Dahl Omnibus.
《独闯天下》《完全出人意料故事集》《两篇寓言故事》以及《罗尔德·达尔选集》出版。

1987　A Second Roald Dahl Selection: Eight Short Stories.
《罗尔德·达尔作品第二次精选:八部短篇小说集》出版。

1988　Matilda and Ah, Sweet Mystery of Life.
《玛蒂尔达》出版;《〈奥妙生活〉等乡村故事集》出版。

1989　The BFG, Danny the Champion of the World, and Breaking Point. Rhyme Stew.
动画片《好心眼儿的巨人》上映;电视电影《世界冠军丹

尼》和《断裂点》播映;《儿童押韵诗的另类焖烧》出版。

1990　*Esio Trot. Dirty Beasts*, *Revolting Rhymes*, and *The Witches*. Roald Dahl dies November 23 in Oxford, England.

《小乌龟成长记》出版;动画片《脏兮兮的野兽故事集》和《反叛性童话集》播映;电影《女巫》上映;11月23日,罗尔德·达尔在英格兰牛津市去世。

附录2

罗尔德·达尔去世后作品出版时间轴

罗尔德·达尔去世后,其作品出版情况(截至2014年)

1991　*The Vicar of Nibbleswicke, Memories with Food at Gipsy House, The Minpins. The Collected Short Stories of Roald Dahl*, and *Roald Dahl's Guide to Railway Safety. The Amazing World of Roald Dahl.*

《尼泊斯威克的牧师》《吉卜赛房舍美食回忆》《树洞小矮人》《罗尔德·达尔短篇故事集锦》《罗尔德·达尔铁路安全指导》以及《罗尔德·达尔的惊奇世界》出版。

1992　*Idealnaya para.*

俄文电影《理想夫妻》上映。

1993　*My Year.*

《我的春夏秋冬》出版。

1994　*Roald Dahl's Revolting Recipes.*

《罗尔德·达尔的另类食谱》出版。

1995　*Lamb to the Slaughter and Other Stories. Pisvingers!.*

《〈宛若羔羊〉及其他故事集》出版;荷兰语电影《Pisvingers!》上映。

1996 *Matilda* and *James and the Giant Peach* movies released.
电影《玛蒂尔达》和《詹姆斯与大仙桃》发行。

1997 *The Great Automatic Grammatizator and Other Stories*.
《〈伟大写手〉及其他故事集》出版。

1998 *The Umbrella Man and Other Stories*.
《〈卖伞男子〉及其他故事集》出版。

1999 *The Enormous Crocodile*.
动画片《大大个头的鳄鱼》上映。

2000 *The Mildenhall Treasure* and *Skin and Other Stories*. *The Wonderful Story of Henry Sugar*
《宝藏风波》发表;《〈人皮刺青〉及其他故事集》出版;《〈非凡亨利〉等故事集》出版。

2005 *Charlie and the Chocolate Factory* and *The Bet. Songs and Verse. More About Boy*.
电影《查利与巧克力工厂》和《非常赌注》上映;《歌曲与诗歌》出版;《更多儿时故事》出版。

2008 *Three Little Pigs*.
动画短片《三头小猪猪》播映。

2009 *Fantastic Mr. Fox*.
电影《了不起的狐狸爸爸》上映。

2010 Musical version of "*Matilda*". *The Missing Golden Ticket and Other Splendiferous Secrets*.
音乐剧《玛蒂尔达》上演;《丢失的金色票券以及其他特棒的隐秘事儿》出版

2013 Musical production of "*Charlie and the Chocolate Factory*".
音乐剧《查利与巧克力工厂》上演。

2014 Audible Audio Edition of *Matilda*, *Dirty Beasts*, *The BFG*, *Fantastic Mr Fox*, *The Enormous Crocodile*, *Revolting Rhymes*, *The Magic Finger*, *The Witches*, *James and the Gi-*

ant Peach, Charlie and the Chocolate Factory, The Twits, Boy: Tales of Childhood, Charlie and the Great Glass Elevator, The Giraffe and the Pelly and Me, Going Solo, and George's Marvellous Medicine. Roald Dahl's Story-Sketcher: Create! Doodle! Imagine!

有声读物《玛蒂尔达》《脏兮兮的野兽故事集》《好心眼儿的巨人》《了不起的狐狸爸爸》《大大个头的鳄鱼》《反叛性童话集》《魔法手指》《女巫》《詹姆斯与大仙桃》《查利与巧克力工厂》《特威特夫妇》《男孩时代：儿时故事》《查利与大玻璃升降机》《我与长颈鹿和小鹈鹕》《独闯天下》以及《小乔治的灵丹妙药》出版发行；《罗尔德·达尔的故事草图本：创作！涂鸦！想象！》。

附录3

《罗尔德·达尔短篇故事品读及汉译探索》全系列目录总览

对英国作家罗尔德·达尔"非儿童类"（个别篇章具有"儿童类"文学特点，但由于是罗尔德·达尔早期作品，也被收录进来，作为研究的对象）短篇故事（小说）进行研究所著系列图书，共分为8卷，每卷包括若干章（至少两章），每章至少分为两节，每节研究1部（个别为半部）罗尔德·达尔的短篇小说。这些小说长短不一、难易各异，按照不同的主题加以编排（不一定很科学）。每一节中，先对作品做引导性的介绍，名为"原作导读"，再给出小说的原文供读者阅读或作为翻译的参考，同时给出语言点及文化层面上的注释，以辅助理解，名为"原作释读"，最后给出探索性的汉语译文，名为"翻译探索"。

第 1 卷

第一章　愿赌服输 ·· 1
第一节　《南方来客》Man from the South ································· 2
一、原作导读 ··· 3
二、原作释读 ··· 4
三、翻译探索 ··· 20
第二节　《赌海沉溺》Dip in the Pool ·· 31
一、原作导读 ··· 32
二、原作释读 ··· 33
三、翻译探索 ··· 48
第三节　《费西先生》Mr. Feasey ··· 59
一、原作导读 ··· 59
二、原作释读 ··· 60
三、翻译探索 ··· 101

第二章　莫惹娇妻 ··· 131
第一节　《宛若羔羊》Lamb to the Slaughter ····························· 132
一、原作导读 ··· 132
二、原作释读 ··· 133
三、翻译探索 ··· 147
第二节　《通天之路》The Way up to Heaven ··························· 157
一、原作导读 ··· 158
二、原作释读 ··· 159
三、翻译探索 ··· 177

第三章　战争创伤 ··· 190
第一节　《美好昨日》Yesterday Was Beautiful ························· 191
一、原作导读 ··· 192
二、原作释读 ··· 193
三、翻译探索 ··· 200

第二节 《如你之人》Someone Like You ············ 205
   一、原作导读 ······························ 205
   二、原作释读 ······························ 206
   三、翻译探索 ······························ 219

第三节 《士兵幻象》The Soldier ················ 228
   一、原作导读 ······························ 228
   二、原作释读 ······························ 229
   三、翻译探索 ······························ 241

第四章 战场硝烟 ···························· 252

第一节 《废墟之中》In the Ruins ··············· 252
   一、原作导读 ······························ 253
   二、原作释读 ······························ 253
   三、翻译探索 ······························ 255

第二节 《坠机余生》Shot down over Libya ······· 257
   一、原作导读 ······························ 258
   二、原作释读 ······························ 259
   三、翻译探索 ······························ 271

第三节 《希腊孤女》Katina ····················· 278
   一、原作导读 ······························ 278
   二、原作释读 ······························ 279
   三、翻译探索 ······························ 313

参考文献 ···································· 338
后记 ······································· 340

第2卷

第一章 乡村风情 ···························· 1

第一节 《霍迪先生》Mr. Hoddy ················· 2
   一、原作导读 ······························ 3
   二、原作释读 ······························ 4

三、翻译探索 …………………………………………… 16
　第二节　《奥妙生活》Ah, Sweet Mystery of Life ……… 24
　　　一、原作导读 …………………………………………… 25
　　　二、原作释读 …………………………………………… 26
　　　三、翻译探索 …………………………………………… 36

第二章　迷雾重重 …………………………………………… 43
　第一节　《当心有狗》Beware of the Dog ……………… 44
　　　一、原作导读 …………………………………………… 45
　　　二、原作释读 …………………………………………… 46
　　　三、翻译探索 …………………………………………… 63
　第二节　《草垛之灾》Rummins ………………………… 75
　　　一、原作导读 …………………………………………… 75
　　　二、原作释读 …………………………………………… 77
　　　三、翻译探索 …………………………………………… 92

第三章　殊异人生 …………………………………………… 104
　第一节　《外科医生》The Surgeon …………………… 106
　　　一、原作导读 …………………………………………… 105
　　　二、原作释读 …………………………………………… 108
　　　三、翻译探索 …………………………………………… 149
　第二节　《善本书商》The Bookseller ………………… 176
　　　一、原作导读 …………………………………………… 177
　　　二、原作释读 …………………………………………… 179
　　　三、翻译探索 …………………………………………… 216

第四章　天真男孩 …………………………………………… 237
　第一节　《猪肉美味》Pig ……………………………… 238
　　　一、原作导读 …………………………………………… 239
　　　二、原作释读 …………………………………………… 242
　　　三、翻译探索 …………………………………………… 274
　第二节　《海龟奇事》The Boy Who Talked with Animals … 295

一、原作导读 ……………………………………… 296
　　二、原作释读 ……………………………………… 298
　　三、翻译探索 ……………………………………… 324
参考文献 ……………………………………………… 343
后记 …………………………………………………… 345

第3卷

第一章　冷嘲热讽 ………………………………………… 1
第一节　《音乐"大师"》Mr. Botibol …………………… 2
　　一、原作导读 ………………………………………… 3
　　二、原作释读 ………………………………………… 5
　　三、翻译探索 ………………………………………… 39
第二节　《品酒"大师"》Taste ………………………… 60
　　一、原作导读 ………………………………………… 60
　　二、原作释读 ………………………………………… 63
　　三、翻译探索 ………………………………………… 85

第二章　意识之流 ………………………………………… 101
第一节　《仅此而已》Only This ………………………… 103
　　一、原作导读 ………………………………………… 103
　　二、原作释读 ………………………………………… 104
　　三、翻译探索 ………………………………………… 113
第二节　《老手之死》Death of an Old Old Man ……… 118
　　一、原作导读 ………………………………………… 119
　　二、原作释读 ………………………………………… 121
　　三、翻译探索 ………………………………………… 138

第三章　科幻色彩 ………………………………………… 151
第一节　《器官实验》William and Mary ……………… 152
　　一、原作导读 ………………………………………… 153
　　二、原作释读 ………………………………………… 155

三、翻译探索 …………………………………………… 197
　第二节　《探声机器》The Sound Machine …………… 225
　　一、原作导读 …………………………………………… 225
　　二、原作释读 …………………………………………… 228
　　三、翻译探索 …………………………………………… 247
第四章　匪夷所思 …………………………………………… 262
　第一节　《创世新灾》Genesis and Catastrophe ……… 263
　　一、原作导读 …………………………………………… 264
　　二、原作释读 …………………………………………… 265
　　三、翻译探索 …………………………………………… 276
　第二节　《折翼天鹅》The Swan ………………………… 284
　　一、原作导读 …………………………………………… 284
　　二、原作释读 …………………………………………… 287
　　三、翻译探索 …………………………………………… 322
参考文献 ……………………………………………………… 342
后记 …………………………………………………………… 345

第4卷

第一章　神秘莫测 …………………………………………… 1
　第一节　《神秘房东》The Landlady …………………… 2
　　一、原作导读 …………………………………………… 3
　　二、原作释读 …………………………………………… 5
　　三、翻译探索 …………………………………………… 22
　第二节　《不应老去》They Shall not Grow Old ……… 32
　　一、原作导读 …………………………………………… 32
　　二、原作释读 …………………………………………… 35
　　三、翻译探索 …………………………………………… 62
第二章　夫妻之间 …………………………………………… 79
　第一节　《貂皮大衣》Mrs. Bixby and the Colonel's Coat …… 80

一、原作导读 …………………………………… 52
　　二、原作释读 …………………………………… 84
　　三、翻译探索 …………………………………… 114
　第二节　《亲密爱侣》My Lady Love, My Dove …… 133
　　一、原作导读 …………………………………… 133
　　二、原作释读 …………………………………… 135
　　三、翻译探索 …………………………………… 158
第三章　弄巧成拙 …………………………………… 175
　第一节　《虚欢一场》Parson's Pleasure ………… 176
　　一、原作导读 …………………………………… 177
　　二、原作释读 …………………………………… 180
　　三、翻译探索 …………………………………… 222
　第二节　《世界冠军》The Champion of the World …… 248
　　一、原作导读 …………………………………… 248
　　二、原作释读 …………………………………… 251
　　三、翻译探索 …………………………………… 294
参考文献 ……………………………………………… 324
后记 …………………………………………………… 326

第 5 卷

第一章　不堪回首 …………………………………… 1
　第一节　《公学遗恨》Galloping Foxley …………… 3
　　一、原作导读 …………………………………… 3
　　二、原作释读 …………………………………… 5
　　三、翻译探索 …………………………………… 30
　第二节　《最后之举》The Last Act ……………… 45
　　一、原作导读 …………………………………… 46
　　二、原作释读 …………………………………… 51
　　三、翻译探索 …………………………………… 100

· 341 ·

第二章　冤冤相报 ·· 134
第一节　《最后颂歌》Nunc Dimittis ····················· 135
一、原作导读 ······································· 136
二、原作释读 ······································· 139
三、翻译探索 ······································· 178
第二节　《复仇公司》Vengeance Is Mine Inc. ············ 202
一、原作导读 ······································· 203
二、原作释读 ······································· 205
三、翻译探索 ······································· 234

第三章　意味深长 ·· 255
第一节　《熏制奶酪》Smoked Cheese ···················· 256
一、原作导读 ······································· 257
二、原作释读 ······································· 258
三、翻译探索 ······································· 261
第二节　《倒立之鼠》The Upsidedown Mice ············· 262
一、原作导读 ······································· 263
二、原作释读 ······································· 264
三、翻译探索 ······································· 267
第三节　《蛇毒解药》Poison ···························· 269
一、原作导读 ······································· 270
二、原作释读 ······································· 272
三、翻译探索 ······································· 289

参考文献 ··· 301
后记 ·· 303

第 6 卷

第一章　物极必反 ·· 1
第一节　《音乐奇猫》Edward the Conqueror ················ 2
一、原作导读 ··· 3

二、原作释读 …………………………………… 4
　　三、翻译探索 …………………………………… 39
　第二节 《魔力王浆》Royal Jelly …………………… 59
　　一、原作导读 …………………………………… 60
　　二、原作释读 …………………………………… 63
　　三、翻译探索 …………………………………… 105
第二章 结局难料 …………………………………… 135
　第一节 《贵妇之颈》Neck ………………………… 136
　　一、原作导读 …………………………………… 137
　　二、原作释读 …………………………………… 139
　　三、翻译探索 …………………………………… 169
　第二节 《人皮刺青》Skin ………………………… 188
　　一、原作导读 …………………………………… 188
　　二、原作释读 …………………………………… 190
　　三、翻译探索 …………………………………… 216
第三章 如堕雾中 …………………………………… 234
　第一节 《怪异乔治》(上部) Georgy Porgy (Part A) …… 235
　　一、原作导读 …………………………………… 236
　　二、原作释读 …………………………………… 237
　　三、翻译探索 …………………………………… 258
　第二节 《怪异乔治》(下部) Georgy Porgy (Part B) …… 271
　　一、原作导读 …………………………………… 271
　　二、原作释读 …………………………………… 273
　　三、翻译探索 …………………………………… 195
参考文献 …………………………………………… 309
后记 ………………………………………………… 310

第7卷

第一章 亦真亦幻 …………………………………… 1

· 343 ·

第一节 《宝藏风波》The Mildenhall Treasure ……………… 2
　　一、原作导读 ……………………………………………… 2
　　二、原作释读 ……………………………………………… 5
　　三、翻译探索 ……………………………………………… 41
第二节 《非洲往事》An African Story ……………………… 64
　　一、原作导读 ……………………………………………… 65
　　二、原作释读 ……………………………………………… 67
　　三、翻译探索 ……………………………………………… 87

第二章 异想天开 ……………………………………………… 101
第一节 《意愿突发》The Wish ……………………………… 102
　　一、原作导读 ……………………………………………… 102
　　二、原作释读 ……………………………………………… 104
　　三、翻译探索 ……………………………………………… 110
第二节 《伟大写手》The Great Automatic Grammatizator … 114
　　一、原作导读 ……………………………………………… 114
　　二、原作释读 ……………………………………………… 116
　　三、翻译探索 ……………………………………………… 149

第三章 功成名就 ……………………………………………… 170
第一节 《非凡亨利》(上部) The Wonderful Story of Henry Sugar (Part A) ……………………………………………………… 171
　　一、原作导读 ……………………………………………… 172
　　二、原作释读 ……………………………………………… 173
　　三、翻译探索 ……………………………………………… 219
第二节 《非凡亨利》(下部) The Wonderful Story of Henry Sugar (Part B) ……………………………………………………… 249
　　一、原作导读 ……………………………………………… 250
　　二、原作释读 ……………………………………………… 251
　　三、翻译探索 ……………………………………………… 293

参考文献 ……………………………………………………… 322

后记 ··· 323

第8卷

第一章　非常之辈 ··· 1
第一节　《搭车怪客》*The Hitch-hiker* ································ 2
一、原作导读 ··· 2
二、原作释读 ··· 4
三、翻译探索 ··· 25

第二节　《捕鼠者说》*The Ratcatcher* ································ 39
一、原作导读 ··· 39
二、原作释读 ··· 41
三、翻译探索 ··· 63

第二章　事与愿违 ··· 78
第一节　《大兵"救美"》*Madame Rosette* ································ 79
一、原作导读 ··· 79
二、原作释读 ··· 82
三、翻译探索 ··· 128

第二节　《小菜一碟》*A Piece of Cake* ································ 159
一、原作导读 ··· 160
二、原作释读 ··· 163
三、翻译探索 ··· 183

第三章　生财之道 ··· 197
第一节　《管家之谋》*The Butler* ································ 198
一、原作导读 ··· 198
二、原作释读 ··· 200
三、翻译探索 ··· 207

第二节　《卖伞男子》*The Umbrella Man* ································ 211
一、原作导读 ··· 212
二、原作释读 ··· 214

· 345 ·

三、翻译探索 …………………………………… 226
第四章　人生之路 …………………………………………… 234
　第一节　《幸运开局》(上部) Lucky Break (Part A) ……… 235
　　　一、原作导读 …………………………………… 236
　　　二、原作释读 …………………………………… 237
　　　三、翻译探索 …………………………………… 265
　第二节　《幸运开局》(下部) Lucky Break (Part B) ……… 281
　　　一、原作导读 …………………………………… 281
　　　二、原作释读 …………………………………… 283
　　　三、翻译探索 …………………………………… 310

参考文献 ……………………………………………………… 325
附录 …………………………………………………………… 327
　附录1　生平时间轴 ……………………………………… 327
　附录2　罗尔德·达尔去世后作品出版时间轴 ………… 333
　附录3　《罗尔德·达尔短篇故事品读及汉译探索》全系列
　　　　　目录总览 ……………………………………… 335
后记 …………………………………………………………… 347

后　　记

  我们对罗尔德·达尔"非儿童类"短篇故事（小说）进行研究和翻译已经持续了六七个年头了。其间，因教学和其他科研的缘由，有所间断，但多数时间是在研读和翻译达尔的这部分短篇小说中度过的。所研读、翻译的达尔这部分短篇作品共计六十篇。

  在研究和翻译罗尔德·达尔这部分作品过程中，历尽了艰辛，特别是在翻译过程中，不时会遇到这样或那样的"坎坷"。达尔在写作过程中，时常会"卖弄"自己所掌握的某些专业方面的知识，如葡萄酒、收藏、音乐、医学等，这就逼着译者硬着头皮去熟悉相应的知识。另外，达尔还偶尔会"显摆"一下自己英语之外的词汇，如法语、拉丁语等，这对于译者来说，未免有些"捉襟见肘"了——有的词，任凭怎么查也不得结果。达尔原文中的某一段有时会罗列出若干的专有名词，本着一丝不苟的研究态度，翻译过程中译者对它们均一一查证——哪怕对其中某些表达已经相当熟悉了。对于这样的"坎坷"，下笔前会来回踱步、反复思量、仔细斟酌，正如鲁迅先生在译完《死魂灵》谈到翻译时所言："我向来总以为翻译比创作容易，因为至少是无须构想。但到真的一译，就会遇着难关，譬如一个名词或动词，写不出，创作时候可以回避，翻译上却不成，也还得想，一直弄到头昏眼花，好像在脑子里面摸一个急于要开箱子的钥匙，却没有。"（鲁迅《"题未定"草·且介亭杂文二集》）

  在研究和翻译罗尔德·达尔的这部分作品过程中，还会遇到语言及文化差异方面的"绊脚石"，处理起来颇费脑筋，正如严复在谈

《天演论》翻译的《译例言》中所言:"新理踵出,名目纷繁,索之中文,渺不可得,即有牵合,终嫌参差,译者遇此,独有自具衡量,即义定名。"另外,在翻译中对于查询无果的地方,也得认真加以思考,甚至经过了很长时间才"创造性"地下笔定论,可谓"一名之立,旬月踟蹰。我罪我知,是存明哲"(严复《译例言》)。由此可见,译事之难,不亚于李太白笔下的"蜀道之难,难于上青天"了!

幸运的是,在对罗尔德·达尔这些"非儿童类"短篇小说进行研究和翻译过程中,我们得到了许多朋友和同事热情的帮助和有力的支持,感激之情无以言表。

对罗尔德·达尔短篇小说的研究和翻译源于英国朋友马礼(他的英文原名叫"Jonathan Rackham",时任渤海大学外籍英语教师)2009年赠送给著者的一本书,书名叫《罗尔德·达尔小说精品集》(The Best of Roald Dahl)。在阅读这本书的过程中,得到了启发,萌生了要研究并翻译作家罗尔德·达尔"非儿童类"短篇小说的念头。我们于2010年9月开始动笔,从此一发而不可收。在对原文理解过程中所遇到的难题,得到了马礼耐心而细致的解答,甚至在他回到英国后,还继续通过电子邮件、越洋电话等方式给予我们热情的解答。在此,衷心感谢好友兼同行的马礼,感谢他的热情帮助!

译文从初稿到成稿,虽经数次校正和修改,仍然存在不少问题。此时,我们的学长兼兄长又兼同事和朋友的刘恩东先生及时伸出了援助之手,对最终的成稿在"忠实"的基础上进行了"通顺"方面的梳理。刘恩东先生虽身为英语教师,但是,其汉语功力不可小觑,令吾等外语研究者难以望其项背,特别是他古汉语的功力,甚至超出很多古汉语的专业研究者。有了我们兄长的梳理和理顺,毛坯一样的成稿方焕发出光彩。兄长对书稿的修改,虽然有时只是增填一个字,或者是删除一个词,但却救译文于"水火"之中。可以说,没有兄长对书稿的理顺,名为"成稿"的译文只能如同一个咿呀学语、走路不稳的婴儿。在此,衷心感谢刘恩东先生,感谢他辛苦的付出!

研究伊始,一个偶然的机会,我们搜索到克里斯廷·霍华德

(Kristine Howard)创建并维护的网站"罗尔德·达尔粉丝网"(Roald Dahl Fans.com),并就罗尔德·达尔有关问题联系过霍华德女士,收到了她及时的回复。整个研究也因霍华德女士的网站而受益匪浅。在此,衷心感谢克里斯廷·霍华德女士,感谢她在网站里所提供的全面而翔实的资料!

同时,我们十分感谢肇庆学院外国语学院及渤海大学外国语学院的领导和同事给予我们热情的帮助和有力的支持!十分感谢哈尔滨工业大学出版社田新华主任在出版方面提供的有力支持!同时感谢为本书的出版而忙碌的所有编辑人员和工作人员!同时,我们十分感谢为本研究提供帮助的所有朋友和同仁!

当然,由于时间和能力所限,错误在所难免,还望读者赐教、斧正,并多提宝贵意见。

对罗尔德·达尔"非儿童类"短篇故事(小说)研究、翻译所成之书,难免泛泛而论,甚至是流于平庸,但是,我们本着扎实做学问、做学问如做人的思想,从起点出发,稳扎稳打,力戒浮躁之风,勿求好高骛远。

记得《礼记·中庸》里有言:"君子之道,譬如行远,必自迩,譬如登高,必自卑。"愿以此语共勉。

著者
张跃伟　王永胜
2016 年初冬